Macromedia® Direct...
For Dummies®, 2nd E...
Keyboard Shortcut...

CW00596963

* = hidden shortcut   ⌘ = Mac Command key/Ctrl = PC Control key   Option = Mac Option key/Alt = PC Alt key

	Command	Shortcut
File menu	New	⌘/Ctrl+N
	New Cast	⌘/Ctrl+Option/Alt+W
	Open	⌘/Ctrl+O
	Close Window	⌘/Ctrl+W
	Save	⌘/Ctrl+S
	Import	⌘/Ctrl+R
	Export	⌘/Ctrl+Shift+R
	Page Setup	⌘/Ctrl+Shift+P
	Print	⌘/Ctrl+P
	Preferences, General	⌘/Ctrl+U
	Quit	⌘/Ctrl+Q
Edit menu	Undo	⌘/Ctrl+Z
	Repeat	⌘/Ctrl+Y
	Cut Cells	⌘/Ctrl+X
	Copy Cells	⌘/Ctrl+C
	Paste	⌘/Ctrl+V
	Paste Special	⌘/Ctrl+P
	Select All	⌘/Ctrl+A
	Find Text	⌘/Ctrl+F
	Find Handler	⌘/Ctrl+Shift+;
	Find Cast Member	⌘/Ctrl+;
	Find Selection	⌘/Ctrl+H
	Find Again	⌘/Ctrl+Option/Alt+F
	Replace Again	⌘/Ctrl+Option/Alt+E
	Exchange Cast Members	⌘/Ctrl+E
	Launch External Editor	⌘/Ctrl+,
View menu	Marker Previous	⌘/Ctrl+←
	Marker Next	⌘/Ctrl+→
	Zoom In	⌘/Ctrl++
	Zoom Out	⌘/Ctrl+minus key
	Ruler	⌘/Ctrl+Option/Alt+Shift+R
	Grid, Show	⌘/Ctrl+Option/Alt+Shift+G

	Command	Shortcut
View menu (cont.)	Grid, Snap To	⌘/Ctrl+Option/Alt+G
Insert menu	Frame	⌘/Ctrl+[
	Remove Frame	⌘/Ctrl+]
Modify menu	Cast Member Properties	⌘/Ctrl+I
	Cast Member Script	⌘/Ctrl+'
	Sprite Properties	⌘/Ctrl+Shift+I
	Sprite Script	⌘/Ctrl+Shift+'
	Movie Properties	⌘/Ctrl+Shift+D
	Movie Casts	⌘/Ctrl+Shift+C
	Font	⌘/Ctrl+Shift+T
	Paragraph	⌘/Ctrl+Option/Alt+Shift+T
	In-Between	⌘/Ctrl+B
	In-Between Special	⌘/Ctrl+Shift+B
	Arrange, Bring to Front	⌘/Ctrl+Shift+↑
	Arrange, Move Forward	⌘/Ctrl+↑
	Arrange, Move Backward	⌘/Ctrl+↓
	Arrange, Send to Back	⌘/Ctrl+Shift+↓
	Align	⌘/Ctrl+K
	Tweak	⌘/Ctrl+Shift+K
Control menu	Play	⌘/Ctrl+Option/Alt+P
	Stop	⌘/Ctrl+Option/Alt+.
	Rewind	⌘/Ctrl+Option/Alt+R
	Step Forward	⌘/Ctrl+Option/Alt+→
	Step Backward	⌘/Ctrl+Option/Alt+←
	Loop Playback	⌘/Ctrl+Option/Alt+L
	Volume	⌘/Ctrl+Option/Alt+M

. . .For Dummies: #1 Computer Book Series for Beginners

COMPUTER
BOOK SERIES
FROM IDG

Macromedia® Director® 5 For Dummies®, 2nd Edition

Cheat Sheet

Keyboard Shortcuts (continued)

* = hidden shortcut ⌘ = Mac Command key/Ctrl = PC Control key Option = Mac Option key/Alt = PC Alt key

	Command	Shortcut
Control menu (cont.)	Toggle Breakpoint	⌘/Ctrl+Option/Alt+Shift+K
	Watch Expression	⌘/Ctrl+Option/Alt+Shift+W
	Ignore Breakpoints	⌘/Ctrl+Option/Alt+Shift+I
	Step Script	⌘/Ctrl+Option/Alt+Shift+↓
	Step into Script	⌘/Ctrl+Option/Alt+Shift+→
	Run Script	⌘/Ctrl+Option/Alt+Shift+↑
	Recompile All Scripts	⌘/Ctrl+Option/Alt+Shift+C
Window menu	Toolbar	⌘/Ctrl+Option/Alt+Shift+B
	Tool Palette	⌘/Ctrl+7
	Inspectors, Text	⌘/Ctrl+T
	Stage	⌘/Ctrl+1
	Control Panel	⌘/Ctrl+2
	Markers	⌘/Ctrl+Shift+M
	Cast	⌘/Ctrl+3
	Score	⌘/Ctrl+4
	Paint	⌘/Ctrl+5
	Text	⌘/Ctrl+6
	Field	⌘/Ctrl+8
	Color Palettes	⌘/Ctrl+Option/Alt+7
	Video	⌘/Ctrl+9
	Script	⌘/Ctrl+0
	Message	⌘/Ctrl+M
	Debugger	⌘/Ctrl+'
	Watcher	⌘/Ctrl+Shift+'
Misc.	*Help Pointer	⌘/Ctrl+?
	*Select range of Cast Members	Shift+click
	*Select non-contiguous Cast Members	⌘/Ctrl+click

	Command	Shortcut
Misc. (cont.)	*Previous Cast Member in the Cast	⌘/Ctrl+Option/Alt+←
	*Next Cast Member in the Cast	⌘/Ctrl+Option/Alt+→
	*Place Cast Member on the Stage	⌘/Ctrl+Shift+L
.	*Move Cast Member one channel lower	⌘/Ctrl+↓
	*Move Cast Member one channel higher	⌘/Ctrl+↑
	*Create new easel in the Paint window	⌘/Ctrl+Shift+A
	*Copy selection	Option/Alt+drag
	*Scale selection	⌘/Ctrl+drag
	*Scale selection proportionately	⌘/Ctrl+Shift+drag selection
	*Constrain horizontally or vertically	Shift+drag selection
	*Nudge selection	Keyboard arrows
	*Zoom in on Paint window	⌘/Ctrl+click in Paint window
	*Zoom out of Paint window	⌘/Ctrl+Shift+click in Paint window
	*Grabber Hand in the Paint window	Spacebar
Keypad	*Play/Stop	+, Enter
	*Rewind	0
	* Step back	1
	* Step forward	3
	* Sound/Disable sound	7
	* Loop/Disable loop	8
	* Reverse video	/
	* Inverse Stage	-

IDG BOOKS WORLDWIDE

Cheat Sheet $2.95 value. Item 0024-4.

For more information about IDG Books, call 1-800-762-2974.

. . .For Dummies: #1 Computer Book Series for Beginners

MACROMEDIA DIRECTOR® 5 FOR DUMMIES®

2ND EDITION

by Lauren Steinhauer

IDG Books Worldwide, Inc.
An International Data Group Company

Foster City, CA ♦ Chicago, IL ♦ Indianapolis, IN ♦ Southlake, TX

Macromedia Director® 5 For Dummies® 2nd Edition

Published by
IDG Books Worldwide, Inc.
An International Data Group Company
919 E. Hillsdale Blvd.
Suite 400
Foster City, CA 94404

Library of Congress Catalog Card No.: 96-76354

ISBN: 0-7645-0024-4

Printed in the United States of America

10 9 8 7 6 5 4 3 2 1

2O/SV/QW/ZW/IN

Distributed in the United States by IDG Books Worldwide, Inc.

Distributed by Macmillan Canada for Canada; by Contemporanea de Ediciones for Venezuela; by Distribuidora Cuspide for Argentina; by CITEC for Brazil; by Ediciones ZETA S.C.R. Ltda. for Peru; by Editorial Limusa SA for Mexico; by Transworld Publishers Limited in the United Kingdom and Europe; by Academic Bookshop for Egypt; by Levant Distributors S.A.R.L. for Lebanon; by Al Jassim for Saudi Arabia; by Simron Pty. Ltd. for South Africa; by Pustak Mahal for India; by The Computer Bookshop for India; by Toppan Company Ltd. for Japan; by Addison Wesley Publishing Company for Korea; by Longman Singapore Publishers Ltd. for Singapore, Malaysia, Thailand, and Indonesia; by Unalis Corporation for Taiwan; by WS Computer Publishing Company, Inc. for the Philippines; by WoodsLane Pty. Ltd. for Australia; by WoodsLane Enterprises Ltd. for New Zealand. Authorized Sales Agent: Anthony Rudkin Associates for the Middle East and North Africa.

For general information on IDG Books Worldwide's books in the U.S., please call our Consumer Customer Service department at 800-762-2974. For reseller information, including discounts and premium sales, please call our Reseller Customer Service department at 800-434-3422.

For information on where to purchase IDG Books Worldwide's books outside the U.S., contact IDG Books Worldwide at 415-655-3078 or fax 415-655-3295.

For information on translations, contact Marc Jeffrey Mikulich, Director, Foreign & Subsidiary Rights, at IDG Books Worldwide, 415-655-3018 or fax 415-655-3281.

For sales inquiries and special prices for bulk quantities, write to the address above or call IDG Books Worldwide at 415-655-3200.

For information on using IDG Books Worldwide's books in the classroom, or ordering examination copies, contact the Education Office at 800-434-2086 or fax 817-251-8174.

For authorization to photocopy items for corporate, personal, or educational use, please contact Copyright Clearance Center, 222 Rosewood Drive, Danvers, MA 01923, or fax 508-750-4470.

is a trademark under exclusive
license to IDG Books Worldwide, Inc.,
from International Data Group, Inc.

About the Author

Lauren Steinhauer

Lauren Steinhauer began his design career in special effects at Universal Studios and his computer career in 1983 in San Francisco with the Lisa, precursor to the Macintosh introduced in 1984. Lauren has since provided multimedia creative services to clients such as Apple Computer, Inc., Claris Corporation, Novell, and Sprint; authored numerous books and manuals on computer-aided design, multimedia development, and World Wide Web design; and led countless computer workshops as a sought-after instructor. Lauren is a faculty member of San Francisco State's prestigious Multimedia Studies Program and offers multimedia creative services through Steinhauer & Associates in the City by the Bay.

Welcome to the world of IDG Books Worldwide.

IDG Books Worldwide, Inc., is a subsidiary of International Data Group, the world's largest publisher of computer-related information and the leading global provider of information services on information technology. IDG was founded more than 25 years ago and now employs more than 7,700 people worldwide. IDG publishes more than 250 computer publications in 67 countries (see listing below). More than 70 million people read one or more IDG publications each month.

Launched in 1990, IDG Books Worldwide is today the #1 publisher of best-selling computer books in the United States. We are proud to have received 8 awards from the Computer Press Association in recognition of editorial excellence and three from Computer Currents' First Annual Readers' Choice Awards, and our best-selling ...*For Dummies*® series has more than 19 million copies in print with translations in 28 languages. IDG Books Worldwide, through a joint venture with IDG's Hi-Tech Beijing, became the first U.S. publisher to publish a computer book in the People's Republic of China. In record time, IDG Books Worldwide has become the first choice for millions of readers around the world who want to learn how to better manage their businesses.

Our mission is simple: Every one of our books is designed to bring extra value and skill-building instructions to the reader. Our books are written by experts who understand and care about our readers. The knowledge base of our editorial staff comes from years of experience in publishing, education, and journalism — experience which we use to produce books for the '90s. In short, we care about books, so we attract the best people. We devote special attention to details such as audience, interior design, use of icons, and illustrations. And because we use an efficient process of authoring, editing, and desktop publishing our books electronically, we can spend more time ensuring superior content and spend less time on the technicalities of making books.

You can count on our commitment to deliver high-quality books at competitive prices on topics you want to read about. At IDG Books Worldwide, we continue in the IDG tradition of delivering quality for more than 25 years. You'll find no better book on a subject than one from IDG Books Worldwide.

John G. Kilcullen

John Kilcullen
President and CEO
IDG Books Worldwide, Inc.

Dedication

To the very special people in my life, including my son Dorian, Eskimo, my mother, my brother Ron, and the rest of my dear relatives, and especially to my Big Brother René (who's the real writer in the family).

Author's Acknowledgments

Many thanks to Mike Kelly at IDG Books for all his great suggestions to the first edition of this book, *Macromedia Director 4 For Macs For Dummies,* to Pam Mourouzis and Gareth Hancock this time around, and to the rest of the hardworking people at IDG Books for putting this all together. Jay Lee provided invaluable advice and assistance with his technical review. Also, thanks to Megg Bonar and to Carol McClendon, Cindy Mannaberry, and Maureen Maloney at Waterside Publishing for giving me the opportunity of putting this book together.

Publisher's Acknowledgments

We're proud of this book; please send us your comments about it by using the Reader Response Card at the back of the book or by e-mailing us at feedback/dummies@idgbooks.com. Some of the people who helped bring this book to market include the following:

Acquisitions, Development, & Editorial

Project Editors: Pamela Mourouzis, Rev Mengle, Michael Kelly

Assistant Acquisitions Editor: Gareth Hancock

Copy Editor: Suzanne Packer

Technical Reviewer: Jay Lee

Editorial Manager: Kristin A. Cocks

Editorial Assistants: Chris H. Collins

Production

Associate Project Coordinator: Regina Snyder

Layout and Graphics: Brett Black, Elizabeth Cárdenas-Nelson, Dominique DeFelice, Cheryl Denski, Maridee V. Ennis, Julie Jordan Forey, Todd Klemme, Anna Rohrer, Gina Scott, M. Anne Sipahimalani, Michael Sullivan

Proofreaders: Kathy McGuinnes, Dwight Ramsey, Robert Springer, Carrie Voorhis, Karen York

Indexer: Sharon Hilgenberg

General & Administrative

IDG Books Worldwide, Inc.: John Kilcullen, President & CEO; Steven Berkowitz, COO & Publisher

Dummies, Inc.: Milissa Koloski, Executive Vice President & Publisher

Dummies Technology Press & Dummies Editorial: Diane Graves Steele, Associate Publisher; Judith A. Taylor, Brand Manager; Myra Immell, Editorial Director

Dummies Trade Press: Kathleen A. Welton, Vice President & Publisher; Stacy S. Collins, Brand Manager

IDG Books Production for Dummies Press: Beth Jenkins, Production Director; Cindy L. Phipps, Supervisor of Project Coordination; Kathie S. Schnorr, Supervisor of Page Layout; Shelley Lea, Supervisor of Graphics and Design

Dummies Packaging & Book Design: Erin McDermit, Packaging Coordinator; Kavish+Kavish, Cover Design

◆

The publisher would like to give special thanks to Patrick J. McGovern, without whom this book would not have been possible.

◆

Contents at a Glance

Introduction *1*

Part I: The Big Picture *9*

Chapter 1: Stars of Director: Graphics, Sound, Movement, and Your CPU 11
Chapter 2: Launching Director: An Application by Any Other Name 19
Chapter 3: Lights, Camera, Action! 43

Part II: Director's Windows of Opportunity *53*

Chapter 4: Casting Coach or Couch? The Cast Window 55
Chapter 5: As Time Goes By: Opening Director's Score Window 73
Chapter 6: Too Graphic for You? Director's Paint Window 91
Chapter 7: Drawing, er, Painting on Director's Paint Window 109
Chapter 8: And Now for Something Completely Different: Text and Field Windows ... 131

Part III: Manipulating Director with More Windows *141*

Chapter 9: Yet Another Set of Tools: The Tool Palette 143
Chapter 10: Getting to Those Scrumptious Palettes: The Color Palettes Window 155
Chapter 11: Your Very Own Digital Video Window 171
Chapter 12: And the Winner of Script of the Year: The Script Window 197
Chapter 13: Messages from Beyond: The Message and Debugger Windows 211
Chapter 14: Twick or Tweak: The Tweak Palette 221
Chapter 15: Your Pals, the Markers Window and the New Window Command 225

Part IV: More Interaction, Please! *231*

Chapter 16: Hey, Kids! Be an Animation Wizard 233
Chapter 17: A Closer Look at Lingo 239
Chapter 18: Showing Off Your 15 Minutes of Fame on Video 257
Chapter 19: You Talkin' to Me? Adding Sound to Your Movie 267
Chapter 20: Cross-Platform Stuff No One Should Need to Know 275
Chapter 21: Shockwave to the Web Wescue 283
Chapter 22: Ready to Wear All Those Hats? 293

Part V: The Part of Tens *299*

Chapter 23: Ten Common Director Questions and Answers 301
Chapter 24: Ten Ways to Add Animation to Your Movies 317
Chapter 25: The Ten Most Important Lingo Words 335
Appendix A: I'm Ready for My Close-up, Mr. DeMille:
            Director 5's System Requirements 343
Appendix B: The Mother of All Resource Lists 345

Index *349*

Reader Response Card .... *Back of Book*

Cartoons at a Glance

By Rich Tennant • Fax: 508-546-7747 • E-mail: the5wave@tiac.net

page 53

page 231

page 9

page 299

page 141

Table of Contents

Introduction 1

What This Book Offers Mac or PC Users Like You 1
Who You Are 2
Icons Used in This Book 3
Conventions Used in This Book 4
Does This Book Cover Everything? 5
How This Book Is Organized 6
    Part I: The Big Picture 6
    Part II: Director's Windows of Opportunity 6
    Part III: Manipulating Director with More Windows 7
    Part IV: More Interaction, Please! 7
    Part V: The Part of Tens 7
What's Next? 8

Part I: The Big Picture 9

Chapter 1: Stars of Director: Graphics, Sound, Movement, and Your CPU 11

What Do You Use Director For? 12
    Following in Walt's mouseprints 12
    Just a Lincoln off the old log 12
By the Way, What the Heck Is Multimedia? 13
    Multimedia is image 14
    Multimedia is sound 14
    Multimedia is movement 15
    Multimedia is your computer 15
        Interactive multimedia 16
        Hypertext 16

Chapter 2: Launching Director: An Application by Any Other Name 19

Reviewing the GUI, Director's Executive Producer 20
    Starting your computer 20
    Your pal, the mouse 21
        Double-clicking 21
        Adjusting mouse tracking 23
    Opening Macromedia Director 23
Stepping Up to the Bar (Graph) 25
    Purging Director's memory 27
    For Mac users only: changing Director's application partition 28

Calling S.O.S. with D.O.L.H. (Director's Online Help) 30
    Director's context-sensitive help 31
    The Help menu 33
The Toolbar 35
Director's File Menu 37
Touring Director's Other Menus 40

Chapter 3: Lights, Camera, Action! 43

All the World's a Stage: Director's Opening Window 43
Wait a Minute! The Darn Stage Is Blank as a Polar Bear in a Snowstorm! 44
    Stage window forever 44
    The incredible, invisible menu bar 44
    Hyperactive windows 45
    Sizing up the Stage 46
    Checks and balances 46
Modifying the Stage 46
    Location, location, location 47
    Pop-up palette 48
Channel Surfing with the Control Panel 48
These Buttons Aren't on My Remote Control! 49

Part II: Director's Windows of Opportunity 53

Chapter 4: Casting Coach or Couch? The Cast Window 55

Calling All Cast Members 55
    Defining the Cast 55
    Adding Cast Members to the Cast window 58
    Internal and external Cast windows 60
        Internal casts 60
        External casts 61
    Linking your imported file 61
    Moving Cast Members around in the Cast window 63
    Editing Cast Members 101 64
        Bitmaps only need apply 64
        External Launcher stuff 65
Exploring the Cast Windows 66
    Custom features 66
    Cast Member Properties button 68
    Director's hard cell 70

Chapter 5: As Time Goes By: Opening Director's Score Window 73

The Score Window: And You Thought NeuroLinguistics 101
  Was Complicated 74
    That's MISTER cell to you, Bud 74
    Icon thingies 74
    Hidden, top-secret channels 78
    Transitions, transitions! (To the tune from *Fiddler on the Roof*) 79

Adding a Cast Member to the Score 80

All This Ink and Not a Drop on Me — Oops 83

Getting Up Close and Personal with the Score
Window Preferences Dialog Box 86

As time goes by: using Space to Time 88

What to do between takes? In-Between Special, of course 89

Chapter 6: Too Graphic for You? Director's Paint Window 91

Oh, No! Thousands of Icon Thingies! 92

Paint window's top row of icons 93

Paint toolbar 94

Director's Paint Tools 95

Lasso tool 96

Selection Rectangle tool 96

Registration tool 98

Eraser tool 99

Hand tool 100

Zoom tool 101

Eyedropper tool 101

Paint Bucket tool 101

Text tool 102

Pencil tool 104

Air Brush tool 104

Paintbrush tool 105

Arc tool 106

Line tool 106

Filled Rectangle, Ellipse, and Polygon tools 106

Rectangle, Ellipse, and Polygon tools 107

Additional Paint window areas 107

Chapter 7: Drawing, er, Painting on Director's Paint Window 109

No, You're Not Limited Just to Black and White 109

How Do I Change the Size of My Lines? 110

When a Graphic's Too Big for Its Own Good 111

Using scroll bars 112

Using the Hand tool 112

Wow! More Special Effects 112

Special commands in the View menu 112

Panel 113

Ruler 114

Grid 114

Onion Skin 114

Special commands in the Xtras menu 118

Installing Xtras 118

Using Filter Bitmap 119

Using Auto Filter 120

Using Auto Distort 121

Exploring more Xtras 122

SuperTechniRamaVision: All about System and Custom Palettes 123
   Using the System palette 124
   Facing problems with the System palette 124
   Living with 16 million headaches 125
   Living with compromise 126
   Compromising, and then compromising again 126
   Checking out those other built-in palettes 128
Who Was That Masked Man? And How Do You Make a Mask, Man? 129
   Creating a mask 130
   Applying Mask ink to a sprite 130

**Chapter 8: And Now for Something Completely
Different: Text and Field Windows** **131**

Bitmapped Text, One Step Away from Pod People 131
Rich Text, Come to Papa 132
Text in a Field 133
The Text Window 133
   Setting tabs 135
   Setting indents 135
The Text Cast Member Properties Dialog Box 136
   The Text Cast Member Name box 136
   The Framing pop-up menu 136
   Anti-alias radio/option buttons 137
   The Unload pop-up menu 137
   Miscellaneous stuff 137
   Searching for text 138
The Field Window 139

Part III: Manipulating Director with More Windows 141

Chapter 9: Yet Another Set of Tools: The Tool Palette **143**

A Brief Explanation of Tool Palette Tools 143
   Painting in Director 144
   Drawing in Director 144
Watch My Lips: T-h-e-s-e A-r-e D-r-a-w-i-n-g T-o-o-l-s 144
   Drawing on the Stage 144
   Modifying a Shape Cast Member 145
      The Shape Cast Member Properties dialog box 145
      The Shape pop-up menu 146
      Shape resizing handles 147
   Checking out the Tool palette tools 149
      Misfit tools 149
      Shape tools 150
      Button-making tools 150
   More Tool palette stuff 153
The Meaning of Life 153
Why You Should Care about This Palette 153

Chapter 10: Getting to Those Scrumptious Palettes:
The Color Palettes Window **155**

Decisions, Decisions, Decisions 155
  The Palette pop-up menu 156
    Director's built-in palettes 157
    Custom palettes 158
  Color Palettes window tools 159
  Color and index numbers 161
  Custom palettes 162
  Hot flashes 164
    Switching palettes in your movie 164
    Achieving that classic look 167
    Babbling on about DeBabelizer 167
The Old H-S-B Thing Again 167
  Hue, saturation, and brightness 167
  Additive and subtractive primary colors 168
  That mysterious 65535 168
  Complementary colors 169

Chapter 11: Your Very Own Digital Video Window **171**

Could You Review That Digital Video Thing Again? 171
  Introduction of digital video 172
  Demands of digital video 172
Digital Video to the Rescue 172
QuickTime Codecs 173
Video for Windows Codecs 177
Preparing QuickTime for Export 177
  Tempo Settings versus Real Time 178
  What color is your pop-up rainbow, er, menu? 178
  Scale options 179
  Sound decisions 180
  Setting up for Real Time digital video 180
What Good Is an Empty Digital Video Window? 181
  Touring the Video window 182
  Setting up your digital video 184
Playing Digital Video Lite 188
  Setting up your window 188
  Preparing the Score 188
  Adding a little Lingo 189
  Testing it out 190
Using Director as a Digital Video Editor 190
  Start from scratch 190
  Prebuilt digital video 191
  A digital video edit 192
    Setting up 192
    Importing the digital movies 193

Chapter 12: And the Winner of Script of the Year:
The Script Window **197**

    Where Good Scripts Go 198
    Script Properties 200
    Script Types 201
    Scripts: The Secret Sauce of Interactive Multimedia 202
        Gu, ghaa, du, uh, ormpf 202
        If you think Lingo's hard, try English 203
        No, Mother, I want to do it myself 203
            Ready-made scripts 203
            Simple scripts 203
            User groups 204
            Scripters 204
    Come On, Try One On for Size 205
        Adding a script to a movie 207
        Testing your scripts 210

Chapter 13: Messages from Beyond: The
Message and Debugger Windows **211**

    The Message Window 212
        Playing with Lingo commands in the Message Window 212
        Tracing the Action from the Message Window 214
    The Debugger Window 217

Chapter 14: Twick or Tweak: The Tweak Palette **221**

    When Mousing Around Just Isn't Enough 221
    Okay, Now Review That X-Y Coordinate Thing 223

Chapter 15: Your Pals, the Markers Window
and the New Window Command **225**

    So What Are Markers Anyway? 225
    A Word about the New Window Command 228

Part IV: More Interaction, Please! *231*

Chapter 16: Hey, Kids! Be an Animation Wizard **233**

    Discovering Animation Wizard 233
    Setting Up for Animation Wizard 234
    Previewing Animation Wizard Effects 236
    Creating Zooming Text with Animation Wizard 236
        A closer look at Animation Wizard 237
        Animation Wizard's basic scenario 238

Chapter 17: A Closer Look at Lingo **239**

Okay, Take a Deep Breath — Lingo's Not That Hard 239
Touring Basic Lingo Concepts 240
    Lingo 240
        Operators 241
        Commands 242
        Functions 243
    Handlers 244
    Events 245
    Messages 246
        Message window 246
    Variables 247
        Local variables 248
        Global variables 248
    Scripts 249
        Movie scripts 250
        Primary event handlers 252
        Frame scripts 255
        Sprite scripts 255
Why You Want to Write Lingo Scripts but Don't Know It 256

Chapter 18: Showing Off Your 15 Minutes of Fame on Video **257**

What You Really Need to Know about Video 257
    Broadcast quality 258
    Multimedia: kiosks, presentations, and CDs 258
    When something's moving, it's hard to see 259
    AV Macs and video boards 259
    Video production 260
        Post-production 262
    Taping your movies 263
Making a Projector (and Why You'd Want to) 264

Chapter 19: You Talkin' to Me? Adding Sound to Your Movie **267**

Where Do I Get All This Stuff, Anyhow? 267
    Sampling your own audio 267
Ready, Set, HeadStart 267
    Sampling sound with an AV Mac 268
    Freeware and shareware 270
    Commercial floppy and CD-ROM collections 270
Where Sounds Go in Director 270
Great Mac Sound for the Price of Good 271
Sync about It 271
    Playing a sound through 271
    Syncing sound to your movie 272

Chapter 20: Cross-Platform Stuff No One Should Need to Know 275

Cross-Platform Which Way? 275
    Now wait, I know I've heard of a cross-platform pack 276
    But I've heard you can use Mac Director
        movies in a Windows projector 276
Prepping Your Director Movies 276
    Following the rules is cool 277
    Stick with the System - Win palette 278
    Fonts R Us 279
    Prep your digital videos 280
Managing Your Files 281
    The project folder 281
    The stub projector 281

Chapter 21: Shockwave to the Web Wescue 283

Why a Web? 284
    Why all the fuss? 284
    Much, much slower than a speeding bullet 284
So How Do I Get Started on the Web? 285
What Hast Thou, Shockwave? 286
    AfterBurner 286
    Shockwave plug-in 287
Okay, So How Do I Use Shockwave? 287
    Prepping your Director movie 287
    Compressing your movie 289
    Making the AfterBurner file 289

Chapter 22: Ready to Wear All Those Hats? 293

Multimedia in Real Life 293
Some of the Roles You Play 295
    Creative director 295
    Art director 295
    Project manager 296
    GUI designer 296
    Lingo programmer 296
    Instructional designer 297
    Program tester 298
Ever Notice All Those Credits at the End of a Movie? 298

Part V: The Part of Tens *299*

Chapter 23: Ten Common Director Questions and Answers 301

How Can I Cut Down the Size of My Movie? 301
What Can I Do to Make Movies Play Faster? 303
What's the Best Way to Speed Up Digital Video in Director? 304

Why Do I Keep Losing Part of My Screen When I Tape My Movies? 305
How Can I Tape Director Movies to My VCR? 305
    Simple, cheap, but not terribly impressive 306
    AV Macs 306
    Video boards 307
Why Am I Getting Weird Colors When I Tape My Director Movies? 307
How Can I Improve the Color of My Movies on Tape? 308
    NTSC palette 308
    A better way to be NTSC safe 310
Can I Set Up My Movie to Play Right on Any Computer? 313
I've Never Done Programming Before. How
   Do I Know My Lingo Scripts Are Okay? 315
Can I Play My Director Movies on a Macintosh and a PC? 315

Chapter 24: Ten Ways to Add Animation to Your Movies 317

Use Animation Wizard's Built-In Special Effects 317
Remember the In-Between Commands 318
    Using In-Between 318
    Using In-Between Special 319
Try Color Cycling 321
    Creating a custom palette 321
    Painting color-cycling artwork 322
    Painting support graphics 323
    Setting up for color cycling 324
    Adding a line of Lingo 325
Buy Good Clip Animation 325
Turn Cast Members into Moveable Sprites 326
Import Digital Videos 326
Import Bitmaps or PICS Files 327
Record Real-Time Animations 328
Use Film Loops 329
Switch Color Palettes 331

Chapter 25: The Ten Most Important Lingo Words 335

Go Command 335
Play Command 336
Pause Command 336
Continue Command 337
Set Command 337
UpdateStage Command 338
DirectToStage Property 338
& and && Concatenation Operators 339
Repeat While and Repeat With Control Structures 340
If-Then Control Structures 342

Appendix A: I'm Ready for My Close-up, Mr. DeMille:
Director 5's System Requirements 343

Appendix B: The Mother of All Resource Lists **345**
    Books 345
    Training 345
    Vendors 346

Index *349*

Reader Response Card .... *Back of Book*

Introduction

1 know, like everyone else, you want to be in the movies. But because Hollywood hasn't been ringing your phone off the hook the last couple of days — or years, for that matter — what better than multimedia with Director 5, the premiere program for creating Hollywood-like movies on your very own PC or Mac. But wait — just the mention of the word Director and, like a .45 caliber Magnum at your temple in a dark alley on Friday the 13th, your palms begin to sweat, your heart rate triples, and you get acne for the first time in 31 years. Director? Me?

You've heard all the stories. Director's hard, like a shot of cheap bourbon at 2 a.m. after a tough case. It's impossible, like the woman who won't forgive you for turning her in — your mother yet. It's rough, like five-day old stubble. (No, I'm not still talking about your mother.) Yes, we've all heard these absurd horror stories.

And they're all true.

Unless you have this book. And you have this book, don't you? At least it's in your hands. Whether you pay for it is between you, your conscience, and that brawny security guard breathing down your neck. Director has a high learning curve; it doesn't hurt to be a rocket scientist with neurosurgery as a hobby. But ordinary people like you and that brawny security guard can understand how to use Director and make smart-looking, successful multimedia productions with a Mac or PC. Best of all, Director 5 has added a portal to Cyberspace called Shockwave so that you can even create movies for the World Wide Web.

What This Book Offers Mac or PC Users Like You

This book is for Mac or PC users. After Director is up and running, it's essentially the same program on either type of computer; where important differences exist, I point them out. If you plan on developing Director movies for both Macs and PCs, you'll need to buy separate copies of Director 5 for Macintosh and Director 5 for Windows.

That aside, I've done everything possible to make this book on Director 5 friendly and inviting. Don't be surprised if you start dating it after a couple of reads.

I'm not going to make all those assumptions that other books make — that you were born knowing a *bit* from a *byte* or what a *Lingo script* is all about. Instead, I break down seemingly impossible tasks into easy, doable steps, making essential features of Director crystal clear. Director 5 has 17 basic windows, give or take, but this book concentrates heavily on the most important ones, including

- The Stage window
- The Cast window
- The Score window
- The Paint window

This book gives you plenty of pictures for reference (get out your crayons) and lots of Director tips and tricks. The last chapter virtually brims with stuff that helps make life more carefree as you read about Director. The last chapter may even clear up your dry, itchy scalp and make your kids behave in public.

Who You Are

This writer's making some basic assumptions about someone who won't ante up more than $24.99 for a book, er, I mean, about someone who buys a book from the . . .*For Dummies* series. I'm assuming one or more of the following about you:

- You're new to computing.
- You're new to animation.
- You're new to multimedia.
- You're new, period.
- You're intimidated by technical jargon.
- You're not interested in technical jargon.
- You don't know what "technical jargon" means.
- You're running a Mac on some version of System 7.
- You're running a PC under Windows 3.1, 95, or NT.
- You've had flashbacks of alien abduction lately.

Icons Used in This Book

Some of the aids included for you in this book are marked with distinctive icons. In fact, if you cut them out really carefully and paste them neatly on acid-free card stock, they make really nifty holiday gifts.

This icon points out optional reading for you budding propeller-heads to ease you into a few technical areas and for trying advanced Macromedia Director techniques.

The Warning icon is meant to alert you to potentially risky or foolhardy software detours and acrobatics. As long as you have good backups — you do make copies of your software, don't you? — the worst that might happen is having to reinstall Director or your operating system. And doting father figure that I am, I'll occasionally remind you to save your work and be sure to eat plenty of leafy, green vegetables.

Your computer is very hale and hardy, which is not to say that you should regularly drop it from a 12-story building. Physically, you can break your computer in only a couple of ways and, even then, only with determination and pluck (you'll find pluck in the notions department of your local drugstore).

Software-wise, you might try something during the course of exploring Director that makes your computer freeze up, display an error message, or behave in some other unusual way, but chances are that it's just a software problem and temporary. Simply restarting your computer clears up at least half of these problems.

Dumb things to do to your computer

Dumb Thing to Do #1

Plugging in or unplugging computer cables while the machine's on. You can easily zap a component on something called the *system board* in your computer. One moment of hedonistic impatience may cost you $1,500 or so to get a new system board.

Dumb Thing to Do #2 (drum roll, please)

The ever popular moving-your-computer-while-it's-running trick, a great way to learn what hard disk head crashes and acid reflux are all about. Inside your computer, your hard drive's spinning at about 5,500 revolutions per minute or faster. Moving a running computer places the delicate read-write heads inside your hard drive at great risk of crashing into your data, about the equivalent of your car crashing into a brick wall at 80 miles an hour.

Throughout the book, you find many suggestions to make working with Director more productive and creative — or to just generally make life easier, like storing avocados in a brown paper bag.

This book is also liberally sprinkled with notes and asides that either clarify a point or seem related — however feebly — to the current topic.

By the way, this book is produced with remarkable state-of-the-art scratch-and-hear technology. When you come to one of these, scratch the icon so that you can read while listening to Ed Ames sing, "Try to remember. . . ." Hah, caught you scratching.

Conventions Used in This Book

This book tries to be more helpful than those other books about Director. On the off chance that you need some information from another computer book, you're sure to run into descriptions that seem puzzling to you because "they" won't bother explaining what "they" mean. However, because I love each and every one of you dearly, *I* explain all.

You're welcome.

Okay, everyone, slip on your enclosed decoder rings. The conventions used in this book include the following:

- **Menu Name⇨Command Name:** For example, "Choose Edit⇨Paste" means "Press the mouse on the Edit menu, drag the mouse pointer down, and choose the Paste command." Sometimes I say, "Go to the Paste command from the Edit menu" or "Choose Paste from the Edit menu." You run into the generic form frequently when you read more technical books.

- **Mac Modifier Key/PC Modifier Key+Character Key:** The Command (⌘) key, Shift key, Option key, and occasionally the Control key are Mac modifier keys. For Windows users, the Control (Ctrl) key usually replaces the Mac's Command key and the Alt key replaces the Option key. By pressing one or more of these modifier keys in combination with a character key, you can use keyboard shortcuts for various menu commands or to apply a specific technique to a selection. For example, "Pressing ⌘/Ctrl+1 alternately hides and shows the menu bar," means, "For a Mac, while pressing the Command key, tap the 1 key; for PCs, while pressing the Control key, tap the 1 key.

  In this book, the Mac's Command key is represented by the special character, ⌘ (Apple's "daisy" icon). By the way, newer Mac keyboards emboss both the daisy icon and the Apple icon on the Command key.

TIP

The Indubitable Rules of Keystrokes

When using modifier keys for keyboard short-cuts, be sure to follow "The Indubitable Rules of Keystrokes," as follows:

1. For Macs, press the Command key (⌘) first; for PCs, press the Control key (Ctrl) first.

2. Press other modifier keys next.

3. Press the character key last.

4. After pressing the complete sequence, release all keys unless specifically instructed not to.

✔ **Bold text:** You'll find text that you are to type at some point in a task in bold characters within a paragraph. For example, I might say "At the C prompt, type **WIN** and press Return to go to the Windows Desktop," meaning that you're to enter the characters W, I, and N in the appropriate field and continue the instructions. Be sure to enter the characters exactly as printed, including uppercase and lowercase letters and spaces. Sometimes stuff you enter is case-sensitive, sometimes not. It's usually safest to type exactly what's printed. (If you see "Simon says," ignore the rest of the sentence; I'm just being silly.)

Does This Book Cover Everything?

Now that we've come to be close, personal friends, you have the gall to ask me, "Does this book have everything anyone ever wanted to know about Director?"

Well, no way.

What won't you find in this book? Laughs for one, as you've already discovered. You won't find an explanation for every command of every window, either. You won't find detailed pontificating on every Lingo command. (*Lingo* is Director's name for its built-in computer language.) You won't find many advanced techniques covered, although I touch on a few in passing as teasers for you prospective propeller-heads out there.

But this book does get you started in a very big way. What this book doesn't cover is more than made up for with clear, concise information about Director 5 essentials for the budding computer user and multimedia and Web designer wannabe. Plus, this book has nice, wide margins to doodle on.

How This Book Is Organized

This book contains three major parts, each part containing several chapters, each chapter made up of billions upon billions of molecules. Makes you think, huh?

You do not need to read this book from cover to cover. I've read it cover to cover for you. Instead, I've written the book from the perspective of a solid reference; this book should summon up images of an overstuffed wingback chair, a crackling fireplace, a Rockwellesque, white-haired grandpa tenderly hugging his grandchild as they peruse a fine, weathered, leather-bound classic together.

Okay, so what you've got in your hot little hand is a floppy, softcover edition; use your God-given imagination, won't you? What I'm trying to convey is that each topic and exercise is relatively self-contained. Using the Table of Contents or the Index, you can go to any topic of interest and find valuable information on the subject in question and plenty of fine, fire-kindling material to boot.

Part I: The Big Picture

In Part I, I ask you to think big. Bigger. That's it. Now you're set to tackle cosmic questions like, "What is the meaning of life?," "Is there absolute good and evil?," and "How do I install this darn software, anyway?" Part I covers all that existential stuff with illustrations and references numerous enough to cut out and use as designer wallpaper. Along the way, you make incredible discoveries, including the fact that *multimedia* really means something. And that the blank screen you first come to in Director actually has a purpose. And a name.

Part II: Director's Windows of Opportunity

After Part I, the book rapidly deteriorates from mediocre to downright useless, unimportant stuff like how to use Director's Cast, Score, Paint, and Text windows. Just reading about the Cast window makes you want to go out and buy a casting couch. After discovering secrets of the Score window, you may be swept up in an overpowering urge to pull on riding britches and shiny black boots and watch creaky, old Erich Von Stroheim movies all night. And I deliberately toned down the Paint window stuff so that you're not inclined to decide that you were born with one ear too many. Finally, if the Text window info doesn't bring out the Hemingway in you, I don't know what will.

Part III: Manipulating Director with More Windows

The richness of Director's windows and commands contributes to the program's reputation for being the premiere multimedia-making application. Part III covers Director's remaining windows with thorough but humorous abandon. In fact, I dare you not to laugh yourself silly as you read about the whimsical Tool palette for creating so-called shapes in Director, the belly laugh-inducing Digital Video window for incorporating digital video movies into your Director productions, and the side-splitting Color Palettes window for color coordinating Director movies to that gaudy underwear you got on your birthday.

Part IV: More Interaction, Please!

Here's the part where you ease into Director's talents for lifting a presentation beyond a glorified side show by taking advantage of your computer's unique powers. Read about how to add special effects to your movies with push-button ease, how to prep your Director movies for the World Wide Web, and how to use Director's computer language, Lingo, to open up a whole new world of interactivity and excess stomach acid.

Part IV is kind of like riding the bobsleds at Disneyland. Something both thrilling and terrifying draws you to the Matterhorn. Except my ride is more thrilling than terrifying, even if you've never thought of using a computer language in your life. For one thing, Lingo is very conversational in tone. In fact, Lingo's simpler than ever, and, believe it or not, you'll be writing Lingo scripts before you know it.

I wind up Part IV by discussing what multimedia is like in the real world and leave you with the burning question, "Do you really want to wear all those hats, and wouldn't that attract a lot of unwanted attention?"

Part V: The Part of Tens

I don't know why, but whenever I think of Part V's name, I can't help picturing Charlton Heston saying it as a line from one of his epics. Can't you just see him exclaiming, "The Part of Tens," his mouth and chin making those distinctively "Hestonian" gestures? Anyway, Part V includes ten frequently asked questions. For example, perfect strangers come up to me all the time to ask, "What's so great about film loops?" That's the kind of exciting life I lead. And so may you, if only you can draw the following picture.

Seriously, Part V also reviews the ten most important ways to add animation to your Director movies and the ten most essential Lingo commands and concepts to become comfortable with.

What's Next?

Aside from paying for the book if you haven't already, the next step is to turn the page and dive right into the task of tackling Director 5. Don't forget that burly security guard.

Attention all readers

The pictures of menus, menu bars, and windows were taken from a Mac running on System 7.5.3, the latest version to date of what is now known as the Mac OS (Macintosh Operating System). If you're running Windows or an earlier release of System 7.0 on a Mac, your screen may differ slightly from the illustrations. If you're running the Mac's previous System, System 6.0, your screen will differ a little more dramatically, but once in Director, much of what you see will be very similar, if not the same. If you're running an even earlier System, shame on you!

Part I
The Big Picture

"AND TO COMPLETE OUR MULTIMEDIA PRESENTATION..."

In this part . . .

1 f you've ever dreamed of creating multimedia of your very own and broadcasting interactive animations on the World Wide Web, there's no better time to dive in with Macromedia Director 5, by far the easiest version of this program to work with since its humble beginning back in 1985.

Even if you just began your computer career, this part preps you for your adventure with introductory chapters, where you can find out why Director is the program of choice for so many multimedia and Web site developers, why you should be nutty enough to join their growing ranks, and what multimedia is all about in the first place.

Chapter 1

Stars of Director: Graphics, Sound, Movement, and Your CPU

● ●

In This Chapter

▶ Exploring uses for Director

▶ Defining multimedia

● ●

*A*t one time, multimedia meant setting up a bank of slide projectors, saying your best prayer, and hoping against hope that everything would work without the benefit of anything approaching a personal computer. In 1984, Apple introduced the first Macintosh, the 128K, with a whopping two programs to explore, MacPaint and MacWrite; if I say so myself, few people then were astute enough to anticipate how dramatically this "toy" was to change our personal and professional lives in years to come.

I wasn't one of them.

My boss at the time dragged me kicking and screaming before I wound up, exhausted, by a Mac 128K, my first computer. I think Peat Marwick's carpeting still shows my heel marks like a jagged scar, leading from drafting table to computer desk. Over time, however, and after several beatings, I learned to love my Mac; the following year, I was rewarded for this change of heart by being allowed to eat lunch and to be among the first to play with a fascinating little program called VideoWorks. This program was destined to evolve into Macromedia Director 5, the premiere authoring tool for cross-platform multimedia.

For those of you new to computing, this book uses the terms *application, program,* and *software* interchangeably. These terms all stand for what makes you break open your wallet at the computer store — what you take home on one or more floppy disks, copy to your hard drive, and use to accomplish various tasks. Perhaps you're using Microsoft Word for word processing and Excel for creating spreadsheets; they're applications, programs, software — same thing.

Director 5 for Macintosh and Director 5 for Windows are nearly mirror images of each other. If you anticipate the need to "port," as multimedia types like to say, your Director movies from one platform to the other, check out Chapter 20, where I summarize common pitfalls to avoid.

What Do You Use Director For?

Some of you in ReaderLand may desperately want to learn Macromedia Director without having the slightest notion why. Okay, I'm going to give you some great ammo to fight back with when your spouse finds out that you just plunked down nearly a grand for a handful of $3^1/_2$-inch plastic squares that you insist are called *floppies*.

Following in Walt's mouseprints

First, you can tell your friends and relatives that you're an animator, just like Walt what's-his-name, because Director's an *animation program* first and foremost. In other words, Director gives you the tools to make presentations that don't just sit there, but actually get up and move around. From its humble beginnings in a log cabin — introduced in 1985 as VideoWorks — Director was built to create a unique type of presentation: eye candy that changes over time.

As you explore the latest successor of VideoWorks, you see that Director 5 offers special windows to help build this kind of presentation with relative ease — if not abandon. For example, you run into the Score window, aptly named because it's very much like a musical score, with distinctive shorthand for recording changes in the presentation from frame to frame. In Director's Score window, you can follow the flow of visual information of your presentation, as well as rearrange and modify this information. In another special window, the Stage, you can play back your masterpiece. And when the throng of admirers comes up and asks, "Where do you go from here?" you can proudly exclaim, "I'm going to Disneyland!"

Just a Lincoln off the old log

How'd you like to have your kids smile up at you and boast to their friends, "My dad's just like Lincoln"? Aside from the distinctive facial features, maybe they recognize in you a yearning to take advantage of Director's *interactive* features to give The People their freedom — freedom to navigate through tons of information by choosing what they want to find out about and having darn good fun at the same time.

To create an interactive movie with Director, you can integrate graphics, music, narration, sound effects, and digital video into your masterpiece; you can also add buttons for deciding what happens next.

Normally, this type of interactive production is reserved for hard-core programmers — you know, those people who all look vaguely like Bill Gates — but Director allows all of us interested in this sort of thing to realize our ideas and present them to others.

Most exciting of all, Director 5 is raring to run on the World Wide Web. With the Shockwave utilities included in Director's package or available on the World Wide Web, you're set to add high-quality animations to the Web experience.

You may have heard Director described as a program that changes data over time. This begs the question, "What is data?" To be honest, I had to look through 12 or 13 glossaries from various technical books in my library before I found one honest-to-goodness definition. Apparently, we're supposed to be born knowing what data is. Well, *data* is information, plain and simple. When combining information with computers, our definition begs to include some kind of translation process so that information becomes a set of signals recognized by your computer. Only then can a computer handle information — moving and modifying it according to your wishes.

When talking about information "changing over time," I don't mean time from a geological or cosmic perspective, but time measured in very small units (30ths of a second) — units so small that you're not aware of moving from one unit of time to the next.

A working definition of *animation* is visual information changing in units of $1/30$ of a second. Director's windows and commands are designed to handle this kind of information, very different from the "static" info that a program like Microsoft Word manipulates. When you type a letter in Word, save the file, and look it over for typos, the document doesn't change on its own; in that sense, it's static information. If it does change, give me a call; I've got the number of a great exorcist for you.

By the Way, What the Heck Is Multimedia?

Even if you already know that you want to create animation with Director, I'll still bet that you probably have a pretty murky concept of what Director's other forte, multimedia, is all about. And "I know it when I see it" just doesn't cut it with those Fortune 500 clients you may want to work for. Trust me.

I admit, defining multimedia is a real challenge; I haven't seen the same definition for multimedia in any two books. Multimedia is one of those slippery things to define, like art, truth, and Aunt Edna's holiday fruitcake. But I'll try to decide on a working definition and to stay away from Aunt Edna's fruitcake.

Working definition of multimedia: *Multimedia* is the presentation of information combining images, sounds, and movement with the power of the computer.

Now, on to exploring my definition one chunk at a time.

Multimedia is image

Multimedia has something to do with images. Imagining multimedia without graphics, movies, artwork, or photographs is hard. Actually, images represent the strongest component of multimedia.

As it turns out, we're visually oriented creatures receiving about 80 percent of the information around us through our sense of sight; compare the richness of our visual life with our sense of smell, taste, or even touch. The other senses are all exquisite, but slip on a blindfold, and you're lost. You've probably seen those figures about how many advertising messages bombard us each day and how much TV we watch (or endure). So commanding visuals are certainly a dominant constituent of multimedia.

Multimedia is sound

But what would multimedia be without sound? Did you know that "silent" movies were never silent? A pianist or organist accompanied screenings, and sometimes a sound-effects man was there in the dark, too, adding thunder, clattering horse hooves, and, of course, gunshots to the melodrama.

Have you ever turned off the audio portion of your TV and watched a movie or commercial without sound? Think of some of your favorite movie scenes and then imagine them without sound. Picture the climactic scene in Spielberg's *Close Encounters of the Third Kind* when the great mothership appears over Devil's Tower, hovering jewel-like above gaping scientists. Imagine the stargate sequence in Kubrick's *2001: A Space Odyssey* without audio. Very different experiences — and not for the better.

So sound, including sound effects, music, and narration, is also a major player in the multimedia game.

Multimedia is movement

In this age of MTV, with its overpowering imagery and movement, color and movement, and creative abandon . . . and movement, movement is an integral extension of the force of imagery that plays such an important part in defining multimedia.

And movement.

In an attempt to stretch the definition of movement, pioneers of multimedia, ahem, myself included, tried incorporating video into productions with clumsy work-arounds, multiple monitors, separate VCRs, laser disc players, controllers, and wires, wires, and more wires. Then a few years ago, Apple Computer turned the world upside down with something called *QuickTime,* allowing multimedia types to add video directly within Director with all the Hollywood claptrap — dissolves, fade-ins, fade-outs, really wild special effects, and, oh yes, some content. QuickTime for Windows and similar technology from Intel and Microsoft have made digital video available for PC users, too.

QuickTime is an addition to the system, an extension in the Mac world or a TSR (Terminate and Stay Resident) program for PCs. By itself, QuickTime does nothing. Find it on the Desktop, try double-clicking its icon, and nothing happens.

Then what does QuickTime do for your computer? Good question. QuickTime extends your operating system to handle the kind of information that changes over time, in the form of a special file type called a QuickTime movie or, as this file type has come to be known, *mooV* (pronounced moo-vee) for the Mac and MOV extension for the PC. In addition to Apple's QuickTime for Windows, you PC types can create *Audio Video Interleaved* (AVI) movie files for your digital video needs, and a number of translators can convert Mac QuickTime mooVs and PC AVI movies into one another.

But here's a point. TV offers photos, graphics, movies, movement, and sounds of every description — and more than a few beyond description. If you've ever caught "Geraldo," you know what I mean. So why isn't TV multimedia? Or movies, for that matter?

One other element completes our working definition of multimedia.

Multimedia is your computer

In Lewis Carroll's *Alice in Wonderland,* the White Rabbit wonders how to begin telling a story to the King and Queen of Hearts. Carroll has the King smugly suggest, "Begin at the beginning . . . and go on till you come to the end: then stop."

Historically, most information has been linear, meaning that you start on page one, march in step through subsequent pages, and, on the last page, as the King of Hearts suggests, you stop. If you graphed the content, you'd wind up with a straight line — that's traditional, linear information and storytelling.

The power of your computer is the digital glue binding the other elements of multimedia together and adding the final touches: *interactivity* and *hypertext*.

Multimedia has something to do with using the computer to give the user, the person before the computer, the freedom to explore information in a "nonlinear" way.

What do you get when you graph interactive multimedia? A graph that looks more like a tree with hundreds or thousands of branches. In fact, many multimedia products feature such a map to help the user navigate through the product.

Interactive multimedia

Defining interactivity and hypertext is as slippery as defining multimedia. Thanks a lot.

When you use computing power to give the user the ability to decide where to start and which direction to go, you add *interactivity* to multimedia.

As you build your presentation in Director, you add interactivity by presenting the user with options in the form of buttons, sliders, and other controls that look like familiar objects in the real world. Here's where knowing at least a little Lingo scripting is important and making a mental note to check out Chapter 25 on Lingo tips and tricks is a good idea.

Hypertext

When you use the power of the computer to add links to text that the user can explore, you create *hypertext* — allowing the user to delve into deeper and deeper layers of information at will. Normally, the user is unaware of how these links work; that is, these links are *transparent* to the user. Ironically, you often go about creating these links with transparent buttons that take the user to deeper levels of information.

Interesting but moldy history of ye olde attempts at interactivity and hypertext

Early insightful experiments in interactivity and hypertext cry out to be cited here. Many illuminated manuscripts, those beautifully gilded pages of hand-drawn text and wondrous illustration from bygone days, feature hypertext in their structure. As you carefully inspect these venerable, delicate documents — put those white gloves on and, please, no sneezing — note the large central block of text, the smaller text to the left, and yet another, smaller block of text to its left. This is hypertext, 12th-century style. In other words, this kind of layout allows the reader to break away from the main text and delve into deeper levels of content on an intellectual whim. Power is transferred to the reader — that's nearly interactive multimedia; just add a gerbil-powered computer and you're off and running.

I've got to include the magical *Tristram Shandy,* a novel by Laurence Sterne published in 1760, in this stopover into antiquity. If you've never read it, do yourself a favor. Beg, borrow, or steal a copy. *Tristram Shandy* is not your ordinary book; describing it makes defining multimedia look like a picnic without ants. There are suddenly blank pages, there are pages with one word on them, there are weird pages. In this inverted Tom Jonesian world, the author tells his story not only with text but with the words themselves — the very pages of the book and how they are or are not laid out. *Tristram Shandy* is certainly an impressive experiment in multimedia, hypertext, and interactivity — the whole shebang, worthy of reading and study.

Chapter 2

Launching Director: An Application by Any Other Name ...

In This Chapter

- Reviewing the GUI, Director's executive producer
- Looking around Director
- Exploring Director's About box
- Purging Director's memory
- Calling S.O.S. with D.O.L.H. (Director's online Help)
- Using Director's File menu
- Touring Director's other menus

*W*hy has the Mac been such a success, making Apple founders Steve Jobs and Steve Wozniak instant holders of savings accounts in excess of $1,000 each and revolutionizing the way you work with and think about computers and software? Most computer pundits agree: Chili's tastier with a big topping of cheddar cheese. Also, they agree that the Mac owes much of its success to its innovative *GUI* (graphical user interface), integral to the Mac since the introduction of the Mac 128K in 1984. Now, of course, a similar approach to interface design is available for PCs with Microsoft Windows.

I lied. Before 1984, before the Mac 128K, the Apple Lisa was around, which was really my first computer. The Lisa stood in all its magnificence like a Mac 128K on steroids, with a 12-inch built-in monitor in place of the 128K's puny 9-inch screen. If the Lisa and Mac had met on the beach, I just know Lisa would've kicked sand in the Mac's little Smiley Face. The Lisa cost $10,000 in pre-1984 dollars, which was a big reason for its demise; those who could afford the Lisa loved it and got a preview of the Mac's Desktop, trash can, menu bar, and icons to boot. And they say money can't buy happiness.

The *GUI* (pronounced goo-ee) is a set of mostly visual cues used to "communicate" with your computer, in contrast to a *CLI,* or command line interface, which is like DOS for PCs, where the user faces a text-based screen, reads lines of data generated by a computer program, and types commands to go to the next step.

The graphical user interface of the Mac OS and Windows includes the following:

- ✔ The Desktop is home base. On the Desktop, you find application and file icons and a menu bar at the top of the screen. These graphic elements come from your computer's chips or from the hard drive.

- ✔ The menus and windows of programs you open and the visual similarity of one program to another.

- ✔ The general "look and feel" of the interface, its friendliness and patience with users — all built-in, of course.

Reviewing the GUI, Director's Executive Producer

One of the most endearing features of a graphic interface is its cozy familiarity. After you learn one program, you probably know 30 to 40 percent of every well-written program out there in ComputerLand. So opening or launching a heavy-duty program like Director 5 is as simple as opening the simplest program you can find. But if you need a quick refresher course in Computer Science 101, use the following section to get up and running.

Starting your computer

For you Mac types, you start one set of Macs with a switch. In compact-type Macs with built-in monitors like the Mac SE and Classic and with some Performas and Mac LCs, chances are you'll find a rocker switch in back and to the left with the Mac facing you. Some oddball Macs like the 660AV and some Power Macs have round buttonlike switches located in the front right panel. Either way, turn on this kind of Mac with the switch.

You start the other type of Mac — Mac II types, some Quadras, some Power Macs, and assorted Performas — from the Power key on the keyboard. The Power key is that wide key at the top left of most keyboards, unless you have a really old keyboard, where you'll probably find the Power key at the top center. Embossed on the Power key is an icon of an arrow, as shown in Figure 2-1.

Figure 2-1:
Power on
your
computer!

Simply give the Power key one good press. Your Mac fires up, and soon you see Mr. Smiley Face, the "Welcome to Macintosh" screen, and finally the Desktop with trash can and icons. What a trash can is doing on *top* of your Desktop I'll never know.

For you Windows types, if your computer's been configured for Windows, starting up takes you straight to the Desktop and all those beautiful icons. If you're starting up from DOS, after the C prompt (C:\>) simply type **WIN** and press the old Enter key to go to the Windows Desktop.

Your pal, the mouse

The humble mouse has actually been around for quite a while. The late '60s saw a growing interest in personal computers, although few people could articulate why they wanted one and what they'd do with one after they got it. While a far-thinking individual, Ivan Sutherland, was working with a primitive graphical user interface astonishingly like what you see today, a gentleman named Doug Englebart was developing an oddball device he called a mouse for working with his computer. Frankly, Englebart's mouse looked more like a giant bar of Ivory soap. Similar devices appeared at Xerox's Palo Alto Research Center in the '70s, where advanced studies on how people use computers were underway; many of its innovative concepts, including the mouse, wound up reflected in today's personal computers sporting graphic user interfaces.

Double-clicking

Double-clicking the mouse is an essential technique when working with Macs and PCs these days, but some people have trouble getting the hang of it. If you click too slowly, your computer doesn't recognize the move as a double-click but as two separate clicks of the mouse, which doesn't give you the desired result.

One way to make double-clicking easier is to adjust the mouse with the Mouse control panel. On a Mac, you find the Mouse control panel under the Apple menu at the top left of your screen. From the Apple menu, choose Control Panels and double-click the Mouse control panel icon, shown in Figure 2-2. In the bottom panel of the Mouse control panel window, shown in Figure 2-3, adjust the mouse's sensitivity to double-clicking. The small round "radio buttons" give you three levels of Double-Click Speed, from slow on the left to medium in the center and fast on the right. If you're a born double-clicker, click the right radio button — hey, no need to brag. The other two radio buttons are for the click-impaired.

Figure 2-2:
The Mouse
control
panel icon.

Figure 2-3:
The Mouse
control
panel on
the Mac.

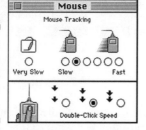

In Windows, double-click the Control Panel icon in the Main program group and then double-click the Mouse control panel icon. In the Mouse control panel, captured to perfection in Figure 2-4, adjust clicking speed with the slider control.

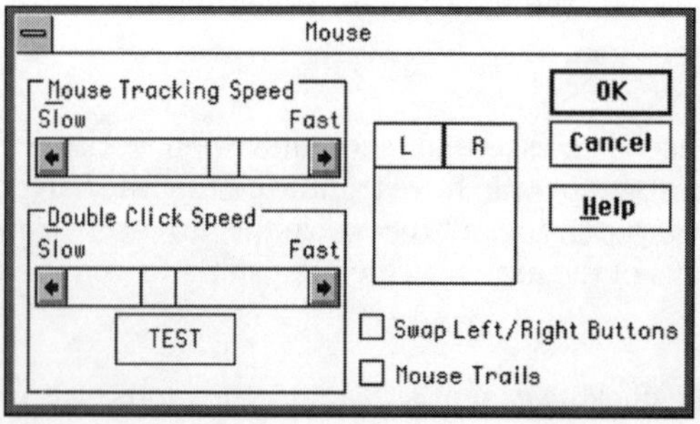

Figure 2-4:
The
Windows
Mouse
control
panel,
where you
can adjust
clicking
speed and
tracking.

Beware default settings!

Sometimes your computer resets itself to settings direct from the assembly line, so-called default settings. This can happen when you do a really good job of zapping the PRAM (Parameter RAM), a common maintenance routine for the Mac, or adjust the BIOS (Basic Input/Output System) on a PC. The default setting for mouse tracking is the slowest setting, intended for using a drawing tablet. If your mouse seems suddenly sluggish, like it's slushing through black strap molasses, check the Mouse control panel and reset it to your favorite speed.

By the way, the easiest and best way to zap the PRAM on a Mac is to beg, borrow, or steal a copy of Tech Tool, freeware available on all the online services, most bulletin boards, and numerous sites on the Web.

Don't try playing with the BIOS on your PC unless you know what it is and exactly what you're doing.

Adjusting mouse tracking

By the way, your Mouse control panel allows you to change how fast your mouse moves around the screen, or *tracks*. If the mouse seems sluggish, adjust the tracking control. If you're working with a tablet and pen-type device instead of the standard mouse, you want the slowest tracking speed for greater control. On a Mac, click one of the tracking radio buttons; for Windows, use the slider control.

One thing that really irks this writer is irk. It's so bland. On a cold, wintry morning, though, nothing is better than a big, steaming bowl of irk; love it with raisins and brown sugar — mmm. Another irksome thing — all those manuals and computer books that tell you to "click the mouse" when the authors really mean "press the mouse." Two completely different techniques. In this book, marvel that it is, I say "press the mouse" to mean exactly that, pressing the mouse button on the standard mouse and *keeping* it pressed. Clicking means pressing and *releasing* the mouse button once. After all, knowing the difference between pressing and clicking keeps us at the top of the food chain.

Opening Macromedia Director

Okay, you're at the Desktop. If you're like normal people — although I doubt it because you paid good money for this book — you've already made an Applications folder (Macs) or program group (PC) the night you wore out your pick-up sticks. The Applications folder/group is probably where you installed Director. Anyway, find Director's custom icon, hand-crafted by Italian artisans for untold generations. (See Figure 2-5.)

Figure 2-5:
Ready to
start up
Director.

From here, select Director by moving your mouse pointer over its icon and clicking once. On a Mac, Director's icon changes its appearance (reverses it if you have a black-and-white screen or darkens it on gray scale and color monitors); that's the Mac's endearing way of showing you that the icon's selected. On your PC, the icon's title reverses.

Now you can go to the File menu and choose the Open command to start Director. But for the truly rugged, high-spirited, and adventurous out there (the kind of computer user who grew up playing with G.I. Joe and eating splinters for breakfast), rev up your engines. Point to Director's icon with the mouse and double-click to issue the Open command. And you thought skydiving without a parachute was macho.

With either method, Director launches and the first window comes into view. Multimedia types call this window the "splash screen." Just knowing this and saying "splash screen" often and in a loud, boisterous voice puts you leagues ahead of multimedia wannabes who actually think hard work and studying will someday pay off.

Finally, with hearts pounding and arms akimbo (I've always wanted to use that phrase), you arrive at Director to find . . .

A blank screen?

This is going to change my life? This blank screen is the beginning of a new career for me? This is why I paid $24.99 for this book — a blank screen? All typical reactions; if I've heard them once, I've heard them once. Trust me; there's more to Director than a blank screen. By the way, this so-called blank screen just happens to be Director's most important window, the Stage, where all the action takes place. More on the Stage in Chapter 3.

Stepping Up to the Bar (Graph)

You can learn some important information about Director by choosing
Windows⇨Inspectors⇨Memory. The bar graph in the Memory Inspector palette
(see Figure 2-6) gives you a quick overview of how well Director is managing
memory for you as you work on a movie.

Figure 2-6:
The Memory
Inspector
palette
displays
Director's
use of
memory in a
bar chart
and allows
you to purge
unneeded
memory to
increase
performance.

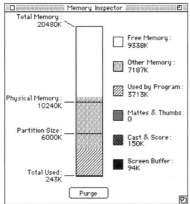

The elements in the bar graph area include the following:

- ✔ **Total Memory:** Indicates the sum of real memory (so-called RAM SIMMs
  installed in your computer) and any virtual memory you may be using.
  Virtual memory is a trick that makes your computer think part of your
  unused hard disk is more memory. You PC types use virtual memory when
  you run in 386 enhanced mode, which pretty much takes care of itself.

- ✔ **Physical Memory:** Reflects the amount of real memory in the form of RAM
  SIMMs installed in the computer. This element of the Memory Inspector is
  visible only when virtual memory is turned on to differentiate physical
  from total memory that includes virtual memory. See the preceding
  paragraph for more on RAM and virtual memory.

- ✔ **Partition Size:** Represents the amount of memory reserved for Director's
  exclusive use. This figure echoes the value set in the Preferred size field of
  the Mac's Get Info box. Windows has no exact equivalent for manipulating
  an application's memory except by increasing the amount of RAM.

Upon opening, Director reserves a specific amount of memory for its
exclusive use, piggy that it is. Once launched, as long as Director runs —
even in the background — the reserved memory remains unavailable to
any other program, the system, or any other component of your computer.

You PC types know it as extended memory, which pretty much takes care of itself. For Mac users, the reserved memory is called the program's *application partition.* Out of the box, the initial or default value of the partition is set to the suggested value, but you can change the value to increase the application's performance. (See the "For Mac users only: changing Director's application partition" section later in this chapter.) More memory = better performance — kind of like presidents.

✔ **Total Used:** Represents the amount of memory being used by the current Director movie.

On the right side of the Memory Inspector, you'll find the following information with corresponding shaded areas in the bar graph:

✔ **Free Memory:** The white section of the bar. Indicates the current amount of unused memory. This is the same value as Largest Unused Block shown in the About This Macintosh box under the Apple menu at the Finder.

✔ **Other Memory:** Indicates the amount of memory used by the system and other applications.

✔ **Used by Program:** Represented on the bar with the light gray section. Indicates how much of Director's program code is currently copied to Director's reserved memory. When launched, only a portion of Director's code is copied into memory.

✔ **Mattes & Thumbs:** Currently 0, begins to take some of Director's reserved memory as you create an animation sequence. This value shows in the bar as a medium gray section. *Matte* refers to a special *ink type* you can give graphics in Director. *Thumbs* refers to the collection of miniature images you see in the Cast window as you develop an animation. Each matte and thumb, or thumbnail image, takes up a small amount of Director's reserve of memory.

✔ **Cast & Score:** This is 0 for a blank Director file, too, but grows as you develop your animation sequence. This value is represented in the bar as a dark gray section. Cast refers to the actual set of graphics and text represented in the Cast window by thumbnail images. Score refers to one of Director's main windows, the Score window, which increasingly takes up Director's reserved memory as you build your animation.

✔ **Screen Buffer:** Represented on the bar as a black section, refers to the amount of Director's reserved memory used to display graphics on the Stage. Screen Buffer size is directly related to the height and width of the Stage window, which you can set and modify in Director at any time from the Modify menu.

Beneath the bar area is the Purge button. The Purge button . . . well, that's what the next section's for.

Purging Director's memory

The Memory Inspector palette gives you critical information about Director's management of memory. Even more unique is the Purge button at the bottom of the palette. When you click Purge, Director tosses out of memory any unneeded data and Cast Members with Purge Priorities (which you can set) other than 0. One thing every animation or multimedia program cries out for when it comes to memory is, "More, more, more!" Purging is one of Director's simplest, built-in ways of freeing up memory.

To purge Director's memory, follow these steps:

1. **Choose Quit from the File menu.**

   What you see on your screen will come closer to matching the following steps if you quit Director first and return to the Desktop.

2. **Double-click Director's application icon to open Director.**

   You arrive at Director's Stage window.

3. **Choose Window⇨Inspectors⇨Memory.**

   Note the striped light gray section in the bar chart in Figure 2-6 and the number below Used by Program. In my example, the value is 3713K. By the way, I've made this section in Figure 2-6 and 2-7 lighter than it really appears on-screen to increase contrast.

4. **Click the Purge button.**

   Note the change in the Used by Program value and the height of the light gray section of the bar. Figure 2-7 shows a drop in value from 3713K to 3257K, freeing up about 500K of memory just in this area of memory. Notice that the Other Memory area and Cast & Score memory use have dropped, too. Congratulations!

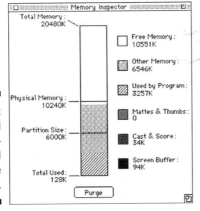

Figure 2-7:
Well
done —
you've freed
up some
memory.

K stands for kilobytes; each kilobyte equals 1,024 bytes of memory. Don't ask why. The number in Figure 2-6 tells you that 3713K of Director's programming code was loaded into memory when you opened the application, only a portion of Director's total code.

After you click Purge, various built-in routines clean up Director's application partition, the amount of memory reserved for the program's exclusive use, and free up memory.

For Mac users only: changing Director's application partition

The amount of memory reserved for a program is often insufficient to run it at maximum efficiency. With a Macintosh, you can increase the amount of memory yourself with the Get Info box. Follow these steps:

1. **Close Director by choosing Quit from the File menu.**

   If this step doesn't take you to the Finder, choose Finder from the Application menu. To modify any program's application partition, you *must* first quit the program. If you ever come to a program's Get Info box and the values in the Memory Requirements panel are grayed out, you forgot to quit.

2. **Choose About This Macintosh from the Apple menu.**

   Note the number to the right of Largest Unused Block. This number represents the memory you have left to play with measured in kilobytes. If the number is 6,000 or less, run to the store and buy more memory. You shouldn't even try to run Director; really, you don't have enough memory. If the number is at least 9000K, click the Close box in the upper-left corner of the About window and go to the next step.

3. **At the Desktop, find Director's icon in the Director folder and select it with one click of the mouse.**

4. **Choose Get Info from the File menu.**

   The Director 5.0 Info window appears, as in Figure 2-8.

   Look at the Memory Requirements panel at the bottom of the Get Info box. The Suggested size is the developer's recommended application partition size and cannot be altered. Notice the value is not in an entry field. Director's suggested size is 9467K.

   The value entered in the Minimum size field limits the smallest amount of memory Director may reserve for itself on opening. The minimum size is in an entry field so you can replace the default value to a smaller number at your own risk. Usually, that's a very bad idea. In my example, the minimum size is set at 5371K. The idea behind the minimum size is to determine the range of memory that you allow Director to work in. In other words, if you decided you wanted Director to reserve between 5000K and 9467K of memory when you open it, you would enter **5000** in Minimum size and leave Preferred size at the default value, 9467. On the other hand, if you wanted to force Director to always open at the preferred size, you'd enter **9467** in the Minimum size field, too.

The value in the Preferred size field is exactly what it says, what the developer would like to see you set Director's application partition to provided you have enough memory. But the trick is to enter an even higher value than the default preferred size for increased performance, especially for high-powered programs like Director.

At this point, I'm going to make some of those assumptions I pooh-poohed in the Intro to my book. One, if you've come this far you have 9000K of available memory (as in step 2). In that case, you would need to *lower* the preferred size in Director's Get Info box to the amount of free memory revealed in the About This Macintosh box in step 2.

Actually for the following example, I'm going to be generous and pretend that you have 16MB of extra memory. No, no need to thank me. I'm also going to assume the preferred size value is currently set to 9467K. Which isn't *too* shabby, but you can do better.

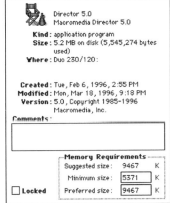

Figure 2-8:
Director 5's
Info
window,
where you
can give the
program
more RAM.

5. **Double-click the field labeled Preferred size to highlight the current value.**

6. **In the Preferred size field, enter a higher value than the default preferred size.**

Don't include a comma or K character. In this example, I want you to enter **9967**.

7. Click the Close box in the upper-left corner of the Director 5 Get Info window.

You just upped Director's application partition by 500K, which is fine for the sake of this example, but . . . remember Real Life? When you're not watching TV? In Real Life, you'd want to set Director's application partition much higher if you've got the memory (and the money). For a typical animation production, you want to set the Preferred size to around 20,000K. That's about 20MB. Yikes!

Calling S.O.S. with D.O.L.H. (Director's Online Help)

One of Director's marvels is its built-in Help system, what multimedia types call online help, meaning that it's available on your computer while you're running Director. You don't have to look up anything in those old-fashioned books. Saying "online help" and "splash screen" loud and often assures you a place in multimedia history. Or maybe psychiatric history. Figure 2-9 show Help's main menu.

From there, you can type a keyword for a search through Help's topics, click one of the large images representing basic help categories, or click one of the buttons very similar to buttons explained in the upcoming section.

Figure 2-9:
The main menu of Director's Help window.

Director's context-sensitive help

Director's online help has more going for it than good looks. It's *context-sensitive help*, meaning that Director can go straight to your topic of interest rather than always landing on its main menu. How does Director accomplish this seeming miracle?

The first step is to transform that ordinary drab mouse pointer into the cool Help Pointer, a cursor that looks like a question mark preceded by a small asterisk. You can access the Help Pointer a couple of ways. Choose Window⇨Toolbar to display Director's new Toolbar feature just under the menu bar and click the Help Pointer icon on the far right. Or press ⌘/Ctrl+?.

Now for the fun, context-sensitive part. Click any window or choose any menu command with the Help Pointer, and Director (usually) takes you right to that topic in the Help window, as in Figure 2-10. In my example, I clicked on the Stage with the Help Pointer, and Director took me to the help section about the Stage window. Notice that you can enter a keyword at the top, which is great fun because Director tries to anticipate what you're typing. As you enter a word or phrase, Director keeps completing your entry in gray characters. If Director guesses right, just stop typing and press Enter; otherwise, continue entering the keyword you want to search for and then press Enter.

Notice the little yellow square in the upper-right corner of the Help window. It represents an electronic stick-on note. Press the square and drag a stick-on note into the Help window, and then write yourself a note! If you don't enter any text, the note disappears when you jump to another page.

Figure 2-10:
One of
Director's
Help
windows.

Table 2-1 summarizes the functions of the items in the first row of buttons at the top of Director 5's Help window, a full collection of tools for maneuvering through Help's contents.

Table 2-1	Help Window Items, Row 1
Item	*What It Does*
Contents button	Takes you to the Director Help Contents window, a main menu with illustrations serving as buttons. Clicking one of the six illustrations takes you to a list of subtopics to explore with a click of the mouse.
Search button	Takes you to the Help Index window with a text field for entering a search topic and a list of topics.
Go Back button	Jumps you back to previous screens in reverse order.
History button	Displays the History palette, where each window you visit is recorded in a scrolling list. Double-clicking a listing takes you back to that window, Alternately, you can highlight a listing and click the View Topic button. Click the Clear button to delete the list.
Previous button	For nostalgia buffs. Each click takes you to the previous window for a specific topic.
Next button	For A-type personalities. Each click takes you to the next window for a specific topic.
Keyword field	Enter beginning characters for a search and notice the Help system trying to guess the rest of the entry with gray letters. When you've seen enough, press Enter.
Note icon	Add a stick-on-style note to the current Help window by moving the mouse over the button. When the cursor changes to a Hand, press and drag a note into the window and type away. Want to trash a note? Drag the note off the window and when the cursor changes to a trash can, release the mouse button.

An intriguing conundrum

To access the Help Pointer, should you press the ⌘/Ctrl+? keys or the ⌘/Ctrl+Shift+? keys? Don't you type a question mark by pressing the Shift key first?

Know what? In Real Life, it doesn't matter. I just mentioned it to pad this section; it was looking a little lean.

Table 2-2 summarizes the function of the buttons in the second row of the Director 5.0 Help window, an echo of the graphical Main Menu that you come to by clicking the Contents button.

Table 2-2	Help Window Buttons, Row 2
Button	*What It Does*
New	Takes you to a list of new features in Director 5. Click on one of the items to go to that topic.
Basics	Takes you to a list of essential Director topic categories, including important windows, techniques, and even troubleshooting. Click a category to explore related topics.
Reference	Takes you to a window of Help's contents organized by menus, an alphabetical list of menu commands, and a list of windows. Click a listing to explore related topics.
Lingo	Takes you to a window brimming with Lingo information, including a definition of Lingo, a list of basic Lingo topics, an alphabetical index, and a list of Lingo topic categories. Click your entry of choice into the magical world of Lingo scripting.
Shortcuts	Takes you to a list of keyboard shortcuts, including the shortcut menu and each of Director's windows. The shortcut menu is the hidden context-sensitive menu that appears when you Ctrl+press an area of Director's interface.
FAQs	Takes you to a list of frequently asked questions (FAQs) on essential topics that you can click to explore further.

As you explore Director's Help system, you find representations of various windows. Clicking different features of a window displays a panel of relevant information. The panels don't include a Close box; to return to the previous window, just click anywhere on your screen, the panel disappears and you are transported back to the Help window.

The Help system is really a mini-application that works with Director. When you want to return to Director, choose File⇨Quit or press ⌘/Ctrl+Q.

The Help menu

Director's help isn't really Director's help. That is, it's Director's help, but it doesn't belong to Director. In other words, h-m-m-m, Director's Help system is really a separate program called QuickHelp. I know you don't believe me, so take a look at the Application menu if you're using a Mac and find QuickHelp listed there. See, I told you.

QuickHelp works with Director but has its own menu. Most of the commands are self-explanatory. I just want to go over some that are different enough.

- **File⇨Print All Topics:** To print out a hard copy of all the help material, choose this command. Great for leveling tables, too.

- **Edit⇨Undo Delete Note:** If you foolishly tossed out a gem of a note, you can reclaim it with this command if you act *immediately* after the trashing incident.

- **Edit⇨Delete Note:** If you mean to trash a note, click the note and choose Edit⇨Delete Note or drag the note out of the Help window. (You'll see the cute hand icon turn into a smelly old trash can.)

- **Edit⇨Copy Topic Text:** Choose this command to go to a scrolling window containing the text for the current topic. You can then choose to copy selected text or the whole shebang (too technical to discuss).

- **Edit⇨Copy Topic as a Picture:** If you want to make your own wallpaper, copy various topics as bitmaps, print them out, color with crayons, and buy wallpaper hanging setup. Great family fun.

- **Find⇨Global Find:** The only difference between this command and entering a keyword to search by is this: You can choose the following Global Find Again command and search repeatedly for the same category. After you type a keyword and press Enter, the keyword disappears.

- **Find⇨Global Find Again:** See the preceding command.

- **Bookmarks⇨Set Bookmark:** Choose this command to create a kind of electronic bookmark for the current topic. A nice feature is selecting a keyboard shortcut from a pop-up menu to return to the marked topic at any time. Bookmarks you create are listed under the Bookmarks menu, too.

- **Bookmarks⇨Edit Bookmarks:** This command takes you to the Edit Bookmarks dialog box, listing all bookmarks in a scrolling field. You can change the name of a selected bookmark or its keyboard shortcut or even delete the bookmark if you feel particularly destructive. You can also click a View button to take you to the page corresponding to the selected bookmark in the list.

- **View⇨Show Notes:** This is one of those infamous toggle commands. Choose once to show your notes. Choose again to hide them. Top security feature. Good thinking, Macromedia. No one's going to figure this one out.

- **View⇨Animation Effects:** This command toggles a zoom effect on and off when you click on some of the pictures in Director's windows.

- **View⇨Director Help:** This one's got me stumped. Send in your best guess to me personally, care of IDG Books Worldwide, Inc.

The Toolbar

Choose Toolbar from the Window menu to view a line of icons that goes clear across the screen, looking incredibly like the facsimile in Figure 2-11. If you're comfortable with the toolbar in Microsoft Word 6.0, you'll like this new feature. It offers lots of basic commands at the click of your mouse.

Figure 2-11:
The Director
5.0 toolbar.

Table 2-3 summarizes the function of each mysterious icon.

Table 2-3		Toolbar Icons
Icon	*Icon Name*	*What It Does*
	New Movie	Creates a new movie. If the current movie hasn't been saved, Director prompts you to save it. Director can show only one movie at a time.
	New Cast	Creates a new Cast window. You may choose to make it an internal or external cast. See "Internal and external Cast windows" in Chapter 4 for more information.
	Open	Displays the Open File dialog box, where you can choose a different movie to work with.
	Save	Updates the current movie to disk, usually to your internal hard drive.
	Print	Displays the Print dialog box with many options, including an Options button with additional buttons.
	Import	Displays the Import File dialog box, where you recruit Cast Members for your movie. For more on importing files, see "Adding Cast Members to the Cast window" in Chapter 4.
	Undo	If you make a mistake and you know it, immediately stop. Do not pass Go. Click once on this icon to step back one giant step to degoof your movie.
	Cut	Removes the selection from the movie and places it in the Clipboard, same as the Cut command in the Edit menu.

(continued)

Table 2-3 *(continued)*

Icon	*Icon Name*	*What It Does*
	Copy	Puts a copy of the selection into the Clipboard, your Mac and PC's little liaison between files and applications.
	Paste	Inserts the current contents of the Clipboard into the current window or insertion point, if appropriate. Grayed out or disabled if not an appropriate command at the time.
	Find Cast Member	Displays the Find Cast Member dialog box, where you can search by Name, Type, Palette, or Usage.
	Exchange Cast Members	Exchanges the selected sprite in the Score window with the selected Cast Member in the Cast window.
	In-Between	Creates intermediate frames from beginning and ending frames you select in the Score window. Check out "What to do between takes? In-Between Special, of course" in Chapter 5 for more info.
	Align	Displays the Align floating palette to line up selected sprites on the Stage in one of nine different ways.
	Rewind	Rewinds the current movie to frame 1, usually what you want to have happen just before you play back your production.
	Stop	Halts playback of the current movie.
	Play	Begins playback of the current movie from the current frame, not necessarily from the beginning of the movie.
	Cast window	Displays the Cast window, where all good actors hope to arrive. The equivalent of choosing Window⇨Cast or pressing ⌘/Ctrl+3.
	Score window	Displays the Score window, where you design and choreograph your movie. The equivalent of choosing Window⇨Score or pressing ⌘/Ctrl+4.
	Paint window	Displays the Paint window, where you create new Bitmap Cast Members or edit imported bitmaps. The equivalent of choosing Window⇨Paint or pressing ⌘/Ctrl+5.
	Text window	Displays the Text window, where you enter so-called rich text. The equivalent of choosing Window⇨Text or pressing ⌘/Ctrl+6.

Icon	Icon Name	What It Does
 📜	Script window	Displays the Script window, where you can play mad doctor conducting cruel and inhuman experiments with Lingo, Director's built-in scripting language. The equivalent of choosing Window⇨Script or pressing ⌘/Ctrl+0 (zero).
 💬	Message window	Displays the Message window, where you can try out Lingo scripts one line at a time, a good "lab" for learning Lingo basics. The equivalent of choosing Window⇨Message or pressing ⌘/Ctrl+M.
 ⋮?	Help pointer	Turns the mouse cursor into America's newest super hero, Help pointer! Choose any menu command or click virtually any location of interest in a window with Help pointer, and you're taken in hand to that very section in Director's built-in, context-sensitive help system.

Director's File Menu

Are you ready to dive into Director's menu bar? Personally, I'd rather go for a pastrami sandwich. To take a look at Director's File menu, press the mouse on File. The File menu drops down, as in Figure 2-12, which is why it's cleverly called a *drop-down* or *pull-down menu.*

File	
New	▶
Open...	⌘O
Close	⌘W
Save	⌘S
Save As...	
Save and Compact	
Save All	
Revert	
Import...	⌘R
Export...	⇧⌘R
Create Projector...	
Page Setup...	⇧⌘P
Print...	⌘P
Preferences	▶
temp	
Quit	⌘Q

Figure 2-12:
Director's
File menu.

Table 2-4 shows you what to expect from each File menu command.

Table 2-4	File Menu Commands
Command	*What It Does*
New⇨Movie	Asks you to save any changes to the current movie, closes the current file, and creates a new movie.
New⇨Cast	Creates a new internal or external Cast window. See "Internal and external Cast windows" in Chapter 4 for more on internal and external casts.
Open	Takes you to the Open dialog box to find an existing Director movie.
Close	Closes any window other than the Stage window, which is always visible for the current movie.
Save	Updates a movie and linked casts that you've already named and saved to the hard drive.
Save As	Opens the Save As dialog box to save the current movie as a new movie on the hard drive.
Save and Compact	Like the Save command, but compresses the movie and removes unneeded data for better performance.
Save All	Updates the movie and all casts, internal and external and linked or unlinked. For more on linked and unlinked casts, see "Linking your imported file" in Chapter 4.
Revert	Returns the current movie to its last saved version on the hard drive.
Import	Allows you to add several graphics file types and sound file types as Cast Members in your Director movie.
Export	Turns a Director file into different external file types.
Create Projector	Creates a stand-alone version of selected movies for distribution.
Page Setup	Sets up a current movie to print with Page Size, Scaling, and Orientation settings.
Print	Allows you to print all or a portion of the current movie, including the content of selected windows.
Preferences⇨General	Allows you to set Stage Size, User Interface options, and Text Units (inches, centimeters, or pixels) and allows you to determine whether to temporarily borrow from unused system memory.
Preferences⇨Score	Allows you to set options like colored cells and drag and drop and to set information in the extended display mode of viewing Cast Members in the Score.

Command	What It Does
Preferences⇨Cast	Allows you to set the maximum number of Cast Members visible in the Cast window, width of each row, thumbnail size, format of Cast Member labels, types of media icons visible, and whether to show Cast Member script icons.
Preferences⇨Paint	Allows you to set the way brushes behave in the Paint window, whether "color cycling" repeats by jumping back from end to starting point or by reversing the sequence of a color cycle, custom line widths, the percentage of Director's blending feature, how fast Lighten/Darken effects work, and the way Director handles changes in color palettes or interpolation. For more on color cycling, check out "Try Color Cycling" in Chapter 24.
Quit	Closes Director and takes you to another open program or to the Desktop.

Well-designed Mac and Windows programs are supposed to share the same look and feel, but even the best of them have individual quirks. Here's a collection of some of Director's idiosyncrasies reflected in the File menu:

- ✔ Director allows only one open movie at a time. When you choose the New Movie command, Director asks you whether you'd like to save changes to the current movie, closes the current movie, and then presents you with the new, blank Director file. In most other programs, you can open as many files as available memory can handle.

- ✔ You can't close the current movie's Stage window. If the only window visible is the Stage window, choosing Close Window from the File menu does nothing, kind of like politicians. Your only options are to switch to another file with the Open command or quit.

- ✔ Director has always been infamous for making heavy demands on your computer's limited memory. Use the Save and Compact command to fall back on when you have nearly completed your animation to bring the size of the file down and to help it copy into memory faster. And remember that the Purge button in the Memory Inspector frees up the maximum amount of memory.

By the way, many of the File commands take you to a window or dialog box featuring a Help button, one more way to access Director's online help, only one step better. For example, if you choose File⇨Import and then click the Help button from the Import dialog box, lo and behold, you come to the Help window for the Import command. No looking up topics or keywords! More of that context-sensitive help.

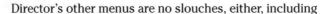

What's an active window?

In the world of graphical interfaces, only one window is available at any one time (with one exception coming up). Whichever window you've just selected is the currently active window; all other open windows are inactive. Looking at title bars is the key to knowing which window is active. On the Mac, the *active window* displays its name in reversed text in the title bar at the top of the window, and gray, horizontal stripes adorn the width of the title bar; in Windows, the title bar of the active window displays the

brightest color of the open windows. In either case, all other open windows become inactive.

Ah, the exception; I'm glad you reminded me. A special window called a *floating palette* appears active at all times and appears to, well, float in front of the regular active window. Director 5's Control Panel and Memory Inspector are examples of floating palettes for the Import command. No looking up topics or keywords! More of that context-sensitive help.

Touring Director's Other Menus

Director's other menus are no slouches, either, including

- ✔ Edit
- ✔ View
- ✔ Insert
- ✔ Modify
- ✔ Control
- ✔ Xtras
- ✔ Window

Some menus that appeared in earlier versions of Director are gone. For example, Lingo, Director's built-in scripting language, doesn't get a menu in the menu bar. Instead, you find two pop-up menus in Script Cast Member dialog boxes, an alphabetical list of so-called Lingo properties and commands, and the same list organized by category. To see them, do the following:

1. **Choose Window⇨Cast or press ⌘/Ctrl+3.**

   The Cast window appears with a row of icons at the top.

2. **Select any Cast Member with one click of the mouse.**

3. Click the Cast Member Script button, the third button from the right.

The Cast Member Script dialog box appears with its own set of icons.

4. Locate the Alphabetical Lingo button with a large L in the center and press to view the alphabetized pop-up menu.

You see an impressive list of Lingo stuff (see Figure 2-13) beginning with operators, and then you see Lingo commands in alphabetical order and with submenus.

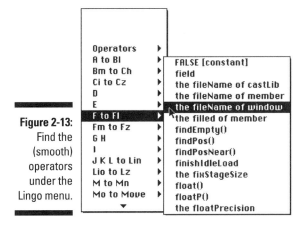

Figure 2-13:
Find the
(smooth)
operators
under the
Lingo menu.

5. Locate the Categorized Lingo button just to the right and press to view the categorized pop-up menu.

Believe it or not, you'll be able to make heads or tails of this mess before long.

For you old-timers, the Palette menu is gone, too. No Paint menu. No Script menu. Actually, you'll find that the menus are much better organized than in previous versions of Director. The menu bar no longer keeps changing which window happens to be active. I get into all the details in upcoming chapters.

Hey, they cheated me out of revert! It's grayed out!

Whoa, pardner. Let's review a basic part of the graphic interface. You've got a new Director file, right? You haven't added a blessed dot to it, right again? So you haven't saved anything to the hard drive — "to disk," as multimedia types like to say.

Now, Revert takes you to the last *saved* version of your file. If you've got no last saved version, you've got no Revert. (You've got no bananas, either, but that's another story.) Director is smart enough to know all this even if the rest of us don't, which is why the Revert command may be grayed out. The technical name for this condition is *disabled.* And, yes, last time I checked, that term's politically correct. Commands that are available to you (not grayed out) are said to be *enabled.* Enabled, disabled. Add these words to your growing vocabulary, and your future's set in stone. Just remember, Hoffa's future was set in stone, too. Or was it his feet?

Chapter 3

Lights, Camera, Action!

· ·

In This Chapter

▶ Introducing the Stage

▶ Traversing the Stage

▶ Sizing up the Stage

▶ Channel surfing with the Control Panel

▶ These buttons aren't on *my* remote control!

· ·

*1*f you haven't had the pleasure (hah) of working in the movie industry, have you ever been to Hollywood and wound up at a free taping of a TV show? Wires, cameras, mikes, more wires, more cameras. And where are they pointing? Sure, at the actors or game show host or talk show host; but, more importantly, the cameras point at the stage. If it weren't for the stage, there'd be no show. I know, you've seen those grainy, old Mickey Rooney films where a convenient barn is always nearby. But no, the world's grown too sophisticated, and you probably can't get fire insurance for the barn, anyway.

All the World's a Stage: Director's Opening Window

As you see when you open Director, the introductory window or splash screen greets you momentarily and then you finally come to the Stage. Just as a stage is vital for TV shows and sound stages, Director's Stage window is *the* window. It's your canvas, where all the action occurs, where your special type of information moving and changing over time plays before your eyes.

Wait a Minute! The Darn Stage Is Blank as a Polar Bear in a Snowstorm!

I see that you noticed the Stage doesn't offer much to catch your attention. If you think it's bad now, just watch this:

1. **Find the ⌘/Ctrl key.**

   These days, the ⌘ key for the Mac or Ctrl key for PCs, one of the so-called *modifier keys* on your keyboard, usually rests just to the left of the spacebar.

2. **Press and hold down the ⌘/Ctrl key.**

   Continue pressing the ⌘/Ctrl key. You're about to perform a keyboard shortcut for selecting the Stage. I know, you're already at the Stage, but watch. . . .

3. **Press 1.**

   (That's the number *1*.) Ah, the menu bar disappears. Now *that's* blank!

Stage window forever

⌘/Ctrl+1, which is a shortcut way of saying steps 1 to 3 above, is what multimedia types call a *toggle* command. Choosing Stage from the Window menu or pressing ⌘/Ctrl+1 alternately hides and shows the menu bar. After all, a menu bar at the top of your animation would be pretty distracting, not to mention unhygienic.

Notice that the Stage window never disappears; it's the one Director window you can't choose to hide.

The incredible, invisible menu bar

On a slow weekend, you can have a great time with Director's menu bar. Press ⌘/Ctrl+1 so that the menu bar disappears. Or should I say *seems* to disappear, because it's really still there! Try it; move the mouse up to where you think the Window menu belongs and, sure enough, the pull-down menu pops into view. All the menus are operational but invisible when you hide the menu bar.

Give yourself ten points for every window you find and then treat yourself to dinner at your favorite restaurant.

Hyperactive windows

If the menu bar is visible, press ⌘/Ctrl+1, find the Window menu, and peek at the Window menu commands. Notice the diamond to the left of the Stage window command, which is Director's coy way of telling you that the Stage is the currently *active* window.

Read all about active window stuff in the sidebar, "What's an active window?" at the end of Chapter 2. Figure 3-1 shows the title bar of an active window.

Figure 3-1:
The title bar
of an active
Color
Palettes
window.

Not counting the Stage window, which doesn't have a title bar, inactive windows lose their horizontal stripes, and the window name becomes grayed out or disabled. The Close box in the upper-left corner and the Zoom box in the upper-right corner disappear as well. (See Figure 3-2.)

Figure 3-2:
An inactive
Color
Palettes title
bar behind
the active
Message
window.

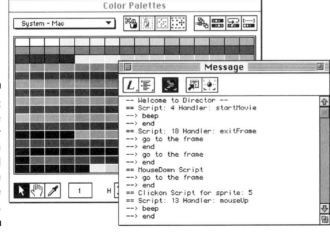

Checks and balances

For a fun time try the following, but be sure that the menu bar is hidden. If the menu bar isn't hidden, press ⌘/Ctrl+1. Display the Control Panel by choosing Window⇨Control Panel or pressing ⌘/Ctrl+2. Press the Window menu and note the check mark by the Control Panel command. The Stage gets a diamond, the Control Panel gets a check. What gives?

Director 5 now makes use of a special type of window called a *floating palette*. The Control Panel is an example of such a palette with a skinny title bar at the top, a Close box in the upper-left corner, and the capability to float in front of other visible, even active, windows. Another peculiar fact about floating palettes in Director: The Close command in the File menu doesn't work with palettes. Try it if you don't believe me.

Modifying the Stage

Options for modifying the Stage window reside in the Movie Properties dialog box. Choose Modify⇨Movie⇨Properties, and the Movie Properties dialog box appears, as in Figure 3-3.

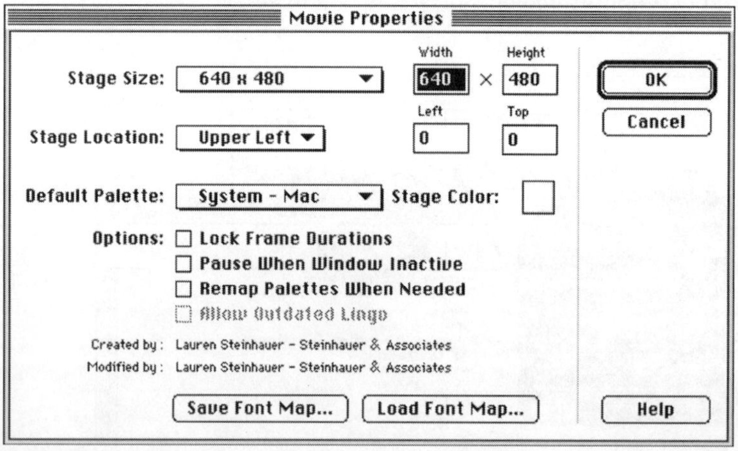

Figure 3-3: The Movie Properties dialog box, where you can modify the Stage window.

Sizing up the Stage

You find a number of size options in the Stage Size pop-up menu, including the following:

- ✔ **512 x 342:** The classic Macintosh size for the so-called compact Mac models including the Mac Plus, Mac SE30, and Mac Classic.

- ✔ **640 x 480:** The standard size for 13- and 14-inch monitors.

- ✔ **832 x 624:** A common size for 16-inch multiple resolution monitors.

- ✔ **1024 x 768:** A common size for 19-inch multiple resolution monitors.

- ✔ **QuickTime 160 x 120:** The famous "postage stamp" size for QuickTime mooVs, often used when computer resources are known to be limited.

- ✔ **QuickTime 320 x 240:** A quarter-screen size often used for CD-ROM publishing because it's large enough to actually see something and small enough to run on all but the slowest computers.

- ✔ **Main monitor:** The Stage adopts the dimensions of the main monitor that you designate with the Monitors control panel.

- ✔ **Multiple monitors:** The Stage can be spread across several monitors to create a "virtual screen." See the "Double your pleasure, double your fun" sidebar later in this chapter.

- ✔ **Custom:** Becomes the selected option when you enter a custom width and height in the boxes to the right of the Stage Size pop-up menu.

Location, location, location

In the world of Director and most other computer programs, the upper-left corner of the screen monitor is called the *origin.* Window locations are measured by using the horizontal and vertical *offset,* or distance from the origin. With that in mind, look at the Movie Properties dialog box options for Stage Location relative to the monitor screen, including

- ✔ **Centered:** Centers the Stage window in the center of the monitor screen.

- ✔ **Upper Left:** Places the upper-left corner of the Stage window at the origin of the monitor screen.

- ✔ **Other:** Enter left and top offsets for the upper-left corner of the Stage window relative to the monitor screen's origin.

For more info on how window locations are measured and used, take a look at "Okay, Let's Review That X-Y Coordinate Thing" in Chapter 14.

Setting a palette other than the standard System palette can have a dramatic effect on all Cast Members seen on the Stage. Select a palette from the Default Palette pop-up menu. For more information on Director's palettes, see "SuperTechniRamaVision: All about System and Custom Palettes" in Chapter 7.

Double your pleasure, double your fun

Running two monitors is great for developing Director movies and multimedia. The idea is to drag all those gorgeous windows to the extra monitor and keep a nice, uncluttered view of the Stage on your main monitor. Makes life nice, easy, and expensive.

You can also use multiple monitors as part of the presentation itself. The monitors become one giant "virtual" screen, with each monitor serving as a port into this magical world.

Some Power Macintosh models have built-in multiple monitor capabilities. Otherwise, you need an extra video card to run each additional monitor for multimedia extravaganzas.

By the way, when you're running two or more monitors, let Director know by choosing Modify⇨Movie⇨Properties and choosing Multiple Monitors from the Stage Size pop-up menu in the Movie Properties dialog box.

Pop-up palette

To the right of the Default Palette pop-up menu in the Movie Properties dialog box is the Stage Color selector. Press the selector to select a color from the pop-up palette.

Multimedia types often measure things with the *pixel* (for Macs) or *pel* (for PCs), short for picture element. A pixel or pel is the unit that makes up the pictures you see on your monitor. A standard for computer displays is a 13-inch monitor measuring 640 pixels width x 480 pixels height. By the way, the resolution of your screen is usually 72 pixels or pels per inch (ppi).

Channel Surfing with the Control Panel

Borrowing metaphors from TV has become very popular in MultimediaLand, especially the VCR metaphor. You see a lot of interfaces that look familiar because the buttons echo controls on your VCR remote. Actually, using the familiar isn't a bad idea in developing animation and multimedia, where communicating quickly and presenting intuitive interfaces are ever-present challenges.

The next Director window to check out under the Window menu is the Control Panel, which sports a familiar VCR interface and duplicates basic commands under the Control menu. These commands include the familiar (Play, Stop, and Rewind) and the not so familiar (Loop Playback). Figure 3-4 shows the Control menu in all its glory.

Control	
Play	⌥ ⌘ P
✓ Stop	⌥ ⌘ .
Rewind	⌥ ⌘ R
Step Forward	⌥ ⌘ →·
Step Backward	⌥ ⌘ ←·
✓ Loop Playback	⌥ ⌘ L
Selected Frames Only	
Volume	▶
Disable Scripts	
Toggle Breakpoint	⇧ ⌥ ⌘ K
Watch Expression	⇧ ⌥ ⌘ W
Remove All Breakpoints	
Ignore Breakpoints	⇧ ⌥ ⌘ I
Step Script	⇧ ⌥ ⌘ ↓
Step Into Script	⇧ ⌥ ⌘ →·
Run Script	⇧ ⌥ ⌘ ↑
Recompile All Scripts	⇧ ⌥ ⌘ C

Figure 3-4:
The Control
menu for all
you control
freaks.

The Control Panel also allows you to

✔ Zoom forward and backward through the frames of your movie.

✔ Set the pace or tempo of your movie.

✔ Select the way you time your movie.

✔ Set displayed time values to real times for the specific computer model running the movie.

These Buttons Aren't on My Remote Control!

The Control Panel is chock full of buttons and icons and more buttons. (See Figure 3-5.) The buttons are pretty *intuitive,* as multimedia types like to say. In other words, you should have an easy time guessing their functions because most of them resemble controls on your VCR remote.

After you click a button, it looks depressed — no, silly goose, not sad, de-pressed as in pressed in if you're running in gray scale or color. If your monitor is set to black and white, the selected button turns into a negative image.

Figure 3-5:
Director's
Control
Panel:
Nirvana for
remote
control
junkies
everywhere.

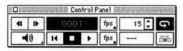

Notice the little black corner in the lower right of some Control Panel buttons, indicating a hidden pop-up menu of options from which you can select with the mouse.

Now go over the buttons in the top row of the Control Panel from left to right:

- ✔ **Step Backward:** Moves you back one frame of your movie with each click.
- ✔ **Step Forward:** Moves you to the next frame of your movie with each click.
- ✔ **Frame Counter:** Displays the current frame of your movie. Period.
- ✔ **Tempo Mode:** Toggles the Tempo panel between frames per second (fps) and seconds per frame (spf) with a pop-up menu.
- ✔ **Tempo:** Displays the current tempo. Increase or decrease the movie's tempo by clicking the up/down arrow controls.
- ✔ **Loop Playback:** Sets your movie to play itself over and over, forever — you'd better like your movie a lot. Actually, you have many outs, like clicking the Stop button in the Control Panel or pressing ⌘/Ctrl+Option/ Alt+period. If you want your movie to play once, click Loop again; the button becomes a straight-line icon.

As if that weren't enough excitement, turn your attention to the Control Panel's bottom row of buttons, described from left to right:

- ✔ **Sound:** Mute your movie's sound level or choose levels 1 to 7 with the button's pop-up menu.
- ✔ **Rewind:** Faster than your VCR or a speeding bullet, clicking Rewind instantly zips you to frame 1 of your movie.
- ✔ **Stop:** One click stops your movie dead in its tracks (no pun intended).
- ✔ **Play:** Start your movie like a pro; one click of the mouse does the job.

✔ **Actual Tempo Mode:** The pop-up menu allows you to see how fast your movie is playing in real or "actual" time and to set how the actual time is displayed: Frames Per Second (fps), Seconds Per Frame (spf), Running Total, or Estimated Total. Running Total gives you the total actual time a movie plays. The Estimated Total setting is considered more accurate for sequences that play longer than a few seconds.

✔ **Actual Tempo:** Displays the actual tempo as set in the Actual Tempo Mode pop-up menu.

✔ **Selected Frames Only:** Click to play only the range of frames selected in the Score window.

Part II
Director's Windows
of Opportunity

In this part . . .

One reason why Director is such a wonderful program to work with is its richness of windows and options therein. In this part, I focus on the major players in the Window Department, where you get to become close, personal friends with Mr. Cast, Mr. Score, Ms. Paint, and that ever popular gad-about, the Text window.

Chapter 4

Casting Coach or Couch?
The Cast Window

- -

In This Chapter

▶ Casting your movie with the Cast window

▶ Adding Cast Members to your movie

▶ A brief tour of the Cast menu

- -

Director's Cast window is how Director types make a casting call in the world of digital moviemaking. All the files on your hard drive get all excited, slap down their copy of *Variety,* and come running to queue up with hearts aflutter, hoping against hope to find themselves among the chosen, on their way to stardom, wealth, and interviews with Robin Leach.

Calling All Cast Members

Now that you know how exciting the Cast window is, take a look at it by choosing Window⇨Cast or pressing ⌘/Ctrl‖3.

Your Cast window appears like a blinding bank of klieg lights streaming into the crisp, Hollywood night sky! Pretty exciting, huh?

Can I believe my ears? Did I hear someone say, "Not exactly"? Hmm, maybe you're not the right file type. Director's pretty picky about the type of file it accepts in the Cast window, you know.

Defining the Cast

First, I'll define the Cast.

Anyone working in the food industry in L.A. No, cut. Over and out. A *Cast Member* is any part of your movie that changes location, shape, or size. As listed in the Import Files dialog box, Macintosh Cast Members include

- ✔ **Picture:** PICT images containing drawings and/or bitmaps.
- ✔ **MacPaint:** Simple 1-bit black and white bitmaps.
- ✔ **Sound:** System 7 sounds, AIFF (Audio Interchange File Format) sound files, and AIFC (compressed AIFF) sound files.
- ✔ **Scrapbook:** Text, graphics, sounds, and QuickTime mooVs in the current Scrapbook.
- ✔ **PICS:** A special file format containing a set of PICTs.
- ✔ **Director Movie:** Any other Director movie, imported as a film loop along with individual Cast Members.
- ✔ **Director Cast:** Cast Members of an external Cast window.
- ✔ **QuickTime:** Digital videos often compressed with various Apple compression schemes (codecs), always imported as linked files.
- ✔ **Text:** Imported text documents and text directly entered in Text and Field windows within Director.

Additional types of Macintosh Cast Members not directly listed in the Import Files dialog box include

- ✔ **Palettes:** Sets of colors optionally imported along with an external bitmap or created directly in Director's Color Palettes window.
- ✔ **Film loops:** A sequence of frames from the Score window copied into one cell of the Cast window as a single Cast Member.
- ✔ **Scripts:** Imported along with Director movies or created within Director's Script window.

The Macintosh version of Director 5.0 is very *Mac-centric*. Even though a PC BMP file is a bitmap, Director won't list it in the Directory when you display the Import Files dialog box and choose Picture or even All Files from the Show pop-up menu. Before attempting to import the file, you first need to convert the BMP file into a Macintosh bitmap with a conversion utility like DeBabelizer.

As listed in the Import Files dialog box, Windows Cast Members include

- ✔ **Bitmap files:** Paintings from programs like CorelPHOTO-PAINT or created directly in Director's Paint window.
- ✔ **JPEG files:** An acronym for Joint Photographic Experts Group, compressed files that can contain 24-bit bitmaps.

✔ **CompuServe GIF files:** An acronym for Graphics Interchange Format, compressed bitmaps with up to 256 colors.

✔ **TIFF files:** An acronym for Tagged Image File Format, high-quality bitmaps often used to save scanned photographs.

✔ **EPS files:** An acronym for Encapsulated PostScript, high-quality drawings or vector-based graphics created with drawing programs such as CorelDRAW! and Adobe Illustrator.

✔ **Photo CD files:** Graphics from Kodak's proprietary scanning service producing a CD-ROM from photographic film formats.

✔ **PC Paintbrush files:** Graphics created with the Paintbrush application, extension type PCX.

✔ **Windows metafiles:** Developed by Microsoft, a graphic container for bitmap and/or vector-based images that can handle up to 24-bit color depth.

✔ **Palettes:** Collections of colors that can be imported or directly created in Director's Color Palettes window.

✔ **Sounds:** WAV (Wave Audio) sound files, AIFF sound files, and AIFC sound files.

✔ **Director movies:** Any other Director movie, imported as a film loop and individual Cast Members.

✔ **Cast files:** Cast Members of an external Cast window.

✔ **Video clips:** Linked digital video Cast Members from QuickTime and AVI (Audio Video Interleave) files.

✔ **FLC and FLI files:** Proprietary animation file types for Autodesk Animator Pro and Autodesk Animator.

✔ **Macintosh PICTs:** The Macintosh metafile format, containing bitmap and/or vector-based graphics.

✔ **MacPaint files:** Simple 1-bit black and white bitmaps.

✔ **Text files:** Imported text documents and text directly entered in Text and Field windows within Director.

Additional types of Windows Cast Members not directly listed in the Import Files dialog box include

✔ **Film loops:** A sequence of frames from the Score window copied into one cell of the Cast window as a single Cast Member.

✔ **Scripts:** Imported along with Director movies or created within Director's Script window.

Of drawings, paintings, PICTs, and PICS

Many years ago, Charlton Heston parted the world of computer graphics into the two realms of drawings and paintings. Drawings come from drawing programs like ClarisDraw for the Mac and CorelDRAW! for the PC. You hear computer nerds refer to this type of file as an object-oriented or vector-based graphic, too. Drawings describe shapes with hidden computer code, are easily enlarged or reduced, and print smoothly at virtually any size on most printers.

Paintings come from Mommy and Daddy paintings, that is, from programs like Adobe Photoshop and Fractal Painter for the Mac and PC, as well as Director's built-in Paint window. Paintings are built up from units of color called *pixels* or *pels* (picture elements), very similar to mosaics made up of individual tiles or magazine photos made up of halftone dots. Also referred to as *bitmapped graphics,* paintings can display very subtle, photographic-like shading and

detail but do not reduce or enlarge well. With low-resolution printers, they print out with distracting ragged edges referred to as the infamous "jaggies."

In the world of Mac, a PICT is an all-purpose file type that may contain a vector-based or bitmapped graphic. A PICS file contains a set of individual PICTs — each PICT stored as a "resource" in the file. Mac files have unique structures called *data* and *resource forks.* When you type a memo, typically the text of the memo goes in the data fork. When you create a PICS file, each PICT you include in the PICS file becomes a resource in the Mac file's resource fork. When you import a PICS file into Director, each PICT resource within the PICS file becomes an individual Cast Member in the Cast window. You can also export a Director movie as a PICS file, turning each frame of your movie into a PICT resource in the PICS's resource fork.

Such power is truly frightening.

Adding Cast Members to the Cast window

You can't wait to add a Cast Member to the Cast. I know the feeling, far stronger than a Big Mac attack. That's what the Import command has been waiting so patiently to do for you.

Import is a pretty common command in most programs and does pretty much the same thing in each program: adds the contents of an external file to the program. Some programs like PageMaker call the Import command the Place command. Same thing.

To add a Cast Member, just follow the Yellow Brick Road, er, these steps:

1. Choose File⇨Import or press ⌘/Ctrl+R.

The Import Files dialog box appears where you can set import options. Notice that All Files is the first option in the Show pop-up menu shown in Figure 4-1. With All Files chosen, you see a list of all importable files on your hard drive. Choosing any other option for Show displays only that file type in the list. PICT is the workhorse file type for the Macintosh. With the Mac, most of the Cast Members you add to Director are PICTs. For PC users, the most ubiquitous file format is the BMP (bitmap) file type.

Figure 4-1:
Options in
the Mac
Import Files
dialog box's
Show pop-
up menu.

Notice the two check boxes at the bottom left of the Import Files dialog box. You can find more on the Linked check box in "Linking your imported file" in this chapter. The As PICT option imports a vector-based PICT into Director as a PICT image. Ordinarily, Director transforms imported PICTs into bitmapped graphics. For more on vector-based files, look back at the sidebar, "Of drawings, paintings, PICTs, and PICS."

2. **Find the desired file in the Directory.**

3. **Click the file(s) in the list that you want to import.**

   You can also choose Add All to import all the files.

4. **Click the Import button.**

   If you import a bitmapped graphic, Director presents the Image Options dialog box, where you can change the file's color depth and palette. Click OK, and Director takes you to the Cast window, where you find the imported file as a new Cast Member in the Cast.

Avoid scrolling through long lists in the Directory and come close to a file by pressing its initial character on the keyboard. For example, if you're looking for a document named PHOTO.BMP in the Directory, press p to select the first file in the Directory beginning with the letter *p*.

You can get even closer to your file, if not right on, by quickly typing **ph** or **pho**. The trick is to type two or more characters quickly enough so that your computer recognizes the key sequence as part of a word.

By the way, this technique works with other scrolling lists, including windows on the Desktop and Director's Help windows.

Director has a few more ways to add Cast Members to the Cast window, including

✔ Painting a new Cast Member in Director with the Paint window tools. You can find more about Paint window tools in Chapter 7.

✔ Entering text in the Text or Field window. Run, do not walk, to Chapter 8 for more info on Text and Field windows.

✔ Creating a Lingo script. For more on Lingo scripting, jump to Chapter 17.

✔ Making a custom palette in the Color Palettes window. (See Chapter 10.)

Think of each Cast Member in the Cast window as a special collection of formatting decisions or "style sheets" that you can apply to any number of frames in your movie. For example, suppose you build a movie with an imported painting across several frames and then decide to change one of the colors of the Bitmap Cast Member from puce to aquamarine. Changing the color of the Cast Member once in Director's Paint window ripples through all instances of the Bitmap Cast Member in your movie. Pretty clever, huh?

Internal and external Cast windows

One of Director 5's most important new features is support for multiple casts for your movies. Now you can work with two types of casts, internal and external casts. For Director old-timers, the closest Director came to an external cast was the one SHARED.DIR file allowed for each movie, where Cast Members and Lingo scripts could be shared among several Director movies.

Use *internal casts* to organize your Cast Members in some meaningful way (all Palette Cast Members in one cast, for example) and reduce the number of cells needed in any one Cast window.

Internal casts

Director 5 starts you off with one internal cast that's saved within the movie itself. Each additional cast you create is added to the movie with its advantages and disadvantages. The greatest advantage of internal casts is never needing to go searching for them; they're intrinsic to the file. You can also organize your Cast Members by using different internal Casts; for example, you can put all Text Cast Members in a Text Cast Member internal cast, all Bitmap Cast Members in another Bitmap Cast Member internal cast, and so on. But you can't share internal Cast Members with other movies. Each new internal cast bloats the Director movie's size and may put performance at risk on slower machines.

External casts

External casts, new to Director 5, are saved *external* to any one Director movie and can be shared among movies common to a production. Another option available to you is to link a new external cast to the movie. Why would you want to do such a ridiculously civil thing?

A *linked cast* opens automatically with its designated movie. Even if you move the cast file inadvertently, Director prompts you to locate the cast on your hard drive. Sounds great, although the prompt could be very distracting during a presentation. Back on the plus side, linked casts are updated whenever you choose Save from the File menu. Unlinked casts need to be saved individually.

Choose Modify⇨Movie⇨Casts to link or unlink selected casts from within the Movie Casts dialog box, as in Figure 4-2.

Figure 4-2:
The Movie
Casts dialog
box, where
you can link
an external
cast to the
current
movie.

Linking your imported file

Choose File⇨Import to display the Import Files dialog box. You find the Linked check box in the lower-left corner. (See Figure 4-3.)

Figure 4-3:
The Linked
check box in
the Import
Files dialog
box.

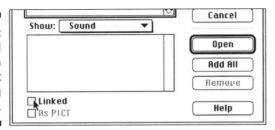

If you leave the Linked check box unchecked, the imported file becomes part of your movie, increasing its size. Benefits? No need to keep track of the imported file; it's part of your movie. On the other hand — no, the other hand — checking the Linked check box gives you a bouquet of advantages, including the following:

✔ Creating a relationship with the imported file so that you can view the file without physically adding it to your movie, keeping the movie file size down.

✔ Automatically updating a linked file after you make changes to the file in its parent application. For example, if you import a Photoshop PICT to Director as a linked file and then later open, modify, and save the PICT in Photoshop, Director automatically updates the linked file the next time you open the movie.

✔ Sharing an external, linked file among several movies without increasing the size of each movie.

✔ Using the Launch External Editor command to open the selected Cast Member's parent application from Director's Cast window. Choose Edit⇨Launch External Editor, as in Figure 4-4.

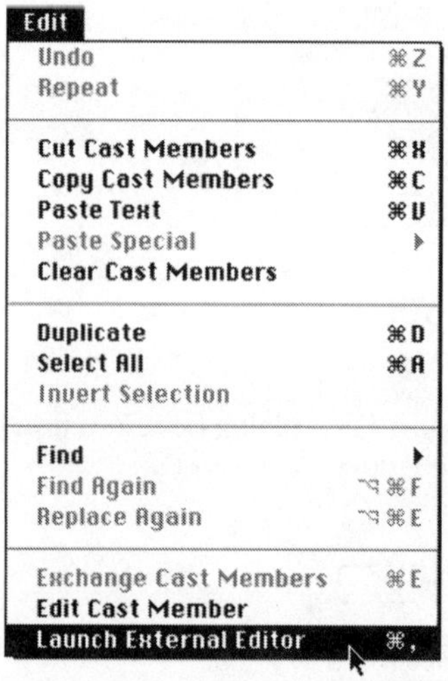

Figure 4-4:
Choose
Launch
External
Editor from
the Edit
menu to
modify a
selected
Cast
Member
with its
parent
application.

Edit	
Undo	⌘ Z
Repeat	⌘ Y
Cut Cast Members	⌘ X
Copy Cast Members	⌘ C
Paste Text	⌘ V
Paste Special	▶
Clear Cast Members	
Duplicate	⌘ D
Select All	⌘ A
Invert Selection	
Find	▶
Find Again	⌐ ⌘ F
Replace Again	⌐ ⌘ E
Exchange Cast Members	⌘ E
Edit Cast Member	
Launch External Editor	⌘ ,

After importing linked files, do a good job of tracking them. If a file's location changes after you import it as a linked Cast Member, the next time you open the movie, Director asks where the heck the file is, spoiling your presentation with catcalls and boos from the disappointed and unruly audience.

The safest way to ensure that Director never loses track of linked files is to create a project folder for each presentation and to keep all linked files and movies in that folder. If you're working on a Mac and you must move a file out of the project folder, take advantage of System 7's Alias command. At the Desktop, select the file, choose File➪Make Alias, and move the alias to a new location.

Whenever you import digital video like a QuickTime mooV or AVI (Audio Video Interleaved) movie, Director automatically links it to the current movie.

Moving Cast Members around in the Cast window

You may want to move a Cast Member from one slot to another in the Cast window. Director helps you out with special cursors to keep you on track and prevent you from making embarrassing mistakes that may turn you into a social misfit. Come along with me on a little tour of this fascinating experience:

1. **Choose Window➪Cast or press ⌘/Ctrl+3 to display the Cast window.**

2. **Move the mouse pointer over the Cast Member that you want to add to the Score window.**

   Notice that the mouse pointer or cursor changes to a grabber hand cursor, illustrated in Figure 4-5.

Figure 4-5:
The mouse pointer changes to a grabber hand cursor when moved over a Cast Member.

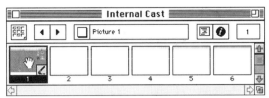

3. **At this point, press the mouse and begin dragging in the direction of an empty cell in the Cast window.**

   A couple of things happen at this point. The grabber hand cursor turns into the menacing Fist cursor, and the Cast Member follows the mouse in ghostly outline form, both visible in Figure 4-6.

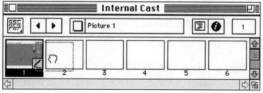

4. When the Cast Member and Fist cursor loom over the chosen cell in the Cast window, release the mouse button.

You've moved your Cast Member from the first cell to the second. I had you make a small detour to show how you can move Cast Members from cell to cell within the Cast window. You're going to make one more detour to see how hard Director goes out of its way to be helpful to you.

When you're dragging a Cast Member from the Cast window and you try to release the mouse at an inappropriate time, the Fist cursor gets tattooed with the international "no way" sign (you know, the circle with the slash through it).

Editing Cast Members 101

Considering how many types of graphics you can import, you may be wondering which Cast Members you can edit directly in Director. Here's the list; it's real long, so I hope you don't get eyestrain:

▌ ✔ Bitmaps

Bitmaps only need apply

Director's built-in editor, the Paint window, can handle only the file type called a *bitmap,* which comes from paint programs like Photoshop or CorelPHOTO-PAINT. A bitmap is just a collection of colored pixels that you can turn on and off or change color with the Paint window's various tools. For more on the Paint window, jump to Chapter 6.

Ah, you're wondering how come QuickTime isn't in my nifty list. You've heard that QuickTime movies are nothing more than a collection of bitmapped images. Almost won the turkey, but not close enough. QuickTime frames may start out as bitmaps, but once incorporated into a QuickTime movie, they're transformed into a special QuickTime format that Director's built-in Paint tools can't modify.

By the way, Director includes PICTs in the Import dialog box, but, when you click Import, Director changes imported PICTs into bitmapped graphics that you can edit in the Paint window. For more on PICTs and bitmaps, see the sidebar earlier in this chapter, "Of drawings, paintings, PICTs, and PICS."

If you're determined to add a real PICT to your movie, you've got two choices:

✔ Before importing the PICT, be sure to check the As PICT check box at the bottom left of the Import Files dialog box.

✔ Or with a PICT already in the Clipboard, click an empty cell in the Cast window and be sure to choose Edit➪Paste Special➪Paste as PICT. If you use the standard Paste command to copy a PICT from the Clipboard to the Cast window, you'll wind up with a bitmap (another way to add a bitmap to the Cast window but not necessarily what you may want to accomplish).

You wind up with a real PICT in your movie, but you can't edit the image in Director's Paint window. Unless . . .

That's where the External Launcher comes in — one of Director's niftiest commands.

External Launcher stuff

When you can't edit a linked Cast Member within Director because the Cast Member is not a bitmapped graphic, or if you prefer to edit bitmaps in another program (like Photoshop or CorelPHOTO-PAINT), use the External Launcher command to connect linked Bitmaps or Sound and Digital Video Cast Members with a compatible application. To establish the connection, follow these steps:

1. **Select the Cast Member in the internal or external Cast window.**

2. **Choose Edit➪Launch External Editor or press ⌘/Ctrl+comma.**

   The Open dialog box appears, where you may locate the application you prefer as the external editor. For example, if the Cast Member you select is a Digital Video Cast Member, you can choose Adobe Premiere as the program of choice for making video edits.

3. **Open the application with the Open button or by double-clicking the program in the Directory list.**

   The application opens and displays the original file, ready for modification.

4. **After you complete your edits, save the file and quit the chosen program to return to Director.**

   Director has now established the connection between the file type you chose in the Cast window and the application you just visited. Director automatically updates the Cast Member in the Cast window and wherever else it appears in the current movie.

Simple, isn't it? You could do this editing stuff in your sleep, right? Now, wake up.

In the Real World, nothing's simple. The one glitch in this editing stuff is the peculiar nature of Macintosh PICTs. A PICT may contain a bitmap graphic or a drawing-type (*vector-based* is another term you hear) graphic. If the image embedded in the PICT is a drawing-type graphic, you can import the PICT as a PICT into your Director movie (see "Bitmaps only need apply" earlier in this chapter) but forget about editing it in Director. Even weirder, you won't be able to connect the PICT to an external editor like ClarisDraw or CorelDRAW!.

What's a computer nerd to do? The ugly truth is that if you want to modify the drawing in the PICT, you need to open its parent application (ClarisWorks, for example), make your changes, and save the update upon quitting. Then reimport the PICT as a PICT in Director the old-fashioned way with the Import command. Whew! I hope someone at Macromedia does something about this for Director 6.

People change their minds. If you decide to change the program of choice as the external editor for a specific file type (bitmap, sound, or digital video), hold down the Option/Alt key before choosing Edit⇨Launch External Editor. Director gives you the Open dialog box again, where you can select a different program.

Why would you want to import a real PICT into Director? Because you can enlarge or reduce PICTs more successfully than bitmapped graphics, and they print smoothly from most printers. Disadvantages? PICTs animate more slowly than bitmaps in Director, and you won't be able to apply Director's special ink effects to a PICT. For more info on ink effects, jump to Chapter 5 and the section, "All This Ink and Not a Drop on Me — Oops."

Exploring the Cast Windows

If you walked through the steps in the previous sections and imported a Cast Member into the Cast window, are you happy now? Good, now that's out of your system, and you can go back to exploring the Cast window itself. Notice the custom features of the Cast window.

Custom features

At the top of the Cast window is a row of buttons and text areas. From left to right, they include

✔ **Choose Cast:** Press to choose a Cast window from the pop-up menu or to create a new Cast window.

✔ **Previous Cast Member:** Each click selects the previous Cast Member. When you get to the first Cast Member, the next click loops you back to the last Cast Member and away you go in reverse gear, again.

✔ **Next Cast Member:** Each click selects the following Cast Member. When you get to the last Cast Member, the next click loops you back to the first Cast Member, where you continue the forward cycle.

✔ **Drag Cast Member:** Press and drag to drag the currently selected Cast Member(s) to the Score window or the Stage. You can also press the Cast Member thumbnail directly and drag it to the Score window or Stage.

The nice feature of the Drag Cast Member button is that you can place a selected Cast Member or group of selected Cast Members even if they are not currently visible in the Cast window. For example, say you have your Cast window set to show six thumbnails at a time; the Cast window currently displays Cast Members 1 to 6, and you select Cast Members 35 to 42 farther down in the unseen set of cells. Use the Drag Cast Member button to place the selection on the Stage or in the Score window.

✔ **Cast Member Name:** Displays the name of the currently selected Cast Member. An imported Cast Member adopts its original filename, but you can change its name in this field at any time.

✔ **Cast Member Script:** Takes you to the Script window for the currently selected Cast Member. In the Script window, you can play with Lingo, Director's easy-to-use, built-in language. Every Cast Member can have a script associated with it.

✔ **Cast Member Properties:** Takes you to the Cast Member Properties window for the currently selected Cast Member, where you can change the name, palette, and purge priority of the Cast Member. For more info on palettes, see Chapter 7. For more info on purge priorities, see Chapter 8.

✔ **Cast Member Number:** Displays the selected Cast Member's cell number. As you import and create Cast Members, Director places them sequentially in the Cast window, but you can always drag one or more Cast Members to other locations in the Cast window.

Super secret menu

One of Director 5's new features is hidden context-sensitive menus, which work on most of Director's windows. For example, to view hidden menus in the Cast window, you Mac types press the Control key. PC types use the right mouse button instead of a key. Everybody, press the mouse on one of the cells of the Cast window. If the cell contains a Cast Member, the secret menu contains a mix of menu commands from the Edit, Modify, and other menus in Director's menu bar. Even a blank cell gives you Paste Text, Import, and Cast Properties commands.

Cast Member Properties button

You can call up the Cast Member Properties window in a number of ways — so
many choices, so little time:

✔ Click the Cast Member Properties button in the Cast window.

✔ Choose Modify⇨Cast Member⇨Properties.

✔ Press ⌘/Ctrl+I.

✔ Super secret way: After signing 15 copies of the enclosed nondisclosure
form, feel free to read the preceding sidebar.

Because the Cast Member Properties button is so essential, the following steps
show you how to take advantage of its options:

1. **Make sure that a Bitmap Cast Member is selected in the Cast window.**

2. **Click the Bitmap Cast Member Properties button.**

   Director takes you to the Bitmap Cast Member Properties dialog box,
   similar to Figure 4-7.

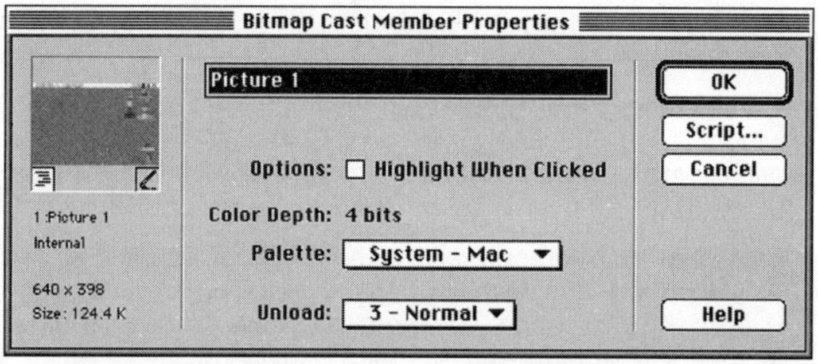

Figure 4-7:
A Bitmap
Cast
Member
Properties
dialog box
bursting
with
information
and options.

Bitmap Cast Member Properties	

Picture 1   OK

Options: ☐ Highlight When Clicked   Script...
                                                  Cancel
1 :Picture 1   Color Depth: 4 bits
Internal   Palette: [System – Mac ▼]

640 x 398
Size: 124.4 K   Unload: [3 – Normal ▼]   Help

In the left panel of the dialog box is a thumbnail preview of the Cast
Member. Underneath is the Cast Member Number, the current Name,
whether the Cast Member is an internal or external Cast Member, its
dimensions, and its size.

In the center panel is the Name field. Notice that Director has even highlighted the name for you so that you can change it on a whim — such
decadence. If you check the Highlight When Clicked check box, the Cast
Member highlights like a button when you press the Cast Member during
playback. Below the Options check box, the color depth is displayed. Next,

the Palette pop-up menu allows you to change the set of colors for the Bitmap Cast Member. Underneath is the Unload pop-up menu, which you can use to alter how Director manages computer memory. In the right panel are OK, Script, Cancel, and Help buttons.

3. **If you're so inclined, type a new name for your Cast Member.**

   The text that Director preselected for you is replaced with the name you enter.

   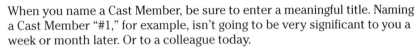

   When you name a Cast Member, be sure to enter a meaningful title. Naming a Cast Member "#1," for example, isn't going to be very significant to you a week or month later. Or to a colleague today.

4. **Press the Palette pop-up menu to view a list of Director's built-in palettes and custom-made palettes.**

   A list of Director's built-in palettes and custom-made palettes appears, as shown in Figure 4-8.

Figure 4-8:
A sparkling array of colors is available in the Palette pop-up menu.

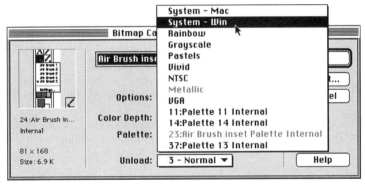

5. **Select the desired palette from the Palette pop-up menu.**

   When you select a new palette, be prepared for a potentially startling color shift on your screen. As soon as you switch palettes, colors on-screen are "remapped" to the new set of colors. For example, if you switch from the regular Mac System palette or the Windows palette to the NTSC palette, you're going to see a big difference in colors. For a full description of palettes included with Director, including the NTSC palette, check out Chapter 10.

6. **Press the Unload pop-up menu.**

   This pop-up menu allows you to modify the way Director *purges* RAM (random-access memory).

Did someone say something about purge? I know, this one's a little scary. You've heard of purges in other parts of the world. That's bad enough, but tell me it's not happening in the good old U.S. of A. But this is a different kind of purge.

Purging in Director is a way of managing memory. When memory runs low, Director starts trashing or *purging* stuff from memory, including Cast Members. The Unload pop-up menu lets you decide what gets tossed and when by selecting a Cast Member from the Cast window, opening the Cast Member Properties box, and setting a purge priority based on the following criteria:

✔ **Priority 0:** Gives a very important Cast Member that is going to be used frequently in the movie Priority 0, meaning, "Never purge Mr. Big Shot from memory. Too important."

✔ **Priority 1:** A little lower on the totem pole than Priority 0; giving a Cast Member Priority 1 means, "Save this puppy for last."

✔ **Priority 2:** The normal setting, meaning, "Expendable but nice. Keep it if you can."

✔ **Priority 3:** The lowest priority; mow 'em down along with gaffers, technicians, accountants, and assistant directors.

Director's hard cell

The Cast window is mainly a set of 32,000 rectangular cells. If you have a screen large enough to display them all, congratulations. (By the way, I know where you can get a great deal on industrial-size sun blocker; give me a call.)

Each occupied cell in the Cast window represents one Cast Member with a thumbnail preview and gives you the following information:

✔ The type of Cast Member

✔ The position of the cell in the window by number

✔ An optional name for the cell

You can learn a lot about a Cast Member by noting its thumbnail's icon(s), listed directly ahead in Table 4-1:

Table 4-1	Cast Member Type Icons
Icon	*What It Represents*
	Bitmap. A painting, may have been imported from a PICT, PICS, MacPaint, Scrapbook file, ClarisDraw file, CorelDRAW! file, or BMP file or created in Director with Paint window tools. May be edited in Director's Paint window.
	Button. Created with one of three Button tools in the Tools window.

Icon	What It Represents
	Digital Video. Typically an imported QuickTime mooV or AVI movie; plays in its own Digital Video window on the Stage. Digital Video Cast Members are always linked to the original external files on disk.
	Field. Text-based Cast Member created with the Field tool in the Tool window or by choosing Insert⇨Control⇨Field. Can be set as editable text during playback, but fields in motion tend to slow down animation sequences.
	Film Loop. A sequence of Director frames organized into a single Cast Member in the Cast window. An imported, unlinked Director movie becomes a film loop, too; each of its Cast Members is added to the current movie's internal cast. Film loops are often used for animations that, well, loop — for example, a bird with constantly flapping wings.
	Linked Movie. A Director movie that has been imported as a linked Cast Member. The linked movie's Cast Members are not added to the internal cast.
	Linked PICT. A PICT imported with the As PICT and Linked check boxes selected in the Import Files dialog box.
	Linked Sound. Imported sound file with the Linked check box selected in the Import Files dialog box.
	Palette. A collection of colors imported with an external graphic file or chosen from the Color Palettes window. Director comes with a set of palettes, but you can also create your own custom palette in the Color Palettes window.
	PICT. A PICT imported with the As PICT check box selected in the Import Files dialog box. You can also copy a PICT to the Cast window from the Clipboard by choosing Edit⇨Paste Special⇨As PICT.
	Script. Each Lingo script you write in the Script window becomes a Script Cast Member in the Cast window or may be added when you import a linked Director movie.
	Shape. A shape created with one of the Shape tools in the Tools window; similar to object-oriented drawings created with programs like ClarisDraw and CorelDRAW!. Shapes use less memory than bitmaps but animate more slowly on the Stage and aren't recommended for movies running on slower computers.
	Sound. An imported sound file from among many file types including SND resources, Windows .WAV sound files, and Macintosh AIFF (Audio Interchange File Format) sound files. AIFF sounds may be linked to the original file on disk. An AIFF sound also plays from disk, reducing the load on memory, and can be used for both Mac and Windows Director movies. For more on sounds, see Chapter 19.

(continued)

Table 4-1 *(continued)*

Icon	What It Represents
A	Text. A Text Cast Member created when you enter text in the Text window. One of Director 5's best new features includes expanded text support for Text Cast Members, including tabs, indents, paragraph formatting, and anti-aliasing. However, Text Cast Members are not editable on playback.
▧	Transition. Each transition effect you select in the Score becomes a Cast Member. For more on transitions, see "Transitions, transitions!" in Chapter 5.
☐	Xtra. A new feature for Director 5, an Xtra Cast Member indicates a plug-in addition to Director's capabilities, including new media types and transitions.

Selecting multiple Cast Members

Director's a little strange when it comes to making multiple selections in the Cast window. Shift-selecting works for most applications, but not for Director. No, that's not good enough for Mr. Fancy Pants Director.

When you need a noncontiguous selection of cells, ⌘/Ctrl-click desired cells, useful for selecting Cast Members throughout the Cast window to drag to the Stage or to change their palettes. However, to make a *contiguous* selection of cells in the Cast window, that is, without jumps, stay with the old Shift-click trick. Click the first cell to highlight it. Move to the last cell to be included in the selection and Shift-click the last cell. You wind up with a contiguous range of selected cells.

Chapter 5

As Time Goes By: Opening Director's Score Window

In This Chapter

▶ Exploring the Score window

▶ Using icons in the Score window

▶ Adding Cast Members to the Score window

▶ Finding the hidden cells

▶ Coloring in the Score window — stay inside the lines!

▶ Manipulating cells

*M*ost programs don't need a Score window. Word processors don't have one. Have you ever heard of a Score window in a desktop publishing program? I don't recall seeing a Score window for PageMaker or QuarkXPress. Why am I talking like Andy Rooney?

Information in other programs doesn't intrinsically change with time. Sure, you return to a PageMaker newsletter or a Word memo to modify it, or maybe you can use it as a template for a new file. But once you make your changes, you can stare at the file night and day and it doesn't change. If it does, you've got the makings for the next Spielberg hit.

From its start as VideoWorks in 1985, Director was designed to handle information that changes over time, information that cries out for a Score-type window. You design your Director movie in the Score window, deciding which Cast Members appear and vanish on the Stage at your every whim. With client approval, of course. Of all Director's windows, the Score window allows you to play director to the hilt.

So hitch up your riding boots and get a good grip on that riding crop. Berets on . . . now! With your best guttural grumbling, shades of Erich von Stroheim resonating in the air, demand that the Score make its appearance this instant. Of course, it helps to go up to the Window menu and choose Score.

The Score Window: And You Thought NeuroLinguistics 101 Was Complicated

Choosing Score from the Window menu calls up the Score window. I've got to admit, it's a mighty intimidating window. Everything has its place for a purpose, though, and soon you'll be reading it like the back of your hand. You can read the back of your hand, can't you? That's a must quality for multimedia types. Good.

The Score window is where you really create your movie. In our culture, lots of stuff moves from left to right: type, days of the calendar, pages of a book, even images. Ever notice how figures in a film moving left to right seem effortless? Film the same scene moving right to left, and it's uphill all the way. Add a little dramatic music, some popcorn, and you've got great dramatic footage. So think of the Score as a graph of time moving left to right in your animation — earlier stuff to the left, later stuff to the right.

That's MISTER cell to you, Bud

The small, white rectangles in the Score window are called *cells*. Cells hold sprites that come from the Cast window and serve as building blocks for the visual timeline that you develop in the Score window. You can change the view of these cells in the Score window. For example, if motion info is most important to you at a particular time in your movie's development, you can switch to Motion view from the Display pop-up menu.

To move one frame to the right in the Score window, press ⌘/Ctrl+Option/Alt+→. Alternatively, just press 3 on the numeric keypad. To move left one frame, press ⌘/Ctrl+Option/Alt+← or press 1 on the keypad.

Icon thingies

I guess you noticed plenty of new icon thingies to explain. Start from the top left of the Score window, shown in Figure 5-1, and note the following:

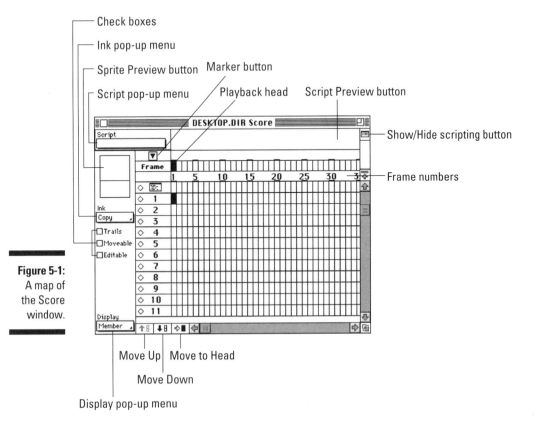

Check boxes

Ink pop-up menu

Sprite Preview button — Marker button

Script pop-up menu — Playback head — Script Preview button

DESKTOP.DIR Score

Script

Show/Hide scripting button

Frame

1 5 10 15 20 25 30 3 — Frame numbers

Ink

Copy

☐Trails
☐Moveable
☐Editable

1
2
3
4
5
6
7
8
9
10
11

Display

Member

Figure 5-1:
A map of
the Score
window.

Move Up | Move to Head

Move Down

Display pop-up menu

✔ **Script pop-up menu:** Below the word *Script,* you see a long, white, shadowed box, which usually means a pop-up menu. When you start adding scripts to your movie, you find them here listed by number and name.

✔ **Script Preview button:** To the right of the Script pop-up menu is a larger area that looks like a button. In fact, it's the Script Preview button, which displays the first two lines of the currently selected script in the Script pop-up menu. A click of the Script Preview button opens the Script window, where you can modify the script to your heart's content — or as much as you can stomach, depending on how you and your internal organs feel about scripting.

✔ **Show/Hide Scripting button:** To the right of the gray Script button (just below the standard Zoom button) is a tiny button to hide and show the two scripting areas described in the preceding paragraphs.

- ✔ **Sprite Preview button:** Below the Script pop-up menu button is a small preview area for the currently selected sprite in the Score window. Its distinctive icon type is displayed in the lower-right corner of the preview area. A thumbnail appears for a bitmap sprite. If the sprite is a script, the Cast Member Number and external or internal label is displayed. Double-clicking the preview area takes you to the Paint or Script window for the sprite, where you can make modifications.

- ✔ **Marker button:** To the right of the Sprite Preview area is the Marker button, which looks like a downward-pointing arrow. With it, you can label specific frames of your movie. You can find out how this works in Chapter 15.

- ✔ **Playback head:** Below the Marker button is the word *Frame,* which marks the row of cells called the *scratch bar.* In the scratch bar is the playback head indicating the current frame of the movie. You can press the playback head with the mouse and drag left or right across the scratch bar to other frames of your movie like the fast shuttle on your VCR remote.

- ✔ **Frame numbers:** Just below the scratch bar is the row of frame numbers. That's it. That's all frame numbers are. I know, you should get more than numbers for a pricey package like Director. But frame numbers are useful, trust me. The numbers break down the Score into sets of five frames; makes counting them real easy.

- ✔ **Ink pop-up menu:** Under the sprite thumbnail is the Ink pop-up menu listing an impressive set of *ink effects* worthy of George Lucas. The idea is to select one or more bitmap sprites and apply an ink effect to them with impressive results with this caveat: Ink effects can seriously slow down the performance of your movie, especially on a low-powered computer.

- ✔ **Trails, Moveable, and Editable check boxes:** Below the Ink pop-up menu are three check boxes that you can turn on for sprites selected in the Score: Trails, Moveable, and Editable. *Trails* leaves a streak of the sprite as it moves around the Stage during playback; *Moveable* allows the user to move a selected sprite while the movie plays — the user can drag a folder into a file cabinet, for example, by using the mouse pointer; and *Editable* refers to field sprites, allowing a user to enter text in a field sprite while a movie is running.

- ✔ **Display pop-up menu:** Below the three check boxes is the Display pop-up menu, used to customize the view in the Score window, similar to changing the view of a window at the Desktop with the View menu.

  For example, when you choose Extended from the pop-up menu, you get larger cells with additional information. You can even customize what info displays in Extended view by choosing File⇨Preferences⇨Score and clicking the items you'd like to include in Extended view.

In Figure 5-2, for example, the first line displays *B* for bitmap and a bullet to indicate the sprite's lack of movement (if the sprite moved to the right in the next frame, you'd see a small right-pointing arrow rather than a bullet); the second line displays 0002 for the Cast number of the sprite; the third line displays COPY for the ink type; the fourth line displays a script code; and the next two lines represent the center of the sprite in pixels measured from the upper-left corner of the Stage window (the zero point).

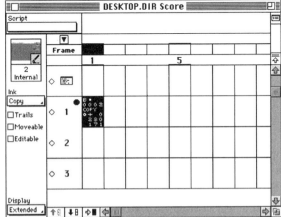

Figure 5-2:
Score
window
cells in
Extended
view.

✔ **Move Up, Move Down, and Move to Head buttons:** To the right of the Display pop-up menu is a row of three utility buttons. From left to right, the Move Up button moves selected sprites up the Score window with each click, the Move Down button moves selected sprites down the Score, and the Move to Head button takes you wherever the playback head currently rests in the Score window.

✔ **Channel numbers:** To the right of the Ink pop-up menus is a column of numbers labeling the visible rows of small, white rectangles or cells that your sprites rest in. For each frame of your animation, 48 total rows or channels are available. Think of channels as plastic overlays used in traditional animation. Going along with this analogy, channel 1 is similar to static background art, such as the canyon where Wile E. Coyote is chasing Road Runner; channel 2 is the second rearmost acetate layer with Road Runner running away from you toward the background; channel 3 is the next layer with Wile E. Coyote tearing after Road Runner; channel 4 is a great yellow cloud of dust that Road Runner and Wile E. Coyote kick up as they race down the canyon. And look, you've got 44 channels left to play with. Wow.

✔ **Hide/Show Channel buttons:** Just to the left of each channel number is a diamond-shaped button that hides or shows the channel.

Use Trails for easy and unusual special effects

Okay, you Roy Rogers fans, happy Trails is a special effect you can apply to a selected sprite in the Score so it leaves a copy of itself wherever it moves on the Stage. In effect, the sprite becomes a brush that paints its own image along its path of movement to build unusual shapes and patterns on the Stage. In addition, when you turn off Trails in a subsequent frame, the same sprite begins to erase its own trail wherever it passes over the trail on the Stage.

You nostalgia buffs can build your own psychedelic "flower power" happenings on Director's Stage. (Don't forget beads, flowers in hair, and tie-dyed bell bottoms.)

Hidden, top-secret channels

Find the column of bold numbers labeling the channels in the Score window. Above the number 1 is the small Script Channel icon representing one of a set of special channels that are hiding but waiting for you to explore them. Pith helmets on now, everyone. To begin your safari through the steaming jungle of hidden channels, notice the small scroll bar in the top right corner of the Score window. At the bottom of the small scroll bar is a special Jump to Top button.

When you click the Jump to Top button, the top five hidden channels zip into view, as in Figure 5-3. Aren't you glad you had your pith helmet on?

Figure 5-3:
Hidden
channels in
the Score
window.

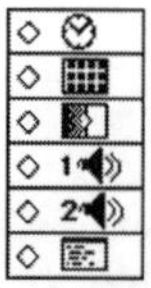

So that makes a grand total of six special channels, as outlined in Table 5-1.

Table 5-1		Special Score Channels
Icon	*Channel*	*Add a Sprite in This Channel to . . .*
⊗	Tempo	Set the pace and add limited interactivity to your movie from the selected frame.

Icon	Channel	Add a Sprite in This Channel to . . .
▦	Palette	Change the set of colors used in your movie from the selected frame.
▨	Transition	Set dissolves, wipes, and other transition effects; by the way, the transition starts on the previous frame.
1◀»)	Sound Channel 1	Play imported sounds including SoundEdit, AIFF, AIFC files, WAV files, and SND resources.
2◀»)	Sound Channel 2	Play left and right stereo sound from stereo-capable Macs (Quadra and Power Mac AV models) and PCs with stereo-capable sound cards.
▦	Script	Scripts in the Score channel activate when the playback head reaches the appropriate frame.

✔ A SoundEdit sound file is the proprietary file type for Macromedia's SoundEdit 16, a Macintosh application for editing sampled sounds. An *AIFF* (Audio Interchange File Format) file is a cross-platform capable sound file type that has been promoted as an industry standard. *AIFC* files are similar to AIFF files but compressed. And *SND* files are bits of code that become part of the movie file itself when imported into a Macintosh Director movie. *WAV* files are a common PC sound file.

✔ If you intend to import and play back sound from both Sound channels, make sure that you Mac types have Sound Manager 3.0 or later installed in your System folder or that your PC sound card supports stereo sound and you have the latest sound driver installed; update drivers with the Drivers control panel in the Windows Program Manager.

✔ Getting into the habit of entering a Tempo setting in the first frame of the Tempo channel for each movie is not a bad idea. Otherwise, Director plays your movie at 15 fps (frames per second), the default tempo setting that doesn't necessarily match your needs. And be sure to floss after each and every meal.

Transitions, transitions! (To the tune from Fiddler on the Roof)

Built-in transitions help you quickly build professional-looking multimedia with Director. You can heighten the drama of a bullet chart by setting a new line of text to dissolve into place on the Stage. Or you can create quick animation effects by *wiping* from one frame to another. I've used this trick to create an animation sequence with only two sprites and one wipe transition.

Imagine a sprite in Frame 1 that looks like a deck of cards neatly squared on the table. The second sprite in Frame 2 depicts the deck fanned out across the Stage. You double-click Frame 2 in the Transition channel and choose Wipe Right from the pop-up menu of transitions. When you rewind your movie with the Control Panel window and click the Play button, the Wipe transition creates a slick illusion that the deck of cards has magically fanned itself.

In case you didn't notice, the Transition pop-up menu gives you over 50 transitions to choose from. In other words, if you think I'm going to cover each one of them in this book, I've got a great piece of property I'd love to show you in a quaint little village called Chernobyl. Anyway, after you've chosen a transition, Director allows you to modify most of the transitions with one or more of the following options:

- ✔ **Duration:** Available for most transitions, you can set a duration in $1/4$-second units.

- ✔ **Chunk Size:** Factory set at the best rate for a particular transition; you're invited to experiment with the number of pixels or chunks affected in the image from one unit of time to the next. Generally, the larger the chunk, the coarser the effect of the transition.

- ✔ **Stage Area/Changing Area:** Some transitions allow you to apply the effect only to the part of the Stage that changes. For example, choosing Changing Area displays a new sprite dissolving into view on the Stage while the background doesn't show any transition effect.

Never set a transition in the first frame of a movie. Transitions are designed to start on the previous frame. When you set a transition in the first frame, no previous frame exists to begin the transition.

Adding a Cast Member to the Score

Have you noticed one thing the Score shares with other windows? Aside from the gizmos, numbers, and icon thingies, the Score's pretty bare when you first open it. You see, Macromedia made a deal with you when you bought Director. Macromedia made the software; you make the movie. You're responsible for putting content into the Score, which is pretty frightening considering those old SAT scores. But you've come a long way, and something that may brighten up that old Score window, aside from a couple of throw rugs and a little paint, is to add a Cast Member. Build your movie by adding Cast Members from the Cast window to the Score like so:

1. **Choose the Stage window by choosing Window⇨Stage or pressing ⌘/Ctrl+4.**

2. **Choose the Cast window by choosing Window⇨Cast or pressing ⌘/Ctrl+3.**

3. **Press the mouse over the Cast Member of choice in the Cast window.**

   Notice that when you first move the cursor over the Cast Member, the mouse pointer transforms from a drab, ordinary arrow into the grabber hand cursor, as shown in Figure 5-4. When you press the mouse button down, it changes into the infamous and diabolical Fist cursor, as shown in Figure 5-5.

Figure 5-4: The grabber hand cursor in the Cast window.

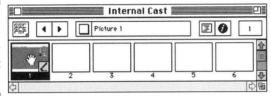

Figure 5-5: The grabber hand cursor turning into the Fist cursor.

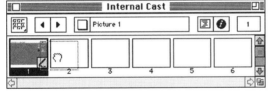

4. **Keep the mouse button down and begin dragging the mouse toward the Score window.**

   Notice the "ghost icon" of the chosen Cast Member following the Fist cursor. As you drag over areas where you shouldn't release the mouse, the cursor changes into the fist with the international "No-No" symbol inside, as in Figure 5-6. Kind of like Robert Mitchum with Love and Hate tattooed on his knuckles in that old black-and-white movie. Now that's macho.

Figure 5-6: The Fist cursor displaying the "No-No" symbol.

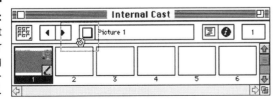

5. With the mouse button still pressed, drag the Cast Member over the Stage window.

The cursor changes back to the regular fist. The cell currently resting under the fist turns black, highlighted with a bold, white border to indicate its readiness to receive your offering. The black rectangle to the right of the word *Frame,* the playback head, follows the mouse cursor as you move left or right. I capture all this fascinating action in Figure 5-7.

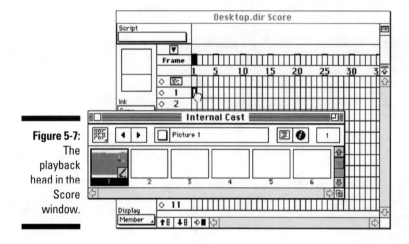

Figure 5-7:
The playback head in the Score window.

6. When you move the Fist cursor over the cell of choice, release the mouse button to place the Cast Member at that location in the Score.

Now a number of events take place at the same time. See if you catch them all; no fair peeking at Figure 5-8, which reflects most of these changes:

✔ Your pants fall down. If not, the program's defective; return it immediately and demand a fresh copy. Pull your pants up first.

✔ Your Cast Member instantaneously appears, centered on the Stage.

✔ A small preview of the Cast Member appears in the upper-left corner of the Score window.

✔ The Step Recording Indicator appears just to the right of the channel number. Creating a movie by dragging Cast Members into the Score window puts Director into so-called frame-by-frame or Step Recording mode.

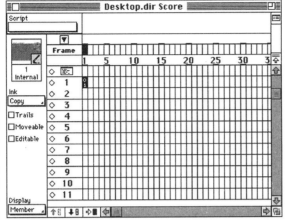

Figure 5-8:
The Score
window
after adding
a Cast
Member.

 Take my advice and tattoo the following on your forehead. Call the contents of the Cast window *Cast Members.* After you drag a Cast Member into the Score window, refer to the Cast Member in the Score as a *sprite.* Hey, I didn't make this up; blame Macromedia. It's the honest truth, I swear. So a bitmap in Cast window is a Cast Member. The same bitmap in Score is a sprite. Good. Cut. Print.

All This Ink and Not a Drop on Me — Oops

I know, I whizzed by that Ink pop-up menu pretty quickly in the "Icon thingies" section earlier in this chapter. Now you can relax, get a cup of coffee, loosen your belt, take off your shoes — wait, better put your shoes back on — and investigate the mysterious world of ink effects in Director.

The most useful and frequently used inks under the Ink pop-up menu include

- ✔ **Copy:** The out-of-box or default ink for sprites, it uses the least amount of memory and is the fastest running ink of all. On the Stage, the sprite is contained in a rectangular *bounding box* that reflects the sprite's maximum width and height. The bounding box is filled with opaque pixels that obscure the background. The color of the pixels is the current color of the Stage's background that starts off as white and is changed by choosing Modify⇨Movie⇨Properties and selecting a color from the Stage Color pop-up menu.

- ✔ **Matte:** Makes pixels surrounding a sprite in its bounding box (the imaginary frame defining the width and height of the sprite) transparent so that the sprite displays a cut-out effect against the background.

✔ **Bkgnd Transparent:** Similar to Matte but turns all background-colored pixels surrounding and *within* the sprite transparent, allowing you to achieve the infamous "donut" effect. You could use Bkgnd Transparent to make a sprite such as a large *A* dance around the Stage. The so-called counter in the center of the *A* appears transparent, allowing sprites and the background to show through. Why the A is dancing around is between you and your conscience.

✔ **Mask:** Similar to Matte but goes a step further. When set up correctly, Mask allows selective background-colored areas in a complex sprite image to remain opaque and still deliver the "donut" effect. For intimate details on the mask-making process, turn to "Creating a mask" in Chapter 7.

TECHNICAL STUFF

Technical drivel about color values

To really understand how ink effects do their magic, you need to understand how a color image appears on your screen. Each pixel you see on your screen is the result of red, green, and blue light mixing together, which is why monitors are often referred to as RGB displays (or as #@%%^&*!! displays when they're not working).

By the way, these red, green, and blue lights come from three tiny electronic "guns" inside your monitor, one for each color, pointed at the phosphorescent surface of your screen. Your color TV at home works basically the same way.

Each color has its own recipe of red, green, and blue light. Where you see a black pixel, no red, green, or blue beams of light strike that particular area of the monitor. So another way of saying black is Red = 0 (for 0 percent), Green = 0, and Blue = 0. Where you see a white pixel, maximum (or 100 percent) red, green, and blue light meet and mix at that precise point on your screen. You can designate white as Red = 100, Green = 100, and Blue = 100.

When you're mixing light together instead of crayons, red and green equal yellow, believe it or not. Here's a simple test to prove I'm right. Rent three standard klieg lights and three filters — red, green, and blue — each about two yards wide. Overlap their mega-volt beacons on the wall of any nearby skyscraper and what do you get in the center? That's right, pure white light. Now turn off the blue klieg light (watch your fingers, those klieg lights get hot). Voilà, a beautiful, diaphanous yellow. And it only cost you a few thousand dollars in equipment and hauling to demonstrate the additive approach to mixing color. Don't worry, it's probably tax-deductible.

So with so-called additive color, any color can be designated with a set of red, green, and blue values. When you select a sprite from the Score and apply the Add ink effect, Director adds the red, green, and blue values of each pixel in the selected sprite to the red, green, and blue values of each underlying pixel. Remember, these values are percentages of color, so you might see a case where adding values gives you a sum over 100 percent. When this occurs with the Add ink effect, Director makes the excess percentage the new value. On the other hand, when you choose Add Pin, you're telling Director to ignore color values over 100 percent, resulting in a number of new colors with 100 percent red, green, and/or blue.

Other inks allow you to create some very unusual effects, especially when two or more sprites overlap, but beware. They can tax your computer's hertzpower to the limit and force your movie to its knees (not a pretty sight). Additional ink effects include

- **Transparent:** Intended mainly for black-and-white screens, makes any background-colored pixels in the selected sprite transparent.

- **Reverse:** Intended mainly for black-and-white screens, black or foreground-colored pixels in a selected sprite become white, and white or background-colored pixels become transparent, revealing the background. With color monitors, color-on-color effects are hard to predict, so save time for plenty of experimentation and breaking of fine china against the wall in fits of aesthetic frustration.

- **Ghost:** Intended mainly for black-and-white screens, black pixels in the selected sprite turn pixels of underlying sprites white and transparent.

- **Not Copy, Not Transparent, Not Reverse, Not Ghost:** Not as in "The check is in the mail . . . NOT," first reverses pixels of the selected sprite and then adds the corresponding ink effect to them.

- **Blend:** Averages the selected sprite's color with the color of underlying sprites, creating a transparency effect.

- **Darkest:** Compares pixels of the selected sprite to the current foreground color and colors only pixels in the selected sprite that are darker than the foreground color.

- **Lightest:** Compares pixels of the selected sprite to the current foreground color and colors only pixels in the selected sprite that are lighter than the foreground color.

- **Add:** Adds the color values of each pixel in the selected sprite to the color values of each underlying pixel. The Add ink effect looks like a blend at first glance but doesn't hold true on close inspection. Also, as its name implies, Add often makes a new, lighter color after the addition, but not necessarily. Some color combinations in Add loop past the highest color value in a palette, white, to the lowest color value, black, or to a subsequent color in the palette, resulting in surprising color changes. Check out the sidebar, "The wild, wacky world of foreground color, background color, and pattern," coming soon to your neighborhood, about colors and their associated values to see how all this works, as if anyone cares.

- **Add Pin:** Similar to Add, but doesn't allow the final color to loop past the highest color value. The result is that many color additions with Add Pin wind up white, the highest color value that a pixel can register.

✔ **Subtract:** Subtracts the color values of each pixel in the selected sprite from the color values of each underlying pixel, resulting in a new color. If the result is a negative value, the color restarts from black to subsequent colors in the palette.

✔ **Subtract Pin:** Similar to Subtract, but doesn't allow a color value to loop back and continue up the scale of color values. Applying Subtract Pin to a sprite often results in many black pixels, the lowest color values that a pixel can register.

Getting Up Close and Personal with the Score Window Preferences Dialog Box

Chances are, you guessed that the Score Window Preferences dialog box, majestically photographed in Figure 5-9, is related to what goes on in the Score window. Glad to see that you're not asleep out there in ReaderLand. Why don't you see what's inside? Display options for the Score include

The wild, wacky world of foreground color, background color, and pattern

When you're exploring ink effects, you need to keep in mind that Director always recognizes a set of three related conditions: current foreground color, current background color, and current pattern. Because inks make use of these two colors and the current pattern in creating their effects, being aware of these conditions can help you anticipate an effect. Even if you're running a black-and-white monitor, you have a current foreground color, black, and a current background color, white. Running color, you can switch from black to a color chip with the foreground color selector and switch from white to another color — including black — from the background color selector in the Paint or Tools window.

When you're painting with solid black paint, the current pattern is simply solid black. If you're considering a waffle pattern in the Pattern pop-up

menu, the pattern itself is black, its negative space white. Running in color mode, the current foreground color replaces black and the current background color replaces white.

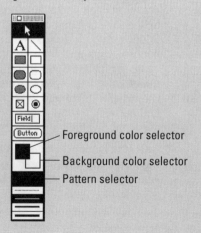

— Foreground color selector

— Background color selector

— Pattern selector

Figure 5-9:
The Score
Window
Preferences
dialog box,
where you
can set
many
options.

```
┌─────────────────────────────────────────────────────────────┐
│ ═══════════════ Score Window Preferences ═══════════════     │
│                                                               │
│  Display Options:  ☐ Allow Colored Cells       ┌──────────┐  │
│                    ☐ Enlarged Cells            │    OK    │  │
│                    ☒ Playback Head Follows Selection └──────┘ │
│                    ☒ Drag and Drop Enabled     ┌──────────┐  │
│                                                │  Cancel  │  │
│  Extended Display: ☒ Cast Member Type, Motion, Blend └─────┘ │
│                    ☒ Cast Member Number                       │
│                    ☒ Ink Mode                                 │
│                    ☒ Script Code                              │
│                    ☒ X and Y Location                         │
│                    ☐ Change in X and Y Location  ┌────────┐  │
│                                                  │  Help  │  │
│                                                  └────────┘  │
└─────────────────────────────────────────────────────────────┘
```

✔ **Allow Colored Cells:** Makes a new option available on the left side of the window so that you can color-code selected cells with a pop-up menu. You don't want to use this option on slower machines.

✔ **Enlarged Cells:** Makes Score window cells larger so that you don't get eyestrain. Nice on a large monitor.

✔ **Playback Head Follows Selection:** If selected, this option makes the playback head follow the position of the mouse pointer as you make a selection. Unselected, the playback head doesn't move until you click in the scratch bar.

✔ **Drag and Drop Enabled:** With this option turned on, you may press a selection of one or more cells in the Score and drag it to another location. Unchecked, you need to do the old Cut and Paste trick to shuffle sprites around.

Another set of options in the Score Window Preferences window affects Extended Display Information when you choose it from the Display pop-up menu, including

✔ **Cast Member Type, Motion, Blend:** Marks the Cast Member type as text, a PICT, or bitmap, followed by a bullet if no motion occurs from the previous frame or an arrow indicating its new position and direction. If you've applied a Blend percentage for the sprite by choosing Modify⇨Sprite⇨ Properties and entering a Blend percentage, that value is also included in the information.

✔ **Cast Member Number:** Shows the Cast Member's position in the Cast window or, if you've chosen to display its name in the Cast window with the Cast Window Preferences dialog box, shows the first letters of the sprite's name.

✔ **Ink Mode:** Shows the ink you chose for the sprite with the Ink pop-up menu in the Score.

✔ **Script Code:** Shows a plus sign if the sprite has a Cast Member script or the number of the script from the Script window.

✔ **X & Y Location:** Shows the location of the sprite's centerpoint relative to the upper-left corner of the Stage window. For more on X and Y coordinates, run, do not walk, to "Okay, Now Review That X-Y Coordinate Thing" in Chapter 14.

✔ **Change in X and Y Location:** Shows the relative change in position of a sprite in movement from the previous frame.

Now that you have a better idea how the Score window and preferences work together, check out how you can easily add eye-catching effects with built-in Director features. Drop by someday, and I'll show you my personal collection of eyes I've caught over the years. Pâté, anyone?

As time goes by: using Space to Time

One of the monster challenges you face when you use Director is to get Cast Members from the Cast window to the Score. Space to Time under the Score menu is the instant coffee of Director commands. This command allows you to select a number of Cast Members from the Cast window and instantly place them as sprites in consecutive frames of the Score. When you choose this command from the Modify menu, the Space to Time dialog box appears. In the Space to Time dialog box, you can set the number of frames separating each sprite as it becomes part of the Score. The default value is 1; you can enter whatever value you please.

Sometimes you want to visually check how a set of selected Cast Members relate to each other by dragging them to the Stage as sprites. What happens when you drag Cast Members to the Stage? Excellent; have a lump of sugar. They're placed in separate channels under the *same* frame in the Score. After you check each sprite's position and possibly modify the location of some of the sprites, you can select the sprites from the Score by dragging out a selection marquee or by pressing Shift and clicking the sprites; then choose Space to Time from the Score menu to rearrange the sprites' cells from consecutive channels to consecutive frames. This action places the sprites in the Space-Time Continuum that Einstein proposed, and the end of the world occurs in a blinding flash of searing heat. Or maybe it just places the sprites in adjacent frames of your movie. Are you brave enough to take the chance?

What to do between takes? In-Between Special, of course

Objects in the Real World don't usually start and stop in equal units of space from moment to moment. For example, imagine a bouncing ball. The ball speeds up or accelerates as it approaches the floor, bounces off the ground with stored up energy, and begins to slow down or decelerate as it reaches its highest point in the air because of the effects of gravity.

Using In-Between Special, you can call up the In-Between Special dialog box and enter a so-called Ease-In value to accelerate a selected sprite as in-between frames are generated. You can also enter a so-called Ease-Out value to decelerate the sprite.

In addition, In-Between Special allows you to set up nonlinear movements for tweened sprites. Just as you need to select beginning and ending sprites for the regular In-Between Linear command under the Modify menu, In-Between Special requires at least one more intermediate sprite to determine the curved "path" followed when Director creates the full set of tweened sprites with In-Between Special.

If little of this makes sense to you, don't worry. The following chapter details working with sprites in the Score, and everything comes together. Trust me. Now, about that great real estate deal in Chernobyl. . . .

Chapter 6

Too Graphic for You?
Director's Paint Window

In This Chapter

▶ Accessing the Paint window

▶ Reviewing some familiar icons

▶ Hammering away at Director's Paint tools

*Y*ou know, Director's pretty generous. For the price of the top animation program in Computerdom, the Macromedia people throw in a pretty slick paint program just because they like you so much. Oh, you think the company may have an ulterior motive? Well, it's a good program anyway.

With the built-in paint program hiding under the Paint window, you can handle any kind of bitmap from 1-bit, black-and-white graphics to what techies call *24-bit images,* meaning graphics with over 16 million colors. How did I get that figure? You don't want to know. (If you'll just burst not knowing, read the sidebar, "Colors, colors everywhere," later in this chapter.)

Director also gives you a number of ways to display and use the Paint window, including

> ✔ **Choosing Paint from the Window menu:** When you want to start from scratch, call up the Paint window and begin splashing away on a blank, electronic easel. Not an easy thing to do, even with a degree from the Sorbonne and the big set of crayons you got for Christmas.

> ✔ **Double-clicking a Bitmap Cast Member:** With one or more Cast Members eagerly awaiting the role of their lives, you can double-click a Bitmap Cast Member's preview in the Cast window and find the actual-size bitmap in the Paint window ready and willing to be edited. This route is a lot easier than starting from scratch. Where did the Cast Member come from? Well, there are Daddy Cast Members and . . . no, that's another story. The Cast Member could be an import from a good collection of clip art, an image

you scanned yourself and saved as a bitmap, a screen shot you took with the old ⌘+Shift+3 trick on a Mac or by pressing the Print Screen key, sometimes labeled PrtSc, on your trusty PC (some keyboards insist that you hold down the Shift key, too), a chart generated from raw data in Excel, or a roll of film that you had your friendly photo dealer turn into a PhotoCD for you.

🖛 **Double-clicking a bitmap sprite in the Score window:** As long as the sprite is a bitmap, you get the Paint window with the bitmap ready for editing in its own cozy easel. See Chapter 5 for more info about sprites.

🖛 **Double-clicking the small thumbnail preview of the currently selected sprite in the Score window:** You wind up with the bitmap staring back at you from the Paint window, anxiously awaiting your latest directorial changes.

Oh, No! Thousands of Icon Thingies!

Okay, hold on. You went to the menu bar and chose Paint from the Window menu or you pressed ⌘/Ctrl+5, the Paint window keyboard shortcut. Now you see icon thingies everywhere staring back at you wondering what *you* are, as in Figure 6-1.

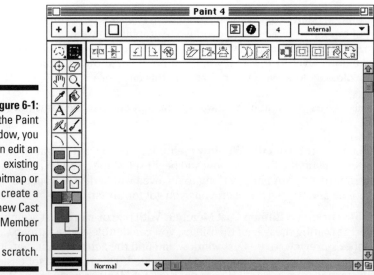

Figure 6-1:
In the Paint window, you can edit an existing bitmap or create a new Cast Member from scratch.

Colors, colors everywhere

Getting over 16 million colors from 24-bit graphics comes from the way computers understand information. In the end, all computers know is number 0 and number 1, a counting system called _binary_, which is why computers make such rotten house guests for the weekend. Boring, boring, boring! Anyway, to your computer, 0 is _off_ and 1 is _on_.

However, various combinations of 0s and 1s, on and off _states_, have unique coded meanings to your machine. To a computer, 24-bit means a number in binary that looks to you like a string of 24 1s in a row. Rocket scientists like to call this value "2 to the 24th power." 24-bit, 24 binary 1s in a row, 2 to the 24th power — they all stand for the same value — 16,384,000.

First, you're exaggerating. The number of icons is far less than a hundred, let alone "thousands." A lot of the icons are standard interface stuff for your Mac or PC. So far, so good. Then there's the mysterious stuff: You have a row of icons just under the title bar of the Paint window. To the left, you see a double column of enticing icons and, below the enticing icons, a number of small panels. You can handle this. If you read Chapter 5, you made it through the Score; you can get through the Paint window.

Paint window's top row of icons

Hello, row of icons in the Paint window. Explore them, if you dare, from left to right:

- ✔ The New Cast Member icon (+ icon) gives you a new electronic easel to paint in with each click; this action also creates a new Cast Member that occupies the next available cell in the Cast window.

- ✔ The Previous and Next Cast Member icons allow you to click through the easels of Bitmap Cast Members in the Cast window.

- ✔ The Drag Cast Member icon lets you drag the contents of the Paint window to the Stage or Score window.

- ✔ The Cast Member Name field shows you the current name of the Cast Member.

- ✔ The Cast Member Script icon (the i icon) takes you to the Cast Member Script dialog box, where you can tinker with Lingo scripts.

✔ The Cast Member Properties icon takes you to the Cast Member Properties dialog box, where you can modify basic options for the Cast Member displayed in the current easel.

✔ The Cast Member Number icon shows you the location of the Cast Member in the Cast window.

✔ The Choose Cast pop-up menu displays a list of Cast windows. Multiple Cast windows, internal and external, are a new feature for Director 5. For more on internal and external Cast windows, see "Internal and external Cast windows" in Chapter 4.

Paint toolbar

Whooh, and that's just the first row. Director 5 sports a whole new wonderland of icons underneath as well. While you're still feeling adventurous, check out this second row called the *Paint toolbar* that allows you to apply various effects to a bitmap with the click of a button. From left to right, the Paint toolbar buttons include

✔ **Flip Horizontal:** Flips the selection in the Paint window along the horizontal axis. If a portrait of your Aunt Tillie was facing left, it's facing right now, her best side.

✔ **Flip Vertical:** Flips the selection in the Paint window along the vertical axis. If a portrait of your Aunt Tillie shows her standing by the porch, now she's standing on her head.

✔ **Rotate Left:** Rotates Aunt Tillie 90 degrees counterclockwise around her center point.

✔ **Rotate Right:** Rotates Aunt Tillie 90 degrees clockwise around her center point.

✔ **Rotate Free:** Rotates Aunt Tillie freely around her center point as you drag the mouse hither and thither.

✔ **Skew:** Places "handles" or tiny rectangles around the current selection in the Paint window that you can use to distort the bitmap along the horizontal or vertical axis.

✔ **Warp:** Places "handles" or tiny rectangles around the current selection in the Paint window that you can use to distort the bitmap in any direction, one handle at a time.

✔ **Perspective:** Places "handles" or tiny rectangles around the current selection in the Paint window that you can drag to shrink or stretch the bitmap horizontally or vertically, giving a three-dimensional effect to the bitmap.

- ✔ **Smooth:** Director's way of eliminating the infamous stairstep appearance common to bitmaps because of the way they are built up with square pixels or pels. Smooth softens edges of the selection by adding pixels of intermediate values to subdue the stairstep effect, often referred to as "jaggies." Another name for smoothing is *anti-aliasing*.

- ✔ **Trace Edges:** Paints a border around the shapes that Director finds in the current selection.

- ✔ **Invert Colors:** Reverses colors in the current selection, turning black to white, white to black, and creating some wild psychedelic neohippie effects with colored artwork. You'll want to find your love beads.

- ✔ **Lighten:** Brightens all shades in the current selection by one step in value. *Value* is the lightness or darkness of an image.

- ✔ **Darken:** Darkens all shades in the current selection by one step in value.

- ✔ **Fill:** Pours the current Foreground color and Pattern into the currently selected shape. Keeping up with all these current events?

- ✔ **Replace:** Exchanges Foreground color paint in the selection with the current Destination color, another color Director keeps track of for making smooth gradations of color and shading.

Director's Paint Tools

Other mysterious icons of the Paint window represent tools to modify a bitmap in the current easel or create a new Cast Member from scratch. Remember, these are Paint tools. You build a graphic by turning on units of "electronic paint" or pixels/pels with the Brush or Pencil tool in the Paint window's easel. It's really like a magician's trick. Step up close to the image and watch it break down into separate pixels with no distinguishable shape. Step away and view the image at a normal distance and the image comes together — a distant cousin to *mosaic art,* what the Impressionists were trying to accomplish with dabs of oil paint and the use of halftones in magazines and newspapers to give the illusion of great tonal depth with microscopic flecks of ink on paper.

Each Paint tool has a so-called *hot spot,* one or more pixels in its cursor from which the "electronic paint" flows like crazy. For example, the Pencil tool's hot spot is right where you'd expect it, at the tip of the pencil point. Knowing where the hot spot is in each tool is important for full control of the image you're building in the Paint window.

This section describes Director's Paint tools from left to right, row by row.

Lasso tool

 Use the Lasso tool to create irregularly shaped selections in the Paint window by dragging the Lasso around the desired graphic. The Lasso's hot spot is at the tip of the free end of the rope. Think of using the Lasso as "roping in" an area that you want to include in a selection.

To modify the way the Lasso tool works, press the Lasso tool in the Paint tool palette to display a pop-up menu and choose one of three options, described in Table 6-1.

Table 6-1	Lasso Pop-Up Menu
Command	*How the Lasso Tool Works*
Shrink	Tightens around the silhouette of a bitmap, eliminating background-colored pixels from the selection.
No Shrink	Sets the selection to include all pixels "roped in" with the Lasso.
See Thru	Sets background pixels within the selection to Transparent ink.

To make a polygonal selection with the Lasso tool, follow these steps:

1. **Option/Alt-click a point outside the target image to establish a starting point for the polygonal selection.**

2. **Click the Lasso tool once for each segment of the polygonal selection.**

3. **For the last segment of the polygonal selection, double-click the Lasso tool to create the last segment and close the polygonal selection shape.**

 To create an identical copy or clone of a selection, Option/Alt-drag the selection to a blank area of the Paint window. Each time you release and then re-press the mouse button, you can Option/Alt-drag a new clone to another area of the easel. If you want to constrain movement horizontally or vertically as you clone a selection, add the Shift key to the set of modifier keys.

Selection Rectangle tool

 The Selection Rectangle tool is another basic selection tool for making, of all things, rectangular selections. When you choose the Selection Rectangle tool, the mouse cursor changes to a crosshair. The tool's hot spot is where the crosshairs intersect. Make a selection by moving above and to the left of what you want to select, pressing the mouse, and dragging down and to the right until the graphic is enclosed in the selection *marquee* (sometimes referred to as the marching ants, although my personal belief is that they're termites).

Modify the way the Selection Rectangle tool works by pressing the tool in the Paint tool palette and choosing one of four options from the pop-up menu, as described in Table 6-2.

Table 6-2	Selection Rectangle Pop-Up Menu
Command	*Behavior*
Shrink	Snaps to the height and width of a graphic, eliminating background-colored pixels from the rectangular selection.
No Shrink	Includes all pixels enclosed in the selection rectangle.
Lasso	Notes the color first pressed and eliminates matching pixels from the selection. Also switches to the Lasso tool.
See Thru Lasso	Notes the color first pressed, turns all matching pixels in the selection and all background-colored pixels transparent, and then switches to the Lasso tool.

The Selection Rectangle tool is also the key to quickly making copies of bitmaps and resizing them, either proportionally or to distort a bitmap horizontally or vertically. Table 6-3 outlines the result of applying modifier keys to the Selection Rectangle tool.

Table 6-3	Using the Selection Rectangle Tool
Action	*Result*
Press Option/Alt and drag a selection	Creates an identical copy, or *clone.* Each time you stop and re-press the mouse, you can press Option/Alt and then drag a new clone to another area of the easel.
Press Option/Alt+Shift and drag a selection	Creates a clone and constrains movement of the clone horizontally or vertically, depending on the direction of the initial move.
Press ⌘/Ctrl and then drag a corner of a selection	Resizes the selection horizontally and/or vertically. Dragging away from the selection increases the selection's size. Dragging into the center of the selection reduces the selection's size.
Press ⌘/Ctrl+Shift and drag a corner of a selection	Proportionally resizes the selection horizontally and vertically. Dragging away from the selection increases the selection's size. Dragging into the center of the selection reduces the selection's size.

One of Mr. Bitmap's most serious disadvantages is how poorly it scales up or down. A bitmap resized in Director's Paint window rarely results in an acceptable image for professional work. Notwithstanding Director's fine built-in Paint

Some kindly advice for scaling graphics in Director

✔ Reducing a bitmap always works better than enlarging it in Director. Whenever possible, create the largest size bitmap needed for a particular Cast Member. You can always duplicate the Cast Member, choose Modify⇨Transform Bitmap, and type a new percentage in the Scale entry field.

✔ If a bitmap is moving, loss of quality is harder to detect and less critical to the eye.

✔ If you know that changing scale is going to be an important part of a Cast Member's role, add the Cast Member to the Cast as a real PICT: From the Clipboard, paste the PICT into the Cast window with the Paste Special command found in the Edit menu. Or import the PICT, being sure to check the As PICT check box in the Import Files dialog box. Then rescale the PICT as a sprite on the Stage by pressing Shift and dragging a corner handle (for proportional scaling).

✔ If you've pulled and stretched a sprite, bitmap, or PICT on the Stage beyond recognition and want to magically turn it back to its original form, choose Modify⇨Sprite⇨Properties and click the Restore button in the Sprite Properties dialog box.

program, the best approach to resizing a bitmap is to use a sophisticated paint program like Photoshop. A program on Photoshop's level calls on highly refined routines for scaling graphics that even allow successful, limited enlargement of a bitmap. *Limited* is the key word.

Registration tool

 In traditional animation, artistes drew their initial sketches on highly translucent paper called *onion skin.* They learned to hold several pages in one hand and, with inconceivable dexterity, flip back and forth through the pages to test the sequence. In a fit of creative exuberance, the artistes christened this technique "onion-skinning." Artists with 12 or more fingers per hand were highly prized, chained to their desks, fed special high-protein diets, and groomed daily with Mr. Ed's horse hair pomade.

Viewing a sequence of bitmaps in the Paint window by pressing the Next Cast Member button is one of Director's equivalents to onion skinning. Each bitmap in the Paint window starts out in life, as it should be, equal under the law and with a registration point centered in the graphic. You can see the registration point of a bitmap by choosing the Registration tool and noting where special dotted lines intersect on the easel. Click the Registration tool to fine-tune a bitmap's registration point.

To test an animation sequence using the Next Cast Member in the Paint window, follow these steps:

1. **If the Cast window is not displayed, choose Window⇨Cast.**

2. **Press Shift and select a range of contiguous Cast Members in the Cast window belonging to a particular animation sequence.**

   If necessary, manually rearrange Cast Members by dragging them into the correct sequence so that they occupy contiguous cells. Director takes care of all the accounting stuff to keep the Score and Stage windows in sync with the changes you make in the Cast window.

3. **Choose Cast⇨Align Bitmaps.**

   This command causes the registration point of selected Cast Members to line up at a common point.

4. **Double-click the first Cast Member of the animation sequence.**

   Director takes you to the Paint window, where you see the Cast Member's bitmap.

5. **Simulate "onion skinning" by pressing the Next Cast Member button and letting subsequent bitmaps pass by.**

6. **If necessary, adjust one or more bitmaps' registration point by clicking in the desired location with the Registration tool.**

After adjusting registration points, you need to repeat steps 2 through 4 to realign the registration points before viewing the sequence, again using the Next Cast Member button in the Paint window.

The Align Bitmaps command works best with relatively small bitmaps of similar shape. If the Align Bitmaps command doesn't seem to work, you may have chosen bitmaps too diverse in size or registration point location; try limiting your selection.

To recenter a bitmap's registration point in the Cast Member, its default setting, double-click the Registration tool in the Paint window.

Eraser tool

 Use the Eraser tool to remove pixels from a bitmap in broad strokes.

Director doesn't allow you to change the shape of the Eraser. For critical, pixel-by-pixel erasing, follow these steps:

1. **Select the Pencil tool.**

2. **Set the background color to the color behind the graphic.**

   For more information about the Background color chip, see "Additional Paint window areas" at the end of this chapter.

3. **Press Option/Alt to paint with the background color and "erase" unwanted pixels by clicking them with the Pencil tool.**

   To instantly erase the entire Paint window, double-click the Eraser.

Some programs are thoughtful enough to warn you when you're about to do something drastic, such as erasing the entire contents of a file or window. They bring up an alert box asking, "Are you sure you want to erase the entire window?" giving you an out by clicking a Cancel button. Not Director. So think twice before using the double-click Eraser trick. Be certain that you want to erase everything in the window.

If you do erase the entire easel by mistake, stop. Do not pass Go. Do not collect $200. Immediately choose Undo Bitmap in the Edit menu or press ⌘/Ctrl+Z to restore the graphic.

Hand tool

 Pressing the Hand tool within the easel of the Paint window allows you to shift the view on-screen so that you can view hidden sections of full-size bitmaps such as screen shots or oversized bitmaps.

A common fear of novice Director types is that moving a bitmap in the Paint window might mess up the position of artwork on the Stage. Director is smart enough to know better. Give Director some credit, will you? Sheesh!

If the position of a bitmap in the Paint window is important to you, press the Option/Alt key and drag the Hand tool around the easel so that you move around the screen without changing the placement of the bitmap relative to the top-left corner of the easel.

Press the spacebar to temporarily change the currently selected tool in the Paint window to the Hand tool. This trick now works with the Text tool in Director 5 as long as you haven't established an insertion point in the Paint window. Once you have, try pressing the spacebar and clicking at the same time. If it works, you've got only one problem; you lose the insertion point and any text you've typed becomes a bitmap. It's a jungle out there.

If you've been scrolling up and down a large bitmap in the Paint window and become lost, click the Next Cast Member button in the upper-left corner of the window and then click the Previous Cast Member button. You'll find the bitmap centered in the Paint window like magic.

Zoom tool

 Each click of the Zoom tool doubles the size of the image in the Paint window while a small window in the upper right of the Paint window displays an actual-size view of the region surrounding the mouse pointer. The actual-size view is displayed to keep you from getting lost at larger magnifications.

To zoom out, press ⌘/Ctrl+Shift and note how the little plus sign (+) in the Zoom tool changes to a minus sign (-). By the way, the Zoom tool echoes the Zoom command in the View menu with a pop-up selection of views to 800 percent.

Eyedropper tool

 Click the Eyedropper tool on a pixel to sample its color and pattern and to set the current foreground color and pattern to the sample.

 Shift-click the Eyedropper on a pixel to match the current background color and pattern to the pixel. Option/Alt+click the Eyedropper on a pixel to match the end or destination color in the Gradient Destination color chip to the pixel. By the way, a *gradient* is simply a blend of colors.

Paint Bucket tool

 Use the Paint Bucket tool to fill an area with the current foreground color and pattern. The tool's hot spot is at the very tip of the paint spilling from its bucket.

If you choose Gradient from the Ink pop-up menu, the Paint Bucket tool also fills an area with the current gradient, set in the Gradient Destination color chip. The Paint Bucket tool is designed to work with solid areas of color, or as techie types like to say, contiguous blocks of pixels. You see, the Paint Bucket's hot spot is sensitive to the color you initially click on; the Paint Bucket is designed to seek out contiguous pixels of matching color.

Double-click the Paint Bucket tool to go to the Gradient Settings dialog box shown in Figure 6-2. The beginning color is defined by the current foreground color; the ending color by the current color chosen as the Destination color chip.

As you can see, Director offers you many options in this dialog box:

✔ Direction of the gradient

✔ Number of cycles in the gradient

✔ Method of producing the gradient

✔ Spread of the gradient, meaning evenly spread or favoring the first or last color

✔ Range, meaning where Director places the beginning and ending colors of the gradient (for example, across the Cast Member versus the window size)

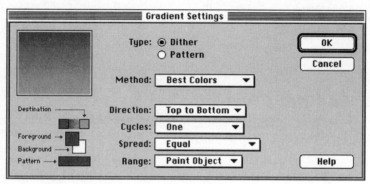

Figure 6-2:
The
Gradient
Settings
dialog box.

Text tool

 The Text tool in the Paint window is for creating text that becomes a bitmap as soon as you do just about anything other than type or set text attributes like Font, Size, and Style.

Try this out:

1. **Choose Paint from the Window menu.**

2. **Click the + button near the upper-left corner of the window.**

3. **Click the Text tool.**

   After you move back to the easel, your mouse pointer should look like the classic I-beam cursor that belongs to word processing programs like Microsoft Word.

4. **At the I-beam, type some text.**

5. **Type a period and then three spaces.**

   Okay, those of you out there who typed "a period and then three spaces," go stand in the corner for at least three hours. And no supper.

6. **Press the Delete key once.**

Why did I have you add three spaces and then delete a space? The sense of power is intoxicating. Actually, just to give you a better view of the insertion point that looks like an upside-down cross. The short horizontal line at the bottom of the insertion point marks what typographer types call the *baseline,* where lowercase characters like *x* and *n* rest on the page.

You should also see a bold, gray border around the text you type. As long as you retain the gray border and the insertion point, you can modify the text in several ways. For example, you can

- ✔ Delete characters to the left of the insertion point one character at a time with the Delete key.

- ✔ Move editable text without losing the border or insertion point by pressing the mouse anywhere within the gray border and dragging.

- ✔ Choose Modify➪Font to display the Font dialog box, where you can change the font, size, vertical spacing (leading), kerning, and color of selected text.

- ✔ Choose Modify➪Paragraph to display the Paragraph dialog box, where you can change the alignment, left and right margins, first indent, and extra vertical spacing of selected text.

- ✔ Double-click the Color resolution indicator to change the scale, color depth, and/or palette of the text with the Transform Bitmap dialog box. After this operation, you lose the ability to edit the text.

- ✔ Press the Pattern chip to change the current pattern. You don't see pattern changes until you change the text to a bitmap.

- ✔ Press the Background color chip to change the current background color; the white space within the bold, gray border that contains the text adopts the new background color. By the way, you don't see background color changes until you change the text to a bitmap.

- ✔ Press the Foreground color chip to select a new current foreground color; selected text immediately adopts the new foreground color.

- ✔ Press the Gradient Destination color chip to set up first and last colors for a custom gradient. This action alone does not modify the editable text. To apply a gradient to the editable text, you need to take one more step, selecting Gradient from the Ink pop-up menu. Also, changes are not visible until you turn the text into a bitmap.

- ✔ Press the Ink pop-up menu to change the current ink effect. Changes are not visible until you turn the text into a bitmap.

Click on a blank area of the Paint window to turn text typed with the Text tool into a bitmap, no different from any other bitmap imported or painted into being with one of Director's Paint tools.

The biggest disadvantage of turning text into a bitmap is losing the ability to edit the text. If you want to make edits, you must literally erase and retype bitmapped text; take care to match the previous artwork and blend the text appropriately into its surroundings.

There's an old saying I just made up: Every cloud has a silver lining. You see, a wonderful advantage of bitmapped text is never having to worry if the right typeface is installed in the user's system, a never-ending concern when using editable text. What if the right typeface isn't installed in the computer? What if the user doesn't have the same typeface? What if you have halitosis? And on and on it goes.

 Avoid poor display of text by choosing a TrueType font or installing Adobe Type Manager to your system and restarting your computer before opening Director. For serious type aficionados who want extra-smooth looking type, consider anti-aliased text, a new feature for Director 5. For more on anti-aliased text, see Chapter 8.

Pencil tool

 Use the Pencil tool for free-form painting. Its hot spot is at the tip of the Pencil point, and it paints with the current foreground color in the Paint window. With the Option/Alt key pressed, the Pencil tool paints with the current background color.

 The Pencil doesn't display the current pattern or the current ink effect; its ink effect is always set to Normal, and it always paints with one-pixel-wide paint. (Must be the Republican in the bunch.) See this section's last paragraph for more on ink effects.

Press the Shift key to constrain the Pencil's movement to straight horizontal or vertical lines.

 Use the Pencil for critical, pixel-by-pixel retouching of a bitmap, too.

Press the ⌘/Ctrl key to temporarily change the Pencil tool or any other tool in the Paint window to Director's Zoom tool.

Air Brush tool

 Use the Air Brush tool to create soft, feathered shapes of color and splatter effects with the current foreground color and pattern.

If you're familiar with Photoshop, you'll be disappointed with Director's Air Brush tool. There's no contest, although Photoshop's Airbrush tool doesn't create the interesting splatter effects that you can achieve with Director's Air Brush, so there. You may just find yourself sneaking away one day from Photoshop to get an effect that you can achieve only in Director.

Double-click the Air Brush tool to display the Air Brush Settings dialog box, shown in Figure 6-3, where you can customize the spray, size of dots, and speed of spraying paint. To modify the Air Brush effect even more, change the current ink effect from Ink pop-up menu.

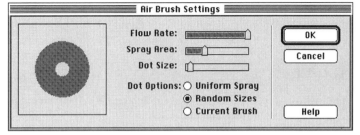

Figure 6-3:
The Air
Brush
Settings
dialog box.

Press the Air Brush tool to reveal a pop-up menu of five customizable Air Brush settings.

Paintbrush tool

The Paintbrush is perhaps Director's most intuitive Paint tool. It looks and acts just like, well, a brush.

When coupled with ink effects like Smudge or Smear from the Ink pop-up menu, you'd swear you're painting with real oil or acrylic paint. Double-click the Paintbrush to display the Brush Settings dialog box shown in Figure 6-4.

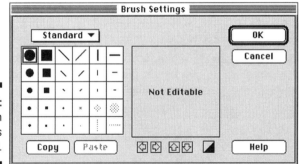

Figure 6-4:
The Brush
Settings
dialog box.

In the Brush Settings dialog box, you can select from 30 installed brush shapes or create custom shapes of your own by pressing Custom in the pop-up menu.

Arc tool

Use the Arc tool to paint curved segments.

Press the mouse to establish the beginning of an arc, drag in any direction to paint the arc on the easel, and release the mouse to complete the arc.

Shift-drag to create a perfect quarter-circle with the Arc tool. Option/Alt+drag the Arc tool to paint an arc in the current background color.

Line tool

Use the Line tool to paint straight lines at any angle in the current foreground color on the Paint window's current easel.

Press Shift and then drag the Line tool to draw horizontal, vertical, or 45-degree angled lines. Press Option/Alt and then drag the Line tool to draw horizontal, vertical, or 45-degree angled lines in the current background color. Stand on one leg to make this look more impressive.

Filled Rectangle, Ellipse, and Polygon tools

Use the Filled Rectangle to paint rectangles, ellipses, and polygon shapes filled with the current foreground color in the current pattern and bordered in the current line width. The border won't display the current pattern.

Hold down the Option/Alt key to paint a filled shape with a border displaying the current pattern, effectively creating a rectangle with no border.

Shift-drag to paint a perfect square or circle. There's no law against tossing in the Option/Alt key to paint a perfect square or circle with a border displaying the current pattern.

Double-click the Filled Rectangle, Ellipse, or Polygon tool to display the Gradient Settings dialog box. For more on the Gradient Settings dialog box, check out the "Paint Bucket tool" section, earlier in this chapter.

Rectangle, Ellipse, and Polygon tools

 Ah, but wait, your little friends have a dual personality. Click the regular Rectangle, Ellipse, or Polygon tool to paint a shape with a transparent fill, bordered with the current foreground color in the current line width. To add a little zip to your life, press the Option/Alt key when painting to add the current pattern to the border. And to make life so exciting that you can hardly stand it, add an ink effect from the Ink pop-up menu. Now that's living on the edge. Whooh.

NOTE

The Polygon tool behaves a little differently than its siblings in the Paint tools palette. Click and drag to establish the first side of the polygon; continue to click and drag to add a side. Double-click the Polygon tool to close the polygon.

Additional Paint window areas

Now, to wake some of you drowsing off in ReaderLand, I'd like you to look at the areas of the Paint window just below the Polygon tools, as in Figure 6-1. Top to bottom, these areas include

- **Gradient Destination color chip:** Allows you to select the beginning and ending colors for a *gradient,* or blend of colors, by pressing the left and right sides of the chip and selecting a color from the current palette. Double-click the chip to go to the Color Palettes dialog box, where you can choose a different palette for the bitmap.

- **Foreground color chip:** Allows you to select the current foreground color by pressing the Foreground color chip and choosing a color from the current palette. The number of colors depends on the current color depth setting of your monitor. Double-click the chip to get to the Color Palettes dialog box, where you can select a different palette for the bitmap.

- **Background color chip:** Allows you to select the current background color by pressing the Background color chip and choosing a color from the current palette. The number of colors depends on the current color depth setting of your monitor. Double-click the chip to go to the Color Palettes dialog box, where you can select a different palette for the bitmap.

- **Pattern chip:** Allows you to select the current pattern by pressing the Pattern chip and choosing a pattern. Double-click the Pattern chip to go to the Pattern dialog box, where you can create custom patterns.

- **Line Width indicator:** Allows you to choose the current line width for Director's Paint tools. To set a custom line width, choose File⇨Preferences⇨Paint, from which you can select a line width of up to 64 points with a sliding control in the Paint Window Preferences dialog box.

✔ **Color Depth indicator:** Displays the color depth of the current bitmap in the Paint window. *Color depth* is techie talk for how many colors a bitmap can display at one time. For example, a 1-bit graphic can show only black and white, while an 8-bit graphic can display up to 256 different colors at one time. Double-click the Color resolution indicator to go to the Transform Bitmap dialog box, where you can, among other options, set the bitmap to a higher or lower color depth.

I lied; 1-bit Cast Members don't have to be black and white. Director gives you a sneaky way to add lots of color to your movie by using just 1-bit graphics. Select a 1-bit sprite on the Stage and give it any color from the Color Palettes pop-up panel in the Tool palette. This is a common trick used by developers working under very tight assumptions about user resources, meaning that you're trying to squeeze lots of color into a Director movie that has to fit on a floppy disk. This is also a great trick if you plan to publish on the World Wide Web, where economy is vital for successful design.

You can "sample" a pattern or brush shape by clicking the mouse anywhere outside the Patterns or Brush Shapes dialog box. Your sample appears in the large panel on the left of the respective window, where you can click individual pixels to further modify the bitmap into a custom pattern.

Director saves custom tiles in the file where the custom tiles are created. However, Director saves custom patterns to the Director 5 Preferences file in the Preferences folder. If you want to archive custom patterns you've created, be sure to back up the Director 5 Preferences file before reinstalling the system software or Director; then restore the archived Director 5 Preferences file after installation.

Just to the right of the Line Width indicator is the Ink pop-up menu, which allows you to choose an ink effect for a selection in the Paint window. Many of the ink effects are similar to the inks available in the Score window, but others, such as Smudge and Smear, are specifically used to expand the potential of Director's Paint tools. Double-clicking the Ink pop-up menu several times gives you a terrific headache as the pop-up menu wildly appears and disappears with each click without taking you anywhere else. Great fun on a slow weekend.

Chapter 7

Drawing, er, Painting on Director's Paint Window

In This Chapter

▶ Setting colors in the Paint window

▶ Exploring mysteries of the Line Width indicator

▶ Handling graphics that are too big for their own good

▶ Making masks, even when it's not Halloween

*O*kay, you've perambulated through the mysteries of the Paint window, although I'm not sure that perambulating is legal in public, at least until the kids are sound asleep. Anyway, there are some people whose ice cream always falls from the cone one minute after they buy it, who wind up with an odd sock at the Laundromat, and who always choose Brand X in those taste tests. For those of you out there in ReaderLand whose Paint window comes up with black as the current foreground color and white as the current background color, let me assure you that Director is a 24-bit program; it can handle over 16 million colors at one time, provided that your monitor, computer, and video card can handle 24-bit color. You Windows 3.1 people are stuck with 8-bit color, I'm afraid, which is just as well. Staying on 8-bit color will help your Director movies run faster.

No, You're Not Limited Just to Black and White

Changing colors is a cinch. The Foreground color chip on the Paint window is actually a pop-up menu. When you press the chip with the mouse, a *palette*, or collection of colors, appears; highlight any one of the colors to make it the new foreground color. It's that simple.

Even if you're set for displaying 24-bit color, or over 16 million colors, you can have only one current foreground color at a time. You paint with this color, unless you alter the Paint tool's behavior with modifier keys.

Director's Paint window also provides you with a Background color chip that's located underneath the Foreground color chip. The Background color chip is a pop-up menu, too.

After you decide on your Foreground and Background colors, you have one other important color option to address. You know which one? Wonderful, here's an extra large lump of sugar. That's right — the destination or ending color in the Gradient Destination color chip, your key to creating gradients or color blends in Director. Both the beginning and ending colors in the chip — tantalizingly alluded to in Figure 7-1 — are actually pop-up menus hiding a full palette of available colors.

Figure 7-1:
The Gradient Destination color chip, your key to creating color blends in Director.

How Do I Change the Size of My Lines?

You're painting with the Line tool, and you're getting frustrated because you can't figure out how to change the size of the line. You've cursed at it, which is usually effective with high-technology equipment, but this time, zippo. You've pouted, but with the same result.

You must have forgotten the Line Width indicator in the Paint window, lovingly hand-painted in Figure 7-2.

The Line Width indicator offers you the following:

✔ **Dotted line:** Click this option to paint an invisible line. The invisible line affects only the shape tools — the Rectangle, Ellipse, and Polygonal tools — and when the invisible line is selected, the shape tools produce an object without a border (useful if you're too lazy to press the Option/Alt key).

✔ **1-pixel, 2-pixel, 3-pixel lines:** Click to choose one of three ready-made line widths for down-to-the-wire, heart-thumping, last-15-seconds-on-the-clock line making.

Choose File➪Preferences➪Paint to go to the Paint Window Preferences dialog box, where you can use a sliding control to select a line width of up to 64 points.

Figure 7-2:
The Line
Width
indicator is
in the lower-
left part of
the Paint
window.

When a Graphic's Too Big for Its Own Good

What's a person to do when a graphic's too big to see everything at once in the Paint window? The following sections give you a clue.

First, you need to view your Cast Member in the Paint window. Should you choose to accept it, you can accomplish your mission in a number of ways:

✔ Find the Cast Member in the Cast window and double-click its thumbnail.

✔ Find the Cast Member in the Score and double-click the sprite.

✔ Select the Cast Member in the Score and double-click the small preview in the upper-left corner of the Score window.

✔ Select the Cast Member in the Score and double-click its sprite on the Stage.

✔ Throw chicken bones on the floor, chanting, "Aboo — abow — aboo" (archaic language predating pig Latin).

Using scroll bars

When a full-size bitmap is too large to see at one time in the Paint window, a wonderful invention should come to mind: scroll bars. A vertical scroll bar is on the right side of the Paint window with an up arrow at the top, a down arrow at the bottom, and a weird little box in between that techies call the *elevator*. Also, a horizontal scroll bar with its own arrows and elevators is located at the bottom of the Paint window.

To see a different portion of the Paint window, you can do any of the following:

 ✔ Click the up or down arrow of the vertical scroll bar.

 ✔ Click the right or left arrow of the horizontal scroll bar.

 ✔ Press and drag the elevator on the vertical or horizontal scroll bar.

Now you know all you ever wanted to know about scroll bars. Aren't you glad you asked?

Using the Hand tool

Another tool that should come to mind when you have a bitmap too large to see at one time is the Hand tool, which lets you drag the bitmap around within the Paint window like a loose sheet of drawing paper. Either choose the Hand tool from the Tool palette or press the spacebar, and any other tool temporarily becomes the Hand tool. One exception: The Text tool won't turn into the Hand tool until you press the spacebar and then press the mouse in the Paint window.

Using the Hand tool changes the location of the bitmap within the Paint window but does not change its position on the Stage or its recorded position in the Score window.

Wow! More Special Effects

When you work in the Paint window, certain commands in the View and Xtras menus become very enticing. I know you're just dying to see what these menus are all about, so dive in; the paint's fine.

Special commands in the View menu

In the View menu shown in Figure 7-3, the bottom four commands relate to the Paint window. These commands include Panel, Ruler, Grid, and Onion Skin.

Monitoring monitor size

The whole topic of working around extra large bitmaps shows why multimedia developer types like monitors larger than the standard 13-inch variety. With a 17-inch monitor or larger, you can place all those tricky windows to the side of the screen and still see the entire Stage, which you probably set to the ever-popular 13-inch size. If you opt to get a larger monitor, find out whether your computer or video card allows you to install extra VRAM, the video RAM that provides a larger screen without losing colors.

Another solution to the large bitmap dilemma is to install a second monitor, not necessarily color,

where you can place all those annoying extra windows and palettes. The prime monitor and any additional monitors can be joined into one virtual screen so that you can literally drag a palette from one screen to the next. Adding another monitor usually means adding another video card to the innards of your computer, although those of you with Power Macs get a bonus — Power Macs are set up for running two monitors without additional add-ons. Check your particular model of Mac or PC to see what you need.

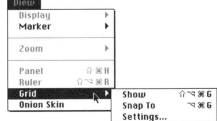

Figure 7-3: The View menu.

Panel

Panel is a *toggle* command, a kind of command that alternates or toggles between turning a command on and off or making a display element visible or invisible, in this case showing or hiding the set of Paint tools on the left side of the Paint window. At times, you may find the Paint tools distracting, so Director is thoughtful enough to include a command that lets you hide the tools whenever you want. Hiding Paint tools with the Panel command is also a way of eking out a little extra real estate on a small monitor. Today, any monitor 14 inches or smaller is considered small.

Ruler

Another toggle command like the Panel command, Ruler allows you to show or hide vertical and horizontal rulers in the Paint window, as shown in Figure 7-4. Notice the dotted line in each ruler; the dotted line marks the current position of the mouse. Strangely enough, the size of the ruler doesn't change when you enlarge the view with the Zoom tool. For accurate measurements, you need to do a little old-fashioned arithmetic based on the current view of the bitmap.

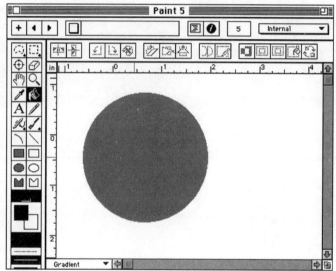

Figure 7-4:
Horizontal and vertical rulers you can show or hide in the Paint window.

Grid

Another new feature for Director 5, the Grid helps you align sprites on the Stage while the Grid's Snap To command, depicted in Figure 7-3, is turned on. The Snap To command makes the Grid magnetic; sprites seem to, well, snap in place, aligning along the Grid's array of squares. The Grid's submenu also includes the Show command, which is another toggle command alternatively showing and hiding the Grid on the Stage. You can choose Settings from the submenu to custom-tailor the Grid to your every whim with the Grid Settings dialog box shown in Figure 7-5.

Shhhh — secret features of Paint window rulers

Notice the small box in Figure 7-4, where the vertical and horizontal rulers intersect in the upper-left corner of the Paint window; it includes the letters in for inches. You can change the unit of measure on the rulers simply by clicking the small box and choosing the appropriate unit. The other units of measure available to you include

- ✔ cm = centimeters

- ✔ Pixel = $\frac{1}{72}$ of an inch (your display's unit of measure)

- ✔ Pica = $\frac{1}{6}$ of an inch (a typographic unit of measure)

The small box also marks the zero point, or origin, of the rulers, where measurement begins. You can set the zero point to any other location by positioning the mouse pointer in either ruler and pressing and dragging to some point on the current easel. Resetting the zero point allows you to take measurements from the center of a bitmap or its upper-left corner or any other arbitrary point on the easel.

To return the zero point to its default setting by using the small box, position the pointer in either ruler and press and drag it into the small box.

Onion Skin

Believe it or not, Onion Skin is not the name of the new John Lynch movie. Onion Skin is a new command under the Paint window's View menu. The Onion Skin and the Onion Skin floating palette are both new for Director 5. The term *onion-skinning* comes from traditional animation; animators hold several pages of translucent paper in one hand and preview an animation sequence by flipping back and forth through the pages.

To begin peeling away Onion Skin's mysteries, call up the Onion Skin palette, depicted in Figure 7-6, by choosing View⇔Onion Skin. Onion Skin is one of those famous toggle commands; next time you choose Onion Skin, the palette will go running off and hide itself. It is a *palette,* a special kind of window that floats in front of all other windows, including the currently active window. For more information about active windows, check out "What's an active window?" in Chapter 2.

Figure 7-5:
Use the Grid Settings dialog box to custom-tailor the Grid to your every whim.

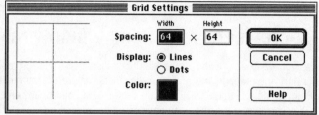

Onion Skin works by displaying Cast Members trailing and following the current bitmap as ghost images in the same Paint window easel. You can specify how many Cast Members are displayed at one time. Normally, these Cast Members represent the frames of a particular animation sequence; use the Onion Skin palette in order to check whether any bitmaps are out of sync or need refining or for tracing purposes.

I bet you're wondering just what those Onion Skin icon thingies are all about. Now you can find out:

✔ **Toggle Onion Skinning:** Click to highlight the icon and turn on onion skinning. Figure 7-6 shows the icon turned on. Click again to turn off this feature.

Figure 7-6:
The new Onion Skin palette allows you to trace over other Cast Members.

✔ **Preceding Cast Members:** Click to display the Cast Members preceding the current bitmap as ghost images in the Paint window. The farther the Cast Members are from the current bitmap, the lighter they appear. Alter the number of preceding Cast Members shown by clicking the up or down arrows or by entering a value.

✔ **Following Cast Members:** Select to display the Cast Members following the current bitmap as ghost images in the Paint window. The farther the Cast Members are from the current bitmap, the lighter they appear. Alter the number of following Cast Members shown by clicking the up or down arrows or by entering a value.

✔ **Set Background:** Looking like Juan Valdez's mountain in Colombia, the Set Background icon allows you to designate any bitmap in the Cast window as the background image. Go to the chosen bitmap in the Paint window by using the Previous Cast Member or Next Cast Member button, select the bitmap in the Paint window by double-clicking the Selection Rectangle tool, and click Set Background in the Onion Skin palette.

✔ **Show Background:** Click this toggle button to display or hide the designated background bitmap.

✔ **Track Background:** If the designated background bitmap has been animated with the Auto Distort command and you want to include the background animation in the Onion Skin view, click the Track Background icon to step through the background bitmap's animation while you use the Onion Skin feature.

Now that you know a little about Onion Skin's features, start putting them to use. The following steps show you how to use the Onion Skin command in the View menu.

Setting the background image

1. **Choose Window➪Paint or press ⌘/Ctrl+5 to display the Paint window.**

2. **Choose View➪Onion Skin to display the Onion Skin palette.**

3. **Using the Previous and Next Cast Member buttons in the Paint window, display the bitmap you want to designate as the background image.**

   The bitmap you want for the background image can be located anywhere in the Cast window. Say you created an animation sequence by using Auto Distort in the Xtras menu. Say the sequence shows a bull's-eye getting warped over ten frames, as though hit by a tremendous force. (See "Using Auto Distort" in this chapter for details on using this command.) Navigate to the beginning frame of the bull's-eye animation.

4. **Double-click the Selection Rectangle tool to surround the bitmap in a selection marquee.**

5. **Click Set Background in the Onion Skin palette.**

Turning on the Onion Skin palette

1. **Using the Previous and Next Cast Member buttons, navigate to the bitmap you want to inspect with the Onion Skin palette.**

   Say you've already made another ten-frame sequence of an arrow being squeezed in half by the force of its forward motion. (You can create this sequence with the Auto Distort command in the Xtras menu.) In the Paint window, navigate to the arrow bitmap that represents frame one of the arrow sequence.

2. **Turn on onion skinning by clicking the Toggle Onion Skinning icon.**

3. **Enter a value or use the small arrow controls to set the number of preceding Cast Members shown as ghost images.**

4. **Enter a value or use the small arrow controls to set the number of following Cast Members shown as ghost images.**

   If you want to leave the background bitmap as a static image, skip to step 6.

5. **If you want to display background animation, click Track Background.**

   As you step forward and backward in the Paint window with the Next and Previous Cast Member buttons in the next step, you see that the designated background image also displays its animation.

6. **Move forward and backward through the bitmaps in the Paint window with the Previous and Next Cast Member buttons.**

   Because you have Onion Skin turned on, you see the set number of previous and next bitmaps relative to the current bitmap as ghost images, and you can now check the animation sequence to see whether it works.

Special commands in the Xtras menu

Director 5's Xtras are basically plug-ins to extend the feature set of programs like Adobe Photoshop and Premiere. Director Xtras come in three flavors: filters, transitions, and new Cast Member types. New Xtras are on the way from third-party developers, or if you're a whiz at programming in C blindfolded, you can make your own Xtras in your spare time. Right.

Installing Xtras

To install a new Xtra filter, locate the Xtras folder/subdirectory in Director's folder/subdirectory. Add the new Xtra filter(s) to the Xtras folder/subdirectory.

Other Macromedia products now feature Xtras, too. If you move the Xtras folder/subdirectory to the Macromedia folder/subdirectory, you make all the Xtras available to any Macromedia program you run. You Mac types can find the Macromedia folder in your System folder; you PC people can find the Macromedia subdirectory in the Windows subdirectory.

In the Xtras menu, reproduced in excruciating detail in Figure 7-7, the last three commands include Filter Bitmap, Auto Filter, and Auto Distort.

Figure 7-7:
You'll find
special
effect
commands
under the
Xtras menu.

> **Xtras**
> Update Movies...
>
> Filter Bitmap...
> Auto Filter...
> Auto Distort...
>
> FileFlex ▶
> PrintOMatic Lite ▶
> Palettes.cst
> Animation Wizard

Using Filter Bitmap

New for Director 5, Filter Bitmap allows you to apply a Director Xtra filter to selected Cast Members in the Cast window or to a selection in the Paint window. Choosing Filter Bitmap displays the Filter Bitmap dialog box, shown in Figure 7-8. You can even add Adobe Photoshop and Premiere filters to the Xtras folder.

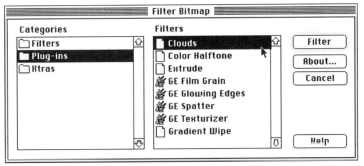

Figure 7-8:
The Filter
Bitmap
dialog box
under the
Xtras menu.

To find the Xtras folder, go to the Finder on a Mac or Program Manager in Windows and open the Director 5 folder. Inside, you'll find the Xtras folder, where all good Xtras go. (The Xtras folder is installed during Director's program installation.)

The following steps guide you through applying a filter to a selection:

1. Display the Cast or Paint window.

2. Make a selection.

In the Cast window, make a selection by Shift-clicking contiguous Cast Members or ⌘/Ctrl-clicking noncontiguous Cast Members. In the Paint window, use the Lasso or Selection Rectangle tool to make a selection.

3. **Choose Xtras⇨Filter Bitmap to display the Filter Bitmap dialog box.**

4. **Choose a Category of filter from the left Directory list in the Filter Bitmap dialog box.**

   To view all available filters, choose All from the Category list.

5. **Choose a specific filter from the right Directory list in the Filter Bitmap dialog box.**

6. **Click Filter.**

   Some filters require specific settings. To access these filter settings, click the Filter button and a dialog box or other control is displayed.

Using Auto Filter

Auto Filter is very similar to Filter Bitmap, but Auto Filter, well, automates the process a bit. Figure 7-9 shows the Auto Filter dialog box, where you decide which filter to apply and the number of frames over which the effect should build incrementally.

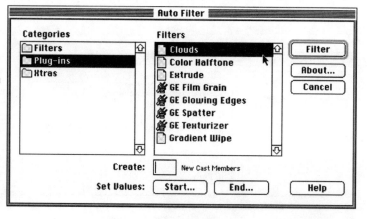

Figure 7-9: Choose Xtras⇨Auto Filter to automatically filter frames incrementally.

The following blow-by-blow account helps you use Auto Filter:

1. **Choose Window⇨Cast or press ⌘/Ctrl+3.**

2. **Select a Bitmap Cast Member from the Cast window, or Shift-select a range of Bitmap Cast Members.**

   To filter part of one Cast Member, choose Window⇨Paint, choose the Selection Rectangle tool or the Lasso, and then select a portion of the current Bitmap Cast Member to alter.

3. **Choose Xtras⇨Auto Filter.**

4. **In the Auto Filter dialog box, double-click the Category of filter you want to use.**

5. **Highlight the Filter of choice in the Filters list.**

6. **Click Set Values:Start.**

   Filter controls appear where you can enter settings for the beginning of the sequence.

7. **Click Set Values:End.**

   Filter controls appear where you can enter settings for the ending of the sequence.

8. **Back at the Auto Filter dialog box, enter the number of New Cast Members you want to create for the sequence.**

   If the box is grayed out or disabled, you have selected a range of Cast Members in the Cast window. Auto Distort applies the filter incrementally to the selection without creating new Cast Members.

9. **Click the Filter button.**

Some filters may task your CPU (central processing unit) to the limit; don't be surprised if filtering takes some time to complete.

Using Auto Distort

You can use Auto Distort to create an animation sequence. Start with a bitmap you've distorted in the Paint window with the effects from the Paint toolbar. (For more on the effects, see "Paint toolbar" in Chapter 6.)

To use Auto Distort, follow these simple steps:

1. **Choose Window⇨Paint or press ⌘/Ctrl+5 to display the Paint window.**

2. **Using the Previous and Next Bitmap Cast Member buttons, find the bitmap you want to distort.**

3. **Double-click the Selection Rectangle tool to create a selection marquee around the entire bitmap in the Paint window easel.**

   If you want to distort a portion of the bitmap, use the Selection Rectangle tool to make a selection. Auto Distort does not work with selections made with the Lasso tool.

4. **Click one of the effects in the Paint toolbar and distort the bitmap using the handles that appear in the selection marquee.**

5. **Choose Xtra⇨Auto Distort to display the Auto Distort dialog box, shown in Figure 7-10.**

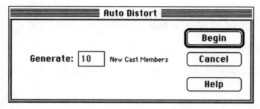

6. **Enter a value in the Generate box for the number of New Cast Members you want Auto Distort to build.**

7. **Click the Begin button.**

Without knowing it, you have created *key frames,* which are beginning and ending frames for a sequence. Auto Distort fills in the difference incrementally by the value you enter in the Generate box in step 6. You wind up with new Cast Members in the Cast window that make up an animation sequence Walt would be proud of. Be sure to take time for a popcorn break after you proudly present your work to the world.

Exploring more Xtras

Under Auto Distort in the Xtras menu, you'll find another set of Xtras, including FileFlex, PrintOMatic Lite, Palettes.cst, and Animation Wizard. (Attention, Director old-timers: Animation Wizard replaces Auto Animate.)

FileFlex

FileFlex comes with Director as an Xtra in the Xtras menu. This simple database program can handle up to 1,000 records. From the submenu, you can choose Database Designer, which lets you lay out a customized database by dragging and dropping field types into the main window.

PrintOMatic Lite

PrintOMatic Lite adds basic printing features to Director 5 movies and requires light to intermediate Lingo scripting. For example, you can write a simple script for a button that says

```
on mouseUp
print "This is a test"
end
```

After you get some Lingo under your belt, you can create something Director calls an *instance.* What's that? At this point, you don't want to know. Just remember that it's more powerful, sounds more impressive, and may even get you that date you've wanted. In other words, later on down the line, it's worth learning. Look over Lingo Chapters 17 and 25 to get your feet wet.

Palettes.cst

Choosing Xtras⇨Palettes.cst displays an external cast of assorted palettes to play with, as you can see hand-engraved in Figure 7-11. For example, you might add a Rainbow Windows palette to the Score if you're developing for a PC or a Cinepak palette, which is a set of colors that works especially well with Digital Video Cast Members compressed with Apple's Cinepak codec. For more information about Digital Video and codecs, see "Showing Off Your 15 Minutes of Fame on Video" in Chapter 18.

Figure 7-11:
Choosing
Palettes.cst
from the
Xtras menu
displays an
external
cast
bursting
with a
variety of
palettes.

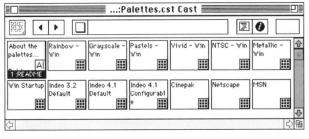

Animation Wizard

The Wizard is ready to show you his tricks. He helps you put together animated presentations at the click of a button or two. He's so helpful, in fact, that I've devoted Chapter 16 to his sly shenanigans.

SuperTechniRamaVision: All about System and Custom Palettes

Something about a known quantity is so comforting, so cozy, so . . . known. I think it's safe to say that people don't really like surprises (except for listeners of Howard Stern, maybe). A surprise birthday party is about as big a surprise as most people can stomach.

Same thing goes for using a computer. Your PC comes with a default set of color schemes. On a Mac, the System palette is a known quantity. It has exactly 256 different colors. White is always the first color, black is always the last. Always. In between is a range of colors — what techies call a *color lookup table* (CLUT), each color in its own specific slot. Windows has its own cozy set of startup colors. No surprises, either.

Using the System palette

You can view this set of palettes or color schemes by choosing Color Palettes from the Window menu. The Color Palettes dialog box appears, looking suspiciously like Figure 7-12.

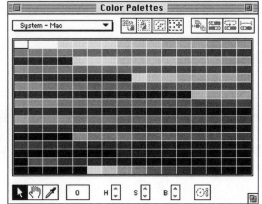

Figure 7-12:
The Color
Palettes
dialog box.

Take a look at the Palette pop-up menu shown in Figure 7-13, and you find a bouquet of palettes. When you choose System - Mac or System - Win from the selection of palettes, you know what to expect. As a multimedia producer, you constantly need to anticipate what the user, the intended audience for your epic, is going to see. Chances are that the user's going to be running off the standard, ubiquitous System palette or startup color scheme.

Facing problems with the System palette

Which is not to say that problems don't arise from sticking with a standard palette or color scheme. The same 256 colors that make you feel so smug also limit you in a critical way — to 256 colors. Some of the problems that the System palette presents you with include the following:

Figure 7-13:
The Palette
pop-up
menu in the
Image
Options
dialog box,
where you
can remap
an imported
bitmap to
the System
palette.

✔ **Poor rendering,** or display, of certain color gradients because of the limited number of colors to work with, depending on specific foreground and destination colors chosen.

✔ **Posterization,** or blockiness, of some areas of scanned photographs and computer-based images, basically because of the same limited color choice problem.

✔ **Artifacts,** or defects, in an image, which are little monsters in a bitmap that don't belong there, created when your computer attempts to display a range of colors that it really doesn't have the resources to create.

Living with 16 million headaches

As a multimedia type, you face a classic dilemma. Use fast, 8-bit color and stay with the System palette of 256 colors. That ensures that the user sees what you intend to show, but the user has to put up with problems like posterization and artifacts, which degrade the aesthetics and effectiveness of your multimedia product.

Or go with 24-bit color, giving you over 16 million colors to play with, nearly photographic quality on a good monitor. But risk suffering a whole new set of performance problems, such as the fact that 24-bit color asks your computer to handle three times the amount of data and computation as 8-bit color. The result? Your multimedia slows to a grinding halt on all but the fastest machines.

Do you really want to run the risk of assuming that your user is running your beautiful multimedia on the latest, greatest computing dynamo the computer industry has to offer? The viewer's machine may turn out to be an old clunker with 1MB of memory, and then your beautiful multimedia is almost all for naught.

Living with compromise

I've heard of this thing called. . .what was it?. . .oh yes, compromise. Director has heard of compromise, too, which it offers in the form of a Method pop-up menu, shown in Figure 7-14, in the Gradient Settings dialog box with several options for rendering a gradient.

Figure 7-14:
The
Gradient
Settings
dialog box,
where you
can create
custom
gradients
for the Paint
window.

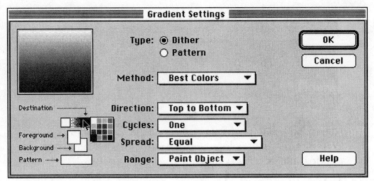

Given a specific set of foreground and destination colors, one rendering method may work better than another using 256 colors. Pattern Best Colors, for example, may work better than, say, Dither Adjacent Colors. It's a visual decision rather than an intellectual one (thank goodness); if one rendering method makes a better-looking gradient, it's the best rendering method.

Another way of compromising — staying with 8-bit color when you want 24-bit, photographic-quality color — is to modify a 24-bit image in a high-level paint program such as Photoshop, Painter, or DeBabelizer by choosing Index color. These programs offer special routines that reduce 24-bit color's 16 million hues to the System's palette of 256 colors. The routine that drops the color depth from 24-bit to 8-bit uses a special trick called *dithering* in an attempt to preserve image quality. Dithering fools the eye into thinking that it sees more colors than really exist in the image. Sometimes the result of dithering is 8-bit color that can pass as 24-bit color; sometimes the result is disappointing.

Compromising, and then compromising again

A better solution when using high-end paint programs such as Photoshop or Painter to reduce colors from millions to 256 is to choose an option called an *adaptive palette*. The result is a graphic no longer based on the System palette or startup color scheme, but on a custom set of 256 colors analyzed by the paint program for optimum effect and combined with a special dithering routine. The result of using an adaptive palette is often an 8-bit image nearly indistinguishable from its 24-bit original.

When you import a bitmap, Director displays the Image Options dialog box, shown in Figure 7-15. This is your chance to import a bitmap's adaptive palette into the Cast window as a new Cast Member. Otherwise, Director remaps the bitmap to the System palette, often with unhappy results.

Figure 7-15:
The Image
Options
dialog box
appears
when you
import a
bitmap into
Director.

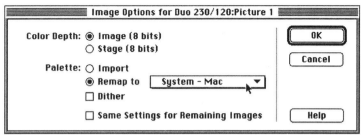

Director gives you a gaggle of options in the Image Options dialog box. For Color Depth, choose between Image and Stage:

- ✔ **Image:** Click this radio/option button to retain the original color depth of the bitmap.

- ✔ **Stage:** Click this radio/option button to change the bitmap's color depth to the current color depth of the Stage.

For Palette, you have the honor of choosing Import or Remap to:

- ✔ **Import:** Click to import a bitmap's palette as an additional Cast Member, especially important for a bitmap with an adaptive palette.

- ✔ **Remap to:** Click to select a palette from the pop-up menu and have the imported bitmap remapped to the selected palette.

Last but not least, the Image Options dialog box gives you two fun check boxes to play with, Dither and Same Settings for Remaining Images:

- ✔ **Dither:** Check to apply a *dithering routine* to the imported bitmap. A dithering routine increases the apparent number of visible colors, similar to the idea of using four process colors in printing to create the illusion of reproducing full-color graphics and photographs.

- ✔ **Same Settings for Remaining Images:** Click to apply the same selection of options to remaining bitmaps listed in the Import Files dialog box.

Checking out those other built-in palettes

Why so many other built-in palettes? In Figure 7-13, in addition to the System palette, you see several other choices.

The following list takes you through the built-in palettes and gives you an idea why they're there and what you can do with them:

- **System - Win:** A palette of colors that transfers between the Macintosh and Windows platforms to help prep your movie for cross-platform compatibility.

- **Rainbow:** A special palette of bright colors, heavy on primary colors, as seen in a rainbow, for special effects and extra-smooth color gradients. Simply add the palette to the Score in the Palette channel.

- **Grayscale:** A special palette of 256 values for extra-smooth grayscale bitmaps and gradients. Add this Palette to the Score in the Palette channel when needed.

- **Pastels:** Another special palette of colors that is "softer" than the standard System palette, lighter and less saturated, with zero percent cholesterol.

- **Vivid:** A special palette similar to Rainbow but not so focused on primary colors. A more sophisticated yet bright set of colors for special effects. Take a look at this palette after drinking 10 or 12 cups of coffee for a real cheap thrill.

- **NTSC:** A special palette for prepping your movie for transfer to video. Novice multimedia types are often shocked at how different a Director movie looks on TV. One of the most dramatic changes in video transfer occurs with color. *NTSC* (National Television Systems Committee) TV, which is the kind of TV you currently watch, can handle only a very limited range of colors and *saturation levels* (that is, how red a particular red really is). For example, colors on NTSC TV above 70 percent of full saturation appear to spread beyond the image and bloom, meaning that the color seems to fluoresce or glow. Other colors simply translate into ugly browns, grays, and greens or make totally unexpected color shifts in the spectrum. So Director supplies you with a set of NTSC-legal colors to help reduce NTSC shock after you transfer your beautiful multimedia to videotape.

- **Metallic:** Another special effects palette of subtly metallic colors, designed mainly for robots that become interested in developing multimedia in their spare time. You haven't heard of robot-brewed multimedia? Well, that's 'cause robots have so little spare time. Workaholics, every one of them, bless their little tin hearts.

✔ **VGA:** A special palette for working with VGA monitors that newer Mac models can easily accommodate. VGA monitors display a color shift from standard Mac monitors; Director's VGA palette attempts to properly translate the color shift. By the way, VGA is dimmed in the Palette pop-up menu if you're not running a VGA monitor, so don't feel cheated or something.

✔ **System-Win (Dir 4):** A palette of colors for movies made with Director 4, which displays colors differently than Director 5. Choosing the standard System - Win palette over this palette, you see a definite and probably unwanted color shift in all graphics.

The best way to work on Director movies intended for video transfer is to work directly with an NTSC monitor or at least to refer frequently to an NTSC monitor during development. The 660AV and 840AV Mac models can switch between your computer monitor and an NTSC TV through the Monitors control panel. Second-generation Power Macs use the Monitors and Sound control panel of System 7.5.3 to send a second video signal to your TV, giving you two displays to work with. Some third-party video cards for Macs and PCs supply a separate port for outputting NTSC signals so that you can work with two monitors at one time. Check the capabilities of your own monitor, computer, and/or video card. Some settling of contents may occur. Over. Out.

Who Was That Masked Man? And How Do You Make a Mask, Man?

One of the most important ink effects available from the Score window's pop-up menu is the Mask ink effect. Matte ink makes the white, rectangular bounding box of a bitmap invisible, allowing the background to show through. But white pixels within the graphic remain opaque, which is not always the effect you want. That's when you want to turn to the more versatile Mask ink effect.

For example, the Matte ink effect on a Text Cast Member such as the letter *A* (that's a capital *A*) doesn't give you the effect you need. In the center of a capital *A* is that little bit of what typographer types call the *counter,* or negative space. It looks like a tiny pyramid and by all rights, the background should show through the counter, too.

When you use the Matte ink effect on the letter, what happens? Sure enough, the bounding box surrounding the *A* sprite turns transparent, and you get a silhouette effect; but the *A*'s counter remains white and defeats the effect you intend to create.

Creating a mask

Follow these steps to create a mask that you can add to a sprite:

1. **Select a bitmap Cast Member in the Cast window.**

   Make sure that an empty cell is to the right of the selection.

2. **Choose Edit⇨Duplicate.**

3. **Double-click the duplicate Cast Member, taking you to the Paint window.**

4. **Choose solid black from the Foreground Color selector (the very last color).**

5. **Select the Paint Bucket tool and click inside the area of the Cast Member that requires the mask, filling its shape with black paint.**

   If the bitmap were a large capital *A,* you wouldn't want to fill the A's "counter," that pyramid shape in the middle of the character.

6. **Choose Modify⇨Transform Bitmap to display the Transform Bitmap dialog box.**

7. **Choose 1 bit from the Color Depth pop-up menu.**

8. **Click the OK button.**

   The Bitmap Cast Member in the Paint window is now a 1-bit graphic, which is exactly what you need to go to the next set of steps. Don't worry, there are only 534 more steps.

   Just kidding.

Applying Mask ink to a sprite

To apply the Mask ink effect to a sprite, follow these steps:

1. **Click the Score window and make sure that the original sprite is still selected.**

   The sprite also appears selected on the Stage.

2. **Choose Mask from the Ink Effect pop-up menu in the Score window.**

After Mask ink is enabled, the area of the sprite that needs the mask displays the original Cast Member; nonmasked areas become transparent, revealing the background.

While pressing the ⌘/Ctrl key, click on a selected sprite on the Stage to reveal the secret Ink Effect pop-up menu. Remember, with the purchase of this book, you agreed to guard this secret with your life. Always read the small print.

Chapter 8

And Now for Something Completely Different: Text and Field Windows

● ●

In This Chapter

▶ Examining different text types

▶ Revisiting the Paint window's Text tool

▶ Looking into Text and Field windows

● ●

*A*lthough people think of multimedia as a visual experience, content in the form of old-fashioned words still plays a big part in most multimedia productions. Working with Director is no exception. A strong textual element exists among all the jumping, gliding, hip-hopping, generally hyperactive sprites on the Stage. In fact, Director 5 has dramatically beefed up its text-based features.

In this chapter, you can explore Director 5's new text capabilities and find out more than you ever wanted to know about bitmapped text, so-called *rich text*, and text in fields.

Bitmapped Text, One Step Away from Pod People

Bitmapped text is fake. It looks like text, reads like text, and even smells like text — kind of musty. Bitmapped text reminds me of those pod people from *Invasion of the Body Snatchers,* that creepy movie out of the '50s where Uncle Ira turns out to be a big cucumber.

Bitmapped text starts out like Uncle Ira, looking for all the world like the genuine article, like text created with a click of the Text tool. But this Text tool comes from the Paint window, which should be a dead giveaway. After you type some text with the Paint window's Text tool and even do some limited formatting and revising, when you're not looking the text turns into, yikes, a bitmap! And it doesn't even have to be a full moon.

Don't get me wrong — bitmapped text can claim many advantages over real text in Director. You never have to worry whether the user has the right fonts installed. Bitmapped text is legally entitled to all bitmap privileges under the Constitution, such as being stretched and pulled like taffy with distortion options from the Paint toolbar or having Xtras filters applied to it ad nauseam for special effects rivaling Industrial Light and Magic stuff. But . . .

Once this kind of text becomes a bitmap, it can't be edited. And bitmapped text looks like heck warmed over when you print it out.

Rich Text, Come to Papa

Rich text is Director 5's name for text you type with the Text tool from the Tool palette or from within a Text window.

Don't confuse the Text tool from the Tool palette with the Text tool in the Paint window that gives you bitmapped text. Two different "animules" completely.

Rich text is the closest thing to word processing-type text in Director 5. In general, it's the text of choice for most movie-making in Director with a feature set worthy of an Oscar, including

- **Paragraph formatting:** Create paragraph-specific formatting choices just like you make in Microsoft Word and other word processing programs, including alignment, line depth (leading), and even kerning (spacing between character pairs).

- **Tabs:** Set real tabs within paragraphs of rich text.

- **Editable text:** Rich text is always editable in authoring mode — that is, while you're making your movie with Director and before you turn the movie into a projector. For more on making projectors, see "Making a Projector (and Why You'd Want To)" in Chapter 18. Rich text in a projector becomes bitmapped text with all its benefits and disadvantages.

- **Anti-aliasing:** Rich text can be anti-aliased or smoothed out with special routines to eliminate the infamous stairstepping effect, or *jaggies,* common to text displayed on a computer monitor. Set text for anti-aliasing in the Text Cast Properties dialog box.

- **Imported text:** Import text from Microsoft Word and other programs that save in RTF (Rich Text Format).

Text in a Field

Create text in a field by choosing Insert⇨Media Element⇨Field or by selecting the Field tool in the Tool palette, as in Figure 8-1, and dragging out a field on the Stage.

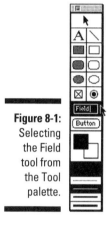

Figure 8-1:
Selecting
the Field
tool from
the Tool
palette.

Text in a field has special uses in Director movies. Use text in a field only if you need editable text during playback of the movie or projector or if text needs to be printed out at high resolution, because of the following limitations:

- ✔ **System dependent:** To display properly, text in a field depends on the right fonts being installed in the user's system. Otherwise, unexpected and potentially disastrous results may occur on playback, causing you to never play the piano again.

- ✔ **Limited formatting:** Text in a field doesn't offer the full formatting features of rich text discussed in the preceding section. You can't apply true paragraph formatting or set tabs and indents to text in a field.

- ✔ **Slow playback:** Text in a field is slower on playback than bitmapped or rich text and can significantly impede performance, especially on slower computers.

The Text Window

Go ahead, choose Text from the Window menu to display the Text window, which should look something like Figure 8-2. The beady-eyed among you who already read Paint window stuff may notice something familiar. If you like, review the top row of identical Paint window icons in Chapter 6.

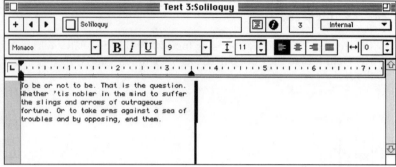

Figure 8-2:
The Text
window,
where you
can type
text with
tabs and
paragraph
formatting.

In the second row of icons, you have lots of formatting goodies to explore. From left to right, they include

- **Font pop-up menu:** Displays all fonts currently installed and available for selection.

- **Bold, Italic, Underscore buttons:** Click to apply one or more of these formatting options to selected text.

- **Size pop-up menu:** Choose any type size from the pop-up menu or enter a value directly in the field.

- **Line Spacing:** Displays line spacing or *leading* of the Text Cast Member in points. Use the up and down arrows to alter the vertical distance from line to line. You can also directly enter a value in the entry box.

- **Left Align, Center, Right Align, and Justify buttons:** Click one of the buttons to set alignment for selected paragraphs in a Text window. Left Align aligns selected paragraphs flush on the left side of the text block, leaving the right side so-called *ragged.* Center aligns selected paragraphs along the midpoints of each line, and Right Align aligns selected paragraphs along the right side of the text block, leaving the left side ragged. Justify stretches each line of selected paragraphs so they are flush on the left and right sides of the text blocks. You often see this effect in magazine design, where two or three columns of text are on a page. Justified text is thought to be more formal and sophisticated than other alignments.

- **Tracking/Kerning control:** Adjusts two similar but distinct types of text spacing. With a block of selected text, increase the general horizontal spacing, or *tracking,* by clicking the up arrow or tighten spacing with the down arrow. Generally, the larger the type size, the tighter the tracking can be. Normally you wouldn't even bother with adjusting spacing for *body text,* like the text you're reading now. You'll want to adjust tracking, though, for headlines and larger, so-called *display-size* text like banners.

Certain character pairs in a block of text are troublesome because of the very shapes of the characters. For example, W and A as in WATER and o and w as in owl have too much space between them compared with the general spacing or fit of most characters. Without adjustment, or *kerning*, these character pairs stand out from the rest of the text, interrupting the flow of text and reducing readability. Good typesetters kern character pairs like A and W. Now you, too, can kern character pairs in Director 5. Simply click in between the characters, and then click the up arrow to increase or the down arrow to decrease character pair spacing. Like tracking, you usually apply these adjustments to text larger than body text.

Under the second row of icons is the Text ruler for setting tabs and indents in rich text. You can hide or show the ruler by choosing View⇨Ruler. To change the units displayed in the ruler, choose File⇨Preferences⇨General and select from Inches, Centimeters, or Pixels from the Text Units pop-up menu.

Setting tabs

The left side of the ruler is called the *tab well*, which cycles through four kinds of tabs with each click: left, right, center, and decimal.

To create custom tabs, follow these steps

1. **Select paragraphs for tabbing in the Text window.**
2. **Click the tab well until you see the kind of tab you need.**
3. **Click once in the ruler just under the displayed text units (inches, for example) to establish each custom tab.**

Change the position of a tab by dragging it to the desired location on the ruler. Remove a tab simply by dragging it off the ruler.

If you don't establish custom tabs, preset tabs are designed to align every half inch on the ruler as with most word processing programs, like Microsoft Word.

Setting indents

Set indents for selected paragraphs by dragging left and right indent markers along the ruler. To set a first line indent, use the control that points down from the top of the ruler.

The Text Cast Member Properties Dialog Box

Click the Text Cast Member Properties icon, the one that looks like an italic "i" in a bowling ball, to display the Text Cast Member Properties dialog box, shown in Figure 8-3, so that you can check out its unique features.

Figure 8-3:
The Text Cast Member Properties dialog box.

The Text Cast Member Name box

In this entry box, you can enter a meaningful name for the Text Cast Member instead of referring to it by its position in the Cast or the Score (which can change over time and cause unexpected results) — or as "Hey, you."

The Framing pop-up menu

From the Framing pop-up menu, meticulously reproduced by Alsatian artisans (see Figure 8-4), you can choose one of three options for text display on the Stage, including the following:

Figure 8-4:
The Framing pop-up menu.

✔ **Adjust to Fit:** Creates a field that automatically adjusts its depth to display the total amount of text in the field.

✔ **Scrolling:** Creates a field with a vertical scroll bar on the right side, allowing you to enter a large amount of text without resizing the text field. The user simply scrolls with the up and down arrows to see different parts of the field's content on playback.

✔ **Cropped:** Creates a text field with a fixed depth regardless of the amount of text typed in the field, although you can manually reshape the field by dragging one of its selection handles (the small black squares in the corners and at the center points of each side of the text field) to reveal more of the text.

Anti-alias radio/option buttons

A new feature for Director that you can apply to Text Cast Members, anti-aliasing is a technique for subduing the stairstepped effect common to text on-screen, often referred to as the jaggies, and to increase perceived sharpness. Under the Framing pop-up menu are three check boxes, including

✔ **All Text:** Click this radio/option button so that all text in the Text window becomes anti-aliased.

✔ **Larger Than:** Click this radio/option button and enter a value in the small entry box to the right so that text in the Text window larger than the entered value becomes anti-aliased.

✔ **None:** Click this radio/option button so that none of the text in the Text window is anti-aliased.

The Unload pop-up menu

Use the Unload pop-up menu to tell Director which Cast Members may be purged or removed from memory when not visible on the Stage. Check out an extended discussion of the Unload pop-up menu in Chapter 4.

Miscellaneous stuff

You find a few other goodies in the Text Cast Member Properties dialog box:

✔ **Text Cast Member Preview:** At the top left is a preview representing the contents of the Text Cast Member, with a Text Cast Member icon in the lower-right corner of the preview.

✔ **Size Indicator:** At the bottom-left corner, Director displays the size in bytes of the Text Cast Member.

  ✔ **Script button:** Under the OK and Cancel buttons, Director provides a Script button to take you to the Text Cast Member's Script window.

  ✔ **Help button:** The ever-popular Help button displayed in all dialog boxes to take you quickly to Director's built-in Help system.

Searching for text

To search for and replace text in the Find Text dialog box, depicted in Figure 8-5, choose Edit⇨Find⇨Text, where you discover the following options:

Figure 8-5:
The Find
Text dialog
box.

```
┌──────────────────────── Find Text ────────────────────────┐
│                                                            │
│     Find:  │hapless harlequins        │   ┌───────────┐    │
│                                           │    Find   │    │
│  Replace:  │hipless hippies           │   └───────────┘    │
│                                           ┌───────────┐    │
│   Search:  Text Cast Members              │  Replace  │    │
│            ◉ Cast Member 3                └───────────┘    │
│            ○ Cast "Internal"              ┌───────────┐    │
│            ○ All Casts                    │Replace All│    │
│                                           └───────────┘    │
│  Options:  ☒ Wrap-Around                  ┌───────────┐    │
│            ☐ Whole Words Only             │   Cancel  │    │
│                                           └───────────┘    │
│                                                            │
│                                           ┌───────────┐    │
│                                           │    Help   │    │
│                                           └───────────┘    │
└────────────────────────────────────────────────────────────┘
```

Selecting Text and Field Cast Members on the Stage

A selected Text or Field Cast Member on the Stage may appear in one of two ways. The situation's kind of schizophrenic and fraught with danger, so be careful.

When you give a Text or Field Cast Member one click, a thin dotted border with handles in the corners and midpoints appears, indicating that the Text or Field Cast Member is selected as an object and not as text. When you move the mouse pointer inside, the cursor remains a pointer, and you can drag the Cast Member as an object to a different location on the Stage or press a handle and drag to reshape the Cast Member.

When you double-click a Text or Field Cast Member on the Stage, the border becomes thick and patterned with striped lines. Afterward, when you move the mouse inside the Cast Member, the pointer turns into the venerable I-beam cursor. You can take this to mean that the Text or Field Cast Member is now in edit mode and you can modify its contents until heck freezes over.

✔ **Find:** Enter the word or phrase you're looking for, the so-called *search string,* here. Include only as much as you're sure that you need and watch out for typos and misspelled words. Click Replace or Replace All to continue.

✔ **Replace:** Enter replacement text when the Find Text command makes a hit.

✔ **Search: Text Cast Members:** Restrict the search to the currently selected Cast Member, the internal cast, or all casts by clicking the appropriate radio/option button.

✔ **Change Again:** Allows you to replace found text with the last substitute text entry made in the Find/Change dialog box.

✔ **Wrap-Around check box:** Makes Director search from the insertion point to the end of the selected field and then search from the first character in the field to the original location of the insertion point, coming full-circle in its search.

✔ **Whole Words Only check box:** Makes Director search for a match of complete words rather than partial words. For example, if you enter *part* as the search criteria with Whole Words Only checked, Director ignores words like *partner* and *partisan* with *part* in them and accepts only the complete word *part* as a legitimate hit.

The Field Window

The Field window, shown in Figure 8-6, is exactly like the Text window. Except it's different — I mean, different in that text you enter in a Field window remains editable during playback of the Director movie and after you have turned a movie into a projector. In other words, if you have text areas in a Director movie that a viewer might fill in, like a questionnaire or a database entry, you need to make these areas with the Field tool in the Tool palette or by choosing Window⇨ Field. For Text window info, see the preceding section, cleverly titled "The Text Window."

Field windows are different from Text windows in what they lack as well. Here's what's missing:

✔ No Ruler

✔ No Justify alignment option to stretch each line to its maximum width

✔ No tracking or kerning options

For a quick overview of what you can and can't do with Director text, keep Table 8-1 handy. I suggest making several copies and stapling them throughout your home.

Figure 8-6:
The Field window, where you can enter text that remains editable during playback and in a projector.

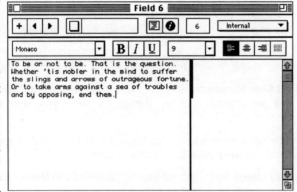

Field 6

Monaco | **B** *I* <u>U</u> | 9

To be or not to be. That is the question.
Whether 'tis nobler in the mind to suffer
the slings and arrows of outrageous fortune.
Or to take arms against a sea of troubles
and by opposing, end them.

Table 8-1 Advantages and Disadvantages of Director Text

Type of Text	Advantages	Disadvantages
Bitmapped	Text shapes are editable pixel by pixel	Not editable for content
	Speedy animation	Poor printing output (resolution frozen at 72 dpi)
		Not searchable with Find commands
		Not recognized as text by Lingo scripts
Rich text	Editable at any time during development	Shapes not editable pixel by pixel during development
	Tracking and kerning options	Font mapping tables for cross-platform movies
	Searchable with Director Find commands during development	
Text in a field	Editable during playback and in a projector	Requires correct fonts installed in the user's system
	Prints at full resolution with smooth character shapes	Slow on playback

Part III
Manipulating Director with More Windows

The 5th Wave   By Rich Tennant

"I found these two in the multimedia lab morphing faculty members into farm animals."

In this part . . .

There's an old saying I just made up: When you're designing multimedia, you can never have too many windows. Someone at Macromedia must agree with me, because they slipped in even more windows with assorted tools to explore while no one was looking. Maybe these windows don't have the glamour of the Score or Cast windows, but boy, would you miss them if they went on strike.

In this part, I walk you through QuickDraw, digital video, 24-bit palettes, H-B-S, scripts and their associated windows, and a gaggle of other intriguing characters just itching to become part of your life.

Chapter 9

Yet Another Set of Tools: The Tool Palette

· ·

In This Chapter

▶ Fiddling around with the Tool palette

▶ Using the shape tools to create and change shapes

▶ Exploring the importance of the Tool palette

▶ Discovering the meaning of life

· ·

*O*ne of the great pleasures of learning Director is plowing through the kazillion windows that the program has to offer — that is, if you also happen to look forward to paper cuts during the day. As if you don't have enough windows to befriend, allow me to present the Tool palette.

A Brief Explanation of Tool Palette Tools

If you've read Chapters 6 and 7, you know that I've talked about Paint tools this and Tool palette tools that. So you just might be wondering, what the heck is the difference? Well, without getting too technical, the Tool palette tools work like ClarisDraw and CorelDRAW!, two well-known computer graphics programs that make mathematical descriptions of shapes like circles, rectangles, polygons, and even freeform shapes. By contrast, when you work in the Paint window, you're putting "digital" paint on a digital easel.

When you use a program like ClarisDraw or CorelDRAW!, you're drawing, not painting. And as much as I hate to admit it, when you use one of Director's tools from the Tool palette, you're really drawing, too, not painting. I feel so ashamed that I didn't bring this up earlier . . . well, not that ashamed.

Anyway, what's the difference between painting and drawing? Read on, my friend.

Painting in Director

In a painting *environment,* to use the big kids' lingo (no pun intended), you add *digital paint* to the page pixel by pixel as you push the Brush or Pencil tool around. Another way of saying this is that you turn on individual pixels on the page that look like a recognizable image from a normal viewing distance. This collection of pixels may look like a circle, an apple, or even text if you use the Paint window's Text tool. But the circle, apple, and text images are all an illusion, smoke and mirrors, nothing but individual pixels glowing on your computer screen that happen to look like a circle, apple, and text. I know, another illusion shattered forever.

Drawing in Director

Imagine that you're drawing in ClarisDraw or CorelDRAW! or, better yet, using one of the Tool palette tools in Director 5. Whether you realize it or not, you're creating a description of an object rather than painting with pixels. Your computer accepts the result as an *object,* or whole entity, not just a collection of pixels that look like something due to a trick of the eye. When you draw an oval with the Circle tool from the Tool palette, you get a real oval; you can click anywhere inside the oval with the mouse pointer and drag the circle around the Stage. Try this on long, rainy weekends; the time just flies by.

Watch My Lips: T-h-e-s-e A-r-e D-r-a-w-i-n-g T-o-o-l-s

What makes the Tool palette tools unique is that they draw shapes or objects, very different from the bitmap-making tools in the Paint window. If the word *object* made you utter, "Huh?" don't worry. In the section coming up, I give you a painless idea of what drawing objects, or what Director calls *shapes,* is all about.

Drawing on the Stage

Functionally, one of the biggest differences between Paint window tools in the Tool palette and those in the Paint window is that you can draw directly on the Stage with a Tool palette tool. Several events occur, actually, when you draw on the Stage with a Tool palette tool. To better understand what happens, set up your screen as follows:

1. **From the Window menu, choose the Tools, Cast, and Score windows.**

2. **Drag the Resize box in the lower-right corner of the Cast window to make the window about two inches square. Click the appropriate scroll bars so that an empty Cast Member cell is visible in the window.**

3. **Drag the Score's Resize box in the lower-right corner toward the center of the window to make the Score window as small as possible.**

4. **Click inside the first empty cell in the Score window.**

5. **Click one of the shaded tools in the second row of the Tool palette.**

6. **From the upper-right region of the Stage, drag the tool diagonally down and to the right about 1^1/$_2$ inches.**

   The Stage is the one window you never have to select. It's always there, like happy, smiley-face sunbeams in California. And, oh yes, like death and taxes.

Notice what happens the nanosecond you release the mouse: Several events occur instantaneously. In fact, if you have an atomic clock handy, it's great fun timing the following as a family project:

✔ A rectangular shape appears selected on the Stage, with small black squares called *handles* at the corners and midpoints of the selection.

✔ Director automatically adds the shape you just drew as a new Shape Cast Member to the Cast window.

✔ Director automatically adds the shape to the first free cell in the current frame of the Score window.

And you thought Director was just another pretty face.

Modifying a Shape Cast Member

As for the type of shape, the shape you just drew directly on the Stage is dramatically different from any graphic you may have created in the Paint window. Well, don't act so smug about it.

For example, when you double-click a Bitmap Cast Member on the Stage, Director takes you to the Paint window, where you can edit the graphic, pixel by pixel.

The Shape Cast Member Properties dialog box

Don't expect Director to take you by the hand and lead you to the Paint window when you double-click a Tool palette shape. What happens when you do? Double-clicking a shape takes you to the Shape Cast Member Properties dialog box, shown in Figure 9-1.

Figure 9-1:
The Shape
Cast
Member
Properties
dialog box
for a shape
drawn with
a Shape
tool.

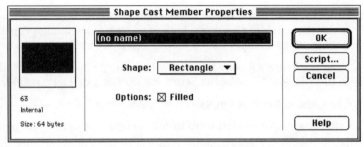

You can easily recognize a Shape Cast Member in the Cast by the icon in the lower-right corner of its cell — like a shape on the Stage, with handles yet.

You can't edit shapes pixel by pixel, but the Shape Cast Member Properties dialog box allows you to modify the graphic in a number of significant ways, including

 ✔ Giving the shape a unique and meaningful identity by entering a name in the Name entry field at the top of the window.

 ✔ Changing the graphic's shape by choosing one of the basic shapes in the Shape pop-up menu under the Cast Member name.

 ✔ Changing the graphic to an unfilled shape by unchecking the Filled check box.

The Shape pop-up menu

Take a look at the Shape pop-up menu, shown in Figure 9-2, featuring four Shape options based on the dimensions of the currently selected shape. You can use the Shape pop-up menu to quickly transform the shape of a previously drawn shape.

Figure 9-2:
The Shape
pop-up
menu.

Shape options in the Shape pop-up menu include the following:

- **Rectangle:** A rectangular shape with 90-degree corners
- **Round Rect:** A shape with rounded corners
- **Oval:** An oval shape
- **Line:** A straight line whose angle reflects the start and stop points of the original shape that you dragged out with a Tool palette tool

Shape resizing handles

Another way of modifying a shape is to resize it by dragging one of its selection handles, as shown in Figure 9-3.

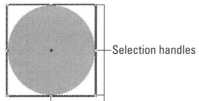

Figure 9-3: The selection handles of a QuickDraw sprite.

Selection handles

Ah, some of you wide-awake types remember that selected bitmap sprites display selection handles, too, and that you can resize them by dragging a handle. However, an advantage of a shape sprite is that you can resize them without jaggies, those infamous stairstepped edges that you get with enlarged bitmaps.

When you want to increase the size of a shape, press one of the shape's handles and drag away from the center of the shape. You should see something like the result pictured in Figure 9-4. If you want to maintain proportions, hold down the Shift key until after you begin dragging a selection handle.

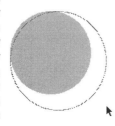

Figure 9-4: Proportionally scaling a QuickDraw sprite by pressing Shift and dragging one of its handles.

The selection marquee and handles disappear and a ghost outline of the sprite grows in size as you continue dragging the mouse. After you release the mouse, the result is an enlarged shape sprite, as shown in Figure 9-5.

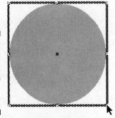

Figure 9-5:
An enlarged
QuickDraw
sprite.

Compare the shape sprite in Figure 9-5 with the bitmap sprite in Figure 9-6, which has been scaled up to similar dimensions. Note the classic and, may I add, ugly stairstepped effect called the *jaggies* that results whenever you try enlarging bitmaps in Director (or any other paint program).

Figure 9-6:
The
infamous
jaggies of a
rescaled
bitmap.

Another important difference between shapes and bitmaps is that shapes are *objects,* self-contained entities that aren't just an assemblage of pixels. Bitmaps look like self-contained shapes; they're really nothing more than a block of pixels that trick the eye into looking like something from a normal viewing distance.

Be careful not to get confused about the difference between bitmaps and shapes when adding Cast Members to the Stage. A bitmap on the Stage takes on some shape-like characteristics. You can click anywhere on a bitmap in the Stage and select the whole bitmap, and, after it's selected, the bitmap displays handles just like its shape-like cohorts.

Director has designed things this way so that we multimedia types can work with bitmaps more easily on the Stage. But double-click that bitmap, get it into the Paint window, and its bitmap heritage comes blazing through. Zoom in and whammo. Pixels! Nasty, slimy, individual pixels that give the whole show away.

Checking out the Tool palette tools

Several of the tools in the Tool palette, smartly reproduced in Figure 9-7, look similar to tools that you find in the Paint window. Read ahead to discover more tools unique to the Tool palette.

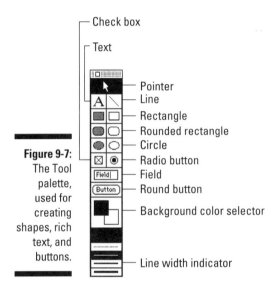

— Check box

— Text

— Pointer
— Line
— Rectangle
— Rounded rectangle
— Circle
— Radio button
— Field
— Round button

— Background color selector

— Line width indicator

Figure 9-7: The Tool palette, used for creating shapes, rich text, and buttons.

Misfit tools

The first tools you meet in the Tool palette are the set of nine tools at the top. Call them misfit tools. From top to bottom, left to right, they include the following:

- **Pointer tool:** The classic mouse cursor moves — interestingly enough — both shapes and bitmaps on the Stage.

- **Text tool:** Click anywhere on the Stage with the Text tool and type rich text, whose unique features include tabs and full-paragraph formatting. The resulting text is the same kind as the text you type in a Text window and then drag to the Stage. The text adopts the current background color in the Tool palette; the text itself reflects the current foreground color.

- **Line tool:** Draws straight lines at any angle directly on the Stage; remember to press Shift and drag to draw a horizontal, vertical, or 45-degree angle line. The line adopts the current foreground color and line width displayed in the Tool palette. While the line is selected, you can change the graphic's color with the Foreground color selector and the line width with the Line width indicator. Notice that line width options in the Tool palette are very limited compared to sizes available for bitmaps in the Paint window. You win some, you lose some. *C'est la vie.*

Shape tools

The second row of tools are the Shape tools with split personalities — filled on the left, hollow on the right. Come to think of it, I have a couple of friends who fit that same description. Anyway, the Shape tools include

- **Rectangle tool:** Allows you to draw a rectangle bordered in the current foreground color or a rectangle filled with the current foreground color. Remember to press Shift and drag to draw a perfect square.

- **Rounded rectangle tool:** Allows you to draw a rounded rectangle bordered in the current foreground color or a rounded rectangle filled with the current foreground color. Remember to press Shift and drag to draw a rounded square shape.

- **Circle tool:** Allows you to draw an oval shape bordered in the current foreground color using an oval filled with the current foreground color. Remember to press Shift and drag to draw a perfect circle shape. And to eat plenty of leafy green vegetables each and every day.

When you double-click a shape created with one of the Shape tools, Director takes you to the Shape Cast Member Properties dialog box. From there, you can change the shape with the Shape pop-up button. For more information on the Shape pop-up button, see "The Shape Cast Member Properties dialog box," earlier in this chapter.

Button-making tools

The next set of tools comprises Director's button-making tools. From top to bottom, left to right, they include the following:

- **Check box button tool:** Creates a check box-style button, as shown in Figure 9-8.

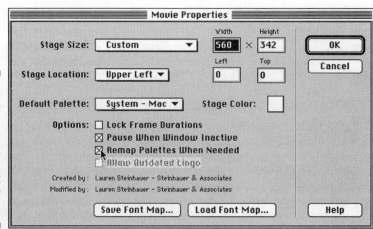

Figure 9-8:
Check boxes
in the Movie
Properties
dialog box
for options
that are not
mutually
exclusive.

During playback, the user may check one or more check boxes, initiating a script inside each checked button that you write in Lingo. Use check boxes, for example, to enable users to change the font, size, and weight of a screen title.

✓ **Radio/Option button tool:** Creates a radio/option button. Figure 9-9 shows radio/option buttons used in the Export dialog box to give you some choices when exporting a Director movie as a QuickTime mooV. Use radio/ options buttons to present a group of options that are mutually exclusive.

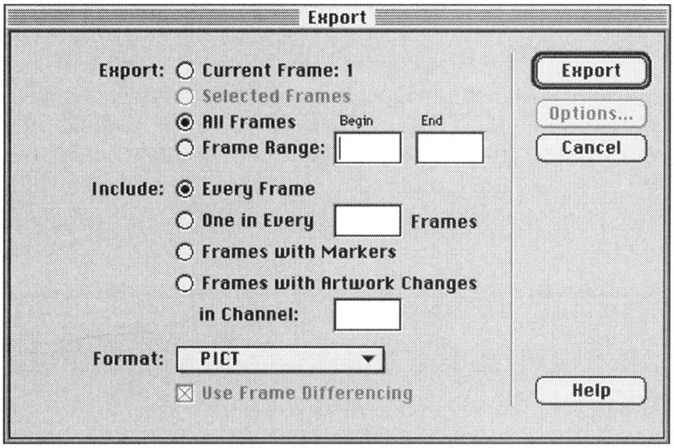

Figure 9-9:
Select
radio/option
buttons in
the Export
dialog box
for options
that are
mutually
exclusive.

During playback, the user may check one of the radio/option buttons from a set, initiating an associated script. You — who else? — are responsible for writing the script that both initiates the desired action and unchecks any other radio/option buttons in the group. For more info on writing scripts in buttons, jump to the "Scripts" section in Chapter 17.

✓ **Field tool:** Select to add text in a field to the Stage. For more on text in a field, jump to "Text in a Field" in Chapter 8.

✓ **Round button tool:** Your plain-vanilla round button tool creates a rounded button, as shown in Figure 9-10, that you can name.

During playback, the user activates an associated script after clicking a round button. Guess who gets stuck writing the script?

You can easily change the button style of a Button Cast Member. Double-click the button to go to its Button Cast Member Properties dialog box, where you can select a different style of button from the Style pop-up menu.

When double-clicking a button to go to its Button Cast Member Properties dialog box, be sure to double-click within the selected button's bold, gray selection border. Otherwise, you'll only place an insertion point in the field area of the button or select part or all of the button name. Very frustrating.

If you can't wait to play with making buttons and adding secret messages in them, what we multimedia types call *Lingo scripting,* peruse Chapter 17. For more on when to use check boxes and radio/option buttons, see the sidebar, "Round versus square: the politics of selection buttons," immediately following this commercial announcement.

Round versus square: the politics of selection buttons

In graphical user interfaces like the Mac OS (Macintosh Operating System) and Microsoft Windows, you find two distinctive styles of buttons for making choices.

Mac radio buttons and Windows option buttons look like this:

> ⦿ Use Movie Settings
> ○ Match Current Movie

When you face a set of options where you may choose only one option to the exclusion of the others — whew, maybe I should have been a lawyer — a well-designed program presents you with a set of radio/option buttons. So the Stage Size panel in the General Preferences dialog box gives you one of two choices: Use Movie Settings or Match Current Movie. Logically, only one option can prevail. When you click your option of choice, its radio/option button adopts the "bull's-eye" style to indicate its standing in the community of selection buttons.

On Macs and PCs, check boxes look like this:

> ☒ Center
> ☒ Reset Monitor to Movie's Color Depth
> ☒ Animate in Background

Check boxes offer you a set of options from which you may pick and choose willy-nilly; these options aren't mutually exclusive. Checked check boxes stand for selected options. Back to the General Preferences dialog box, you can check the Center option. And Reset Monitor to Movie's Color Depth. And Animate in Background. Or if you're anal-retentive, none of the above.

A selected check box isn't really checked. It's "Xed." I think of something checked looking like, well, a check. Anyway, I don't know of anyone who goes around saying, "I Xed the check box." Maybe it sounds too much like a naughty word. But if you want to instantly establish yourself as a free thinker and all-around character, here's your golden opportunity.

More Tool palette stuff

Beneath the nine tools at the top of the Tool palette are the following areas:

- **Foreground color selector:** Allows you to select the current foreground color from the current palette of colors when you press the selector area.

- **Background color selector:** Allows you to select the current background color from the current palette of colors when you press the selector area.

- **Pattern pop-up menu:** Allows you to select the current pattern from a set of patterns when you press the pop-up menu area.

- **Line Width indicator:** Allows you to set the line to invisible or to one of three different widths by clicking the desired option.

The Meaning of Life

Oh, yeah, the meaning of life. Who knows?

Why You Should Care about This Palette

Why should you care about the Tool palette? Because it's there. And because its features are very useful. I've listed a number of reasons why — not necessarily ten reasons, so no drum roll please:

1. **You can paint — excuse me — draw directly on the Stage.**

2. **You can type directly on the Stage.**

3. **You can search and replace text typed with the Text tool while developing your movie.**

4. **You can easily edit text typed with the Text tool while developing your movie.**

5. **You can instantly change the shape of a shape, manually or by using Lingo commands, to create magical transformations during playback.**

6. **You can instantly change the color of a shape, manually or by using Lingo commands, to create magical color changes during playback.**

7. **Field text prints at high resolution, making it the text of choice for printing out storyboards for client approval or for reports generated by a multimedia product that you've produced with Director.**

8. Lingo scripts can recognize, modify, or manipulate text typed with the Text tool.

9. You can reduce or enlarge a shape right on the Stage without getting the infamous stairstepped effect known as the jaggies.

10. Shapes and text take up less memory than bitmapped equivalents.

Well, what do you know? Ten reasons! Okay, I'll take that drum roll after all. *Yes!*

Chapter 10

Getting to Those Scrumptious Palettes: The Color Palettes Window

....

In This Chapter

▶ Creating a custom palette

▶ Working with the Color Palettes window

▶ Using the Apple Color Picker

▶ Discovering the mysteries of 65535

....

*T*hroughout this book, I talk about sets of colors, called *palettes,* that you use to develop movies with Director. Surprise — palettes have their very own window. And some clever devil at Macromedia named it, of all things, the Color Palettes window.

Decisions, Decisions, Decisions

To see your very own Color Palettes window, choose Window➪Color Palettes and, like magic, the Color Palettes window appears, bearing an uncanny resemblance to Figure 10-1. (Remember, this figure is only an artist's representation, not the real thing.)

When Director first brings up the window, it's tiny. Real tiny. Click the Zoom box in the upper-right corner of the window to fill the screen with the Color Palettes window. Simply click the Zoom box again to return the window to its original size.

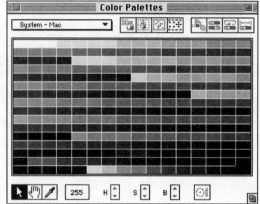

Figure 10-1:
The Color
Palettes
window,
where you
can choose
from built-in
and custom
palettes for
the current
movie.

The Color Palettes window reflects the current palette. If you have a number of custom bitmap sprites in the Score and run from one to the other with the mouse, the palette in the Color Palettes window updates to the current palette. You can change the current palette by selecting a different palette from the Palette pop-up menu in the Color Palettes window.

Before finding out how the Color Palettes window contributes to your Director movies, you should make sense of all the goodies in the window.

Okay, so the Color Palettes window isn't quite as imposing as, say, the Score window, but it's very important in its own little way. You'll find the Color Palette pretty useful after you learn about its various features.

The Palette pop-up menu

When you click the box near the upper-left corner of the Color Palettes window, a menu pops up, as in Figure 10-2, revealing nine built-in palettes and any custom palettes belonging to the current movie.

Figure 10-2:
The Palette
pop-up
menu, in
which you
find nine
built-in
palettes and
any custom
palettes.

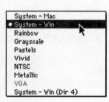

Director's built-in palettes

Here's a look at the ten built-in palettes listed in the Palette pop-up menu shown in Figure 10-2:

- **System - Mac:** This is the Mac's *default* palette, which is the palette the Mac chooses right out of the box while it's still warm. Your desktop and most program interfaces are based on this palette of 256 standardized colors. Most of the PICTs that you import into Director display these same 256 colors.

- **System - Win:** A collection of 256 colors intended to translate well when porting bitmaps between a Mac and a PC.

- **Rainbow:** A bright collection of 256 colors meant to flower forth images of doves, angels, and big, fluffy clouds shimmering before your galvanized eyes. Great for kiddie games.

- **Grayscale:** Sometimes nothing's better than a beautiful set of colorless values, from pure white through incremental shades of gray to deepest velvet black. That's when you choose the good, old Grayscale palette for photographic-quality, black-and-white images in your movie.

- **Pastels:** A collection of 256 colors inspired, no doubt, by watching too many Barney adventures. A plethora of soft, snugly, coochie-coo colors for designing disposable undie packaging.

- **Vivid:** Whoever designed this set of colors needs to cut way down on the coffee. These are 256 *very* bright colors. The word *vivid* actually pales in comparison to the Vivid palette of colors.

- **NTSC:** A special collection of colors meant to translate well when copying (or *printing to video,* as multimedia types are apt to say) your Director movie.

- **Metallic:** An interesting collection of colors that definitely brings to mind thoughts of rusting tin cans, Robbie the Robot, and auto derbies. Not for everyone, but that's what makes life a confusing mess. (Just kidding.)

- **VGA:** Grayed out in Figure 10-2, this set of *VGA* (Video Graphics Array) colors is available only when a VGA monitor is running off your computer.

- **System - Win (Dir 4):** A collection of 256 colors for movies that started out in life as Director 4 files. Director 4 handled colors differently enough under Windows that if you switched a Director 4 movie to Director 5's standard System - Win palette, you would notice a distinct and probably unpleasant color shift.

Free to be NTSC

Novice multimedia types are often alarmed at how dramatically colors change after videotaping their work and playing it back on a real TV. *NTSC* is a set of standards for TV broadcasting that was adopted, while the crust of the earth was still cooling, by a stodgy group of frustrated, old media moguls called the National Television System Committee. Back in the dark ages (1953), there were a number of ways to transmit and receive color television, but some people thought that there needed to be some basic specifications, lest chaos prevail.

Until contemporary debate over standards for high definition and wide-screen television, NTSC standards dictated the quality of color images broadcast to the huddled masses yearning for cable to be free. The NTSC standards include a limited range of colors, bringing you back to the NTSC palette, a collection of 256 NTSC-legal, or safe, colors. None of these colors is so bright as to *bloom,* or fluoresce, beyond an image's outline on the TV screen, and none is far enough removed from NTSC's *gamut,* or color range, that it could transform into an unexpected color.

Custom palettes

Look at the very bottom of the Palette pop-up menu in Figure 10-2, just below the gray rule demarcating the built-in palettes from the custom palettes. You see the line 33:Palette 33, a reference to a custom palette that tagged along with a bitmap I imported into Director while you weren't looking.

When an 8-bit (256-color) bitmap is built on a set of colors other than the System palette, the bitmap carries custom color info in a secret place within its own file. To import a bitmap that has a custom palette, follow these steps:

1. **Choose File⇨Import.**

2. **Select the desired bitmap from the Directory dialog box, and click Import.**

   Director displays the Image Options dialog box — showoff that Director is — boasting that it knows you're trying to sneak in a bitmap with special colors. In this dialog box, re-created in Figure 10-3, Director asks you to decide on a few options.

Figure 10-3:
The Image Options dialog box that appears after you import a bitmap.

Image Options for Duo 230/120:Picture 1

Color Depth: ● Image (4 bits)
        ○ Stage (4 bits)

Palette: ○ Import
    ● Remap to   System - Mac ▼

☐ Dither
☐ Same Settings for Remaining Images

    OK
    Cancel
    Help

3. For Color Depth, you can choose between Image and Stage:

- **Image:** Click this radio/option button to retain the original color depth of the bitmap.

- **Stage:** Click this radio/option button to change the bitmap's color depth to the current color depth of the Stage.

  Choose the Image option to import a bitmap in its original color depth.

4. For Palette, you have the honor of choosing between Import or Remap to:

- **Import:** Click to import a bitmap's palette as an additional Cast Member, especially important for a bitmap with an adaptive palette.

- **Remap to:** Click to remap the imported bitmap to a new palette you select from the menu that pops up.

  Choose the Import option to import a bitmap's custom palette as an additional Cast Member.

5. The Image Options dialog box gives you two fun check boxes to choose from — Dither and Same Settings for Remaining Images:

- **Dither:** Check to apply a *dithering routine* to the imported bitmap. The dithering routine increases the apparent number of visible colors, similar to the idea of using four-process colors in printing to create the impression of full-color graphics and photographs.

  If you're importing a bitmap with a custom palette, leave Dither unchecked. Applying a dithering routine to the custom palette would likely change the quality of the custom colors.

- **Same Settings for Remaining Images:** Click to apply the same selection of options to remaining bitmaps listed in the Import Files dialog box.

6. Click OK.

Color Palettes window tools

In the upper right of the Color Palettes window (see Figure 10-1) is a row of special tools, including

 ✔ **Reserve Selected Colors:** Protects colors you select in the Color Palettes window. Shift-select a block of colors or ⌘/Ctrl-select noncontiguous colors. (By the way, you can combine these selection techniques in one selection.) Use this command to reserve a set of colors for special effects like *color cycling* (an easy method of creating animation that I discuss in

Chapter 24). For example, if you animate a bitmap of a roaring fireplace with color cycling, you don't want the color blend created for the fire effect to appear in other bitmaps. Choose Reserve Selected Colors to avoid using these colors in anything but the fire sequence.

 ✔ **Select Reserved Colors:** Selects all colors in the current palette designated as reserved colors. Use this option to take the next step to "cancel your reservation" by clicking Reserve Colors and clicking the No Colors radio/ option button in the Reserve Colors dialog box.

 ✔ **Select Used Colors:** Tallies up the colors in the bitmap displayed in the Paint window and automatically selects them in the Color Palettes window. This option is grayed out in Figure 10-6 and probably on your screen because it is dependent on three conditions: The command must have a bitmap in the Paint window (whether or not the Paint window itself is visible); the Color Palettes window must be visible; and the Color Palettes window needs to be the active window.

 ✔ **Invert Selection:** Selects the unselected colors and deselects the selected colors in the Color Palettes window. On long, rainy weekends, I pass the time very quickly by selecting and inverting colors over and over again; in no time, it's Monday morning. Try it.

 ✔ **Sort:** Displays the Sort Colors dialog box, shown in Figure 10-7, where you decide how to sort the selection of colors by clicking one of three radio/ option buttons: Hue (by red, for example, rather than blue or green), Saturation (by intensity or purity of color), or Brightness (by lightness or darkness of color).

 ✔ **Reverse Sequence:** Reverses the order of a contiguous block of selected colors. Try Reverse Color Order on the gradation of grays in the System palette at the tail end of the colors. Your computer won't allow you to move or modify black (index number 255) or white (index number 0). The moment you reverse colors in one of the default palettes, Director forces you to the Create Palette dialog box. The big bully.

 ✔ **Cycle:** Shifts a contiguous block of selected colors one color over with each issue of this command. Rotate Colors reproduces what happens to a block of selected colors in color-cycling animation, only more slowly. If you're having trouble picturing what happens, think of a selection of colors as a rosary of color, each color a bead in the chain. Each time you choose Rotate Colors, you shift the rosary by one bead; that covers all the Catholics out there. Now, there are these worry beads. . . .

 ✔ **In-Between:** Creates a blend of colors between the beginning and ending colors of a contiguous block of selected colors. If you look back at the System palette, notice that it lacks a contiguous block of smoothly graduated colors; the key to creating effective color cycling animation is to create a custom palette with a wide range of blended colors. You can select the block of colors either by dragging through colors or by clicking a beginning color and then Shift-clicking the ending color with the Arrow or Hand tool.

What do you know? You've got a bottom row of icons, too. Life _is_ good.

✔ **Arrow tool:** Your basic mouse pointing and selection tool. Click in the Color Palettes window with the Arrow tool to make a single selection. Drag the Arrow tool through a block of colors in a palette or Shift-click a range of colors to make a contiguous selection. ⌘/Ctrl-click colors to make a noncontiguous selection.

✔ **Hand tool:** Use the Hand tool to move a selection in the Color Palettes window. Drag a selection with the Hand tool to another area of the palette. As it passes over colors, the Hand tool highlights the color directly beneath its pointing finger, which is where the first color in the selection lands when you release the Hand tool. After you move colors in one of Director's ten default palettes, Director presents the Create Palette dialog box. If you move a noncontiguous selection, Director deposits them as a contiguous block of colors when you release the Hand tool.

✔ **Eyedropper tool:** Common to many high-powered paint programs, including Photoshop, the Eyedropper tool allows you to _sample_ a color anywhere on the Stage. Sampling means that you can record a color's percentage of red, green, and blue light that makes up all colors on an RGB monitor. Suppose you're working with the System - Win palette and you have an image of a bright sun on the Stage; you click the brightest area with the Eyedropper tool, and the fifth color from the top-left of the color chip selector area becomes highlighted. The number to the right of the Eyedropper tool changes to 5 to display the color's _index number._ For more information about indexed color, see "Color and index numbers" in this chapter.

✔ **Index Color number:** Gives the index number of the currently selected color that represents its position in the CLUT (Color Lookup Table) currently in use. A CLUT is another way of referring to colors when you're running your monitor in 8-bit color mode, giving you 256 colors from index number 0 to 255. Index number 0 is always white and index number 255 is always black in Mac and Windows CLUTs.

✔ **H-S-B (Hue, Saturation, Brightness) controls:** Modify the selected color in the H-S-B color model. If the current palette is the System palette, the nanosecond you begin clicking one of these controls, Director takes you to the Create Palette dialog box, where clicking OK automatically creates a new custom palette.

✔ **Color Picker:** Takes you to the so-called _color wheel,_ where you can run wild, making up your own colors.

Color and index numbers

Most of the Color Palettes window is taken up by the set of colors making up a particular palette. (Yes, you're still in Figure 10-1.)

Have you noticed something striking? (No, running out of beer doesn't count.) White is always the first color in the upper-left corner of the palette, and black the last. In other words, white is always index number 0, and black is always index number 255. Always and forever. You can bet your life on it — just don't bet mine. You never know when some computer maker is going to slip up and put black in the center or something.

Anyway, this black-and-white thing applies to all Director's default and custom palettes. That's right, your computer doesn't allow you to move or modify white or black, regardless of how weird the other colors in your custom palette happen to look.

In the System - Mac, System - Win, and System - Win (Dir 4) palettes, things get even more draconian. Each color is always the same color in its respective position and always has the same index number for identification. Of course, this boring predictability is the whole point of a System palette. The only problem is that Real Life and even the world of the imagination don't always fit so neatly into this predefined handful of colors.

Custom palettes

If you ever need colors that aren't in one of Director's default palettes, you can create a custom palette. Follow these steps to create your very own palette:

1. **Choose Window⇨Color Palettes.**

2. **Click the Zoom box in the upper-right corner to fill the screen with the Color Palettes window.**

3. **Choose System - Mac from the Palette pop-up menu if you are using a Mac; choose System - Win if you are on a PC.**

   One exception is if you're working with a Windows Director movie that was originally created with Director 4. To match its colors in Director 5, choose the System - Win (Dir 4) palette.

4. **Double-click a color you can live without.**

   On a Mac, the Apple Color Picker, shown in Figure 10-4, appears. On a PC, Windows' Custom Color Selector, shown in Figure 10-5, appears.

   In the Apple Color Picker, notice that the color you double-click shows up in the large color sample under Define a new color, is marked in the color wheel itself with a small circle, and is displayed broken down into its components in H-S-B (hue, saturation, brightness) and R-G-B (red, green, blue) values. In Windows' Custom Color Selector, the selected color appears in the Color|Solid panel, is marked in the large color space with a crosshair-like icon and is shown broken down into its components in H-S-L (hue, saturation, luminance) and R-G-B values.

Both windows display two main color models or spaces used in the multimedia industry: H-S-B or H-S-L (essentially identical models) and R-G-B. (Just in case you're interested, nearly all computer monitors use RGB color to create the images on your screen.)

Few people think of colors as numbers like the ones in Figures 10-4 and 10-5, but numbers add a certain precision to the whole business of defining a color. For example, I might think of a special color, a kind of British racing green that's very difficult to describe accurately. Instead of trying to put the color into words, I can pass on the color's components in one of the color models so that it reproduces fairly accurately on your monitor.

Figure 10-4:
On a Mac, double-clicking a color in the Color Palettes window opens the Apple Color Picker.

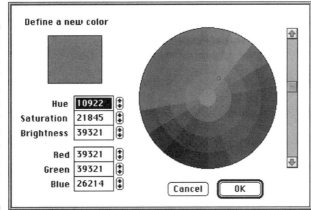

Figure 10-5:
On a PC, double-clicking a color in the Color Palettes window opens Windows' Custom Color Selector.

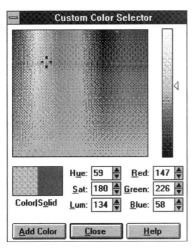

5. Enter new RGB or H-S-B (H-S-L) values.

If that great Austin Healy green sounds appealing to you, try the following RGB values in Apple's Color Picker: 8963 for Red, 14928 for Green, and 20129 for Blue.

For you PC types, try the following RGB percentages: 86 for Red, 72 for Green, and 69 for Blue.

6. Click OK.

As soon as you click OK, Director knows that you made changes to a default palette, and it displays the Create Palette dialog box, shown in Figure 10-6, where you can christen your own custom palette with a meaningful name. Or a silly name.

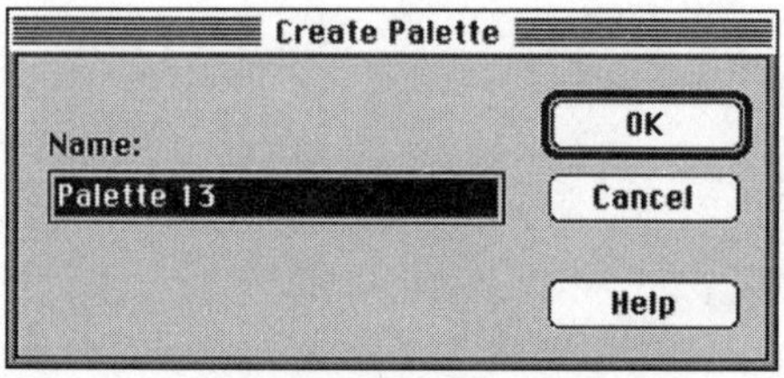

Figure 10-6:
After you make a change to a palette, the Create Palette dialog box appears.

7. Enter a name for the new palette in the dialog box and click OK.

With a click of the mouse, you add a custom palette to the list under the Color Palettes window and a Palette Cast Member to the Cast window.

Hot flashes

I'll bet my mother's hot water bottle that you see an iridescent flash when switching palettes. It's not one of Director's most fetching traits. To avoid the flash, try adding a transition to the Transition channel in the same frame in which you place the custom palette. The Transition palette is just underneath the Palette channel in the Score window. The Frame Properties: Transition dialog box appears, as shown in Figure 10-7.

Switching palettes in your movie

I can think of at least three reasons why you may want to switch palettes in a movie; there are probably 5,895 other reasons, give or take.

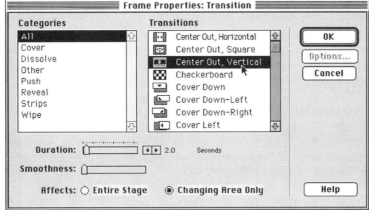

Figure 10-7:
The Frame
Properties:
Transition
dialog box,
where you
can choose
from a wide
range of
transition
effects.

Adaptive palettes

Big Number One reason is due to the limitations of the default System - Win and System - Mac palettes. Their 256 colors just don't do justice to photographs, for example, displaying millions of colors, scanned into your computer and then reduced to 256 paltry colors. Often, the result resembles a graphic technique called *posterization,* in which light and shade variations are reduced to a few solid blocks of color. Sometimes, you may actually want this effect. It can be very dramatic, graphic, and artful. But not if you're aiming for realism and photographic quality.

That's when you go into Photoshop, open the scanned photo, and choose Indexed Color from the Mode menu. A dialog box appears, giving you a number of choices for reducing colors to a limp 256. But one special choice, called the *Adaptive method,* creates a custom palette that optimizes results. Amazingly, the altered bitmap with a 256-color adaptive palette often looks almost as good as the original photo. Director tries to do the same thing with imported bitmaps. After you click Import in the Import Files dialog box, the Image Options dialog box appears with options named Remap and Dither that approximate what Photoshop can accomplish, although not as well.

Wonderful as Director may be, Photoshop's the expert at remapping bitmaps. So if you choose the Photoshop route, be sure to click the Import radio/option button in the Image Options dialog box. The imported bitmap and its palette become new Cast Members in the Cast window.

Better performance through plastics, er, 8-bit graphics

Why would you want to reduce all those beautiful 16 million colors to 256 colors? Well, that's reason number two for making a custom palette. 24-bit graphics are gigantic; they slurp up room on your hard drive and stretch your poor machine's computing power above and beyond its limit. Unless you can count on developing and running your movie on the latest, greatest computing dynamos Apple and IBM have to offer with umpteen gigabytes of storage and a terabyte or two of memory chips, the most common solution is to drop colors. Either go with the System palette's interpretation of your image or let Director handle it with the Remap option. Or you can try Photoshop's adaptive palette method.

Color cycling

By the way, the third reason I can think of for creating a custom palette is color cycling. If you're downright antsy to find out more, jump to "Try Color Cycling" in Chapter 24. Just keep in mind that the color cycling palette is a limited palette, and you may want to swap back to your regular palette after color cycling is finished. Be sure to add your regular palette to the Palette channel in the Score at the appropriate frame.

After you place your bitmap on the Stage, the bitmap may look weird, almost psychedelic. Okay, all together, "Like wow, man, yeah, psychedelic." Now that you've got that out of your system. . . .

To properly view the bitmap on the Stage, you need to add its custom Palette to the Palette channel in the Score window. Add the Palette Cast Member to the Palette channel in the same frame where your bitmap makes its appearance in the Score. Until you change palettes again, Director continues to use the custom palette, which may or may not be what you want. If not, add your regular palette, probably the Mac or Windows System palette, to the Palette channel at the appropriate frame.

Only a few transitions really overcome the flashing that occurs when switching palettes. I've used the Dissolve, Pixels Fast transition set to Changing Area with great success. How did I find the transition that works the best? Trial and error. To save you the pain, I experimented and experimented, night and day, day and night. And to what end? To end up a shell of a man with a good transition. Aargh.

Achieving that classic look

Another technique that helps when you plan to switch Palettes is to choose File➪Preferences➪General and check Classic Look (Monochrome), as in Figure 10-8.

Choosing Classic Look helps Director's performance because the interface becomes black and white and doesn't need to be updated every time you switch palettes. It uses less memory, and many developers find the black-and-white interface less distracting, too.

Babbling on about DeBabelizer

There's dithering, and then there's *dithering*. Great as Director may be, Photoshop and other high-end paint programs offer dithering routines that produce superior results. A fascinating, peculiar, irritating, and necessary program called DeBabelizer from Equilibrium does a particularly excellent job of dithering bitmaps for the Macintosh platform.

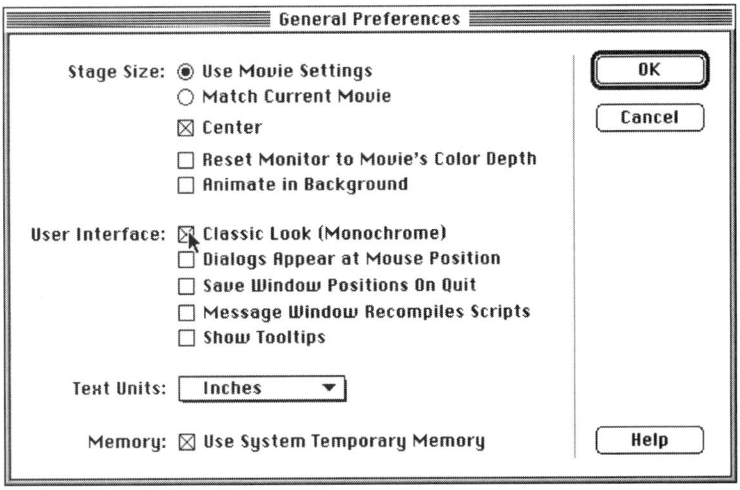

Figure 10-8:
Check
Classic Look
in the
General
Preferences
dialog box to
prevent
Director
from having
to update
the interface
with every
Palette
change.

```
┌─────────────────────── General Preferences ───────────────────────┐
│                                                                    │
│  Stage Size:  ◉ Use Movie Settings          ┌──────────────┐      │
│               ○ Match Current Movie         │      OK      │      │
│                                             └──────────────┘      │
│               ⊠ Center                      ┌──────────────┐      │
│               ☐ Reset Monitor to Movie's Color Depth│ Cancel │   │
│               ☐ Animate in Background       └──────────────┘      │
│                                                                    │
│  User Interface: ⊠ Classic Look (Monochrome)                      │
│                  ☐ Dialogs Appear at Mouse Position               │
│                  ☐ Save Window Positions On Quit                  │
│                  ☐ Message Window Recompiles Scripts              │
│                  ☐ Show Tooltips                                   │
│                                                                    │
│  Text Units:  ┌─ Inches        ▼ ┐                                │
│                                                                    │
│  Memory: ⊠ Use System Temporary Memory      ┌──────────────┐      │
│                                             │     Help     │      │
│                                             └──────────────┘      │
└────────────────────────────────────────────────────────────────────┘
```

DeBabelizer solves one of the most irksome enigmas that comes up when using two or more palettes in a Director movie. How can images common to Director sequences with different palettes appear at the same time on the Stage? DeBabelizer can analyze a wide range of color requirements in different images and create what it calls a *Super Palette* that is usually a terrific compromise palette for all the images. This is the palette you want to import as a Cast Member along with the special bitmaps themselves. As you're saving the bitmaps in DeBabelizer, be sure to save the files in PICT2 with CLUT file format from the pop-up menu in DeBabelizer's Save As dialog box.

The closest equivalents to DeBabelizer for the PC are a utility program called HiJaak and Photoshop itself.

The Old H-S-B Thing Again

Earlier in this chapter, I took you on a tour of the Apple Color Picker and the Windows Custom Color Selector to create a custom palette. During the tour, you discovered that on-screen colors are described with two different color *models,* or systems: H-S-B (H-S-L) and RGB.

Hue, saturation, and brightness

H-S-B stands for hue, saturation, and brightness — not an old vaudevillian team that worked with seals — one of the major color models that multimedia types use to develop products. Take another look at the Apple Color Picker in Figure 10-4 or the Windows Custom Color Selector in Figure 10-5 and see how the H-S-B (H-S-L) model relates to colors in its color space.

In the H-S-B color system, *Hue* refers to pure color. Picture a distinctive color in your mind; that's a hue. As a color changes hue in the Apple Color Picker, it moves around the circumference of the color wheel. In the Windows Custom Color Selector, the crosshair-like icon in the rectangular color space moves horizontally through its landscape.

Saturation refers to intensity of hue. How red is a particular red? A washed-out or pastel red is less saturated than pure red, candy red, or apple red. In the Apple Color Picker, as a hue becomes less saturated, it moves closer to the white center of the color wheel. In the Windows Custom Color Selector, pure hues are at the top; as a hue becomes less saturated, it moves closer to the bottom of the color space.

Think of *Brightness* as the amount of light shining on a hue. When you turn off lights in a room at night, all hues go black, even yellow. When you set Brightness to 0 in the Apple Color Picker dialog box, you're turning off all the lights. The Apple Color Picker visualizes this scenario with the "elevator" in the scroll bar sliding to the bottom. The Windows Custom Color Selector features a similar scroll bar to visualize the brightness level of a color.

Additive and subtractive primary colors

Remember school? You learned that the primary colors are red, yellow, and blue. Close, but no turkey. Actually, you need to work with two different sets of primary color schemes when playing with color. Additive primaries — red, blue, and green — are for working with pure (or incident) light, such as the light that your monitor uses. That's why monitors generally use red, green, and blue (RGB) light. Mix all three colors at the highest saturation and brightness levels and what do you get? White light. If you're a fan of the theater, those lighting technicians use the same scheme to light the stage; when the director wants a golden glow on her leading man and lady, the lighting crew had darn well splash red and green spots on them to make yellow light. That's the wacky world of additive color for you.

On the other hand, when you're dealing with light reflected off objects, you turn to subtractive primary colors: cyan, yellow, and magenta — printers' colors or *process colors*. In the desktop publishing world, printers customarily sneak in black as a fourth color to add bite to the printed image.

That mysterious 65535

In Figure 10-4, the Apple Color Picker, the selected hue happens to be pure red, as red as you can get on an RGB computer screen. Below the H-S-B values, RGB mode represents the same hue with red at maximum, the mysterious value 65535, while green and blue are set to 0. With saturation and brightness in the H-S-B color model turned up all the way, the additive and subtractive primaries are evenly divided in 60-degree intervals around the color wheel with pure red at number 0, pure green at 21845, and purest blue at 43690; subtractive primaries work out to pure cyan at 32768, pure yellow at 10922, and pure magenta at 54614. All based on 65535 divided by 6. And boy, wouldn't you love to know why? That makes two of us, because I haven't a clue.

I lied. Actually, I have a good idea why that mysterious 65535 keeps coming up. The Apple Color Picker is designed to handle up to 16-bit color. One way of defining 16-bit color is 2 multiplied by itself 16 times, which is "2 to the 16th power." Which is, ta da, 65536. Isn't all this math stuff bringing back fond memories of old school days, wilted peanut butter sandwiches, and the school bully grinding your new glasses into the pavement at recess? Anyway, you may have noticed that it's not a perfect match. Since computers start counting from 0, subtract 1 and the remainder becomes . . . 65535! That's 65536 hues to click through, each color with its own identifying number in the H-S-B system.

The Windows Custom Color Selector uses a different scheme from Apple's Color Picker and specifies RGB colors in percentages. To change Apple Color Picker RGB colors with values from 1 to 65535 into Windows RGB percentages, use the following formula. Yikes!

Percent = 1.00 – (Apple Color Picker number / 65535)

If you'd studied your math instead of the redhead next to you, I wouldn't need to tell you that this means, "Divide each Apple Color Picker RGB number by 65535. Subtract the result from 1.00, and that should get you close to the number in RGB percentages." Now, where's my apple?

Complementary colors

You can also use the Apple Color Picker to find *complementary* colors. Four out of five rocket scientists agree that a complementary color is the color that creates white light when added to the original color. The technique for finding a color's complement is simplicity itself with the Apple Color Picker. After choosing a color either by clicking on the color wheel or entering values in H-S-B or RGB mode, find the complementary color directly opposite on the color wheel. You can build color schemes around opposing colors that are scientifically guaranteed to be pleasing to the eye. If you have great color sense, don't bother. But if, like many developers, you need help in putting together pleasing colors, this technique can at least point you in the right direction. Unfortunately, the Windows Custom Color Selector doesn't work with the technique.

Or try a group of three complementary colors, which is what primary colors are. To make things more interesting, start with a more subtle color and then find its complements by finding the other two colors a third of the way around the color wheel in each direction. For example, say you decide on a yellowish color by eye-clicking hither and thither on the color wheel. Better yet, click hither and yon. You note that in H-S-B color mode, the color you pick is Hue 14626, a little more interesting than pure yellow. To find a set of complementary colors, imagine dividing the color wheel into thirds like a pie, starting at your yellowish color. The other two "slices" wind up at around hues 36338 and 58316. To make things more interesting, brighten one hue by moving your choice in toward the white center of the color wheel and darken another color by scrolling down with a couple of clicks to the down arrow. The colors are no longer perfect, but that's okay; the result is visually more exciting.

Have you noticed that computers start counting with 0? For example, 8-bit color gives you 256 colors, but the first color is index number 0 and the last color index number 255. Also, on a Mac, the Apple Color Picker offers 65536 hues in H-S-B color mode, but the first hue is 0, the last 65535. You see this kind of thing very frequently when working with your computer. A little safety tip: Don't let it throw you, especially if you wind up programming for NASA.

Chapter 11

Your Very Own Digital Video Window

In This Chapter

▶ Reviewing digital video

▶ Setting up your movie for digital video

▶ Getting close and personal with codecs

▶ Exporting your movie

▶ Touring the Video window

▶ Playing digital video in Director

▶ Using Director as a movie editor

*D*epending on who you speak to, digital video is either the biggest thing since sliced bread or a sham technology, doling out postage stamp-sized, cataract-inducing animations to a swelling crush of catatonic multimedia wannabes swayed by a movement more subversive than Tupperware parties. Where lieth the truth?

Could You Review That Digital Video Thing Again?

Adding video to the rest of the mix that multimedia is made of has been the dream of developer types for some time. We tried all sorts of Rube Goldberg, Scotch tape, and rubber band kinds of solutions. Some actually worked, but none turned out to be as on target as digital video in the form of Apple's QuickTime and Microsoft's Video for Windows.

Introduction of digital video

In 1993, Apple introduced QuickTime to the world. Depending on your perspective, QuickTime was a major event on the same plateau as the invention of writing, movable type, and teflon-coated frying pans; "nice"; or insignificant. Old-time videographers laughed at the stamp-sized images everyone was suddenly showing on their monitors and the poor quality of the video images. Similar comments belittled Microsoft's entry into digital video, Video for Windows, an extension to the Windows interface.

But critics missed the point. QuickTime and Video for Windows technology was destined to improve; more important, digital video gave birth to *desktop video,* allowing anyone with a computer the opportunity of accessing and manipulating video-style information with the ease of using text and still graphics.

Demands of digital video

Remember contemplating your navel in the '60s and '70s? Okay, contemplate video for a moment. Video is a radically different type of information compared to traditional computer information. Most critical of all, video *changes over time.* Video presents a new image approximately every thirtieth of a thecond — excuse me, second. If you're asking your computer to "read" video or record video, you suddenly make enormous demands on your software and hardware.

Now consider the size of a video-style file. A good rule of thumb is to count on about 27MB (megabytes) per second of video. 27 MEGABYTES! Sorry, I lost it for a second, but I'm all right now.

Without getting too technical, consider the demands that a second of video, about 30 frames, makes on your hardware, keeping in mind your computer's many so-called *bottlenecks,* areas that slow down performance regardless of how fast a machine you have. To make things more interesting, video-style information often includes sound effects, narration, and/or music. Not only are you asking your computer to take care of this additional burden, but you're also asking the machine to somehow synchronize sounds to images. What does your machine do if video with sound is running on a slow computer? Does the whole movie slow down so that the speaker sounds like Forrest Gump on Prozac? Or does the narration get completely out of sync so that your movie looks like a really bad Ninja film? What's a budding Steven Spielberg to do?

Digital Video to the Rescue

Maybe now you can see why Apple developed QuickTime and Microsoft gave us Video for Windows. Technically, they're extensions to the operating system, an INIT in the parlance of Mac lovers and a TSR (Terminate and Stay Resident) for the PC users in the crowd. The icon of QuickTime is reproduced in Figure 11-1. QuickTime is included with Apple's latest, greatest system update for Macs. Otherwise, it's available free in any number of CD-ROM discs these days. Oh, and Apple actually sells QuickTime kits for Macs and Windows. Video for Windows comes with Windows 3.1 and Windows 95.

Figure 11-1:
The QuickTime icon, Apple's extension for digital video.

However you get digital video into your machine, you restart your computer, and ka-boom! Nada. Nothing. Not a darned thing. Your computer doesn't rev up like a Lamborghini or double in speed. Zip.

You find yourself asking, "Self, what's the big deal about digital video, anyway?" Well, the video extension e-x-t-e-n-d-s your system. In and of themselves, QuickTime and Video for Windows don't do anything you'll notice. Digital video works its magic after you launch a video-type program, such as Adobe Premiere. Then the extension shifts into overdrive with special video capabilities.

QuickTime Codecs

QuickTime contains a number of built-in compression schemes. Multimedia types like to call them *codecs* for *co*mpression/*dec*ompression or *co*der/*dec*oder, depending on who you talk to. In Director, you meet QuickTime and Video for Windows' codecs when you save a movie as a digital video file to your hard drive. You can import digital video into Director, but you may also choose to turn your Director production into a QuickTime mooV by using the Export command under the File menu.

After you choose Export from the File menu, Director takes you to the Export dialog box, shown in Figure 11-2. Notice that Director gives you some powerful options under this dialog box, including which frames to export: a single frame, all frames, or every fifth frame, if you so choose.

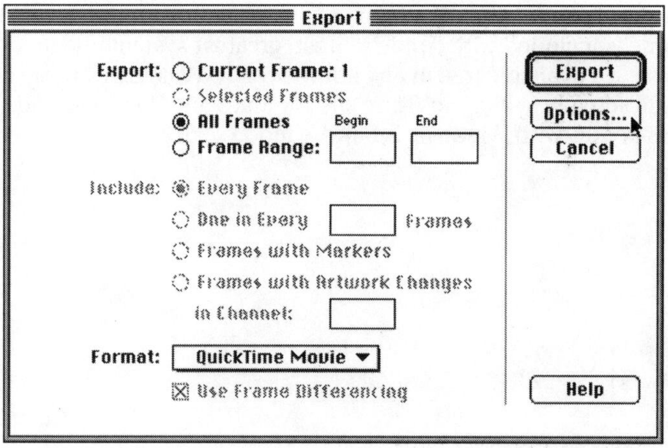

Figure 11-2:
The Export
dialog box,
where you
may choose
to turn your
Director
movie into
QuickTime,
PICTs, a
Scrapbook
file, or a
PICS file.

Focus now on the Format pop-up menu and the Options button in the upper-right corner of the Export dialog box. If you choose QuickTime Movie from the Format pop-up menu straight away, you're telling Director that you accept the default, out-of-the-box setting for your QuickTime mooV, and you miss the opportunity to custom select a codec. So your first step after arriving at the Export dialog box is to click the Options button. Director takes you to the QuickTime Options dialog box, shown in Figure 11-3, to introduce you to your set of QuickTime codecs.

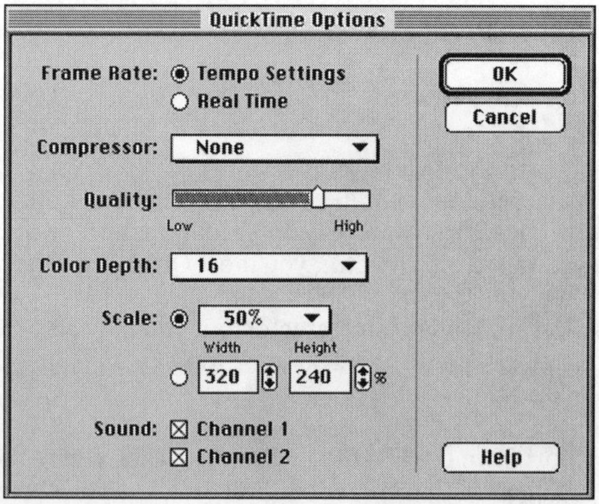

Figure 11-3:
The
QuickTime
Options
dialog box,
where
Director
offers you a
choice of
codecs for
turning your
movie into
QuickTime.

Pressing the Compressor pop-up menu displays a list of codecs, as shown in Figure 11-4.

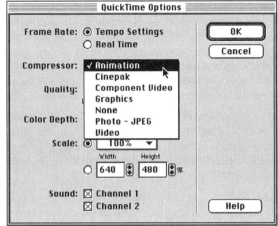

Figure 11-4:
The list of
QuickTime
2.1 codecs
under the
Compressor
pop-up
menu.

The set shown in Figure 11-4 is QuickTime 2.1's current list of codecs for the Macintosh, each designed to compress a specific type of file. They include the following:

✔ **Animation:** This codec's main purpose is compressing computer animation, such as a sequence created in a 3-D program that takes you on a tour of a make-believe city existing only on computer. This type of file has unique characteristics that the Animation codec is designed to compress most efficiently.

✔ **Cinepak:** This is the codec of choice for many developers and is especially useful for preparing QuickTime movies destined to run off a CD-ROM. The Cinepak codec takes a long time to compress information into a QuickTime mooV; figure about two minutes per frame on average. But, once compressed, Cinepak mooVs decompress quickly on playback and look very good. Developers often choose to compress their work overnight with the Cinepak codec in combination with utilities allowing batch compression (that is, compressing a log or list of selected QuickTime files).

In addition to controls for setting the degree of compression for the Cinepak codec, some QuickTime applications and utilities — not including Director, unfortunately — allow you to set the *data rate* (how much information is sent to the Mac or PC) in kilobytes per second. For example, using a useful shareware utility called MovieShop, you'd want to set a QuickTime mooV's data rate to around 90 kilobytes per second for QuickTime destined to play on older, single-speed CD-ROM drives and around 150 kilobytes for double-speed CD-ROM drives. If you're interested, you can find MovieShop on various commercial online services, bulletin boards, and the Internet. An excellent commercial product that does even more is called MovieCleaner.

✔ **Component Video:** For you to better understand the Component Video codec, I need to give a mini-lecture on how real TV works. What we receive on our real TVs is *composite video,* meaning that the image-making signals are essentially mixed together, as opposed to separate red, green, and blue signals. Real TV attempts a translation back to red, green, and blue data for the picture tube to work properly, but there's that old saying about stuff losing something in translation. TV is a perfect example.

Video composed of separate red, green, and blue signals is called *component video* and results in significantly higher image quality than composite video. When you're about to make a QuickTime mooV from a component video source, the Component Video codec is the one to go with to save all the extra info that component video offers.

✔ **Graphics:** This is the codec of choice for 8-bit graphics; that is, bitmaps that display 256 colors, and a special situation for at least two reasons and possibly 3,472 more. First, QuickTime is optimized to display thousands of colors. And second, 256-color bitmaps are limited in color range. The Graphics codec is developed to achieve good compression and optimum results with 8-bit graphics, resulting in few *artifacts* (flawed pixels in the image) that typically occur during the compression process.

✔ **None:** I'll give you one guess. You got it: This selection turns off all codecs and results in a QuickTime mooV with no compression. None offers the highest quality QuickTime results but is a practical choice only if you own behemoth hard drives with names like Bruiser and Powe-r-r-r-r-r-D-r-r-rive, accessorized with a Cray (as in lightning speed) computer or two.

✔ **Photo - JPEG:** Developed for compressing full-screen, 24-bit (16 million) color *still* images. Now you may be asking yourself, "Self, why offer still-image compression in a movie-making program?" Well, it's important to remember that part of the beauty of QuickTime is its capability to incorporate virtually all file types into the Movie file type, including still images. For example, you can use a series of still images, such as a tour of famous paintings from the Louvre in Paris, as a QuickTime sequence, compressed with the Photo - JPEG codec and spliced together in Director with other QuickTime sequences, each compressed at its optimum value with the best codec.

✔ **Video:** The Video codec offers fast compression and decompression for files with moving images and sound. Moving images present special problems for compression schemes because all the pixels that make up the image tend to change from frame to frame. All this change disables what any self-respecting compression scheme tries to do: namely, cut down on info by recording only what changes from frame to frame.

Of these codecs, QuickTime for Windows currently offers two Apple codecs, Video and Cinepak, plus None and Intel Indeo Video R3.2. The Intel Indeo Video codec is very similar to the upcoming description of Cinepak.

Notice the Quality slider under the Compressor pop-up menu back in Figure 11-3. The slider is used to set the degree of compression. (I'm working on a Quality slider for Congress.) In general, you aim for the highest possible quality by selecting the least amount of compression, but you have to balance quality against frame rate and image size. If a large video window and/or high frame rate are paramount, you need to consider compromising on quality by upping the compression rate.

 Some developers use QuickTime for purposes other than making digital movies. Because QuickTime can incorporate still-image file types such as PICT files and sounds, you may want to consider using QuickTime as a way of archiving various file types into one QuickTime standard. Use no compression or the Animation codec, which is sometimes used to organize and store high-quality PICTs. An additional benefit of this kind of QuickTime archive is easily taping animations to video, one PICT per frame, the so-called single-frame technique that some high-end video recorders offer.

Video for Windows Codecs

Video for Windows, Microsoft's solution to digital video, offers its own set of codecs for the PC, including

- **MPEG-1:** An acronym for Motion Pictures Experts Group, MPEG-1 is designed to display full-screen, full-motion video. The hitch is that creating and viewing MPEG-compressed video is dependent on installing a pricey MPEG decompression board. Top boards run from $4,000 to $15,000, give or take a few pennies. Free MPEG viewers are now available for the PC and Macintosh that allow you to view but not compress MPEG movies at half-size (320 x 240). You can download these viewers over any number of bulletin boards or commercial online services like America Online and the Internet.

- **MPEG-2:** A new and improved version of MPEG-1 with a price tag to match. MPEG-2 boards start around $85,000, give or take a lunch.

Preparing QuickTime for Export

Take another look at the QuickTime Export Options dialog box in Figure 11-3. If you've read the sections in this chapter, you checked out the Compressor pop-up menu and learned about QuickTime 2.1's various codecs and how to adjust the amount of compression with the Quality slider, keeping in mind the inverse relationship between image quality and amount of compression. Now you can become close, personal friends with the dialog box's other features.

Tempo Settings versus Real Time

Director gives you a choice between Tempo Settings and Real Time when saving part or all of your Director movie as digital video. Choose Tempo Settings to create a digital video movie based on sprites in the Tempo channel of the Score window. Be warned that using regular transitions in the Transition channel and/or Palette transitions helps determine a digital video's file size and playability. Choose Real Time to duplicate playback of your movie from a specific computer.

Digital video has a big advantage over Director when it comes to playing the same movie on different computers. Exported as digital video, a Director sequence of 30 frames with a tempo setting of 15 frames per second plays back on any computer at precisely two seconds, with good sync between video and audio. The same sequence played as a Director movie may or may not play back in two seconds. Depending on machine type, color depth, and a number of other factors, the Director movie will run at different speeds on computers of varying performance.

The big difference is that Director is frame-based while digital video is time-based. Director plays all frames of a movie no matter what, even if it limps to an agonizing crawl on an old, festering computer. Digital video keeps a sharp eye on time, dropping frames rather than getting picture and sound out of sync.

What color is your pop-up rainbow, er, menu?

Your next consideration is setting the desired color depth in the QuickTime Options dialog box. Keep in mind that color depth options are dependent on the chosen codec. For example, choose the Animation codec from the Compressor pop-up menu and you'll find a complete choice of color depths under the Color Depth pop-up menu, as shown in Figure 11-5; choose Graphics for your codec and only 256 colors will be available.

You can create your digital video in black and white, although I don't recommend it. The result is dithered black-and-white frames, possibly justified when considering as wide an audience as possible. There's just one problem: It's ugly, although it might make an interesting special effect.

You can choose 256 colors, which multimedia types call 8-bit color. However, if you read my rantings in the previous section on codecs, the Graphics codec is specifically engineered to optimize 8-bit (256 colors) digital video.

Anyway, you can move up to thousands or even millions of colors. Keep in mind that QuickTime is optimized for thousands of colors, what developer types call 16-bit color. As tempting as millions of colors sound, 24-bit digital video makes enormous demands on a computer. And experts agree that only three people in the whole world can tell 16-bit from 24-bit color. And I'm not telling.

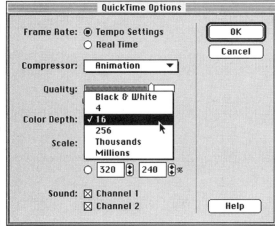

Figure 11-5:
The Animation codec allows a complete choice of color depths from the Color Depth pop-up menu.

If you're planning on cross-platform compatibility, better stay with 8-bit color. An army of pre-Windows 95 users out in the world are limited to 256 colors.

How do you export a color Director movie as a gray-scale digital video? You don't. Within Director, you can import the color digital video, place it into the Score, and then set the Palette to Grayscale in the Palette channel of the Score window. Thinking positively, it's relatively easy and all done in Director. The downside? All other sprites in the same frames turn gray along with the digital video until you change palettes again. The best way to create a gray-scale digital video is to turn to a utility program like MovieShop for the Mac or a heavy-duty application like Premiere for Macs and PCs, open the color digital video, and then save it as a gray-scale movie. For more on the Score window, see Chapter 5. For more on switching palettes, see Chapter 10.

Scale options

Director gives you several ways to scale your QuickTime movie. Choose a value from the Scale pop-up menu, shown in Figure 11-6; or choose Other and enter a specific percentage in the Scale dialog box, reproduced in Figure 11-7. You can also enter Width and Height values manually, or click the little up and down arrows that are visible in Figure 11-3.

In Real Life, only a handful of dimensions work well with digital video, all based on the classic 4-to-3 screen ratio inherited from the film industry since silent screen days, passed on to television and now digital video. The proportions of the ubiquitous 13-inch monitor, 640 x 480 pixels (or *pels*), reflect this 4-to-3 ratio; you can derive other dimensions by simply halving these values again and again until you arrive at the stamp-sized video window that started it all in 1993, a whopping 160 x 120 pixels.

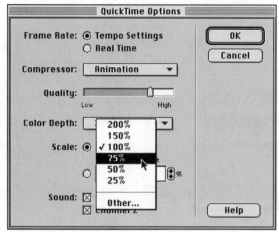

Figure 11-6:
The Scale pop-up menu in the QuickTime Options dialog box.

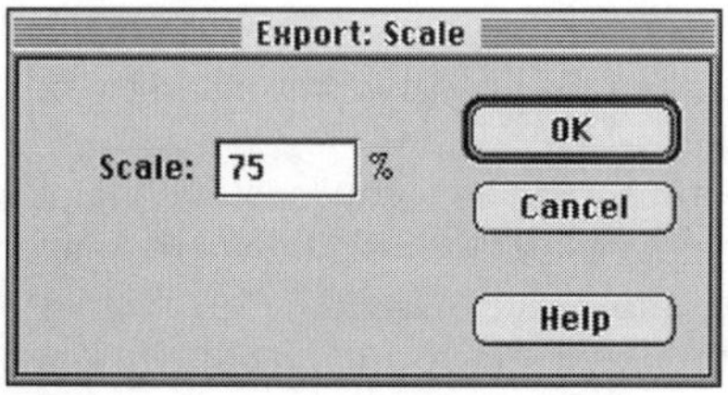

Figure 11-7:
The Scale dialog box.

Sound decisions

You may choose to include sound channels along with your animations by clicking the appropriate check boxes. In Figure 11-3, I decided to include both channels of sound. If your computer doesn't support stereo sound, only one sound check box will be enabled anyway.

Setting up for Real Time digital video

Use the following steps to prepare your digital video for Real Time playback:

1. **Turn off all Lingo commands by choosing Control⇨Disable Scripts.**

2. **Establish a beginning tempo for the movie by double-clicking the Tempo channel in frame 1, clicking the Tempo radio/option button in the Set Tempo dialog box, and sliding the Tempo control to 15 fps, a standard rate for on-screen animation barring high-end equipment, pronounced EXPENSIVE. Click OK.**

3. **Set desired tempos in other frames of the Tempo channel, as in step 2.**

4. **Set desired transitions in the Transition channel by double-clicking the Transition channel in the respective frame, scrolling to the preferred transition in the Set Transition dialog box, and customizing the transition with its specific set of check boxes and other controls. Click OK.**

5. **Uncheck Loop Playback in the Control menu.**

6. **Rewind the movie with ⌘/Ctrl+Option/Alt+R.**

7. **Make popcorn.**

8. **Salt and butter popcorn.**

9. **Play the movie with ⌘/Ctrl+Option/Alt+P.**

10. **At the conclusion of the movie, choose File⇨Export.**

11. **Be sure to click Options in the Export dialog box and check the Real Time radio/option button in the QuickTime Export Options dialog box.**

12. **Select an appropriate codec from the Compressor pop-up menu.**

    To review codecs and their uses, jump back to the "Codecs" section earlier in this chapter.

13. **Make any other desired modifications to Director's default settings in the QuickTime Options dialog box and click OK.**

14. **Make any other desired modifications to Director's default settings in the Export dialog box and click Export.**

15. **Play back your digital video to test results.**

16. **Clean fingers of salt and butter from popcorn.**

By the way, Lingo is Director's built-in programming language that's a lot easier to use than you might think. Why do you think I devote two precious chapters (17 and 25) to it in this book?

What Good Is an Empty Digital Video Window?

It's time to dive into using digital video in Director with the infamous Video window. When you choose Video from the Window menu, surprise! It's blank. That outrageous price that Macromedia wants for Director, and you get a blank window, as blank as Figure 11-8.

Try copying a bitmap and pasting it into the empty Video window; you can't. Sure, it's a great practical joke. It'll keep you entertained for a couple of hours, but then it dawns on you. You realize that you *can* use a blank Video window in Director to glue together snippets of *other* videos.

Figure 11-8:
An empty
digital Video
window.

By the way, you may open as many Video windows in Director as your memory or RAM allows — more RAM, more windows.

After you import a digital video, you can use all the standard Copy, Paste, and Clear commands under the Edit menu to move, rearrange, and delete frames within the Video window and *between* Video windows. Until you get Adobe Premiere, you can edit video in Director. And with Shockwave, Director's plug-in for the Web's premiere browser, Netscape Navigator, you're set for doing cutting-edge animation in Cyberspace! For more on Shockwave and the Web, turn to Chapter 21.

When you export a Digital Video Cast Member cut and pasted together in Director as a digital video file, the result is what we multimedia types call a "flattened" file, meaning that all the bits and pieces it took to put the Digital Video Cast Member together in Director are now part of the final digital video file, independent of the original sources.

Touring the Video window

Take a closer look at that blank Video window. Most of the features look familiar; some are unique to this window. Notice that the top row of buttons duplicates precisely what you find in the Paint window. To review Paint window buttons in psychoanalytical depth, take one giant step back to Chapter 6.

The Video window buttons, from left to right, include the following:

- ✔ New Cast Member
- ✔ Previous Cast Member
- ✔ Next Cast Member
- ✔ Drag Cast Member
- ✔ Cast Member Name
- ✔ Cast Member Script
- ✔ Cast Member Properties
- ✔ Cast Member Number

The only unique area of this window is the row of controls at the bottom. These controls are actually a standard feature called, of all things, the *controller*. Digital movies usually appear with the controller, although you can hide it in most programs, including Director. Notice how similar the controller buttons are to VCR or remote control buttons. From left to right, the controller features the following:

- **Sound Control:** Press to adjust the sound, from off to full volume, with a sliding control. Sound may be adjusted during playback. If no slider appears when you press the Sound Control button, the original digital video has no soundtrack, or it wasn't imported along with the graphics for any of 5,392 reasons.

- **Play and Stop:** Click to begin video playback. On playback, the button changes its icon to a square and functions as the Stop button.

- **Scroll Bar:** Press and drag to the right to fast forward or to the left to fast rewind as with the shuttle control on some VCRs.

- **Step reverse control:** This moves the digital video back one frame for each click of the mouse.

- **Step forward control:** This moves the digital video forward one frame for each click of the mouse.

- **Resize box:** This is like the Resize box on most windows. Press and drag to manually resize the Video window's dimensions.

If you don't want to assume the person viewing the digital video knows how to use a controller, you have two options. Either include a Help area somewhere on-screen, or hide the controller by unchecking the Show Controller check box in the Digital Video Properties dialog box and include a custom Play Movie button somewhere on-screen that issues the Lingo play command. See Chapter 17 for more on Lingo commands.

Unfortunately, there's no simple play command for digital video in Director. In the "Playing Digital Video Lite" section of this chapter is a method for playing a video from a button that avoids a lot of Lingo scripting. It looks like a lot of work, but the whole process goes pretty quickly when you're setting it up.

Make the distinction clearly in your mind between a Digital Video Cast Member in the Cast window, its sprite placed on the Stage, and its Video window — three very different views of the same object, as shown side-by-side in Figure 11-9. By the way, Figure 11-9 shows an impossible situation in one respect: All three windows are active, when in Real Life only one window may be active at any time. Don't let this throw you.

Figure 11-9:
Three faces
of an
imported
digital video
movie:
its Digital
Video Cast
Member,
its sprite
viewed on
the Stage,
and its
Video
window.

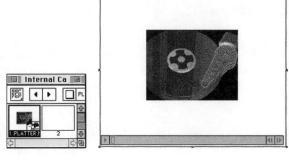

The first view, from left to right in Figure 11-9, shows an imported digital video as a Cast Member in the Cast window. Note the row of Cast window buttons at the top, the Cast Member's telltale thumbnail size, its cell number under the thumbnail followed by as much of the name as can show in Geneva 9-point type, and the Digital Video icon in the lower-right corner.

The second view in Figure 11-9 is the Digital Video Cast Member's sprite on the Stage. Notice the selection rectangle and handles that appear when you select the sprite. Displaying the controller at the bottom of a Digital Video sprite is optional; you may hide it by selecting the Cast Member, clicking the Cast Member Properties button, and unchecking the Controller check box.

The third view in Figure 11-9 shows the Digital Video Cast Member's Video window. Display it by double-clicking a Digital Video Cast Member in the Cast window or its sprite on the Stage. Notice the telltale Add button at the top of the window and the Digital Video's permanent controller. Director doesn't allow you to hide a Video window's controller any more than its Close box, Zoom box, or Resize box.

Setting up your digital video

Click the Digital Video Cast Member Properties button, and Director takes you to the Digital Video Cast Member Properties dialog box, depicted with excruciating accuracy in Figure 11-10.

The Digital Video Cast Member Properties dialog box gives you important information on a Digital Video Cast Member. In Figure 11-10, the digital video is Digital Video Cast Member 1. At the top, Director gives you the Digital Video

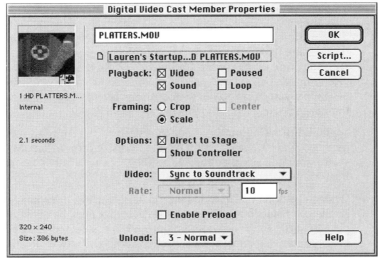

Figure 11-10:
The Digital
Video Cast
Member
Properties
dialog box
offers a
number of
options for
modifying a
Digital Video
Cast
Member.

Cast Member's name, which may be different from the source file's name on the hard drive; remember, you can rename a Cast Member in its Properties dialog box at any time. Underneath the name is the video's address or path on the drive. At left, Director informs you that the digital video runs for 2.1 seconds, its dimensions are 320 x 240, and its file size is 386 bytes. In addition to all this info, Director offers you a flock of options at no additional expense.

Playback options include

✔ **Video check box:** Check to show the video sprite on playback. An un-checked Video check box hides the video track. With only the controller showing, you can still click the Play button to play an audio track.

✔ **Sound check box:** Check to enable any sound tracks embedded in the video sprite.

✔ **Paused check box:** Check to keep the video sprite from automatically playing when it appears on the Stage; you can then click the Play button on the controller at any time. With the check box unchecked, Director plays the video sprite when it appears on the Stage.

✔ **Loop check box:** Check to make the digital video jump from the last frame to frame one and replay, continuing to loop until you click the controller's Stop button.

To stop a digital video, press the spacebar. Press the spacebar again to resume playback. By the way, this keyboard shortcut works with most QuickTime-related programs.

The Framing options include

- **Crop radio/option button:** Click to turn the video sprite's *bounding box* (the outline that highlights when you select the sprite) into a frame showing more or less of the sprite as you drag the bounding box by a selection handle into various dimensions. If the sprite's controller is set to be visible, you can crop out the controller along with unwanted parts of the image.

- **Scale radio/option button:** Click to resize a video sprite by its selection handles. Shift-drag a selection handle to resize proportionally. Regain a sprite's original size by choosing Modify➪Sprite➪Properties and clicking Restore.

- **Center check box:** Check this option to center the video sprite within the dimensions of its bounding box. If the Center check box is disabled (grayed out), then the Crop radio/option button is not selected, as in Figure 11-10. Once you select Crop, the Center check box becomes enabled.

Additional options include

- **Direct to Stage check box:** Checking this box forces Director to play the video sprite at the highest layer, regardless of its real channel position in the Score.

  Each frame of a Director movie contains 48 channels to work with, like transparent layers one on top of the other. Channel 1 is the furthest back, like a background layer; channel 48 is the closest layer to you. Playing digital video in the closest or highest channel maximizes playback speed because Director doesn't have to deal with the possibility of calculating the effect of other sprites overlapping the video sprite.

  Two rules are associated with this option. First, no other sprites can be in higher channels in the Score when you call on this option, and second, the only acceptable ink type is the default ink, Copy. In other words, when you need to apply a custom ink type to a video sprite, or you want other sprites overlapping or crossing a video sprite in your animation, don't use Direct to Stage. You may cause the magnetic fields of the North and South Pole to swap places, causing havoc throughout the world and some really bad traffic jams.

- **Show Controller check box:** Only enabled after you check the Direct to Stage check box, the Show Controller check box displays a digital video's controller, the subject of the next section.

- **Video pop-up menu:** Choose Sync to Soundtrack to play video at its original rate even if frames are dropped. Or choose Play Every Frame, No Sound to prevent dropped frames.

✔ **Rate pop-up menu:** This is available if you choose Play Every Frame from the Video pop-up menu. Select a rate from the pop-up menu: Normal, Maximum, or Fixed. Enter a value in the entry box to the right.

The Fixed rate option only works properly when the entire digital video plays at the same frame rate. Some digital videos vary frame rate from sequence to sequence.

✔ **Enable Preload check box:** Checking this box automatically issues a Lingo command, preLoadCast, that initiates the copying process into memory before Director plays the video sprite.

Director has two ways to call up digital video information from the source file to play back on the Stage. The slower way is to read one frame of the source file from disk, display the frame on the Stage, read the next frame, display it, and so on. The faster method is to copy the entire source file into memory or, in a limited memory situation, copy as much of the file as possible to memory, and then play the digital videos from memory. The faster method is where the Enable Preload into RAM check box comes into play.

Be sure to uncheck the Enable Preload into RAM check box when you anticipate or need to assume a low-memory situation.

When you import a digital video, Director always sets up the source document as a *linked* file; the Digital Video Cast Member that appears in the Cast window refers to the external digital video on your hard drive when you play back the video sprite in the Stage window.

✔ **Unload pop-up menu:** Choose one of the Purge Priority options, as shown in Figure 11-11, for the Digital Video Cast Member.

For detailed information about Purge Priority options, jump back to Chapter 4.

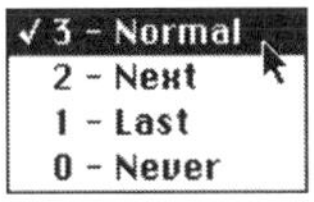

Figure 11-11:
The Unload pop-up menu for setting when a Cast Member is cleared from memory.

Playing Digital Video Lite

Hold onto your seats. You're about to enter the eerie, scary world of LINGO! Actually, you'll do just fine. You can try out all the basics of Lingo by reading Chapters 17 and 25. But to get your feet wet, try this section first, Digital Video Lite. Goes great with low-fat pancakes, too.

First, you need to set up a new Digital Video Cast Member in the Cast window that has only the first frame of the video you'd like to play.

Setting up your window

1. **Choose Window⇨Cast and double-click the digital video you'd like to play to bring up its Digital Video Cast Member window.**

2. **Click the Cast Member Properties button and check that the Paused check box is *not* checked.**

3. **Click OK.**

4. **Choose Edit⇨Copy Video.**

   Basically, you've copied the first frame of the video, known as the *poster* because it acts as a preview image for the file.

5. **Click the Add button in the Digital Video Cast Member window to display a blank Digital Video Cast Member window.**

6. **Click the new Digital Video Cast Member *in the Cast window* and choose Edit⇨Paste Video.**

7. **In the Save As dialog box that appears, name the new digital video something original, like** Poster. **Using the Directory window, select the location where you'd like to save the file, and click Save.**

Preparing the Score

Now you need to set things up in the Score window.

1. **Using the Score window's playback head, move to the frame where you'd like to insert a digital video.**

   Remember the frame number and the channel. You'll use the same channel throughout the rest of these steps.

2. **Drag your video from the Cast window to the Score, noting the channel number.**

   Of course, placing your video in the Score also centers the video on the Stage.

3. **While the digital video is highlighted in the Score, choose Edit⇨Copy Cells.**

4. **Highlight the frame that is two frames to the right of the frame you chose in step 1 and choose Edit⇨Paste Cells.**

5. **In the Cast window, highlight the original full-framed digital video.**

6. **Choose Score⇨Switch Cast Members.**

7. **Highlight the original video in the Score, noting its frame number, and choose Edit⇨Copy Cells.**

   The next part's a little dicey. You need to guess approximately how many frames your animation runs. For example, if your movie is running at 15 *fps* (frames per second), and you guess that the digital video runs for 3 seconds, that's 45 frames.

8. **Guess the number of frames your digital video takes and add that number to the frame number you noted in step 7.**

9. **Whatever number you arrive at in step 8, highlight that frame and choose Edit⇨Paste Cells.**

   You're preparing to use the In-Between command in the Modify menu.

10. **Press Shift and click the first copy of the full-framed video to select the range of frames you guessed the video would take to play completely.**

11. **Choose Modify⇨In-Between.**

Adding a little Lingo

Remember, I said that these steps avoid *a lot* of Lingo; avoiding it altogether is hard.

1. **Return to the frame where your digital video is, noting the frame number, and double-click the Script channel in the same frame.**

2. **Type** go to the frame **and click the Script window's Close box.**

   When you play the Director movie, this line of Lingo locks you in this frame until another command tells Director to do something else.

3. **Choose Window⇨Tools and select the basic Button tool.**

   For more on the Tool palette, page back to Chapter 9.

4. **Drag out a button at the bottom of the Stage and enter a name for the button where you see the blinking insertion point: for example,** Play Movie.

5. **Click the outline of the button to select it (so that it displays selection handles), press ⌘/Ctrl+I to display its Properties dialog box, and click the Script button.**

6. **In the button's Script window, type** go to frame.

7. **Add a space and then the number of the frame where the real full-framed digital video begins; then click the Close box.**

Testing it out

Now you're ready to test your work.

1. **Choose Control⇨Play or press ⌘/Ctrl+Option/Alt+P.**

   What should happen? Your Director movie should play to the frame where your digital video (in this example, "Poster") appears. Director waits until you press the button you created (in this example, "Play Movie"). When you finally do decide to press the button, the Lingo command hidden in the button jumps you to the full video and plays to its conclusion, *providing* you guessed correctly about the number of frames it would take. If you didn't guess correctly, go to step 2.

2. **Add some additional frames to the set of duplicate frames allowing your digital video to play to completion and retest.**

Using Director as a Digital Video Editor

If you don't have an honest-to-gosh digital video editing program like Adobe Premiere or one of the other fine products on the market, you can use Director itself as an editor. Of course, Director wasn't meant to be a dedicated video editor, so don't expect to replicate all the wondrous special effects you've heard about; but for basic editing, cutting, and pasting, Director works just fine. In a way, it offers some features that those fancy editing programs lack.

To use Director as an editor, you need to start with some digital video. In other words, opening the Paint window, creating a masterpiece on a blank easel, copying it, and trying to paste your graphic into a blank Video window just doesn't work. Try it if you don't believe me. Gjeeeech.

Start from scratch

Remember that old saying about, "Where there's a will . . ."? Just as soon as the words leave my lips (that is, my keyboard), I find myself backtracking on them a bit. Director actually does provide a way to create a digital video from scratch — it's a roundabout way, but it works! For example, you decide to develop an animation sequence in Director, maybe the old-fashioned way, one drawing at a time, making small, incremental changes to your actors (or sprites, as we Director types call them) from frame to frame. You build your sequence over the days, the weeks, the months. You forget to make your car payment; they tow your car away. You build your sequence. Your spouse leaves you; your children run away. You build your sequence, fine-tuning each frame to perfection until you have ten frames Disney would be proud of. Sure, you've sacrificed a little, but hey, that's the path of the true artiste.

Anyway, you've got your ten frames. Then again, maybe you're not so dedicated. You decide to use Director's Animation Wizard features, discussed in Chapter 16. You build an animated bullet chart. The topics fly in; the bullets fly in. Full color, stereo sound, with just a couple of clicks of the mouse. You seriously consider CinemaScope but finally pass on that one. Either way, one drawing at a time or taking advantage of Director's built-in animation capabilities, you build your ten frames. Then you realize what makes the darned thing so powerful is the sync between graphics and sound. Now, you *did* swipe that musical intro from *Star Trek: The Next Generation*, didn't you? So what if you spend some big time in a maximum security federal penitentiary; you're an artiste, willing to sacrifice a little for your art. A few years in the slammer's nothing compared to building ten great frames Disney would be proud of.

What I'm trying to say is, Director is a frame-based application. With a lot of tweaking and perspiration, you can make graphics and sound sync pretty well together. Wondrous as Director is, however — kiss, kiss — the application is just not designed to do the job as well as digital video. Digital video is time-based. Digital video was developed to play at a user-set rate, to stay in sync with any accompanying soundtracks, and to drop frames if necessary in order to accomplish its mission, should it so choose to accept. Impossible, you say? No, digital video works very well indeed for synchronizing graphics with soundtracks. So why not export your ten frames as a digital video, resolve any sync problems, and, if you want to stay with Director as the software "engine," simply re-import your video back into a Director movie? Now for your editing pleasure, you have the best of both worlds: digital video's time-based technology and Director's interactive and Web publishing capabilities.

Prebuilt digital video

Another way to use Director's built-in video editing features is to start with some prebuilt video. A list of sources might include the following:

✔ **Your own digital videos:** That's what AV Macs and PC video boards are all about, complete with Video In and Video Out ports, Stereo Sound In and Out ports, and *DSP* (Digital Signal Processor) chips on the system board, along with other special computer stuff to digitize *analog video* (your videotapes) into digital info that your computer understands and Director can display in a Video window.

✔ **Freeware and shareware digital video:** You say you don't have a camcorder, a VCR, or talent? All the major commercial online services, such as America Online, CompuServe, and Prodigy, have tons of digital video for you to *download* (copy to your computer through an inexpensive modem). And don't forget the Internet. Many videos are freeware with unlimited usage rights granted to you by the originator; other files may be shareware-style files where you're obliged to send in a relatively low fee for ownership and/or usage, or perhaps a licensing fee per one-time usage of the video based on the honor system. In these legally combative times, it's important to read all fine print and completely understand the contract you're agreeing to before adopting someone else's work for your own.

Freeware doesn't necessarily translate into "no strings attached." Always read the fine print. How do you think I wound up getting married twice?

✔ **Digital video on floppy and CD-ROM media:** Countless sources of third-party commercial digital videos and still images on floppies are on the market. Better yet, purchase a CD full of digital video. A CD-ROM disc can store up to 650 megabytes of info, and its shelf life is longer than your own. Assuming the image and sound quality is high, prices for CD-ROM collections are usually very reasonable. Again, check and double-check usage rights before you purchase anything. My recommendation is to look for unlimited usage to get your full money's worth, unless you just can't live without that CD full of one-time usage kitties lapping up milk, ripping sofas, sinking needle-sharp, little fangs into toes, and so on.

A digital video edit

Okay, say your client, Mr. Big, wants you to re-edit some scenes from a couple of digital videos and make Director the "engine" that plays the files. Mr. Big wants to use Director because he has plans for you to add some animation and interactivity to the project about a month from now. Here's a basic plan I recommend following:

Setting up

1. **Make a project folder by choosing File⇨New Folder at the Mac's Desktop or the Windows Program Manager.**

2. **Name the folder.**

3. **Add your mooV(s) to the folder.**

   Figure 11-12 shows a couple of digital videos, HD_CU.MOV and PLATTERS.MOV, ready for editing.

By the way, CU stands for close-up, as in "I'm ready for my close-up, Mr. DeMille."

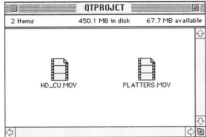

Figure 11-12:
Two
QuickTime
mooVs in
their own
project
folder on the
Desktop.

Importing the digital movies

1. **Highlight Director's icon on the desktop.**

2. **Choose File⇨Open or double-click Director's icon.**

3. **When you arrive at Director's blank Stage window, choose File⇨Import.**

4. **In the Import Files dialog box, click Desktop.**

5. **From the Show pop-up menu, choose QuickTime.**

   Your view should look close to Figure 11-13.

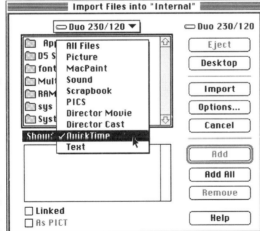

Figure 11-13:
Selecting
QuickTime
from the
Show pop-
up menu in
Director's
Import Files
dialog box.

Selecting the right file type from the Type pop-up menu in the Import dialog box is very important. Choosing the wrong file type could wind up hiding the very files you're looking for.

Notice the absence of a Link To File check box under the directory in the Import dialog box after you choose QuickTime from the Type pop-up menu. This is because Director automatically imports each QuickTime mooV as a *linked file,* meaning its content doesn't become incorporated into the Director file. Only a link pointing to the source file is established; when playing a Digital Video sprite, Director reads QuickTime info from the original file in the project folder on the Desktop.

6. **Double-click the project folder in the Directory.**

7. **Double-click each mooV you want to import. If you want to import all mooVs in the folder, be lazy and click Add All.**

Clicking the Add All button in the Import Files dialog box imports all files shown in the open folder in the directory. After you decide which Image Options to select, Director returns you to the Stage, where you find the Cast window with your Digital Video Cast Members in place, as in Figure 11-14.

Figure 11-14:
Digital
Video Cast
Members in
the Cast
window
after being
imported.

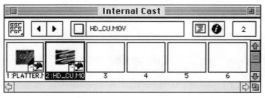

Notice the tiny Digital Video icon in the lower-right corner of each thumbnail.

Displaying the Cast Members' Video windows

1. **Double-click the first Cast Member to display its Video window.**

2. **Option/Alt+double-click the second Cast Member to add its Video window to the screen.**

Why the Option/Alt key? If you simply double-click the second Cast Member, it replaces the first Cast Member in the current Video window, and you wind up with only one Video window on display, which probably isn't what you want at this point. Don't let Director fool you, though. After Option/Alt+double-clicking, the second Video window may land in exactly the same place as the first Video window. Just follow the next step.

3. **Move the new Video window by its title bar to the right of the first Video window.**

Making a new Video window

1. **Press Option/Alt and click the second window's New button (with the + icon) to display a new Video window.**

2. **Move the new Video window to the right of the first two windows and assemble all three windows, as in Figure 11-15.**

Editing together a new Digital Video Cast Member

1. **To select a range of frames, Shift-drag your digital video's scroll bar in the controller, as in Figure 11-16.**

   Notice that the selected range of frames appears black in the controller's scroll bar.

2. **Choose Edit⇨Copy Video to copy the selected frames.**

3. **Click the empty Video Cast Member in the Cast window.**

4. **Choose Edit⇨Paste Video.**

   As soon as you choose Paste Video, Director automatically presents you with the Save As dialog box, depicted in Figure 11-17, so you can save the new digital video to your hard drive.

5. **Enter a name for the new file and click OK.**

Digital videos always import as linked files, so they can be shared among a number of Director movies without adding to the size of your complete presentation. Also, edits you make to digital videos with programs like Premiere are automatically updated in Director because the video files are linked to their Director documents.

After you've copied the first frame(s) into the empty new video window, it's just a matter of more cutting and pasting from one video window to the next directly in the Stage window. By picking and choosing sequences from among several video windows, you can edit together a new digital video epic right in Director

Figure 11-15:
Three Video
windows
lined up in
preparation
for digital
editing in
Director.

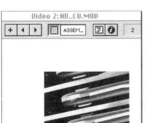

Figure 11-16: Selecting a range of frames in a Video window by pressing Shift and dragging the controller's scroll bar.

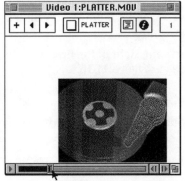

Figure 11-17: Director presents you with the Save As dialog box after you paste video into a new Digital Video window.

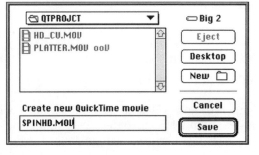

Chapter 12

And the Winner of Script of the Year: The Script Window

In This Chapter

▶ Sampling Director's secret sauce

▶ Creating a script by the seat of your pants

▶ Adding a script to a movie

*N*o doubt about it. There's excitement in the air. The crowd's restless, the fans are pushing, shoving, scratching, and straining to get autographs. Eyes flashing, flashbulbs bulbing. I've never seen anything like it. For tonight's the night all bits and bytes have been waiting for. Dressed in their little tuxedos and sequined evening gowns, the members of Computerdom's royalty have convened once more in their annual ritual of mutual back-patting.

Now is the moment. The envelope is torn. We're always tearing the envelope around here. Pouty lips mouth incomprehensible words among the rising din of apprehension. And what's that? Yes, the winner is of script of the year is . . . the Script window!

Well, it's all over now until another 1,892,160,000 ticks pass by. (By the way, computers keep time in ticks per second, 60 ticks per second.) There's nothing left but streamers tossed carelessly to the floor, a rainbow of confetti strewn in the aisles, an empty champagne glass here and there. Wait, slurp, now no empty champagne glasses here and there.

So the Script window won, again. I'm not surprised. The Script window is one of the more important windows Director 5 has to offer. In fact, the Script window and the scripts it contains are the keys to Director's interactive possibilities.

Where Good Scripts Go

Script windows are important because that's where you write Lingo *scripts*, snippets of text containing Lingo commands. By the way, Lingo is Director's built-in programming language.

If the Script window isn't visible, check to see if your eyes are shut. If not, choose Window⇨Script from Director's menu bar or press ⌘/Ctrl+0 (zero). Director presents the Script window, looking amazingly like Figure 12-1.

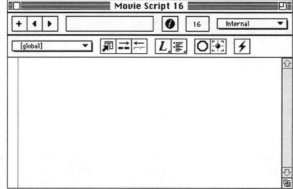

Figure 12-1:
A Movie
Script
window,
where you
can type
Lingo scripts
for your
movie.

In addition to all the accoutrements of a basic window, just beneath the title bar you find a row of buttons. They're the same as Mr. Paint window's buttons, with one exception: The Script button is missing because you are already at the Script window. You can read about the rest of these buttons in Chapter 6.

The stuff in the second row, the Script toolbar, now they're really different. Let me perambulate through them from left to right:

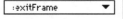

 ✔ **Handler Name pop-up menu:** A handler is a number of Lingo lines beginning with *on* followed by a space and the name of the handler (on mouseDown, for example), followed by one or more Lingo commands, and ending with the word end in its own line. Once you write a slew of Lingo handlers, you'll find them all listed in the Handler Name pop-up menu, a veritable Who's Who of Lingo handlers.

 ✔ **Go to Handler button:** The Script window is like a miniature word processor. Somewhere in the window is an insertion point. If it's in a line that refers to a handler, clicking Go to Handler takes you directly to that handler.

✔ **Comment button:** Just about every computer language includes some way of making notes to yourself within the lines of code. Click Comment to add the comment operator (—) to the beginning of a line, marking the line as a comment as opposed to a line of Lingo. Director ignores comment lines; it's a good idea to be generous with them.

 ✔ **Uncomment button:** Clicking Uncomment removes the comment symbol (—) from a line of text in the Script window.

 ✔ **Alphabetical Lingo pop-up menu:** Pressing this button reveals a list of operators and commands in alphabetical order, as in Figure 12-2.

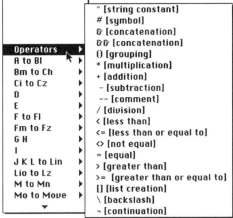

Figure 12-2:
Reveal
Lingo's
Operators
and
commands
by pressing
the
Alphabetical
Lingo
button.

 ✔ **Categorized Lingo pop-up menu:** Clicking this reveals a list of Lingo stuff organized by categories like Navigation, Movie Control, and User Interaction.

 ✔ **Toggle Breakpoint button:** This sets or clears a *breakpoint,* a special marker like a giant bullet point to the left of a line in the Script window. As Director executes a script, it stops at each toggle breakpoint and takes you to a new Director window, the Debugger, where you can analyze a handler that's not working properly. See Chapter 13 for more Debugger info.

 ✔ **Watch Expression button:** The Watch Expression button and the new Watcher window work together to keep track of what expressions and variables stand for while you're playing back a movie. Expressions and variables are Lingo stuff that usually stand for some kind of value. For example, I might invent a variable called myValue and write some Lingo to make myValue stand for the value 20. When you're developing a movie, it's often important to know what expressions and variables stand for from frame to frame because expressions and variables often change values over time. Add an expression and variable you want to keep track of to the Watcher window by clicking the expression or variable in the Script window, then clicking the Watch Expression button. Once added to the Watcher window, the expression or variable is updated as your movie plays back.

 ✔ **Recompile Script button:** Click to recompile and test all handlers in the current movie. Lingo is too conversational for your computer to understand, so Lingo needs to be *recompiled* or translated into machine language before your computer actually executes Lingo handlers.

Script Properties

In the Script Cast Member Properties dialog box, you find important info about the script you're currently exploring. Display the Script Cast Member Properties dialog box by clicking the Cast Member Properties button in the top row of Script window buttons, as in Figure 12-3. Take a look at the dialog box's layout, shown in Figure 12-4, including the following:

Figure 12-3:
The Cast Member Properties button in the Script window.

Figure 12-4:
Click the Cast Member Properties button in the Script window to go to the Script Cast Member Properties dialog box.

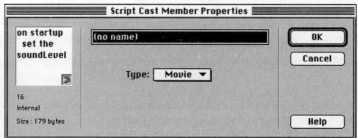

✔ **Script Preview:** The square panel in the upper-left corner of the dialog box. Displays the first few lines of the script. Note the Script icon in the lower-right corner of the Script Preview panel.

✔ **Cast Member Name:** (no name) is the default name Director gives a new Script window. It's not a bad idea to give a script window a meaningful name.

✔ **Cast Member Number:** Each Script window sits in the Cast window as a Script Cast Member with its own location number — in this case, 16 — displayed just below the Script Preview panel.

✔ **Cast Type:** Tells you whether the Script window belongs to an internal or external cast. See "Internal and external Cast windows" in Chapter 6 for related info.

✔ **Cast Member Size:** Tells you the size of the Cast Member in bytes, basic computer stuff nobody knows anything about.

✔ **Type pop-up menu:** Displays three types of scripts you can write for a Director movie: Movie, Score, and Parent.

Script Types

The Type pop-up menu in the Script Cast Member Properties dialog box is the key to making what Director types call a *movie script*, meaning a Script window that contains a set of commands intended to be available anytime during playback of a Director movie. As Figure 12-5 shows, three types exist: Movie scripts, Score scripts, and Parent scripts.

Figure 12-5:
The Type pop-up menu in the Cast Member Properties dialog box, where you choose the type of script for your movie.

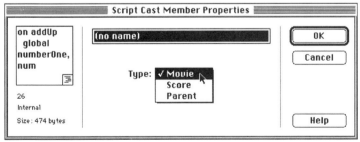

Movie scripts are often initialization-type scripts that set up the movie on startup. Movie scripts may check the type of computer running the movie; set the color depth of the monitor; set other critical values, such as the sound level and the beginning palette from a number of different Palette Cast Members; and generally prepare the movie for optimum playback.

A Score script refers to scripts found in the Script channel of the Score window. They activate only when the playback head enters or exits a particular frame during playback. For example, a Score script in frame 15 may kick in a timing routine that jumps the playback head forward 10 frames to a special animation sequence if you don't press the mouse or a key on the keyboard within 30 seconds.

Here's another example: A Score script placed in frame 10 may read `go to frame 1,` causing the playback head to jump back repeatedly to the first frame of the Director movie so that the movie *loops,* or repeats, until some special condition is met. For a thorough discussion of Score window features, hop back to Chapter 5. For a thorough discussion of conditions, read *The Physicians' Desk Reference.* Boy, are there a lot of conditions. Some are really disgusting.

Parent scripts are more complicated and not within the scope of this book. But after you have some Lingo under your belt, remember to check out how Parent scripts work. Just as a teaser, they allow you to make something like a template for a script and apply that script with unlimited variations to your movie. Maybe in Son of Director 5…

Scripts: The Secret Sauce of Interactive Multimedia

If your main interest in purchasing Director and reading this book is taking advantage of Director's interactive features, sooner or later you need to take the plunge and face the terror of terrors. Right, I'm talking about . . . *programming!*

Gu, ghaa, du, uh, ormpf

Programming. For the technically challenged, the very thought turns hands to jelly, voices to high-pitched squeals, and normally intelligible adults into zombie-like nightcrawlers uttering phrases like, "Gu, ghaa, du, uh, ormpf." I know. I've been there. I know the cold beads of sweat breaking across the forehead, the trembling hand turning to the chapters on code, programming, scripts, variables, and so on.

There's an old saying I just made up: Sometimes you can be your own worst enemy. This thing about scripting is a perfect example. Think about it. Out there in Real Life, thousands and thousands of people no smarter than you are making a good living at scripting. They buy nice homes, drive great cars, and find the perfect spouses; people think they're smart. And all because they do scripting. The only difference between them and you is that they're them and you're you. Also, they've broken past that invisible barrier that exists only in the mind.

If you think Lingo's hard, try English

If all I've said so far hasn't touched you, consider this: Humans are born to use language. Somehow it's in our genes. Learning English — which I'm still working on — means learning thousands of words and gosh knows how many rules about how to meaningfully put these words together in an infinite number of ways (syntax). Do you see my point? Learning English was a monumental accomplishment. Trying a language like Lingo, the key to scripting, involves learning a list of commands that fits under one menu in Director's menu bar and a handful of other concepts. Child's play. And remember, adding scripts to your movies is the key to all those interactive goodies. So find a three-year-old child and begin scripting.

No, Mother, I want to do it myself

Just because you want to use Director's interactive features doesn't necessarily mean that you have to write all the scripts yourself. You can do a number of things to make your scripting life easier.

Ready-made scripts

A number of scripts are *out there* for you to use, requiring only the most rudimentary knowledge of how a script should look and where to place one in your Director movie. Where do you find these scripts? Well, in this book, for one. Although my intention in this book is only to give you a friendly nudge in the scripting direction, I do include some sample scripts that you're welcome to use. In Appendix B, I recommend free and commercial resources available to you. Of course, Macromedia includes a full set of demos and tutorial files on all Director 5's features, including Lingo. Be sure to look over the demos and tutorial files, not only for scripting but also for graphic and interface design. And don't forget the support Macromedia includes with your purchase of Director — a veritable bonanza of technical resources.

Simple scripts

After you overcome any negative mind-set you may have had, try grasping scripting fundamentals and writing some easy scripts. Believe it not, the most frequently used scripts are often extraordinarily simple. Take the go command, one of the most frequently used Lingo commands. Tack on the word *to* and a frame number, and you've created a powerful line of Lingo that jumps the user from one frame to another of your choosing. I discuss this option in more detail in Chapter 17.

User groups

Computer and Director user groups meet on a regular basis throughout the states with enormously generous members more than willing to help you through tough scripting problems. User groups are a place to receive and share information, make contacts and some friends, and keep in touch with what's going on in the rest of the multimedia world.

One of the most famous Macintosh user groups is BMUG, Berkeley Macintosh User Group, listed in Appendix B. BMUG holds frenetic, high-energy meetings and has tons of freeware and shareware software on floppies and CD-ROMs, with a software directory that looks more like the telephone book for greater New York. If you're not lucky enough to live near Northern California, call User Group Locator at 800-538-9696 for a user group in your area. They'll even help you start your own user group with a free starter kit.

Online services, bulletin boards, and the Net

Online services — such as America Online, CompuServe, and Prodigy — and bulletin boards like BMUG abound in the ether, brimming with sample scripts, utility software, roundtable discussions, and technical help for scripting wannabes. The Internet, America's newest techno love affair, offers tons of resources for Director scripting and technical aid. You just might wind up cybertalking with Mr. Macromedia Director himself, Marc Cantor, gadfly, entrepreneur, bon vivant, and founder of Macromedia. By the way, you'll find a list of resources in Appendix B.

Scripters

Without being facetious, I'm going to suggest something shocking: hiring a professional programmer. My goal in this book is twofold. One, I'd love to nudge you into trying scripting for yourself. Until you try it yourself, you may find it hard to realize or even believe how much fun and creative scripting can be. All this book or any other book can do is walk you through scripting essentials. From then on, scripting becomes a process as creative as the visual arts. We have only so many colors to work with, but for thousands of years, artists have been combining them in seemingly endless variety to produce unique and creative results. The same thing applies to scripting.

Also, I want to show that you don't need to do scripting to create winning multimedia with Director. In fact, more often than not, multimedia development in the real world is a team effort, much like filmmaking. Ever sit through those eternal credits at the end of a movie? All those people contributed to the film;

no one person could possibly have done everything. The same approach applies to multimedia. It helps to know your strengths and a little about scripting so that you know whether what you want to accomplish is reasonable. I talk more about the team nature of multimedia in Chapter 22.

Come On, Try One On for Size

Ready for some fun? Are you set to have the time of your life? Okay, let's script. Say you've been developing a business presentation for a mysterious client, Mr. Big. Actually, you're not sure what business Mr. Big is in, but it involves lots of calls from public phones, wearing dark suits and sunglasses, and meeting someone holding a bass cello carrying case at the airport every few weeks. Everyone loves your presentation, but Mr. Big contracts you again to add some scripting so that he doesn't have to work so hard presenting the darn thing. The presentation will look a lot slicker, and Mr. Big won't have to stand up from his gold-plated, wing-back chair so often. Anyway, he makes you an offer you can't refuse.

The movie is called INTRO.MOV. Mr. Big wants it to go automatically to a new movie, US_INC.MOV. Sounds pretty exciting already, let me tell you. Anyone have a megadose of No-Doz handy?

Actually, this scenario's pretty common in producing Director presentations. The question is, how do you go to another movie smoothly? Can this be done with Lingo in the first place? See, here's one good reason to learn something about Lingo even if you never write a script in your life.

After Mr. Big begins INTRO.MOV, he wants to jump from frame 35, the last frame, to the second Director movie, have it play automatically, and then return to the first movie.

Okay, here's how you'd handle an assignment like this. Remember, this mini-tutorial is just an example, a simple template for you to use as an aid for working with Director and Lingo scripts. Also remember that if you mess up, you may be wearing cement boots at the bottom of San Francisco Bay.

1. **Make a new folder for the project by choosing File⇨New Folder from the Mac's Desktop or double-clicking File Manager and choose File⇨Create Directory on a PC.**

    Making a project folder/directory where you place all files is usually a pretty good idea. Otherwise, keeping track of everything, especially linked files, can become pretty hairy.

2. **Give your folder/directory a meaningful name and return to the Desktop or to File Manager.**

   For example, I named my project folder MR_BIG.

   If you're planning on cross-platform compatibility, follow DOS file-naming conventions on a Mac; limit the filename to eight characters followed by a period and a three-character extension. The extension *MOV* stands for a digital video; *DIR* stands for a Director movie. See Chapter 20 for a table of common extensions and more on cross-platform issues.

3. **Add the essential contents of Director's application — including the Director application, Director 5 Help, and Director 5 Resources — to the new folder/directory.**

4. **Add all movies and linked files to the project folder/directory.**

   Some of the files may be from different folders in your internal hard drive. Others may come from external drives and possibly CD-ROM clip art collections. See "Linking your imported file" in Chapter 4.

5. **For PC users, skip to step 7. On a Mac, open the project folder and artistically arrange the main movies and supporting files, as in Figure 12-6.**

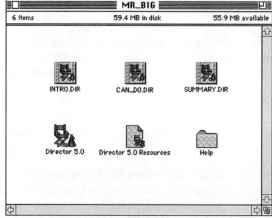

Figure 12-6:
The layout
of the
MR_BIG
folder.

The layout of icons is very deliberate. At the top, I place the Director movies representing the entire presentation. The gears and pulleys running the presentation — Director and its auxiliary files — are underneath the movies. You can resize the window so that only the starting movie is displayed in the window. The layout is purely aesthetic, in case the audience watching the movie sees the open project folder.

The content of the folder is important, too. When you tell Director to find a file, the first place Director looks is just inside its own folder, the *root level* of the folder, so placing necessary movies in the Director folder is especially important for a presentation when you want everything to go as smoothly as possible.

6. **Resize the project's window; shrink the window so that only the Director movies are visible, as in Figure 12-7.**

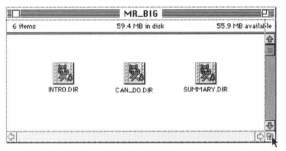

Figure 12-7: Resizing the MR_BIG window so that only Director movies are visible.

7. **Open the main movie in your project folder/directory.**

Adding a script to a movie

The following steps show you how to create an exitFrame handler telling Director to go to the next movie and play it. The handler kicks in when the playback head leaves the frame containing the handler. Use the play command to tell Director to play the movie named in your handler and then return to the place where the play command was issued.

1. **If the Score window isn't visible, choose Window⊅Score or press ⌘/Ctrl+0 (zero).**

2. **Locate the frame in the movie where you want to place your script.**

   In Figure 12-8, I'm getting ready to select frame 35 in the movie INTRO.MOV.

3. **Double-click the Script channel in the frame where you've decided to add the script.**

   Director displays the blank Score Script window, as shown in Figure 12-9.

   If Director provides you with a couple of lines of text, that's a good sign; it means Director likes you. Actually, it happens automatically. The first line of a Score script is set to `on exitFrame`, as in Figure 12-9, one of the most common types of handlers you'll use in Director. For right now, script and handler mean the same thing.

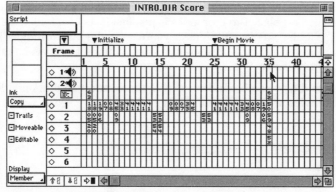

Figure 12-8:
Locating
frame 35 in
the Score
window of
the Director
movie
INTRO.DIR.

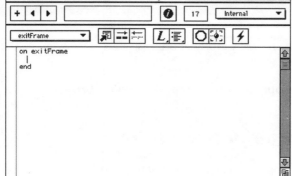

Figure 12-9:
Double-
clicking a
cell in the
Script
channel of
the Score
displays the
Score Script
window.

What does *exitFrame* mean? Well, Director knows when you're about to go to the next frame of a movie. The line on exitFrame tells Director to carry out any commands in the Score Script for that frame as the playback head leaves, or *exits,* the frame. The other line Director gives you automatically in the Score Script window, end, is simply required to end a script. That's Rule #5,793: Whenever you write a handler in Director, the last line must end with the word end.

Notice one other thing: Director sets you up with a blank second line, too. The vertical line shown in Figure 12-9 between the two lines of script isn't a character. It represents the blinking insertion point Director provides so that you can start typing immediately. Such decadence.

4. **Type** play movie, **followed by a space, and then the name of your movie surrounded by plain quotation marks (").**

The play movie command looks for a movie by name on the hard drive and opens the movie. The play movie command needs the name of a movie surrounded by regular quotes to operate successfully.

Trying to use the play movie command without the name of a movie prompts an alert from Director. After you write a script with something missing, misspelled, or containing some syntax problem, Director presents you with a script error alert, as shown in Figure 12-10. This is Director's attempt to be helpful and *debug*, or troubleshoot, a problem script for you. Without getting technical about what an *operand* is, notice the alert tells you that Director expects it in the script. (In this example, the operand missing is the name of the movie you want to play.) The alert includes the name of the problem command, `play movie`, and the question mark confirming that something's wrong. When you click Script to return to the Score Script window and correct the problem, Director kindly provides the blinking insertion point at the end of the bad line.

Figure 12-10:
Director
alerts you to
any script
errors.

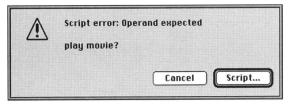

In my example, the completed line would now read

```
play movie "US_INC.MOV"
```

Important: Quote marks in scripts are the plain-vanilla variety, the same character you type to specify inches. Don't even think of adding fancy quotes (", ") in a script. You'll reverse the polarity of the Earth's magma and everything will be sucked into the blackness of outer space, where no one can hear you say, "How embarrassing."

5. **Click the Close box in the upper-left corner of the Score Script window to save the script.**

6. **Choose File⇨Save to update the Director movie.**

The play movie command works by zipping to the movie named in the script, playing the movie, and — provided that no command is found at the last frame of the new movie — returns to the first movie following the frame where play movie was issued.

Congratulations, Professor Higgins. You've just written your first Director script. Anyhow, you haven't taken one critical step: testing your work. Always test your scripts thoroughly. Try to mess things up. Everyone else will.

Testing your scripts

1. Choose File⇨Open.

2. Select the movie in the Directory containing the play movie command and click Open.

3. Press ⌘/Ctrl+Option/Alt+P to play the Director movie.

4. Check that Director executes the exitFrame handler, goes to the second movie, plays it, and returns to the first movie following the frame where play movie was issued.

Now, where's that bottle of champagne?

Chapter 13

Messages from Beyond: The Message and Debugger Windows

In This Chapter

▶ Playing with beeps

▶ Testing Lingo commands

▶ Watching your movie from the Message window

▶ Debugging the bugs

*O*ne thing you can say of Director is that it doesn't lack windows. The Stage window is always hanging around. It's the one window you can't hide. Sure, you can change its dimensions in the Movie Properties dialog box under the Modify menu, but you can't close the Stage window. It doesn't even have a Close box.

Aside from the Stage window, you'll probably do most of your work in the Score window, the timeline of your movie. You may also do a lot of work in the Cast window, depending on how many files you import and whether you like to rearrange the Cast Members every half hour so that things look nice and neat. After you take the plunge and start making handlers in Lingo — Director's built-in language — you'll find yourself in a Script window for one Director object or another.

After you start working with Lingo and the Script window, you may find that the Message and Debugger windows are your best allies. Macromedia designed them to be your very own digital pals.

The Message Window

When you start using Lingo commands, the Message window is a great way to play with bits and pieces of Lingo — as long as you use the Message window from the perspective of playing a game and having a great time while discovering the idiosyncrasies of a somewhat bizarre language. After all, you're trying to communicate with your computer and its little chips of silicon, and if that's not bizarre, I don't know what is.

Why am I making this suggestion? Frankly, because delving into Lingo can be as frustrating as taking up any new language — just like that French class in college where you weren't allowed to speak a word of English the moment you stepped inside the room. The properties, commands, and other Lingo stuff you read about are just tools. If you're an artist, after you get the hang of holding a pencil comfortably in your hand, it's up to you to draw something beautiful, powerful, or terrifying with it. Beyond a basic mastery of Director's tools, including Lingo, you'll need to use the tools creatively. Even after using Lingo commands for a while, you'll still need to experiment. The Message window is great for letting your creativity fly because it gives you instant feedback.

Playing with Lingo commands in the Message Window

I'm sure you've heard your system beep many times. You can enter a Lingo command in the Message window to make that beep happen at the drop of a hat. Open the Message window by choosing Window⇨Message or press ⌘/Ctrl+M. Note the warm `Welcome to Director` message in Figure 13-1.

Your Message window includes a blinking insertion point, a signal from your computer that it's waiting for you to start entering text in the window. To play with one of Lingo's commands in the Message window — the beep command, for example — you need follow only two basic rules. First, type the command, and then press Return or Enter. It's that easy in the Message window.

Figure 13-1:
The Message window, where you can experiment with Lingo commands.

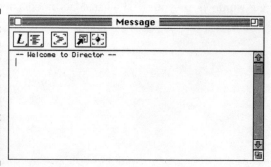

```
-- Welcome to Director --
|
```

After you take a few minutes to memorize the basic rules just listed, try the beep command in the Message window. Type **beep** and press Return or Enter.

Director plays the System beep. *Instant* feedback. That's what makes the Message window so great. You don't need to create a button or even call up the Script window.

The beep command is a kind of command that accepts optional information modifying its result. Lingo types call this optional info a *parameter.* The beep command accepts an optional value followed by a space and the word *times* after its name and plays the System beep accordingly. For example, type **beep 2 times** and press Return or Enter.

Great, Director plays the system beep two times. I can see the power going to your head already. But as you go along with your Lingo career, you learn that some words are just window dressing to make Lingo sound more conversational. I'll let you in on a big secret; Director doesn't really need the word *times.* For example, type **beep 2** and press Return or Enter.

Director still beeps twice, so the word *times* is really just smoke and mirrors. Now, sometimes you may forget the proper *syntax,* or arrangement of words, when writing Lingo scripts. Just for laughs, enter **beep for 2 times** and press Return or Enter. Director objects to the word *for* and presents you with a nasty-looking script error alert, as in Figure 13-2. Try it yourself. You'll laugh.

Figure 13-2:
Director presents you with a script error alert when you try to get away with bad Lingo.

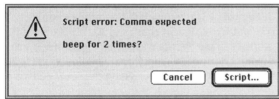

Notice what the script error alert says and doesn't say. According to the alert, Director expects a comma in the line of Lingo. Then the alert repeats the line you typed, `beep for 2 times`, and adds a question mark. That's the problem with many script error alerts. Part of the message may be nonsensical, another part too ambiguous to be of much use. The script error alert doesn't say anything about it being wrong to use the word *for* in the beep command. So you need to take an error message with a grain of salt, accept the fact that something's wrong with the line of Lingo, and find out whether the alert gives you any solid clues pointing to the problem and its solution.

Often the problem with Lingo is a simple typo. Carefully look over the command for any misspelled words. After that, the problem is typically a syntax problem, meaning that you didn't write the Lingo command in the right order or you left out a necessary parameter.

Tracing the Action from the Message Window

You eagle-eyed readers out there in ReaderLand may have caught me. I haven't mentioned a very distinctive feature of the Message window. Right, the row of five intriguing icons at the top of the window. Actually, four of them are covered in "Where Good Scripts Go" in Chapter 12, but I'll review their names and then focus on the Trace button unique to the Message window.

From left to right, the Message window icons are

- ✔ Alphabetical Lingo pop-up menu
- ✔ Categorized Lingo pop-up menu
- ✔ Trace button (not covered in Chapter 12)
- ✔ Go to Handler button
- ✔ Watch Expression button

 When you click the Trace button, shown at left, Director logs messages and scripts in the Message window as they occur in your movie on playback. Without getting too technical, *messages* are descriptions of what Director-types call *events*. For example, every time you click the mouse, you generate a mouseDown event and a mouseUp event that refer to the action of the mouse button. Director describes these events with mouseDown messages and mouseUp messages. You only have to worry about ten different types of messages in Director. For more details on message types, see the "Events" section in Chapter 17.

 A script in its own window is made up of one or more *handlers*. A handler is comprised of a number of Lingo lines beginning with on followed by a space and the name of the handler (on mouseDown, for example), followed by one or more Lingo commands, and ending with the word end on its own line.

With the Trace button in the Message window turned on, the Message window logs scripts as they're executed. One way of thinking of a script is like a customized mousetrap waiting for one particular type of "mouse" or message to trap. The message travels through the Cast Members of your movie and their associated scripts, through a maze called the *message hierarchy*. A script beginning with the line on mouseDown is a custom trap just waiting for a mouseDown message to pass by. At that time, the mouseDown script catches or traps the mouseDown message, preventing it from traveling through the rest of the message hierarchy, and the script is executed.

All this craziness is what the Message window records — as it happens — when you turn on the Trace button, as in Figure 13-3.

Figure 13-3: With the Trace option turned on, the Message window records scripts as Director executes them on playback.

Why turn on the Trace button in the first place? Well, it's a great way to kill a rainy weekend. Just turn on your Trace button, settle down with a hot cup of java, and, before you know it, it's Monday. Didn't someone once say, "Time's fun when you're having flies"?

Anyway, the more conventional reason to turn on the Trace button is to help uncover a problem area in your movie — a process that Lingo types call *debugging,* a crucial part of the development process when you're trying to iron out all the kinks, a topic covered later in this chapter.

The Trace feature is pretty clear when it detects a problem. It slams on the brakes, and your whole movie comes to a screeching halt. Take a look at Figure 13-4. The Message window has recorded the following:

- ✔ The Welcome message
- ✔ The name of the next handler, startup
- ✔ The startup handler being executed (what —> means)
- ✔ A kind of comment in the Message window with Trace on (what == means), that startup comes from a handler in Script window 16
- ✔ The name of the handler, startup, again
- ✔ A list of commands inside the startup handler as they are executed, and so on

Figure 13-4:
The Trace
button's
recording
function
helps
uncover
problem
areas in the
script.

```
▤☐ ▤▤▤▤ Message ▤▤▤ ▥▧
L▐〒, ▦ ▨⊡
   -- Welcome to Director--        ⬆
startup
--> startup|
== Script: 16 Handler:
startup
--> set the soundLevel to 7
--> set the colorDepth to 8
--> preLoadCast 5
--> beepSound
== Script: 6 Handler:
beepSound
--> beep 2
--> end
== Script: 16 Handler:
startup                           ⬇
.                                 ▣
```

If the script abruptly stops while you're using the Message window, Director is telling you that it has found a problem in the last line. In addition, just to hit you over the head with it, Director probably brings up a script error alert such as the one shown in Figure 13-5. Director tells you that it has found a script error; in this case, a property hasn't been found in the first line of the handler `go to the frames`.

Figure 13-5:
A Script
error alert
informing
you of a
problem line
of Lingo
scripting.

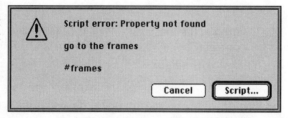

```
⚠   Script error: Property not found

     go to the frames

     #frames

                  [ Cancel ]  [ Script... ]
```

When you encounter an error, look for typos and syntax problems. The line `go to the frames` in the error message is a form of Lingo's go command that allows the movie to continue playback but keeps you in the same frame, except in this case, there's a typo. It should read `go to the frame` without an *s*. That's the kind of error the Message window can help point out to you, as if your computer were playing charades with you. First word. Sounds like . . .

The Debugger Window

One of the less-enjoyable chores of making multimedia is *debugging,* trouble-shooting an ailing script. Director 5 makes the chore a lot more tolerable with the new Debugger window, shown in Figure 13-6.

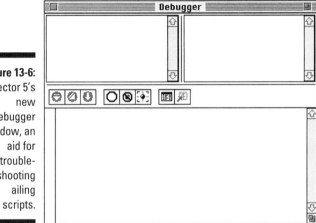

Figure 13-6:
Director 5's
new
Debugger
window, an
aid for
trouble-
shooting
ailing
scripts.

Director provides a bouquet of options for opening the Debugger window.

- ✔ Choose Window⇨Debugger.

- ✔ Add a breakpoint in a Script window. The Debugger appears automatically when Director encounters a breakpoint in a script. (See Chapter 12.)

- ✔ Some error messages include a Debug button, as shown in Figure 13-7. Click Debug to display the Debugger window with helpful information, as in Figure 13-8.

Figure 13-7:
A script
error
message
including
the Debug
button.

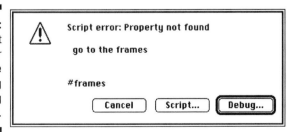

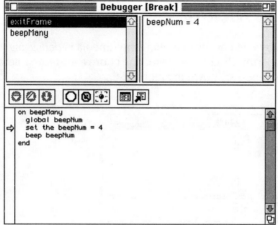

Figure 13-8:
The
Debugger
window with
some
trouble-
shooting
hints.

Although the Debugger can't often tell exactly what the problem is, it provides tools to lead you to the solution of a scripting dilemma.

- ✔ **Handlers History pane:** A list of the handlers in trouble appears in the upper-left scrolling field of the Debugger window.

- ✔ **Script pane:** Director displays each problem handler in the large field of the Debugger window one at a time in the order in which Director encounters the handlers. Notice in Figure 13-8 that an arrow points to the very line causing a problem in the current problem handler. (Don't count on always seeing this arrow.)

- ✔ **Variable pane:** The Debugger window displays values (variables and properties) related to the problem handler currently being debugged in the upper-right field. See Chapter 17 for info on variables and properties.

Director 5 blew it in one respect. Even though you can make a selection in the three fields included in the Debugger window, you can't correct handlers in the window. To edit a handler, you must click the Go to Handler button, the last button on the right, to go to the handler's Script window. Blech!

The Debugger window's row of eight buttons, which aid you in troubleshooting a problem handler, includes from left to right:

- ✔ **Step Script:** Executes the current line of the problem handler and then stops at the beginning of the next line. Step Script does not jump to so-called *nested handlers* (a handler that calls a handler). Use Step Script to determine whether a suspect line contributes to the problem or causes incorrect values to be computed by watching for changes in the Variable pane of the Debugger window.

✔ **Step into Script:** Executes the handler as Director normally executes Lingo, line by line with each click of the mouse, jumping to nested handlers and back to the main handler until the Debugger stops and flags a problem.

✔ **Run Script:** Executes handlers consecutively until the Debugger encounters a problem, at which point the movie stops and the Debugger attempts to display troubleshooting info in one or more of its three panes.

✔ **Toggle Breakpoint:** One of those goofy toggle buttons. Click once and Toggle Breakpoint adds a bullet-like breakpoint to the currently selected line in a handler; click again and the breakpoint is removed. Director stops playback at every breakpoint and displays the Debugger window.

✔ **Ignore Breakpoints:** Click for the Debugger window to ignore any breakpoints encountered in all handlers within a movie.

✔ **Watch Expression:** Click to add a value (variable or expression) selected in the currently displayed problem handler to the Watcher window. See Chapter 12 for more info on the Watcher window.

✔ **Watcher window:** Click to display the Watcher window, which keeps track of different types of values as a Director movie plays back. (See Chapter 12.)

✔ **Go to Handler:** Click to go to the currently selected handler's Script window, where you can alter the handler.

Chapter 14

Twick or Tweak: The Tweak Palette

In This Chapter

▶ Having fun with the Tweak palette

▶ Reviewing the x-y coordinate thing

*W*hat can you say about a window that is about the size of a thumb with tiny cryptic boxes inside and a button with a silly name? It has got to be the funniest window — palette, actually — in all Directordom. In fact, I'm going to up the Tweak palette rating from funny to hilarious.

Anyway, the Tweak palette is actually useful.

When Mousing Around Just Isn't Enough

The Tweak palette is under the Modify menu. Choose it and up comes the . . . heh, ha-ha, hee-hee-hee, oh hah-ha. Excuse me, I just can't help myself. Self-control, Lauren Steinhauer.

Okay, after you've got the (hee) Tweak palette up and running, it doesn't look very (ha-ha) impressive. But sometimes moving an object with the mouse is a royal pain. In the early days of computers, someone once likened using the mouse to drawing with a cake of soap. Ergo, the Tweak palette, as shown in Figure 14-1.

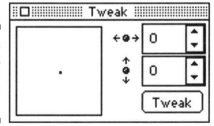

Figure 14-1:
The Tweak window, a laugh a minute.

Notice the zeros in the two boxes in the upper-right corner. You say you're having a hard time finding them? Ho-ho-ho. Hee-hee. Please, my sides. Oh, yes, the values, right. These are the x and y coordinates of the *Cartesian plane*. For an explanation of a Cartesian plane, check out the next section; it may also save your reputation at your next cocktail party (pronounced *beer bust*).

Have you run into the term *sprite* yet? (No, not the drink.) Cast Members on the Stage are referred to as sprites. Okay, with a sprite on the Stage that you'd like to move in small steps, try the following:

1. **Click the sprite on the Stage.**

2. **If the Tweak palette is not visible, choose Modify⇨Tweak.**

   At this point, make believe that the sprite starts out sharing the same coordinate values displayed in the Tweak palette.

3. **Press halfway between the dot in the center of the square and the upper-right corner of the Tweak palette.**

   A thick, black line emerges from the center of the square and values appear in the small boxes on the right side of the Tweak palette, as in Figure 14-2.

Figure 14-2:
The Tweak window displaying how far and in which direction a selected sprite is to be displaced.

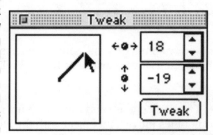

4. **Keeping the mouse button down, drag the mouse in various directions.**

   Note how the thick, black line follows the mouse and how Director continuously updates the values. By the way, you're not limited to staying inside the small dimensions of the Tweak (ha-ha-ha) palette.

5. **If you haven't tried it, drag the mouse beyond the Tweak palette.**

   The black line doesn't visibly extend beyond the Tweak palette but clearly follows the movement of the mouse, and the x and y coordinates continue to update, as in Figure 14-3.

Figure 14-3:
The Tweak
window can
record x
and y values
beyond its
small
dimensions.

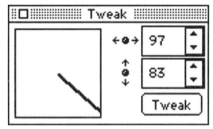

6. **Click the mouse when the Tweak palette indicates values close to how much you'd like to move the sprite.**

7. **Click Tweak.**

Note how the selected sprite moves according to the values displayed in the Tweak palette. Each time you click the Tweak button, the sprite moves again by the values currently shown in the Tweak palette.

Please keep in mind that the values displayed in the Tweak palette are *relative* values, meaning that they don't show a selected sprite's actual location on the Stage but merely how far up, down, or across from its current location the sprite moves with a click of the Tweak button.

Okay, Now Review That X-Y Coordinate Thing

Back in the moldy old 17th century, a Frenchman by the name of Renatus Cartesius was working on a number of grand projects, especially changing his name. Better known as René Descartes, he's given credit for establishing the foundation of analytic geometry and for the famous saying, "Never put Descartes before the horse." Or was it, "I think, therefore I am"?

Anyway, you're interested in Descartes for his creation of a coordinate system used for pinpointing any location on a flat surface. Horizontal locations are set along the x axis and vertical locations along the y axis. You can designate any point on a surface by giving its location along the x and y axes. Starting from an origin at 0,0 (0 for x and 0 for y), locations move in a positive direction down and to the right and negative directions up and to the left. If this stuff confuses you, you can check out Figure 14-4 to get a better idea.

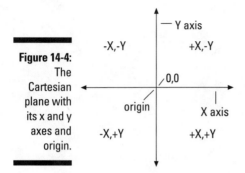

Figure 14-4:
The
Cartesian
plane with
its x and y
axes and
origin.

In fact, click inside the Tweak palette and drag up and to the left of center of the square and note the negative x and y coordinates displayed in its little boxes. In Director and most other programs, the origin is in the upper-left corner of the screen, so all x and y coordinates remain positive. Of course, the units of measure can be anything from inches, millimeters, and typographers' points to *pixels,* the unit of measure of the (ha-ha-ho) Tweak palette. I can't take (hee-hee-ha-ha) it anymore. I'd better go on to the next chapter. Oh, my sides.

Chapter 15

Your Pals, the Markers Window and the New Window Command

In This Chapter

▶ Creating markers

▶ Using the New Window command

*N*ever let it be said that Director lets you down. Out of the kindness of its heart, Macromedia Director gives you umpteen windows, and then it gives you even more. The Markers window is a note to yourself, a permanent ID for key frames in your movie, a printable outline, and a great dessert topping, too.

Introducing your pal and mine: the Markers window.

So What Are Markers Anyway?

Think of markers as bookmarks, only better. Why is that so important, you ask? Good question; have a lump of sugar. Well, for one thing, markers help organize your movie in the Score window and flag important or key frames, as in Figure 15-1. Also, you can add a name and note for each marker in the Markers window that prints out at high resolution, so you can distribute the notes as an outline to members of your design team and clients.

Another great feature about markers is that their names and notes stay with their frames even when you shuffle frames around as you edit a movie. For example, if you have a movie that's 30 frames long, and you add three frames to the beginning, frame 30 becomes frame 33. A Lingo script that refers to frame 30 now affects or references the wrong frame, the frame that used to be frame 27. On the other hand, if you write a Lingo script that refers to the contents of a frame by its marker name, the Lingo script will always be correct. Markers move with the contents of their frames even after you add or delete other frames in the Score.

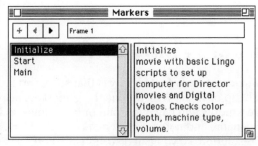

Figure 15-1:
The Score
window with
markers for
frames 1, 10
and 17.

As you orchestrate your Director movie in the Score window, mark important frames by pressing the Markers button (where the arrow pointer is at in Figure 15-1) and dragging a marker above the Frame channel you want to mark. Review frames in Chapter 5.

To name a marker and add a note, display the Markers window, hand illuminated with Old World craftsmanship in Figure 15-2, by choosing Window⇨Markers, pressing ⌘/Ctrl+Shift+M, or simply double-clicking one of the markers in the Score.

Figure 15-2:
The Markers
Window,
where you
can name
markers in
the Score
window and
add notes to
pass long,
rainy
weekends.

At first, the Markers window is blank as a polar bear in a snowstorm. (Drop me a line, I'd love to hear *your* favorite trite phrase.) To name the marker, click within the right scrolling field of the Markers window.

Beware: The Markers window is slightly flaky. Regardless of how many markers you may place in the Score window, the Markers window *appears* blank before you enter some text. But the window is not really blank. For each marker you create, Director reserves a line in the left field. For example, if you create three markers in the Score and call up the Markers window, you'll find that you can highlight the first three lines in the left field one at a time even though the lines are blank. They're just waiting for you to fill them in at your leisure. By the way, note that as you click a blank line, the playback head in the Score jumps to the corresponding frame.

Sometimes the window appears with an insertion point ready and waiting for you to enter text in the right scrolling field, sometimes not. If not, manually click the right scrolling field. Sometimes the Markers window doesn't accept a click in the right scrolling field. If so, click the left field in the Markers window first, and then click the right scrolling field. Life is weird.

After you highlight one of the blank lines in the left field of the Markers window, establish an insertion point in the right scrolling field of the Markers window and enter a name for the marker in the first line. If you want to add a note, be sure to press Return and begin your note on the *second* line. Remember, Director considers any text in the first line part of the marker name. Be sure to press Return to separate the marker name from its accompanying note. Repeat this process for each marker you want to name and describe with a note.

You can toggle between the Markers window and the markers in the Score by pressing ⌘/Ctrl+W to close the Markers window and double-clicking a marker in the Score to reopen the Markers window. (This is another great way to make a rainy weekend fly by.)

To print the contents of the Markers window, choose the Markers window. Then choose File⇨Print and consider the options in the Print dialog box, shown in Figure 15-3. Choose Marker Comments, for example, from the Print pop-up menu and decide whether you want the currently selected markers, all markers, or a range of marker comments printed. When you're ready, click Print.

When you start writing numerous Lingo scripts in a movie, you can use the go command with a frame's marker name to add meaning to the line of Lingo. For example, instead of saying in Lingo, `go to frame 10` — which doesn't say much — you can say instead, `go to marker ("Finale")`. Director moves the playback head to the frame marked `Finale`. With luck, some dynamite special effect starting on that frame is just waiting to kick in and sweep the members of your audience off their feet.

Use only plain quotes whenever you enter programming code. Director is very picky about this. In the example line of Lingo, `go to marker ("Finale")`, be sure to use plain old-fashioned quote characters (Shift+apostrophe), not fancy beginning and ending quotes (", ").

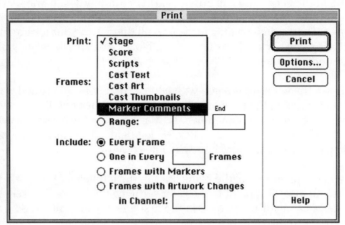

Figure 15-3:
Choose Marker Comments from the Print pop-up menu in the Print dialog box to output comments as high-resolution text.

A Word about the New Window Command

The New Window command in the Window menu only works with a Text, Cast, Video, or Script window when the window is active. New Window creates another window representing the same Cast Member.

New Window is great when using Director to edit QuickTime mooVs, either to use in a Director movie as a Digital Video Cast Member or to export as a stand-alone QuickTime mooV. For more information about digital video and QuickTime, jump back to Chapter 11.

In Chapter 11, I discuss cutting and pasting a new QuickTime mooV together. During this editing process, calling on the New Window command can be very useful, especially for a long sequence. After choosing Window⇔New Window for an active Video window, you can use the new window to move to a different part of the QuickTime mooV, as shown in Figure 15-4.

Suppose that one window shows frame 1 of the sequence, as usual. In the second window, you may fast forward to the middle of the sequence and cut and paste between the beginning and middle sequences to a third blank Video window. Even high-powered QuickTime editing programs like Adobe Premiere have a hard time duplicating the ease of this kind of editing.

You need to understand that the original and duplicate windows refer to the same Cast Member, so edits in either window directly change the Cast Member. You should remember this fact especially when editing Video windows in Director because the original source file is always linked to the Cast Member. Edits in Director actually change the original external file on disk.

Figure 15-4:
Two different views of the same Digital Video Cast Member, thanks to the New Window command.

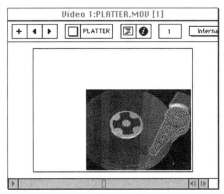 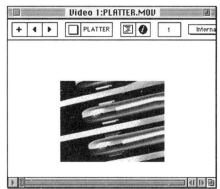

Press Option/Alt when you choose New Window from the Window menu for a Text, Script, or Field window to create a new window of the same Cast Member. Otherwise, the Text, Script, or Field window is replaced with a blank new window.

Part IV

More Interaction, Please!

The 5th Wave   By Rich Tennant

OK—NOW SIT BACK AND GET READY TO EXPERIENCE THIS MEMO.

MULTI-MEDIA FAXING LAB

In this part . . .

When the Altair 8800, the world's first personal computer, hit the stands on the cover of *Popular Electronics* back in 1975, people couldn't wait to busy their hands assembling it. Funny thing was, no one could say why, or what they were going to do with all that silicon after they slapped it together.

If you've got the same kind of trouble articulating why you were just born to do interactive Director stuff and whip up stunning animations for the World Wide Web with Shockwave, Part IV has a haystack full of fodder for you, from making animated presentations with Animation Wizard with the push of a button to why learning Lingo should be high on your To Do list, just under "Change underwear."

Chapter 16

Hey, Kids! Be an Animation Wizard

In This Chapter

▶ Introducing Animation Wizard

▶ Setting up Animation Wizard

▶ Creating animation effects

*O*ne of the easiest, most pleasant ways to get into animation is with Director 5's Animation Wizard Xtra. It's about as close as you can get to instant animation. Be sure to stir thoroughly.

Discovering Animation Wizard

A whole slew (or is that a gaggle?) of wondrous text effects are hiding in the Xtras menu under the name Animation Wizard. By choosing Xtras⇨Animation Wizard, something like Figure 16-1 should appear.

By choosing from Banners, Zooms, Credits, and Bullets, deciding from a bouquet of options, and clicking the Create button, you tell Director to create the required sprites, place them in the Score, and set you up for flying, zooming, and gesticulating text and chart graphics.

The fun doesn't stop after all this frenetic action is set up for you. The objects are now on the Stage and in the Score, ready and waiting for you to modify them. (Find Stage info in Chapter 3, Score info in Chapter 5.) You can add gradients (color blends) and effects to bullets for a 3-D effect, fudge bars in a chart closer together, or replace the out-of-the-box graphic with a new glitzy one using the Switch Cast Members command in the Score menu. (Read more than you ever wanted to know about Cast Members in Chapter 4.) Let Director do the leg work; then add the final spit and polish yourself.

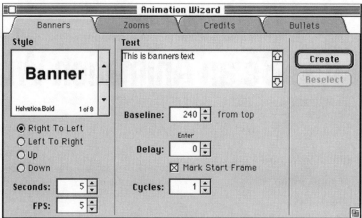

Figure 16-1:
Animation
Wizard,
hiding under
the Xtras
menu,
allows you
to build
push-button
animation.

Setting Up for Animation Wizard

Getting to Animation Wizard is pretty easy. But first, be sure that you have a variety of fonts in your system. After all, you're dealing with text effects; it doesn't hurt to have great fonts handy for inspiration. Try a variety of styles. Think in terms of contrasts; for example, a sans serif font like Helvetica or Avant Garde with a serif font like Palatino or Goudy and a mix of display type, unusual, ornamental, and heavy-weight fonts for graphic impact.

At the same time, getting carried away is easy. The general rule is to be careful when you use more than two different types of fonts in one screen.

Be conservative with the number of fonts you install at one time. Too many fonts bloat the system, making your Mac or PC work harder than it should. More important, Animation Wizard includes a preview feature based on the number of fonts installed in your system. In other words, if you have 50 fonts installed, you may find yourself clicking back and forth though 50 previews in Animation Wizard (gosh knows how many times) before you decide on a font for your effect. See "A closer look at Animation Wizard," later in the section.

If ever there was a time you wanted a product called *ATM* (Adobe Type Manager) installed in your system, this is it. ATM works with PostScript fonts to build screen text on the fly at any point size you choose. Spot PostScript fonts by the couplet of files per font you install in your system, the screen font that looks like a little suitcase, and the printer font that usually looks like a laser printer. The suitcase font provides a limited number of font sizes for displaying the font on-screen, usually from 8 to 24 point. Without ATM, your goose is cooked if you need anything larger than 24-point text. That's where ATM comes in to save the day. The result? No more infamous *jaggies,* those ugly stair-stepped diagonal lines so common to bitmaps displayed on-screen. If you're not using ATM yet, get it and will it to your progeny. Trust me. And be sure that, with Director 5, you have at least Version 3.8 for your Mac or 3.0 for Windows.

You can also use TrueType fonts to get rid of the jaggies that occur with fonts displayed at large screen sizes. These days, Apple and Microsoft include a standard set of TrueType fonts with their operating systems. You can purchase any number of additional TrueType fonts, too. What's so great about TrueType fonts? They have ATM-like routines built into them; a similar technology builds the screen font on the fly at the required size so that you and your family avoid the social stigma of jaggies. By the way, if you decide to add fonts to your system, you need to quit Director first.

You PC types can use the Fonts Control Panel as usual to add or delete fonts in Windows. For you Macaholics, if you're unsure about fonts, check Table 16-1 to find out where your fonts are and how to add them to your computer.

Table 16-1	Where Do Fonts Go in My Mac?	
System Version	**Where Fonts Go**	**Add a Font by**
6.08	Screen fonts in System file	Using Apple Font/DA Mover
	Printer fonts in the System folder	Dragging over the System folder
	TrueType fonts in the System folder*	Dragging over the System folder
7.0	Screen fonts in the System file	Dragging over the System folder
	Printer fonts in the System folder	Dragging over the System folder
	TrueType fonts in the System file	Dragging over the System folder
7.1–7.5	All fonts in the Fonts folder	Dragging over the System folder

*System 6.07 and 6.08 require a TrueType INIT to use TrueType fonts.

With System 7, your Mac recognizes the type of font that you're installing and where the file(s) should go in the System folder. You see an alert box, asking whether you'd like your Mac to continue. Click OK and grab a cup of java.

After you add a *limited* number of great-looking fonts to your computer, open Director and choose Xtras⇨Animation Wizard. Notice the index card metaphor organized by type of animated presentation.

Animation Wizard effects are push-button animation sequences that Director builds for you in a matter of seconds. All you have to do is replace placeholder text with your own text and set options with various controls including buttons, sliders, and pop-up menus. That's part of the fun of using Animation Wizard features; don't be afraid to experiment.

Previewing Animation Wizard Effects

Rather than trying to describe Animation Wizard's effects with mere words, I'll show you how to preview quickly them for yourself.

1. **First, call up the Score window by choosing Window⇨Score or press ⌘/Ctrl+4.**

2. **In an empty channel of the Score, click frame 1.**

3. **Three channels down, click frame 25.**

   Now you've selected frames 1 through 25 in four consecutive frames of the Score. Animation Wizard's smart, but not smart enough to select frames for you. Look over Chapter 5 if you need to review the Score, channels, or frames.

4. **Choose Xtras⇨Animation Wizard.**

5. **Click Banners, the first effect, and go along with the default settings.**

   Previewing works best if you go in order of the effects.

6. **If the Reselect button is enabled, click Reselect.**

7. **Click Create.**

8. **Press ⌘/Ctrl+1 (one) to hide all windows and view the animation.**

9. **Press ⌘/Ctrl+Option/Alt+P to play the movie.**

   Now you can preview the animation for yourself. For each additional effect, press ⌘/Ctrl+1. If the Score window is in front of Animation Wizard, click on any part of Animation Wizard's window peeking through, click the next effect, and repeat steps 6 through 8. The last effect, Bullets, is a little flaky. You may have to start with step 2 to preview it.

The next section, "Creating Zooming Text with Animation Wizard," shows you in detail how to set up a Zooms effect with Animation Wizard, the most complex of the four types of animations available. I'm sure that you can figure out the small differences between setting up the other effects.

Creating Zooming Text with Animation Wizard

I've hinted that Animation Wizard effects are push-button heaven, like some decadent dream out of the '50s when people envisioned the coming age of automation and a push-button world of leisure. You've probably seen the images in old movies and commercials. Push a button, and your bed gets made by silent and invisible mechanical hands; the bed somehow swings into the wall, leaving no seams. Push another button, and a tray of steaming food slides into view from a stainless steel slot, utensils set properly, and a flower and vase popping into place by themselves. Yes, it's the Food-O-Matic, folks, in a Jetsons-style nightmare.

A closer look at Animation Wizard

Take a good look at the interface for Animation Wizard's Zooms effect, shown in Figure 16-2. I picked this effect to demo because it displays the largest number of options and types of controls.

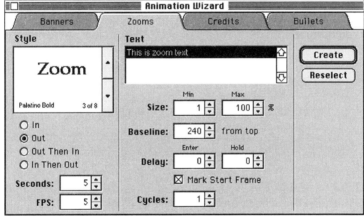

Figure 16-2:
Animation options available for the Zooms effect.

The general scheme of things goes as follows:

✔ **Style:** In the upper-left corner, you find a preview of the current font with its name in the lower-left corner of the Style panel and the number of fonts previewed in the lower-right corner. The size of the previewed font is the same text size that appears in the animation. Click through fonts with the up and down arrow controls on the right side of the Style panel.

✔ **Text:** To the right of the Style panel are one or more lines of sample text in a generic type style. Each style of effect calls for its own specific layout: *Credits* calls for a mix of bold and regular weight type on each line and extends several lines of text; separate bold from regular weight text with a colon (:). *Bullets* calls for a bold title as the first line and regular weight lines of bulleted text underneath. Remember, each line needs its own channel reserved and selected in the Score. Chapter 5 tells you all about the Score and channels.

✔ **Entry fields:** As with Zooms text, you see entry fields for Size, Baseline, Delay, Seconds, FPS (frames per second), and other details of the effect. Try the default values if you like and change them later. Part of the fun of Animation Wizard is experimenting.

✔ **Radio/option buttons:** Provided to give you one choice among several options.

✔ **Check boxes:** Provided to give you one or more choices among several options. For example, check Mark Start Frame so that Animation Wizard puts a marker in the Score window at the first frame of your animation. Not found in the Zooms effect, try Animate Title in the Bullets effect to make the title move in addition to the bullet points. Easy, right?

Animation Wizard's basic scenario

Animation Wizard is kind of like a mad, push-button utopian dream. Basically, you go through a grueling couple of bouts of button-pushing. Here's the basic scenario:

1. **Click the effect you want to build in Animation Wizard: Banners, Zooms, Credits, or Bullets.**

2. **Replace sample text in Animation Wizard with your own text.**

   By now, you should know that typing automatically replaces selected text anywhere in Cyberspace. Same thing here. Couldn't be easier unless you train Igor, trusty but aromatic assistant, to do the typing for you.

3. **Set all optional values and conditions in the entry fields, radio/option buttons, and check boxes.**

4. **Choose Window⇨Score and select the number of channels needed for your animation.**

   Remember, each line of text in Animation Wizard requires its own channel. Remember channels? The horizontal sequence of cells in the Score window?

5. **Press Create.**

Did that go by too fast for you? Really, that's it. Director takes over, creates all the frames for you, sets up the Score, adds Cast Members to the Cast window and sprites to the Stage, and throws in a manicure and pedicure to boot — no extra charge.

Chapter 17

A Closer Look at Lingo

In This Chapter
▶ Dealing with Lingo
▶ Creating handlers
▶ Working with scripts

*L*ingo's something you have to talk yourself into, like putting on a tie, washing the car, or getting married. You may have heard scary stories about Lingo. They're all true.

Just kidding. It's not as bad as it used to be. Lingo's a lot more like everyday speech in Director 5. Of course, if you're still working on everyday speech . . .

Anyway, if you need a morale booster, jump back to Chapter 12. I show you that learning Lingo is something a four-year-old child can handle. So if you have a four-year-old child handy, you're all set. You can even try the sample script in that chapter and live to tell about it.

This chapter delves more deeply into Lingo than Chapter 12 and gives you some essential information about using a computer language. You can use this background info for getting started with just about any programming language, in fact.

Okay, Take a Deep Breath — Lingo's Not That Hard

As programming languages go, Lingo's a breeze. Lingo's referred to as a *high-level computer language*, meaning that it sounds and feels like everyday conversation. The opposite of Lingo is a low-level programming language like *machine language*, in which you wade through 0s and 1s, or *assembly language*, which uses hexadecimal code (a numbering system with 16 digits). How would you like to cozy up to stuff that looks like 5765 6C63 6F6D 6520 746F 2040 6163 696E 746F 7368 for eight or ten hours at a stretch? That's hexadecimal, by the way, for "Welcome to Macintosh."

Although Lingo feels conversational, the experience of learning Lingo is very close to tackling a foreign language with its special rules, distinctive syntax, and unique set of words to learn, small in number though they may be in Lingo. Oh, yes, *syntax* is the way words are arranged to form meaningful clauses or sentences. Lewis Carroll had a great time playing with syntax in *Alice in Wonderland* when he wrote, "'Not the same thing a bit!' said the Hatter. 'You might just as well say that "I see what I eat" is the same thing as "I eat what I see"!'" Or was that the Disney version?

And don't forget Director's online help. I don't attempt to cover everything about Lingo, not even all the basics. Use this chapter as a kind of social event without the booze to turn Lingo from stranger to warm acquaintance. When you encounter something you don't understand while playing with Lingo, remember to choose Help. Better yet, press ⌘/Ctrl+?, and Director's special Help cursor appears. If you're working in the Script window, the Lingo pop-up menus are never more than a click away. Choose a problem Lingo item under the menu with the special Help cursor, and Director takes you right to that topic in Help. For a refresher course on Director's built-in Help system, jump back to Chapter 1.

Touring Basic Lingo Concepts

Now, I'm going to take you on a whirlwind tour of some basic programming concepts that apply to Lingo and most other computer languages. If something doesn't make sense, take a break, wash the cat, and feed the car. Then return to this book, reminding yourself that plenty of people no smarter than you use Lingo every day for fun and profit.

Lingo

Lingo is Director's built-in programming language. Director hasn't always had a language. Its auspicious beginning as VideoWorks in 1985, one year after Apple introduced the Macintosh, gave Mac types a delightful black-and-white animation program to play with, but without Lingo and interactivity. Later, special editions of the program called VideoWorks Interactive introduced Lingo to the world. I characterize the first versions of Lingo as "difficult" and, between you, me, and the wall, I'm being generous. VideoWorks Interactive was always flaky, causing numerous freezes and all-around mayhem on the Mac.

Today's program is a far cry from its VideoWorks days. Director 5 is a slick, solid program on the Mac and PC, and Lingo is conversational and approachable. Lingo is still a computer language, and the time has come to face a few unusual characteristics all programming languages share, including Lingo.

If something doesn't make sense, don't worry. It doesn't mean that your IQ is slipping. It's new, that's all; with time, it all comes together. Trust me.

Operators

With the Script or Message window active, check out the Alphabetical Lingo pop-up menu. The first item you see is Operators with its submenu, as shown in Figure 17-1.

Figure 17-1:
Lingo's list
of Operators
under the
Alphabetical
Lingo icon in
a Script
window
or the
Message
window.

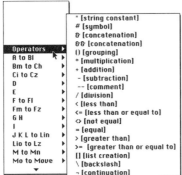

On second look, many of the symbols shown in the Operators submenu should be familiar. They're arithmetic operators like +, –, =, and *. In fact, in your halcyon school days, the teacher probably referred to them as *arithmetic operators*. Lingo's other operators are simply an extension of the same idea. You'll find a set of *comparison operators* in the submenu, too. For example, < means "less than," and >= means "greater than or equal to." You can use these operators in a line of Lingo to compare one value with another. Table 17-1 contains basic explanations of the operators in the order listed in the Operators submenu.

Table 17-1	The Operators Submenu	
Operator	*Function*	*Example*
#	Used to create a symbol instead of a variable for increased speed	Put #Lauren into firstName
&	Used to "glue" text, values, and variables together in a line of Lingo	Set the text of cast "Welcome Message" = "Hello," & firstName & "."

(continued)

Table 17-1 *(continued)*

Operator	*Function*	*Example*
&&	Same as above but automatically adds a space character between two elements	Set the text of cast "Welcome Message" = "Hello ," && firstName & "."
()	Forces Director to execute enclosed operators first in a list of operators	$5+(^9/_3+1)/4$
*	Multiplies one value by another	235*29
+	Adds one value to another	356+25
−	Subtracts one value from another	9 − 3
—	Disables a line of Lingo in a handler to include notes in a script	— The following line gets the machine model running Director
/	Divides one value by another	956/18
<	Less than	85+1<92
<=	Less than or equal to	90+2<=92
<>	Not equal	$^{85}/_2$<>92
=	Equals	85+15=100
>	Greater than	85+20>100
>=	Greater than or equal to	85+15>=100
[]	Used to specify items in a special Lingo form called a *list*	["Sunday", "Monday", "Tuesday", "Wednesday", "Thursday", "Friday", "Saturday"]
¬ (Option+ Return on Macs, Alt+ Enter on PCs)	Use as a "continued on next line" character in a Lingo script, not read as a return character Condition" = "God help us."	If moneySpent > moneyEarned, then ¬ set the text of cast "Financial

Commands

A *command* is a direction telling Director to accomplish a specific task during playback. All programming languages, including Lingo, have commands. In Director, the commands are listed alphabetically by initial letter in the Alphabetical Lingo pop-up menu after Operators, as shown in Figure 17-1. When you scroll to the initial letter of interest, a submenu appears and you can drag the mouse horizontally to choose one of the listed commands.

The go command is one of the most frequently used commands. When Director encounters a go command in the Script channel of the Score window, it executes the command like the stolid genie that it is. If you tell Director to go to frame 15 with a line of Lingo that reads `go to frame 15` in the Script channel of frame 10, the nanosecond Director lands on frame 10 the playback head jumps straight to frame 15, no questions asked — as long as you didn't leave behind any typos and your syntax is correct. Director's an uppity kind of genie, that's for sure. You know what they say: Give a genie an inch, and he'll walk a mile for a camel.

Functions

A *function* tries to pass itself off as an ordinary old command but makes itself conspicuously different with a telltale giveaway: A function always returns a value. For example, the function `the date` returns the current date as recorded by your computer's internal clock. Similarly, `the /time` returns the current time. Commands are hyper. Functions are mellow; they must have been developed in California.

You can use the Message window when you want to try out a function from the Lingo pop-up menu.

1. **Choose Window⇨Message to open the Message window.**

   Notice the Alphabetical Lingo pop-up menu in the upper-left corner of the Message window. Both the Script and the Message windows display the Alphabetical Lingo pop-up menu.

   You need to use a Lingo command, often the put command, with a function to get a result in the Message window. Otherwise, Director doesn't know what to do.

2. **Choose put from the P submenu, as shown in Figure 17-2.**

   The phrase `put expression` appears in the Message window on its own line. *Expression* is just a placeholder and appears selected because Director expects you to replace the expression with something meaningful.

   The put command finds some information and then places or "puts" it in the Message window.

3. **Choose a function from the Lingo pop-up menu.**

   For example, choose time from the T submenu and the phrase `the time` replaces the selected placeholder `expression`. By the way, *the* is another giveaway that *time* is a function; you'll find plenty of *the*s as you use functions — the time, the date, the key, and so on. Ad nauseam. *E pluribus unum.*

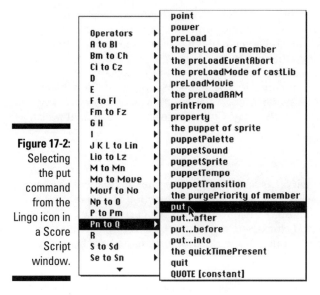

Figure 17-2:
Selecting
the put
command
from the
Lingo icon in
a Score
Script
window.

4. **Press Return to execute the line of Lingo in the Message window.**

   Underneath the line of Lingo you entered, Director displays the current time prefaced with two hyphens to indicate that the command was executed. The two hyphens actually represent one of Lingo's operators, the comment operator, which marks a line of text as a note rather than an instruction.

By the way, a function has one of two forms. For example, you'll see the date function as `the /date` and `date()`. Same thing.

Handlers

A *handler* is three or more lines of Lingo that follow a very strict format, as in

```
on exitFrame
go to frame 15
end
```

Line 1 always consists of *on,* a space, and then the name of the handler. In this example, `exitFrame` is the name of a built-in handler that you use often in the Script channel of the Score. An exitFrame handler activates as the playback head in the Score window leaves the frame that contains the exitFrame handler.

The name of the handler *must* always be one word. In other words, you can't have spaces in the handler's name. A well-established convention is starting the name of a handler with a lowercase letter. You can add words to the name of the handler by capitalizing the first letter of each additional word *without* adding spaces. For example, you can name a handler *getARandomNumber.* Notice that the name of the handler is technically still one word even though you can read it as a phrase or sentence. You may also use an underline to separate words. Director reads a handler name like *get_A_Random_Number* as one word, too.

Line 2 of a handler begins the list of Lingo commands used in the specific handler. In the earlier example, you find only the go command. In some complex handlers, the list of commands may be half a page or more in length.

The last line, line 3 in this case, is always end. It's that simple, folks.

Events

Director echoes the way your computer works. Probably all that empty space inside your machine. Your computer is waiting to serve you and nervously checking whether you've pressed a key on the keyboard or clicked the mouse so that it can respond appropriately. Pressing a key on the keyboard or clicking the mouse is an *event.*

Director behaves the same way on playing back a movie. While a movie is playing, Director constantly checks for events that may be occurring. It checks for 14 types of events:

- **activateWindow event:** When a window becomes active
- **closeWindow event:** When the active window is closed
- **deactivateWindow event:** When the active window is no longer active
- **enterFrame event:** When the playback head enters a frame in the Score
- **exitFrame event:** When the playback head leaves a frame in the Score
- **idle event:** A nonevent, when no event is occurring during playback
- **keyDown event:** When you press a key on the keyboard
- **keyUp event:** When you release a key on the keyboard
- **mouseDown event:** When you press the mouse button down
- **mouseUp event:** When you release the mouse button
- **startMovie event:** When a movie begins to play back
- **stopMovie event:** When a movie stops playing

  ✔ **timeOut event:** Another kind of nonevent, when an event does not occur at an anticipated time

  ✔ **zoomWindow event:** When a window's zoom button is clicked

These are the only events you have to worry about, trust me. I could make up more if that would make you happy. But out of the box, Director is stuck with these 14 events. Period. Over and out.

Messages

Each time one of the 14 events occurs, Director sends out an alarm or message. With a keyDown event, Director releases a keyDown message. A mouseDown event gets a mouseDown message.

Message window

You can actually view these messages as they occur, and you don't even have to drink a six-pack with the Coneheads. Just call up the Message window from the Window menu, be sure to check the Trace button, and play your movie. Figure 17-3 shows the Message window in action, displaying messages in a scrolling list as a movie plays.

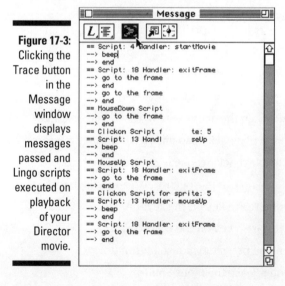

Figure 17-3: Clicking the Trace button in the Message window displays messages passed and Lingo scripts executed on playback of your Director movie.

Useless message passing stuff

By now you must be asking yourself the burning question, "Self, where does Director send all these messages?" To understand how messages behave in Director, imagine a department store that gets more exclusive the higher up you go in the elevator. At the top floor, you find only the most elegant, expensive, one-of-a-kind items imaginable. At the bottom is bargain basement time, the cheapest stuff with the broadest appeal possible. In between, items get more exclusive with every floor. If you buy something at the top floor, you don't bother visiting the floors below. Otherwise, you ride the elevator to the next floor down and find out if anything has your name on it. And so it goes until you wind up frantically flinging stuff out of giant bins in the basement.

Same thing with message passing. Messages flow from the highest to lowest level. If no handler exists in the button to "catch" the mouseDown or mouseUp message, the message takes the elevator and heads for the next floor down, a handler in the Score channel. If a mouseDown or mouseUp handler in the Script channel of the current frame exists, the message activates the handler, or it's back on the elevator heading for bargain basement time. You find movie scripts in the basement, the most generic, all-purpose type of handler available in your movie. By making the analogy of movie scripts and bargain basements, I don't mean to imply that movie scripts are unworthy. In fact, movie scripts contain some of the most important handlers in a movie precisely because of their broad availability. For more on movie scripts, see the "Movie scripts" section later in this chapter.

Variables

A *variable* is a little bit of memory you reserve and name to store a value. In a handler, you might enter the following line:

```
put 10 into theNum
```

That single statement accomplishes three things:

- Declares a variable. (*Declare* is programmerSpeak for "create.")
- Names the variable *theNum*.
- Stores the value 10 in the variable.

It's that simple; don't make it any more complicated.

You might decide to create another variable in the same handler with an additional line:

```
put "Lauren" into firstName
```

This line tells Director to put Lauren into firstName. Notice that when storing a value such as 10, no quote marks are required. To store words, such as *Lauren, cat,* or *dog,* quotes are required to tell Director the value is *literal,* which means that the value of the word stored is the word itself. You need to use quotes to differentiate a literal from the same group of characters (word) used as a variable.

For example, you might enter the following line in a handler:

```
put "Lauren" into cat
```

In this case, you *declare,* or create, a variable, name it *cat,* and store the word "Lauren" in the variable. Remember, a variable is just an arbitrary name you give to a little bit of memory in your computer.

Local variables

When you declare a variable named *cat* in a handler by entering a line such as the examples shown in the preceding section, you create a *local variable* — local because it's recognized only in that one handler. If you decide that you want to add a line in another handler that takes the value of cat and puts it in a text sprite, Text Cast Member 1, you might enter something like the following:

```
set the text of cast 1 = cat
```

But Director objects, saying that you're trying to use a variable that doesn't exist. The only handler that knows that the variable *cat* exists is the original handler in which you created the variable. You need to use a special kind of handler called a *global variable.*

Global variables

Global variables are variables that may be called in any handler of your movie, ergo *global.* To make a global variable, simply type **global**, a space character, and the name of the variable, usually in the second line of a handler. That's all there is to it. Staying with the example of using the variable *cat,* you might type a couple of lines to a handler as follows:

```
global cat
put "Lauren" into cat
```

Now, whenever you want another handler to access the value stored in the variable *cat,* just be sure to add **global cat** under the first line of the other handler, too, and any other handlers that might need the current value in cat.

Scripts

A *script* is the text in a Script window that consists of one or more handlers. Say you have a button on the first frame of a movie. The Script window has a mouseUp handler and a custom handler named *getARandomNumber*. The mouseUp handler moves the playback head to a new frame. The *getARandomNumber* handler generates a random number with the random function that determines the number the mouseUp handler uses to move the playback head. These two handlers form a script in the Button Cast Member Script window. It's that simple. (See Figure 17-4.)

Figure 17-4:
Two
handlers in
the script of
a Button
Cast
Member.

To briefly explain what this script accomplishes, the *getARandomNumber* handler declares a global variable, discussed in the previous section, named *theResult*. The handler uses the random function to pick a random number, in this case, a number from 1 to 10, and places the number into *theResult*. The mouseUp handler also declares the global variable so that it can use the number stored in *theResult*. The mouseUp handler calls on *getARandomNumber*, gets the random number from the global variable, and tells Director to move the playback head to the random frame number that is generated by *getARandomNumber*. You might have a different image on each frame so that the person viewing the movie may see a different image each time he or she presses the button.

Where a specific script resides in your movie determines the type of script and how "accessible" the script is (or what floor it's on in my department store analogy in the preceding sidebar, "Useless message passing stuff"). In a sense, some scripts, such as movie scripts, are listed in the Yellow Pages so that everyone knows about them and can call on them. Other scripts, such as button scripts, have unlisted numbers because they're intended to be used in very restricted situations. Types of scripts are discussed in the following sections.

Movie scripts

Most *movie scripts* are a set of initialization handlers that set primary event handlers, load values into memory, and generally set up the movie for playback. Using the startMovie message, a movie script might typically look like Figure 17-5.

Figure 17-5:
A typical
movie script
in a Movie
Script
window.

This initialization movie script in Figure 17-5 translates as follows:

- ✔ Line 1 says: Make a handler called *startMovie*.

- ✔ Line 2 says: When the movie starts, name a part of memory *stateFlag* and make it a global variable so that the value the variable holds is available to any other handler that declares *stateFlag*.

- ✔ Line 3 says: Set the color of text inside Button Cast Member 1 to white.

- ✔ Line 4 says: Start timing down from 360 ticks, or 6 seconds (and if nothing happens within 6 seconds, do the timeoutScript handler defined elsewhere in the movie).

- ✔ Line 5 says: Put the starting value, 0, into a reserved part of memory you named *stateFlag*, telling Director whether a user has pressed the button since the movie began. Another handler in the button declares the global variable, *stateFlag*, and sets *stateFlag* to 1 the first time the person running the movie presses the mouse over the button.

Movie scripts want to be available to everyone, everywhere. Movie scripts and primary event handlers are the most accessible scripts in your movie. In my department store analogy (see the preceding sidebar "Useless message passing stuff"), you find movie scripts in the bargain basement. They're the scripts that advertise in the Yellow Pages so that everyone knows about them.

To make a movie script, follow these steps:

1. **Choose Window⇨Script.**

2. **If not blank, click the New Script button (the + icon) in the upper-left corner of the Script window.**

3. **Click the Script Cast Member Properties button (the i icon).**

4. **In the Script Cast Member Properties dialog box, choose Movie from the Type pop-up menu.**

5. **Click OK to return to the blank Script window.**

6. **Enter your movie script handlers and commands.**

   For example, you might enter one or more of the following commands in a startUp handler:

   ```
   on startUp
   set the soundLevel to 7
   set the colorDepth to 8
   preloadCast 5
   end
   ```

   The soundLevel indicates the current volume from 0 for off to 7 for ouch, the highest sound level. Using the set command, you set the sound level to its highest setting.

   The colorDepth indicates how many colors your monitor is currently displaying. In the second command line, you set color depth to 8 bits, giving you 256 different colors.

   PreloadCast is a Lingo command that copies designated Cast Members into RAM before they appear on the Stage for improved performance. The third command line copies Cast Member 5 into RAM; maybe it's a big digital video.

7. **Close the Script window with ⌘/Ctrl+W.**

   A dialog box appears if there are problems with your script and you can debug your work. Chances are it's a typo or syntax problem.

8. **Press ⌘/Ctrl+Option/Alt+P to play your movie and test the handler.**

By the way, you can have more than one movie script in a movie.

Primary event handlers

Actions in Director are generally considered events. Director always knows when an event occurs. Four specific actions a user can do in Director are so basic they've been named *primary events*. The four primary events are

- **keyDown Event:** Whenever you press a key on the keyboard
- **mouseDown Event:** Whenever you press the mouse button
- **mouseUp Event:** Whenever you release the mouse button
- **timeOut event:** Whenever a specific duration of time passes without an anticipated event occurring

Director allows you to write a handler for each of these primary events. You can write a keyDownScript, a mouseDownScript, a mouseUpScript, and a timeOutScript for your movie. Had I designed Director, I would have stuck with the term *handler.* But someone in his or her infinite wisdom named them *scripts;* don't let that confuse you — they're handlers. Usually, you write these special handlers as part of a *movie script,* explained in the preceding section, "Movie scripts."

Primary event handlers execute whenever a primary event occurs during your movie's playback. To help you understand the unique consequence of including a primary event handler in your movie, consider what occurs without a primary event handler in your movie. An example of a regular mouseDown handler in a button is

```
on mouseDown
beep 2
end
```

Clicking the mouse over the button generates a mouseDown message. The mouseDown handler in the button acts like a trap, "catching" the mouseDown message. Director beeps twice because the command is activated. The mouseDown message ends there, echoing the meaning of the third line of the handler, end. No other handler gets triggered by that particular mouseDown event.

On the other hand, when you add a mouseDownScript to the movie, the mouseDown Script executes every time the mouse is pressed, even if the mouseDown event triggers a button that would normally trap the mouseDown message.

For example, you can write a mouseDownScript to randomly change the color of a button's text label (the name of the button the user sees on the Stage) each time the user clicks the button. If you need to create a button, page back to "Checking out the Tool palette tools" in Chapter 9.

First, add a script to a button so that it beeps when pressed. Follow these steps:

1. **On the Stage, click a button to which you would like to add a script.**

2. **If you have given the button a text label, skip to step 4; otherwise, double-click the button sprite on the Stage.**

   The button sprite now displays a wide, striped selection border and a blinking insertion point in the center of the sprite.

3. **Type a text label for the button sprite.**

   This label appears to a user as the button's name (usually indicating its function).

4. **Choose Modify⇨Sprite⇨Script.**

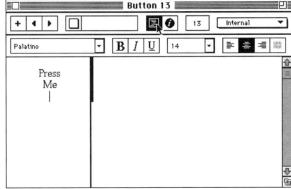

Figure 17-6:
Pressing the
Cast
Member
Script
button in a
Button Cast
Member
window.

The Script window for the button appears with the handler on mouseUp already entered on line 1, a blank second line ready with the blinking insertion point, and end automatically entered on the third line.

5. **Type your command line(s) at the blinking insertion point, in this case beep 2, and then click the Mac's Close box or double-click the Windows Control menu box.**

The following set of steps shows you how to add a script to the Score so that you remain in the same frame while the movie plays back:

1. **Choose Window⇨Score.**

   In frame 1, notice the sprite representing the button on the Stage. The frame just above the sprite is the Script cell for frame 1.

2. **Double-click the Script channel in frame 1.**

   The Script window for frame 1 appears with the handler "on exitFrame" already entered on line 1, a blank second line ready with the blinking insertion point, and "end" entered on the third line.

3. **Type** go to the frame.

Go to the frame is a special version of the go command that keeps the user in the frame that the command was called from, even though the movie is playing.

4. **Click the Mac's Close box or double-click the Windows Control menu box in the Script window.**

Now that you've set up your button and frame 1 with a couple of simple scripts, you can write a primary event handler that kicks in with a mouseDown message even if a button you click executes its handlers. Without a primary event handler, the mouseDown message would stop at the button and never reach a movie script.

Say you decide to make the primary event handler — to change a button's color when pressed — a startMovie type handler.

1. **Choose Window⇨Script.**

2. **Type** on startMovie **for the first line.**

3. **For the second line, enter a mouseDownScript.**

For example, `set the mouseDownScript to "set the foreColor of cast 1 = random(255)"` changes the color of the button's name to different colors each time the button's pressed.

You just accomplished the first part of the line, `set the mouseDownScript to`, establishing the current handler for a mouseDown event, one of four primary events in Director.

The next part of the line, `"set the foreColor of cast 1`, uses the set command to change the foreground color of cast 1, referring to the button you made, Cast Member 1 in the Cast window. The foreground color of the button is the color of the text you typed in the button.

The last part of the line, `= random(255)"`, is one of those functions I mentioned earlier in this section. You're telling Director to return or pick a random number from 1 to 255 and to change the foreground color of the button to that random number each time the user presses the mouse. In Lingo, colors are set by number.

4. **For the third and final line, type** end.

Press ⌘/Ctrl+Option/Alt+P to play back your movie; you can test your scripts by clicking the button several times. The button should beep and its text label should change color each time. If you click the background, the button's text label should still change color without beeping, thanks to the mouseDownScript.

Cast Member scripts

A *Cast Member script* is exclusive to the Cast Member. Director executes handlers in a Cast Member script after you click the Cast Member's sprite on the Stage during playback.

To make a Cast Member script, follow these steps:

1. **Choose Window⇨Cast.**

2. **Select the Cast Member in the Cast window.**

3. **Click the Script button at the top of the Cast window.**

    Director takes you to the Cast Member Script window.

4. **Enter Lingo commands between** on mouseUp **and** end.

    Try playing with the beep command or, if you feel up to it, checking out the set foreColor of cast command in the preceding selection on primary event handlers.

5. **Click the Mac's Close box or double-click the Windows Control menu box.**

6. **Press ⌘/Ctrl+Option/Alt+P to play your movie and test the handler.**

Frame scripts

Frame scripts are scripts you enter in the Frame channel of the Score window. They execute when the playback head reaches the frame in which a frame script occurs.

To create a frame script, just double-click the Script channel cell for the intended frame. The Script window for the respective frame appears with on exitFrame entered for you on the first line, a blank second line ready to go with the blinking insertion point, and end entered for you in the third line. Simply complete the handler and click the Mac's Close box or double-click the Windows Control menu box to create a frame script for the respective frame.

Sprite scripts

When you drag a Cast Member onto the Stage from the Cast window, you create a sprite of the Cast Member on the Stage and a sprite in the Score. A sprite script is a script for that particular sprite in that particular frame of the Score. Director can execute a sprite script when the person viewing the movie clicks on the sprite during playback or when the mouse pointer touches the sprite on the Stage.

Here's how to make a sprite script:

1. **Choose Window⇨Score.**

2. **Select the sprite in the Score.**

3. **Click the Script box at the top of the Score.**

4. **In the Script window that appears, add lines of Lingo between the first line,** on mouseUp, **and the last line,** end.

5. **Press ⌘/Ctrl+Option/Alt+P to play your movie and test the handler.**

Why You Want to Write Lingo Scripts but Don't Know It

As you can tell from my whirlwind tour of Lingo, adding simple Lingo scripts to a movie elevates the Director experience to a dramatic new level for you and whoever is watching your movie. With Lingo, you can check the type of machine running your movie, set the color depth of the monitor, fade in a sound, fade out a sound, adjust the volume of the sound, and at least two or three other things, actually hundreds, probably thousands.

Most important of all to you multimedia types out there in ReaderLand, you can add a level of interactivity to your movie only accessible through scripting with Lingo. When you learn to "make your movie make decisions" with conditional statements using "if-then" lines of Lingo to branch to one of several different possible options — at random, if you so choose — and use repeat statements and a number of other advanced scripting techniques, you're well on your way to developing fully interactive products for multimedia and the Web with Director 5. Bon voyage!

Chapter 18

Showing Off Your 15 Minutes of Fame on Video

In This Chapter

▶ Using video with Director

▶ Defining broadcast quality

▶ Producing video through post-production

▶ Creating projectors

*O*ne of the fantasies that draws people to multimedia is The Big Show. All your friends gathered 'round, anticipation etched in foreheads, necks straining forward, eyes glued in envious approbation to the Big Monitor, waiting dry-lipped for you to make the sign that The Big Show is about to begin. Your relatives, too, are there. Picketing the show, but they're there just the same. It's The Big Show, and you've got room in your heart for everyone tonight. You make your sign, the lights dim, and The Big Show begins.

Director makes *your* Big Show possible with its capability to display and edit digital video and export Director files as QuickTime mooVs. Knowing as much as you can about video and your computer's capabilities to manipulate video information can't hurt. In that spirit, I offer a potpourri of topics to chew on. Just don't spit on the floor, okay?

What You Really Need to Know about Video

Wow, what a dream. But it's a dream that can come true with today's technology. This part of the book is intended as a primer on video — what you can and can't do without spending mucho moola. It's also meant as another inspirational speech with a clear message: "Don't let anyone talk you out of your dreams."

Broadcast quality

Unless you dream of doing state-of-the-art video, you don't need to concern yourself with reaching broadcast quality, whatever that is, or spend oodles of money on equipment trying to attain broadcast quality. In fact, you can do a lot with stuff you can buy at your local electronics store. And I'm talking professional-level work. Plenty of professionals work with Hi-8 and Super-VHS equipment these days. I wouldn't drop below that level, but who doesn't have a camcorder these days?

Having more professional equipment certainly doesn't hurt. The latest and greatest toys are the digital camcorders from Sony and Panasonic with a super-fast means (called FireWire) of transferring digital video to your hard drive. But you shouldn't feel that you *must* wait until you can spend $500,000 on equipment. Don't listen to all the naysayers who tell you, "You can't do it," "You don't have enough equipment," and "You don't have enough experience."

By the way, you can always do this thing called *renting.* If you can't or simply don't want to make heavy purchases, consider renting equipment on an as-needed basis. And don't forget service bureaus, which offer a lot of resources and services — including high-powered workstations, video digitizing, and other multimedia goodies — at reasonable rates. Look up your local service bureaus in the Yellow Pages under "Desktop Publishing and Service Bureaus."

Multimedia: kiosks, presentations, and CDs

Much of what multimedia types produce is not meant for broadcast in the first place. Most of the output is intended for intimate viewing conditions, including kiosks, event-type presentations, CD-ROM publication, and the newest kid on the block, the Web.

Presentations are either displayed on giant 37-inch monitors (also great for getting an even tan) or projected onto a large screen with an LCD panel and an overhead projector. But I'm not talking CinemaScope here; the experience is still relatively intimate.

When you display video in kiosks and live presentations, plan to run the video from a hard drive whenever possible because of the drive's speed advantage over backup devices and CD-ROM drives. In fact, the videos should really be stored on an AV-type hard drive such as those manufactured by Micropolis. These drives are especially fast and optimized for playing long streams of information, which is the nature of video.

When prepping video for CD-ROM projects, be sure to watch the so-called data rate, a measure of how much information is being read by the computer per second. Although triple and quad-speed CD-ROMs are increasingly popular, most developers err on the safe side and use a double-speed CD-ROM data rate as their standard. This means you want to keep the data rate down to 300KBps (Kilobytes per second). You can use Cinepak compression on the Mac and PC to lower the data rate to this amount. For more on Cinepak and other video compression schemes, see Chapter 18.

As of this writing, excitement over the Web is at an all-time peak and doesn't seem to be slowing down. Good multimedia types of all persuasions are stoking the insatiable kiln of industry like so many briquettes getting ready to participate in this new Gold Rush. As a bona fide owner of Director 5 and Shockwave, you're ready to take the plunge and pan, pan, pan. (Find out more about Shockwave in Chapter 21.) When you're prepping video or multimedia in general for the Web, data rate must drop dramatically. Figure 2K per second of video, so a 30-second video would have to be no larger than 60K, which is pretty challenging. You need to drop frame rate, size and color depth. And compress, compress, compress.

When something's moving, it's hard to see

Funny thing about a moving object: It's hard to see. Actually, it's blurry. Ever see something filmed or taped in slow motion? What's the single most striking common denominator of all the images? Blur. They're all blurred. In fact, one of the telltale features of stop-motion animation has been — until recently — an absence of blur. Watch King Kong again. Wondrous as the animation work may be, you know it's stop-motion animation partly because the images of old Kong are *too* sharp. Even master animator of bygone days, Ray Harryhausen, working on his Sinbad epics, couldn't escape *this sharpness thing,* as a former president might say.

So have animators slaved away to find a system producing sharper animation? No, they've developed techniques to blur their work. What I'm trying to say is that an image in motion must not be held to the same critical standards as a still image. What I'm *not* saying is, "Forget quality."

AV Macs and video boards

If you're careful and thoughtful, you can do professional work with AV Macs and PCs equipped with a video board. Their built-in capabilities allow you to convert incoming video into a real TV video signal so that you can copy or "print" to videotape.

Your monitor uses a color scheme called *RGB,* for electronic guns in the picture tube that paint the image on your screen with additive color (red, green, and blue light). Real TV is known as *NTSC TV,* set for a number of technical reasons to a limited range of colors and level of quality. For more information about NTSC TV and related color issues, see Chapter 10.

In the Mac world, AV Power Macs are even more capable than their Quadra cohorts for working with digital video. If you are seriously interested in digital video, you should consider a Power Mac 8500 running at 120 MHz or the even faster 9500. In addition, Mac clones are now surfacing from various third-party vendors, from simple but powerful configurations to hefty workstation models featuring multiple CPUs, just right for digital video.

For you PC types, get the fastest Pentium PC and video card you can afford. Miro, a company in Palo Alto, California, markets the miroMOTION video board for Macs and PCs promising full-frame animation at a full 30 frames per second for under $1,000.

The information in this section is only meant to give you a reference point as you consider your specific needs and research what's available in the marketplace and what direction the technology is heading.

Video production

This section contains some tips to help you produce and digitize video. You also find some post-production tips. The tips in this section should help you maximize performance of an AV Power Mac or Pentium-based PC equipped with a video board and assist you in producing high-quality digital video.

Videotaping masters

When videotaping master tapes, be sure to think about the following:

- ✔ Shoot master video with at least Hi-8 or Super-VHS equipment.
- ✔ Use the highest quality tape you can afford.
- ✔ Clean recording heads before taping.
- ✔ Use the best, most heavily shielded cables you can afford. Avoid cheap cables that degrade images.
- ✔ Use good lighting but avoid over- and underexposure.

    At minimum, use one light behind the subject, one main light angled in front of the subject, and a third light often close to the camera as a fill. Use a fill light in sunlight or a reflector, even white foam core, to bounce fill light into shadows. Get a subscription to *A/V Video,* a great trade magazine that features solid tips on shooting and lighting in every issue.

- ✔ When videotaping, use static shots whenever possible and a tripod for steadiness.

    Use *static* shots, where the camera doesn't move, because most compression schemes note the differences from frame to frame and only record the differences when turning video into digital information. In a panning shot, each frame changes completely, defeating compression technology. For more information on compression schemes, skim over the "Codecs" section in Chapter 11.

✔ Avoid close-ups of people to maximize compression. People tend to move, twitch, gyrate, and generally squirm, giving you the same kind of problem a panning shot presents.

Before digitizing video

Here are some things that you should do before you digitize video:

✔ Clean recording heads before playback.

✔ Install the best cables you can afford. Avoid cheap cables that degrade images.

✔ Use the S-video ports on both VCR and your AV Mac or video board for highest quality digital video.

✔ On a Mac, turn off all so-called System extensions by going to the Desktop, pressing Shift, and choosing Special⇨Restart. Keep the Shift key down until you see the "Welcome to Macintosh, Extensions off" message. Restarting also frees up more of your computer's memory.

For a PC, you need to remove TSR (Terminate and Stay Resident) programs with a memory manager or actually alter your AUTOEXEC.BAT and/or CONFIG.SYS files; if this process sounds too frightening, make friends with the local DOS guru and have him or her help you with this project.

✔ Place a floppy disk in the floppy drive. Otherwise, your computer regularly checks for floppies during digitization, slowing things down.

✔ Use the fastest and largest drive you have for saving digital video. You can compare hard drive speeds with freeware programs available online. One of the best programs for the Mac is MacBench 3.0. For you PC types, try DRYSTONE FOR WINDOWS, which you can download from http://www.shareware.com/ on the Web or an online service.

Better yet, break down and buy an AV type drive — a Micropolis AV drive, for example. An AV drive is specially designed to handle the steady stream of information that video requires. Also, AV drives have redesigned maintenance routines that don't interrupt data flow, unlike the routines in regular hard drives.

✔ Install the latest drivers for your drives. Check with the manufacturer; for Macs, get drivers compatible with System 7.5.3's new SCSI Manager 4.3, the combination of which dramatically increases performance of the drive. Check on the latest Windows drivers from Microsoft and third-party vendors.

✔ If possible, repartition the storage drive with the formatting software that came bundled with the product. At least optimize the drive.

The Format command in most commercial formatting programs does a low-level format on the hard drive selected in the program. Choose the Initialize command in Apple HD SC Setup to low-level format a hard drive for a Mac or use a commercial formatter like Silverlining or FWB Hard Disk Toolkit.

Remember: Low-level formatting and partitioning destroy all information on the disk. Be sure that you have solid backups for everything on the disk before you low-level format it.

If low-level formatting isn't practical, optimize the drive with Norton Utilities Speed Disk or a comparable optimizing program. Optimizing eliminates file fragmentation. It also results in a large, contiguous block of disk space to write to, contributing to maximum hard drive performance.

Digitizing video

When you digitize video, be sure that you keep these things in mind:

- ✓ If possible, don't use compression while digitizing master tapes.

- ✓ If possible, digitize video separately from audio to help increase your computer's performance.

  Chances are that whatever program you use to digitize video offers commands somewhere in the menu bar to choose video, video and audio, or just audio. Eliminating one of the demands on your computer's processor achieves better performance all around.

- ✓ Consider smaller sizes for the Video window. In Director, you can use a still image for the background and a small Video window for the digital video with a matching background to "trick" the user into thinking the size of the video is full screen.

- ✓ Consider installing a dedicated video board. For a Mac with a NuBus slot, consider VideoSpigot AV to dramatically increase performance. For PCI Macs, video boards are just beginning to appear. A board by Miro offers full-frame, 60 field per second performance. Miro offers similar boards for PCs. Check the resources in Appendix B.

Post-production

During post-production, pay attention to the following:

- ✓ If possible, refrain from compression until the final edit.

- ✓ Use Cinepak compression for digital video destined for CD-ROM. Try a setting of 90 kilobytes per second for older, single-speed CD-ROM machines and 150 kilobytes per second for double-speed CD-ROM machines.

- ✓ Consider making the Video window smaller by using the trick explained in the preceding set of tips. Blend the video's background with the matching background of a still image to create the illusion of a screen-sized video window.

Taping your movies

With Director movies using "hand-made" art — made from bitmaps painted in the Paint window or in Photoshop or Fractal Painter and with artwork from 3-D modeling programs— your movie contains original art as sharp as a tack, as crisp as your computer can handle. You don't need to concern yourself about signal loss and image degradation that inevitably occur when converting images from life to digital information. In this sense, you're leagues ahead of the game. The challenge is copying your pristine movie to video.

For Director movies destined for transfer to video, be sure to use the NTSC palette in the Color Palettes window. The NTSC palette is a collection of NTSC-safe, or *legal,* colors that do not tend to change when you transfer the movies to videotape. *Illegal* NTSC colors tend to change dramatically on video, turning muddy or becoming over-saturated and causing *blooming* — a condition in which the color spills over into the rest of the screen.

I'm making an assumption at this point. Either you have an AV Mac with a video out port or a PC with a video board from one of a number of vendors. Or you're planning to buy a video board that supplies a video out port in the very near future. You can't get around this hardware requirement because, ordinarily, computer video and NTSC video don't mix any better than oil and water. The video your computer uses to display Director on-screen is vastly different from the NTSC signal needed to tape to video. Some hardware is needed to make the translation.

Video boards aside, basically you have two options. You can tape your Director movie in "real" time — meaning as the movie actually plays back from your computer, signals streaming from the S-Video out port of your computer to the S-Video in port of your VCR or camcorder. Or you can tape your movie with more control one frame at a time, which requires a special VCR like the Sony EVO-9650 that accepts control signals from one of Director's *XObjects* — a set of external routines you can load for extending Director's capabilities.

If you go with the real-time option, remember that Director is frame-based; it's designed to show every frame, and it slows down rather than drop even a single, precious frame. Better to export the movie as a digital video and import it back as a Digital Video Cast Member because digital video is time-based and designed to play back at the right speed, giving the sound track priority over image to maintain sync. Take a gander at "Sync about It" in Chapter 19 for a detailed look at synchronization issues.

The problem *now* is that digital video drops frames running from a slow computer to keep in step with the soundtrack. (What's the expression — six of one, half a dozen of the other? You can't win for losing? Please, send me *your* favorite trite expression; I'll be happy to include it in my next book.) The point is, you need to decide what's more important to you and the project, a few dropped frames or slowed animation on tape.

Making a Projector (and Why You'd Want to)

You find the Create Projector command in the File menu. With this command, you can create a stand-alone application called a *projector* that incorporates selected movies and plays them so that the user doesn't need a copy of Director or the original files to view the production. In addition, Director compresses the movies and turns lines of Lingo into assembly code, protecting your scripts from prying eyes. Follow these steps to make a projector:

1. **After your movies are ready, choose File⇨Create Projector.**

   The Create Projector dialog box appears, as shown in Figure 18-1. On the left is the Directory, where you locate movies to include in the projector.

2. **Highlight the movie you want to play first in the projector and click Add.**

   Director adds the movie to the Playback Order field on the right side of the Create Projector dialog box.

3. **If you want to add the entire list of movies displayed in the Directory, click Add All.**

   Director adds all movie files currently displayed in the Directory to the Playback Order field.

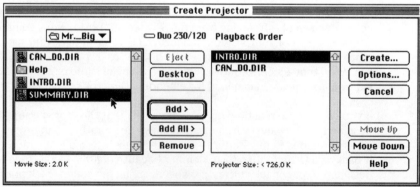

Figure 18-1: The Create Projector dialog box, where you decide which movies to include in a projector.

4. **If you want to change the position of a movie in the Playback Order field, highlight the movie and click Move Up or Move Down.**

5. **Click Options.**

   The Projector Options dialog box appears, as shown in Figure 18-2. The Projector Options dialog box includes the following options:

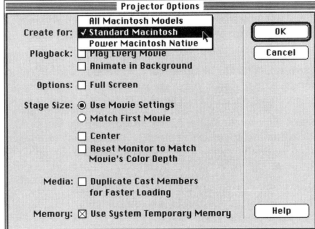

Figure 18-2:
The
Projector
Options
dialog box,
where you
select
playback
options for
a new
projector.

- **Create for:** Choose the platform for the projector from the pop-up menu. You Mac people have a choice between Power Macintosh Native, Standard Macintosh, and All Macintosh models (a so-called "fat binary" version that contains code for standard Macs and Power Macs). PCs users may choose between Windows NT and 95, and Windows 3.1 (that plays with poorer performance on Win NT and 95).

- **Playback:** With Play Every Movie checked, the projector plays every movie displayed in the list field of the Create Projector dialog box. Unchecked, the projector only plays the first movie listed in the Create Projector dialog box.

  If a projector is playing a list of movies and you want to exit the movie currently playing to go to the next movie, press ⌘/Ctrl+. (period). To quit, use the old standby, ⌘/Ctrl+Q.

- **Animate in Background:** Checked, the projector continues playing even if you return to the Desktop or open another application. Unchecked, the movie stops until you click the movie's window again.

  Some movies, especially interactive movies, are designed to continue playing until the user stops the movie with ⌘/Ctrl+. (period) or quits with ⌘/Ctrl+Q. Either shortcut exits you from the projector. Movies designed to stop at the last frame automatically quit the projector.

- **Options:** With Full Screen checked, the projector plays the movies at full screen size, except for the menu bar that remains visible at the top of the display.

- **Stage Size:** If you choose Use Movie Settings, the projector resizes the Stage area for the Stage size set for each movie in the Preferences dialog box. With Match First Movie selected, the Stage remains the same size throughout playback.

- **Center:** Checked, the projector plays each movie in the center of the screen. Otherwise, it plays each movie in the location set in the Preferences dialog box of Director when each movie was created.

- **Reset Monitor to Match Movie's Color Depth:** Checked, the projector automatically sets the monitor's color depth to the color depth used when the movie was created in Director. Otherwise, the projector plays the movie at the monitor's current color depth.

- **Media:** With Duplicate Cast Members for Faster Loading checked, the projector runs faster by avoiding keeping Cast Members in memory. Instead, the projector makes copies of Cast Members as they appear in the movie(s).

- **Memory:** Checking Use System Temporary Memory makes unused System memory available to Director when the application partition is exhausted. See Chapter 2 for info on Director's application partition.

6. **Click the desired options in the Projector Options dialog box and then click OK.**

7. **Click Create.**

   The Save Projector as dialog box appears.

8. **Enter a custom name for the projector.**

9. **In the Directory, navigate to where you'd like the projector saved and click OK.**

10. **At the Desktop, find the projector and double-click its icon to test playback.**

Remember to always test your work!

I'll give you another great reason for making a projector, even if you have no intention of letting someone else see it: Make a projector to copy the movies to video. The projector's size is minuscule compared to loading Director to play your movies; and the movies themselves are compressed. Your chance of successfully recording them to tape in real time is greatly increased.

You're welcome.

Chapter 19

You Talkin' to Me? Adding Sound to Your Movie

● ●

In This Chapter

▶ Where you acquire sound

▶ Where you store sound files

▶ How to use smaller sound files

▶ All about sync (not including the kitchen kind)

● ●

*Y*ou may be asking yourself, "Self, add sound to my movie? Okay, I'm all for that, but . . ." Then all the questions come pouring into mind. How do I add sounds to my computer? Where can I go for canned sounds? How can I get my mother-in-law to like me? And so on.

I can't help with the in-laws, but this chapter gives you a bevy of tips to help you add quality audio to your Director movies.

Where Do I Get All This Stuff, Anyhow?

Sound? What am I, a producer? As a matter of fact, that's exactly what you become when you get involved in multimedia: a multimedia producer, a wild mix of Hollywood and Silicon Valley. So knowing sources for audio becomes pretty important. With a little thought, a number of possibilities come to mind.

Sampling your own audio

With an AV Mac, you're all set to sample sounds. On a PC, you need to buy a sound card like Sound Blaster Pro by Creative Labs or Pro AudioSpectrum by Media Vision for sampling sound. *Sampling* uses an ADC (Analog to Digital Converter) to translate audio into digital information, 0s and 1s, the only thing your computer really understands. The higher the sampling rate, the better the sound: 16-bit digitized audio offers near CD-quality results.

The right connections

AV Macs, some Performas, and most PowerBooks have input for sound in the back; it's the connection with the MIC icon on top. Sound cards for the Mac and PC provide their own input and output ports. You can get your audio from a number of sources: VCRs (most hi-fi VHS decks have terrific audio specs), CDs, and even your camcorder. Hi-8 and SuperVHS camcorders offer impressive if not professional levels of audio specs. Connect either the headphone output or RCA jack output of your audio source to your computer's sound port.

Be prepared with a slew of adapters. Radio Shack and most stereo shops have a wide selection of adapters, but remember this: Side-by-side to Murphy's Law somewhere, a Universal Rule of Adapters states that you never have the adapter you need. I'd relocate if I were you, cat and all, closer to Radio Shack, just for some peace of mind.

Anyway, the Mac 660AV and 840AV feature stereo sound, but they sport a single mini-type stereo Sound-In port. So skip to your handy electronics shop and get a stereo RCA plug-to-stereo mini-plug adapter. The RCA cables go into the adapter, the adapter goes into the Mac, and you're all set for sampling fun. Apple's latest products, the PCI Power Macs, sport RCA plugs for sound.

Double-check that you're using *line* output for records, if you still have any left. Frankly, I think that you should donate them to the Smithsonian. You can find adapters for them, though, at stores like Radio Shack. The main problem with capturing sound is signal loss, inevitable with analog-to-digital conversion.

Be sure that you have the right to use someone else's audio professionally. You don't want to violate any copyright protection; it's not right, and it's against the law. Check whether the audio is in the public domain, that you've been granted *written* permission to use the material, or that purchasing the audio gives you the right to use it in a commercial product or public performance. Even then, did you pay for one-time only use (a *drop needle fee*) or unlimited usage?

Sampling sound with an AV Mac

But how do you actually sample or digitize sound after you're all connected? AV Macs come with a program called FusionRecorder, used for making QuickTime movies. You can use QuickTime technology to record audio only, and there's no law against a QuickTime mooV with only an audio track. In FusionRecorder, simply turn off its video capabilities. The only other decision to make is the sampling rate. The following lists various sample rates and the acceptable uses for them. Remember, the higher the sample rate, the better the sound.

 ✔ **48 kHz:** The AV Mac's highest sample rate in kHz, which stands for kilohertz, or 1,000 hertz, a way of describing the number of sound waves that pass a fixed point, referred to as *frequency* and a determinant of pitch quality. Use for sampling music, especially from CDs, to obtain highest playback quality.

- **44 kHz:** Next highest sampling rate. Use for sampling music from non-CD sources.

- **24 kHz:** Use this sampling rate or higher for narration and sound effects. This special sampling rate is available mainly for the Geoport Telecom Adapter used with AV Macs for modem and fax features.

- **22.05 kHz:** Use this sampling rate or higher for sampling narration and sound effects.

Another common sampling rate is 11 kHz, not directly available when sampling with an AV Mac. Many utilities are available for "downsampling," to turn sound sampled at a high sampling rate — 44 kHz or 22 kHz, for example — into 11 kHz, which is considered acceptable for narration; although higher is always better. You'll also see 7.5 kHz listed in these downsampling utilities, but this sampling rate is for desperation time only: for example, if you *must* fit tons of audio in Director movies that *must* fit on a double-density floppy.

Why use lower sampling rates at all? The lower the sampling rate, the smaller the sound file. With extended narration and musical scores, sound can dramatically swell a movie's size. Later in this chapter, in the section, "Great Sound for the Price of Good on Your Mac," I show you a way to get double the sound quality at half the file size on a Mac. Unfortunately, I'm not aware of a similar program in the PC world.

Sampling sound without an AV Mac

By the way, if you don't have an AV Mac or use a video board-endowed PC, you can install a sound card, such as the Audiomedia card from DigiDesign for the Mac or Sound Blaster for Windows, in the expansion slot of your computer. Many sound cards offer features equal to or surpassing an AV Mac's capabilities. Some cards add considerably more professional features, so results are truly CD-quality audio.

If you don't have an AV Mac or an expansion slot (where extra goodies go inside your computer), or you don't want to make an investment in a sound card, you can sample sound with an external "box." For the Mac, Macromedia's MacRecorder digitizer comes bundled with SoundEdit 16, a very capable sound-editing program. The MacRecorder plugs into the serial port of your Mac and allows you to sample audio from a built-in microphone, an external microphone, or line output. You can even use two MacRecorders to sample stereo sound using both serial ports. Similar devices are available for PCs.

Disc-To-Disk

Disc-To-Disk is a great commercial program that allows you to "copy" sound directly from a CD, giving you the highest possible quality because it's a digital-to-digital data transfer, avoiding analog-to-digital signal loss that occurs when you send analog output from a CD (that's right, it's no longer digital by then) to your Mac with RCA type audio cables. PC users: Sorry, but as far as I know, nothing equivalent to Disc-To-Disk is available for you at this time.

Make sure that you've paid those royalties!

Freeware and shareware

Commercial online services, such as America Online, CompuServe, and Prodigy, and Internet sites have vast libraries of sampled sound to *download* (copy via a modem to your computer). The Internet's the latest craze, and who knows the types of sound you can find there? Most freeware audio allows unlimited usage, but you'll want to double-check the privileges granted you by the owner and read all the fine print.

Commercial floppy and CD-ROM collections

Vast numbers of music and sound effect collections are on the market on floppies and CD-ROM discs. Of course, CD-ROM collections offer a number of advantages over floppies, including storage capacity, shelf life, and sound quality. Combined with the capabilities of Disk-To-Disk software, discussed earlier in this chapter, CD audio offers the highest quality transfer to your hard drive. Again, check and double-check usage rights before you purchase anything. My recommendation is to look for unlimited usage to get your full money's worth.

Where Sounds Go in Director

Just as you can import graphics into your movie, you can import sound files. In the Import Files dialog box, you have an opportunity to import a sound as a linked file, referenced by a movie during playback but not actually incorporated into the movie itself. Your other option is to incorporate the sound into the movie. Either way, the sound winds up as a Sound Cast Member in the Cast.

One way to determine which option to choose is to consider that *incorporated* sounds must load completely into memory before being played, and that they become the property of that one movie. A *linked* sound file like an AIFF sound file plays from disk, reducing memory requirements and remaining available to share among several movies. A special advantage of an AIFF sound file is its portability, meaning that you can use the same AIFF sound file for Mac and Windows Director movies.

In a Mac, sounds incorporated into a Director movie become part of the *resource fork* of the file, the place where sounds and other types of resources are stored. In MacLand, sounds are stored as resource type *snd*. PCs have no equivalent of the Mac resource fork.

Great Mac Sound for the Price of Good

Wouldn't it be great to play 44 kHz sound at a 22 kHz storage and memory price? Or 22 kHz sound, great for narration, at an 11 kHz price? If you own a Mac, you can achieve the impossible with a wonderful little shareware utility called Sound Mover, created by Riccardo Ettore. It's available for downloading to your Mac from most commercial online services, bulletin boards, and the Internet.

If you remember Font/DA Mover from System 6.8, you're familiar with Sound Mover's interface, a window with a left and right scrolling field and a button underneath each field. Pressing Option and clicking the left Open button opens a pop-up menu that allows you to choose the type of sound file you want from your hard drive. When sounds are listed in the left directory, you may copy any sound to a file you find in the right directory. After selecting a sound from the left scrolling field, if you ⌘+Option+click the Copy button, Sound Mover copies the sound while cutting the size of the file in half without lowering the quality of playback.

How does Sound Mover achieve this miracle? Basically, the utility copies every other byte of sound information. Four out of five physicians claim that they can't hear the difference between the original 44 KHz file and the 22 KHz file. Try it, you'll like it.

Sync about It

Synchronizing sound to picture is every multimedia type's nightmare, although digital technology makes this task a lot easier than it used to be. When you think about it, much of the sound you hear around you and in movies and TV isn't synced sound at all. Background noise, most special effects, and musical scores aren't synced to the degree people expect of lip-synced sound. Even then, if someone's head is turned away from the camera, or if a figure is moving or in the distance, sync becomes a much less critical issue.

Playing a sound through

Before running, maybe you'd better learn to crawl. How do you play a complete sound file in Director? Adding a Sound Cast Member to one cell in the Score's Sound channel doesn't do it. Try it; you'll hear the narration, music, or sound effect for an instant, and, as soon as the playback head moves on to the next frame, the sound dies.

To play a sound from beginning to end, you need to add the same Sound Cast Member to as many cells needed in the Sound channel to play back the sound from beginning to end. Not enough cells and the sound dies before the end of the piece; too many cells and you waste valuable cells in your movie. Remember, Director sees a block of cells with the same Cast Member as one "performance" of the sound. To play the sound again, leave at least one cell blank between the first and second performance of the sound.

You can use the In-Between command under the Modify menu to fill a block of cells with a Sound Cast Member. Place a Sound Cast Member into the frame where the sound begins. Choose Edit⇨Copy Cells and make a guess how many frames the sound takes to complete. Shift-click on that frame in the Score. Choose In-Between from the Modify menu to fill the selected frames with the sound and test the sound's duration by playing back your movie.

You can also play with different Tempo settings for a selected block of sound cells. Changing Tempo doesn't change the sound itself, but rather the number of frames needed to play the sound from beginning to end.

Remember, sync is one of those ticklish areas dependent on the speed of your computer's processor. Slower machines need different settings than Power Macs and Pentium PCs.

Syncing sound to your movie

Following are some tips for synchronizing sound to sequences in your movie, be it music, narration, or creepy sound effects.

- Make sure that your audio is clear and well recorded. You don't want to start with source audio that has lots of noise, pops, or other distractions. When you sample audio, digital "noise" degrades the result (especially on lower-end sampling devices or settings). Also, pay close attention to audio levels; digital audio is very sensitive to high recording levels. The settings you use for your VCR or cassette player may sound very distorted when applied to digital sound.

  You want to record as *hot* (AudiophileSpeak for loud) as possible without going into the danger zone of your sound-level meter. Find the loudest part of your audio track, set the levels to that segment, and then record.

- Try changing Tempo settings for various blocks of sounds in the Sound channel of the Score window. Select a block of cells in the Sound channel that contain the same Sound Cast Member. Double-click the Tempo channel in the first frame of the selected sound cells and set the Tempo with the slider control in the Set Tempo dialog box.

When using Tempo settings to sync sound to Director animation, use the slowest machine that you anticipate the movie will play on. Working the other way around, you lose sync as you move to slower machines and the frame rate drops while the sound plays on. Remember that Director is built to play every frame of your movie; the movie slows down on slower computers instead of dropping frames.

✔ If you've developed an animation sequence that you're syncing sound to with the In-Between or In-Between Special commands under the Modify menu, try redoing the *tweening* with a different number of frames between the key frames. To review the tweening technique and In-Between commands, jump back to Chapter 5.

✔ If you own a digital video editing application like Premiere, export your Director movie with sound as a digital video. In Premiere, picture and sound are in separate tracks, and you can take advantage of special tricks that the program offers, like shortening or lengthening audio passages to sync sound to picture without distorting the sound. If you need to run the final video from Director, re-import it as a Digital Video Cast Member to play back in its own Video window while maintaining the sync you established in Premiere. Remember, digital video was built from the beginning to maintain sync between audio and picture, even dropping frames if necessary to maintain sync.

Chapter 20

Cross-Platform Stuff No One Should Need to Know

∙ ∙

In This Chapter

▶ All the dirt on the cross-platform pack

▶ Following the rules is cool

▶ Managing your files

∙ ∙

*O*ne of the reasons people buy Director is to get the four manuals that come with the package. They're great for leveling tables. Another reason is Director's capability to produce multimedia on different types of computers and operating systems, so-called *cross-platform* capabilities.

When you're ready to produce multimedia for Macintosh and IBM-compatibles, you need to know lots of stuff. In this chapter, I get you started with tips on compatibility issues and how to manage your files.

Cross-Platform Which Way?

In a perfect world, you'd buy one program, whip up a multimedia extravaganza overnight, and offer it to every computer-using market you could find. Heck, you'd be happy to sell it to people who don't have a computer. That's the American way.

Now for Real Life. Director 5 is as much a cross-platform program as any out there on the market and then some. But it doesn't match the utopian picture previously described. To do serious cross-platform work with Director, you need to purchase — now sit down — Director 5 for Macintosh *and* Director 5 for Windows.

Now wait, I know I've heard of a cross-platform pack

That's right, Macromedia offers a cross-platform pack. Some people assume that the pack contains a special cross-platform edition of Director 5. Know what's inside? One copy of Director 5 for Macintosh and one copy of Director 5 for Windows, plus assorted manuals for leveling tables. You might save a few pennies with the bundle, but you're still buying two copies of Director.

In the testing phase of a cross-platform project, some developers are tempted to use emulation software like SoftWindows from Insignia Solutions, which makes your Mac think it's a PC, or MacOpener from DataViz, which tricks your PC into opening Mac files. You can also purchase hardware from companies like OrangePC that does the same kind of trick. Frankly, Macromedia doesn't encourage this practice and highly recommends testing Director 5 for Windows on a PC-compatible and Director 5 for Macintosh on a real Mac or Mac clone.

But I've heard you can use Mac Director movies in a Windows projector

This is another source of confusion about Director's cross-platform features. Director movies, the files you save with the Save command, are platform-independent files. Within some limitations, you can open a Macintosh Director movie on an IBM-compatible and a Windows Director movie on a Mac. The same thing goes for making a projector. As long as you stick to some guidelines, you can add Mac movies to a Windows projector and vice versa.

So far, so good. The catch is that projectors are platform-dependent files. Once you turn movies into a projector, they run only under the platform that built the projector, so a Macintosh projector runs only under the Mac operating system, and a Director for Windows projector runs only under Windows. And you probably want to distribute your work as a projector. When your movies are protected as a projector, the Lingo scripting is converted to a low-level language that only your computer and Carl Sagan understand, and the user doesn't need to buy Director 5 to play your movies. See "Making a Projector (and Why You'd Want To)" in Chapter 18 for more information.

Prepping Your Director Movies

The real trick to doing cross-platform work with Director 5 is prepping your Director 5 movies. By following my guidelines, you can develop your movies on either platform, Mac or PC, and safely "port" (don't you love this stuff) over to the other platform.

Following the rules is cool

Although Mac users have more latitude in what they can name their files, most developers strongly suggest staying with PC file-naming conventions for cross-platform work. I'm going to be even stricter with you and ask you to stick with what are called ISO-9660 naming conventions. You may vaguely remember seeing the term ISO-9660 somewhere. If you own a CD-ROM drive, you're right. ISO-9660 is the name of one of the files that should be in your system to communicate with the CD-ROM drive.

The ISO-9660 file-naming convention calls for three parts: a filename, a period, and an extension. Following these rules pretty well guarantees compatibility across platforms and for CD-ROM publishing. It doesn't hurt on the Web, either, when you prep your movies for the Internet with Shockwave. See Chapter 21 for more information.

These naming conventions are very strict. To work properly, they must be followed to the letter, no pun intended. (Or was it intended?)

In more detail, here's how to name your movies for cross-platform work:

- ✔ **Filename:** Begin the filename with a letter, not a numeral. The filename can be up to eight characters long including *only* capital letters A through Z, numerals 0 through 9, and the underscore (_) character (which you get by pressing Shift+hyphen).

- ✔ **Period character:** The period character is reserved for separating the file name from the following part, the extension. Do not try to substitute colons, semicolons, ampersands, or avocados for the period. These symbols do not work.

- ✔ **Extension:** Follow the period with a three-character extension, sticking with the same filename rules. And not just any extension. Stick with the standard extension for standard files. Director movies end in *DIR,* PICTs with *PCT,* and QuickTime movies with *MOV.*

Refer to Table 20-1 for common file types and their extensions.

Table 20-1	File Types and Extensions	
File Type	*Windows*	*Mac*
Director movies		
Unprotected movies	DIR	DIR
Protected movies	DXR	DXR
Animation files		
Autodesk Animator files	FLI	FLC

(continued)

Table 20-1 *(continued)*

File Type	Windows	Mac
Bitmap images		
Bitmap	BMP	BMP
Device Independent Bitmap	DIB	DIB
Encapsulated PostScript	EPS	EPS
GIF	GIF	GIF
JPEG PICT	JPG	JPG
Kodak Photo CD	PCD	PCD
Paintbrush	PCX	PCX
PICT	PCT	PCT
PICT	PIC	PIC
MacPaint	PNT	PNT
TIFF	TIF	TIF
Windows Metafile	WMF	WMF
Digital videos		
Video for Windows	AVI	AVI
QuickTime for Windows	MOV	MOV
Sound		
AIFF	AIF	AIF
WAVE	WAV	WAV

Stick with the System - Win palette

Director 5 comes with a set of palettes to start you off. For cross-platform work, add the System - Win palette to the Palette channel in Frame 1 right from the start and leave it there whether you're working with a Mac or PC. You may see a slight shift in colors from one platform to the other, but generally I think you'll be happy with the results. One exception is if you're working with movies that began as Director 4 movies; because Director 4 handled colors slightly differently from Director 5, go with the System - Win (Dir4) palette to avoid embarrassing color shifts.

Is this going to stifle you? Is it going to limit your free-ranging creativity? Of course, but that's part of working in the cross-platform world. Actually, limitations often stir the creative force within, forcing solutions you never would have dreamed of ordinarily.

A corollary to staying with the System - Win palette is sticking with 8-bit color. Out go those beautiful 24-bit PICTs that glow with all the fire of a room-size transparency. They'd create heck on earth for you and your movies. Director 5 supports 24-bit color on the Stage for Mac and Windows 95 platforms, but again, use only 8-bit graphics. Trust me.

Believe it or not, Windows and the Mac operating system share some things in common. When displaying 256 colors (8-bit color depth), both operating systems fix white at slot 0 and black at slot 255, locking them so that you cannot modify them. But Windows goes farther. Windows reserves the first ten and last ten colors of the current palette for GUI (*graphical user interface*) elements. These colors are called static colors. You may modify static colors between black and white, but not black and white themselves.

Two cross-platform issues this setup affects are Director's Fade to Black and Fade to White effects. Because black and white are locked, they don't work with fade effects available in the Stage Properties: Palette dialog box. If you intend to use fades in a cross-platform movie, avoid solid white (slot 0) and solid black (slot 255) pixels in the graphic. If you must use these colors, create a custom palette by making color slot 1 pure white and slot 254 pure black, duplicate black and white colors that work with fades. Then remap the graphic to your custom palette. Refer to "Creating a custom palette" in Chapter 24.

Fonts R Us

Fonts represent a problem area even without the added complexities of cross-platform development. Even when the platforms are the same, if the user doesn't have the right fonts installed in the computer — or if you and the user have the same fonts but from different type vendors — havoc reigns on your beautiful Director movie wherever you display so-called rich text. To review rich text, skip to "Rich Text, Come to Papa" in Chapter 8. Basically rich text is word-processing text that relies on the fonts currently installed in the system. Very tricky.

Director gives you a way of mapping fonts from one platform to another by modifying the FONTMAP.TXT file in the Director folder or directory. But it's a little technical and a little tricky, too.

The safest, easiest way to work around the problem is to stick with *bitmapped* text, text you enter with the Text tool in the Paint window. See "Text Tool" in Chapter 6 for more on using the Text tool.

You can also convert Director's other types of text into bitmaps when you've completed development by selecting a Text Cast Member in the Cast window and choosing Modify⇨Convert to Bitmap. If you must use editable text, the safest strategy is to stick with boring old Helvetica and Times.

Prep your digital videos

QuickTime mooVs may be used in Director movies for cross-platform projects. However, you need to coax mooVs with a little preening by using one of several programs and converter utilities. You need a program that "flattens" or converts the QuickTime mooV to a cross-platform format and makes mooV *self-contained,* independent of any linked files.

MoviePlayer 2.1, the icon of which is portrayed at left, is a ubiquitous little program for the Mac that can handle both assignments. To convert a QuickTime mooV, do the following:

1. **Open MoviePlayer 2.1.**

2. **Choose File⇨Open and open the QuickTime mooV from the Directory.**

3. **After test playing the mooV, choose File⇨Save As to display the Save As dialog box shown in Figure 20-1.**

4. **Click the Make movie self-contained radio/option button.**

5. **Check the Playable on non-Apple computers check box, which is MoviePlayer's term for "flatten."**

6. **Click Save.**

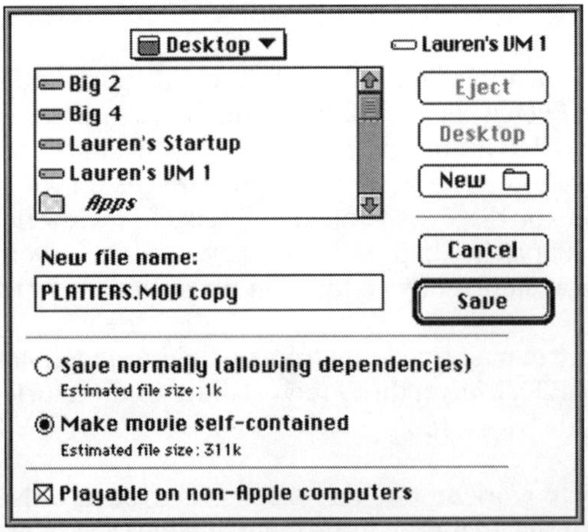

Figure 20-1:
MoviePlayer
selections
to make
your
QuickTime
mooV self-
contained
and
flattened.

▦ Desktop ▼	⊂ Lauren's UM 1
⊂ Big 2	Eject
⊂ Big 4	Desktop
⊂ Lauren's Startup	
⊂ Lauren's UM 1	New 🗀
🗀 *Apps*	

New file name:

PLATTERS.MOU copy

Cancel

Save

○ **Save normally (allowing dependencies)**
   Estimated file size: 1k

◉ **Make movie self-contained**
   Estimated file size: 311k

☒ **Playable on non-Apple computers**

PC owners do not have the option of using MoviePlayer to make a mooV self-contained and flattened. PC users can, however, use a QuickTime for Windows package that Apple sells, which includes a conversion utility, or Adobe Premiere. Open Premiere and find your QuickTime mooV in the Open dialog box. Choose File⇨Export⇨Flattened Movie and click Save. Premiere flattens the mooV and makes it platform-independent. That's it.

You don't have to pay a lot to get a program designed for prepping QuickTime. FlattenMooV is a shareware program that carries a paltry $10 price tag and does a great job. Contact Robert Hennessy at 39495 Albany Common, Unit B, Fremont, CA 94538.

Managing Your Files

One of Director's best features, linking external files to a movie, is also problematic. It's a great feature because you can share information and graphics among several Director movies when the files aren't imbedded in one movie alone. But the catch is that you had better keep track of those linked files. If Director can't find the files, you're in deeper than you know.

QuickTime mooVs are always imported as linked files. The external files must tag along with your Director movies.

The project folder

When you include linked files in a Director movie, the original external files must be available and locatable for a presentation to play back properly. The best solution to this file management dilemma for cross-platform work is to put everything in one folder or directory, which I would call a *project folder*.

Everything goes into the project folder: the Director application and its assorted folders or the projector; any digital video like QuickTime and AVI movies; external sound files; external casts; and other movies called by the main Director movie. Everything. To pretty things up a little, you can arrange the icons you want the user to see in one area of the folder's window and resize the window so that all other files are hidden.

The stub projector

A more technical way of handling file management for cross-platform work is to create what's known as a "stub" projector, a little movie that automates initialization and maintenance stuff that should be taken care of before, during, and after a movie's playback. In this case, you'd make a stub projector to keep Director on top of its ancillary files by working with two of Lingo's functions, the searchPath and the pathName, and a Lingo command, append.

Because a Director movie looks for external Cast Members before reading Lingo scripts, design your production so that the stub projector plays first and does its magic with the searchPath function.

Suppose Mr. Big hires you to make a CD-ROM disc entitled "How I Made a Killing in the Cement Business" and you produce a gorgeous cross-platform production for him. Using the backslash (\), the PC convention for directory (*folder* for Mac-ites), you create two folders/directories. In one, \MOOVS, you store all the QuickTime demos; in another, \AIFFS, you archive important speeches that Mr. Big has given about cement.

Follow these steps to make a stub projector:

1. **Open Director and choose File⇨New⇨Movie.**

2. **Choose Window⇨Script or press ⌘/Ctrl+0 (zero) to display the Movie Script window.**

3. **Enter the following, line for line, substituting the appropriate names.**

```
on startMovie
   append the searchPath, the pathName & "MOOVS"
   append the searchPath, the pathName & "AIFFS"
end
```

4. **Choose Window⇨Score or press ⌘/Ctrl+4 to display the Score window.**

5. **Double-click the Script channel for Frame 1 to display the Score Script window and enter the following, line for line:**

```
on exitFrame
   go to movie "INTRO.DIR"
end
```

6. **Choose File⇨Save As and save the movie, giving it a clever title like CLICK_ME.DIR.**

7. **Choose File⇨Create Projector to display the Create Projector dialog box.**

8. **Find the movie in the left directory and double-click to enter it in the right directory.**

9. **Click Create and name the projector CLICK_ME.DXR. (DXR is the extension for a projector.)**

10. **Put the movie INTRO.DIR and the stub projector CLICK_ME.DXR in the root directory of the CD-ROM. Director shouldn't have any trouble accessing linked files on playback.**

Chapter 21

Shockwave to the Web Wescue

. . . .

In This Chapter

▶ Director in Cyberspace

▶ The shocking truth about Shockwave

▶ Testing your movie in Netscape Navigator

. . . .

*T*he World Wide Web. The World Wide Web? Where have I heard that before? Only everywhere. The Web is the latest and greatest thing, and just about no one saw the phenomenal interest in the Web coming. Corporate types are scrambling to find someone like you to help them get on the Web with attitude. And everyone, and I mean e-v-e-r-y-o-n-e, wants to have his or her very own Web page. Most of the time, they're not even sure why. . . .

Shockwave is the Web utility that everyone's talking about. Shockwave plays Director movies within Netscape Navigator and Internet Explorer, two popular Web *browsers* used to explore the depths of Cyberspace. Actually, Shockwave is a pair of utilities: AfterBurner, a compression program exclusively for Director movies; and the Shockwave plug-in that you add to the Plug-ins folder of your Web browser to play Director movies on the Web. Macromedia has also added Internet-related commands to the Lingo language that are beyond the scope of this book. For in-depth coverage of these new Lingo commands and lots more, see "Net Lingo Spoken Here!" in Chapter 14 of Greg Harvey's *Shockwave For Director For Dummies* (IDG Books Worldwide, Inc.), at your friendly bookstore now or soon. (The book, not Greg.)

Now that I've got you salivating, where do you find Shockwave? If you've got Director 5, you've got Shockwave. You'll find Shockwave inside your Director 5 folder in the Goodies or Utilities folder. The folks at Macromedia haven't made up their minds yet.

If you haven't received your Director 5 upgrade and you're dying to try the tips in this section, download Shockwave from Netscape's Web site at `http://home.netscape.com/`. Important: You need to download the Shockwave plug-in and AfterBurner separately. For some mysterious reason, Netscape is not bundling them together into one download. Nice products, though.

Why a Web?

The World Wide Web is just one small segment of the Internet, *the* network of networks — a sprawling, global, twisting conglomeration of cables, modems, gateways, servers, and software that has its roots in the Cold War of the '50s.

The Web, as it has come to be affectionately called, is the new kid on the block. Proposed as recently as 1989 by Tim Berners-Lee, a researcher for a giant laboratory in Geneva, the Web has come to be the most popular area of the Internet.

Why all the fuss?

Well, compare the Web to the Internet. Using the Internet directly requires endless lines of a cryptic computer language known as UNIX. I'm talking about programming code, reams and reams of code, reminiscent of how early PCs required users to know DOS (Disk Operating System) to get anything done. In other words, the Internet is for nerds (affectionately said), not real human beings. That's why the Internet was a secret for so long.

In contrast, the Web is a graphic environment with all the advantages of the Macintosh OS (operating system) and Windows. Rather than typing lines of commands, you work with icons representing objects, find the one you want, point with your mouse, and click. And people like working with pictures rather than keying in arcane code. Researchers at Xerox PARC (Palo Alto Research Center) — where most of the innovations that surfaced in the form of the first Macintosh had their beginnings — learned that years ago. Xerox PARC taught us a great many lessons about computer design, but the biggest one was that people enjoy working with pictures.

Another thing about people: We're never satisfied. Pictures alone aren't good enough anymore. They have to jump and flex and snatch us by the throat and yank us into unknown virtual realms. We want to see an animated World Wide Web. That's the dream, but what's the reality?

Much, much slower than a speeding bullet

By any standard, Web technology is slow. It's slower than a CD-ROM drive, a floppy drive, or the simplest of networks. In terms of speed, the Web is directly opposed to what animation and multimedia demand — high speed. One minute of uncompressed video takes up 27MB of information. Said another way so you really hear the numbers I'm talking about, to view one minute of video on the Web coming through your phone line, you need to squeeze 27MB of information through the whole mess of a system in under a minute. If you're already set up for the Web, try copying or *downloading* a simple file to your computer. I started my last download oh, around the time of the Great Depression.

So How Do I Get Started on the Web?

Aside from a basic computer setup, you need some hardware and software to enter the wacky world of Cyberspace:

- ✔ **Modem:** You need to purchase a modem, and only one kind will do. Demand your right as an American citizen to buy a 28.8 baud modem with V.34 plus protocol. It's the fastest in regular modem technology, and you won't be happy with anything less.

- ✔ **Internet service provider:** Your Internet service provider (ISP) becomes your liaison with the Web. Ordinary human beings don't connect their computers directly to the Web but to the service provider's servers, which connect you to the Web. Look for an organization that offers service to the Web (not all ISPs do), unlimited usage, and 1 to 2MB of their storage space for your very own Web page. Look for a monthly rate of around $20, give or take.

  If you're new to the Web, a *newbie* as they say, an easier route to connecting is America Online (AOL). When you sign up, AOL gives you 10 free hours to play with no obligation; if you decide to keep the service, the rate's under $10 a month including five hours of connect time plus 2MB of storage for your own Web page, and AOL's software includes it's own Web browser. By the time you read this, you should be able to use Netscape Navigator, the premiere Web browser, with AOL, too.

- ✔ **Web browser:** A Web *browser* is an application that allows you to see all those beautiful Web pages everyone's talking about. A browser is a kind of interpreter that translates a list of funny-looking lines of nonsensical text into readable text and graphics on a Web page. Netscape Navigator is about as good as browsers get.

  You need Netscape Navigator 2.0 or newer or Microsoft's Internet Explorer, especially to work with Shockwave. Basically, Navigator is free for review forever, or until Netscape changes its policies. You download (transfer) it from Netscape's Web site (at `http://home.netscape.com`) or get it from one of a number of CD-ROM collections of Web-related material. If a friend has a copy, don't underestimate the power of whining. When you sign up with an Internet service provider, the company should supply you with Netscape Navigator or a comparable browser and other Web goodies. If not, I'd report them immediately to the UnAmerican Activities Committee.

What Hast Thou, Shockwave?

Don't worry, the rest of this section isn't in neo-Shakespearian prose. Here's where Director and Shockwave step into the Web picture. Now look all you want, you won't find a Shockwave command anywhere in the menu bar. That's because Shockwave hasn't been seamlessly integrated into Director's interface yet. At this time, Shockwave is a type of external file called a *plug-in* that you add to a browser's Plug-ins folder.

Only the latest and greatest browsers work with Shockwave. I'd stay with Netscape Navigator or Internet Explorer from Microsoft. Download Netscape at `http://home.netscape.com` and Internet Explorer at `http://www.msn.com/`.

I'm going to give you a nice, informal introduction to Shockwave and the two external utilities it is comprised of, the Shockwave plug-in and AfterBurner. When you're ready for more, consider *Shockwave For Director For Dummies.*

Where does the Shockwave plug-in, well, plug in? That's where Netscape Navigator 2.0 — the hand-crafted folder of which is smartly reproduced in Figure 21-1 — takes center stage. To install the Shockwave plug-in, just drag it into the Plug-ins folder inside the Netscape Navigator directory/folder and you're set.

Figure 21-1:
Netscape
Navigator
and its
famous
Plug-ins
folder,
where you
install
Shockwave.

AfterBurner

AfterBurner's sole task in life is to dramatically compress your Director movies, one very effective solution to the problem I posed earlier on: How do you squeeze massive quantities of information through ordinary phone lines?

Compression is the key to everything you see and hear on the Web. The two types of graphics you encounter on the Web, GIF (Graphics Interchange Format) and JPEG (Joint Photographic Expert Group) files, represent other compression schemes. High-quality audio is just beginning to be heard, thanks to new applications for the Web like RealAudio 2.0 that have been engineered to compress sound for the Web. But AfterBurner is a specialist, reserving its powers for your Director movies alone.

Shockwave plug-in

The Shockwave plug-in recognizes Director 5 movies you've prepared with AfterBurner, discussed in the previous section, and displays your movie as part of the Web page itself. This kind of graphic is called an in-line graphic as opposed to a graphic showing up in a separate window.

Macromedia has made adding high-quality animations to Cyberspace simplicity itself with the Shockwave plug-in. You can start adding exciting animations and multimedia to the Web now, without using any Lingo, although skimming over Chapters 17 and 25 can't hurt. Exciting as other new Web technologies — like Java, JavaScript, and VRML (Virtual Reality Markup Language) — may sound, they ask a lot in return. With Java, for example, you need to learn a high-level, full-blown programming language at least as difficult as C++. JavaScript is a subset of the Java language, easier to learn than Java but still not exactly intuitive. And VRML is a markup language like the Web standard, HTML (HyperText Markup Language), no Sunday picnic either.

High-level means that the language is conversational and designed for us *human beans* to read and understand. *Low-level* languages like Assembly language are meant for computers to understand.

Okay, So How Do I Use Shockwave?

Be sure to install the Shockwave plug-in by dragging it into Netscape Navigator or Internet Explorer's Plug-in folder.

Prepping your Director movie

Be aware of a number of Director DOs and DON'Ts when preparing to compress your movies with AfterBurner, including the following.

Director DOs

Do keep the original Director movie small. AfterBurner does a great job of compressing your movies to about half their original size or better, but it needs all the help it can get. Figure 2K per second as a safe rate of compressed playback on the Web, so your uncompressed movie should average about 4K per second.

How do you figure your movie's rate? Divide your uncompressed movie's size in kilobytes by its playback time in seconds. You're looking for the value 4 as the result. For example, if your movie runs 30 seconds and its file size is 120K, divide 120 by 30. Perfect, you get 4. If you get a larger value, try reducing the movie with upcoming tricks. I know, 120K is a small movie considering that a blank Director file starts out at around 20K. Take Steve Martin's advice: Get small.

Try the following tricks to trim down a movie's file size:

- A movie's size is directly related to how large Bitmap Cast Members are on the Stage. Paint or import smaller Bitmap Cast Members and resize them larger on the Stage by Shift-dragging a corner selection handle.

    Are they going to look as good enlarged? No, but at this point in the Web's history, you're not aiming for broadcast-quality work.

- Use lots of 1-bit Cast Members; better yet, do the whole movie in 1-bit color.

    1-bit color? Right, you normally think of 1-bit color as only black-and-white graphics, blech; but in Director you can color a 1-bit bitmap on the Stage with the Tool palette. Select the bitmap and choose a color in the Foreground Color selector in the Tool palette. Other 1-bit bitmaps appearing in the same frame can be set to different colors.

- Create Cast Members with tools from the Tool palette instead of painting or importing bitmaps for nearly kilobyte-free graphics. For more info, see Chapter 9.

- Use lots of short film loops to enrich the animation in your movie. See Chapter 24 for more on film loops.

- Use sound, but think small: small sampling rates, small file size, small durations.

    Think 11.025 kHz sampling rate when you're digitizing sound with your AV Mac or with your sound board and try looping short sound clips to create longer audio sequences. Take a look at Chapter 19 for more sound tips.

Director DON'Ts

Shockwave doesn't recognize the following:

- Movies-in-a-window, an advanced feature of Director 5

- The "Wait For" option in the Tempo channel

- Custom menus, another advanced Director feature

- XObjects, external extensions to Director

- XCMDs and XFCNs, two other types of external extension that come from Apple's HyperCard environment

✔ The MCI command for Windows users

✔ The open, openDA, and closeDA commands

✔ The open window and close window commands

✔ The saveMovie command

✔ The importFileInto command

✔ Any filename and path properties

✔ The printFrom command

After you're satisfied with your Director movie and you save the latest changes to disk, choose File⇨Save and Compact, forcing Director to do some important housecleaning. File size drops dramatically, especially if you've been working on the movie for a long time.

Compressing your movie

After you prep your movie, you're ready to move on to AfterBurner, the file compression part of Shockwave.

Making the AfterBurner file

1. **Double-click the AfterBurner folder/directory to display the goodies inside, as shown in Figure 21-2.**

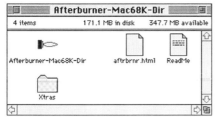

Figure 21-2:
The goodies
inside the
AfterBurner
folder/
directory.

2. **Double-click AfterBurner, which takes you to a simple Directory dialog box.**

3. **Find your Director movie and double-click the file.**

   The dialog box changes to a Save As dialog box so that you can choose where to place the compressed file. AfterBurner changes the extension from DIR to DCR.

4. **Click Desktop.**

5. **Rename the AfterBurner file, if you're so moved, and click Save.**

A progress window appears entitled "Burning" followed by the name of your movie.

6. When AfterBurner finishes, return to the Desktop.

At the Desktop, locate the AfterBurner file. The file for a movie called HOHOHO is pictured in Figure 21-3.

Figure 21-3:
If you follow my steps for compressing a Director movie, you'll find the AfterBurner file on the Desktop.

Testing an AfterBurner file

After compressing a Director movie with AfterBurner, test your movie in Netscape Navigator.

You don't need to be connected to the Web to use Netscape Navigator or any other Web browser.

1. Double-click Netscape Navigator.

Netscape Navigator tries to connect to its home page on the Web when you open the program. If you don't have a modem or it's not on (or if a problem arises), you see an alert letting you know that Navigator tried to do its job. Just click OK and continue.

When you arrive at Netscape Navigator, you see a Web page, as shown in Figure 21-4. In the top-left corner, find the line `Go to`. To the right is a long horizontal box, an entry field with the words, `http://home.netscape.com/` inside. This is Netscape Navigator's Web address, called a URL (Universal Resource Locator). You're going to replace it with the address of your AfterBurner file on the Desktop. Yes, you can see and test Web pages without being on the Web.

2. Click in the Go To field and press ⌘/Ctrl+A to select the contents.

3. Carefully type the following:

```
file:///
```

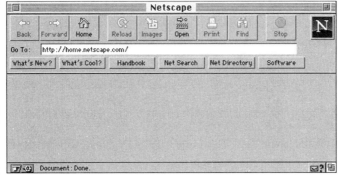

Figure 21-4:
Netscape
Navigator's
graphic
interface,
where you
can test
your
AfterBurner
file.

4. **Immediately after the third slash, type the name of your hard drive.**

In my case, I'd type **Lauren's%20HD**.

Here's where it gets a little dicey. Netscape doesn't recognize a common, ordinary old space character (the one you type with the spacebar).

5. **Replace any spaces in your hard disk's name with** %20.

%20 is the ASCII (plain text) equivalent of the space character. That makes Netscape happy.

After I complete step 5, I'd see `file:///Lauren's%20HD` in the Go To field.

6. **Immediately after what you've entered so far, type:**

```
/Desktop%20Folder/
```

7. **Finally, add the name of your AfterBurner file exactly as shown in its title.**

What you now see in the Go To field is the address of your file on the Desktop, Web style. If you typed everything correctly, you're one step away from viewing your movie. If I had an AfterBurner file called HOHOHO.DCR on my Desktop, for example, its address in the box would look like

```
file:///Lauren's%20HD/Desktop%20Folder/HOHOHO.DCR.
```

8. **Press Enter.**

If all's well, Netscape goes to the address in the Go To field, opens the AfterBurner file, and displays it in the Web page — thanks to the Shockwave plug-in. If nothing happens, you may get some kind of error message from Netscape. Message or not, the problem is probably just a typo in the Go To field. Check your work and try again.

Enjoy!

Chapter 22

Ready to Wear All Those Hats?

In This Chapter

▶ Multimedia in real life

▶ Some of the roles you play

▶ Ever notice all those credits at the end of a movie?

*T*he image of the lone wolf is very appealing to a lot of people — the maverick, the loose cannon, the independent producer, the radical, *The Man with No Name,* Newt Gingrich. As red-blooded, all-American types, we're drawn to the image. We see ourselves like Gary Cooper in *High Noon,* facing the enemy alone on a dusty street in some God-forsaken town. We hear Sinatra crooning in the background about doing it "my way." We honor the entrepreneurs and the athletes who buck all odds to become winners.

When it comes to multimedia, we want our name and our name alone to be called when it's time to hand out the awards. But that's not always the best way to do things in Real Life.

Multimedia in Real Life

At San Francisco State University, where I give a number of multimedia courses, I break up the class in one of the last sessions into groups of four or five students and have each group develop an idea for a *kiosk,* or a self-standing computer setup, used to easily maneuver through a lot of information. To pass the class, they must work together as a team, producing a so-called *alpha version* of the kiosk by the end of the day.

An alpha version of a multimedia project is the equivalent of the TV advertising world's traditional storyboard, where a sequence of stills suggests the direction of a commercial's story line and how its images flow. Sometimes, the alpha version *is* a storyboard. More often, the alpha version is a nonfunctioning placeholder, shown on-screen for graphics, text, sound, and animation to give your clients a better idea of what they have in mind — that is, what you think they have in mind and what you have in mind, plus any suggestions you don't think they would mind.

One student plays the part of creative director, giving the project a unique and consistent point of view. Another takes on the role of project manager, helping the team stay on track and meet deadlines. A third student provides graphics and production support, because multimedia is inevitably reliant on the visual, despite its broader appeal to all the senses. A fourth team member develops the *GUI* (graphical user interface) for the project.

Essentially, this classroom example is multimedia in Real Life, that experience that occurs between TV shows. Aside from an occasional opportunity to develop a project alone, perhaps because of the modest size of the project or, more likely, the modest size of the budget, multimedia development requires a joint effort by a creative team with extraordinarily diverse backgrounds.

Even with a small project, the client may require such tight deadlines that one person — given all the required skills and services — can't possibly complete the assignment alone. In fact, the demands of the project may compel you to develop a team, against your desire to play all parts. One of the images the growth of multimedia has resurrected has been that of the renaissance person of the 21st century: artist, artisan, programmer, computer guru, entrepreneur, good cook, able to leap tall buildings in a single bound. Every now and then, you see an article in one of the computer magazines about being a renaissance man or woman, and how you need to prepare yourself to handle any and all demands of a multimedia project.

Well, grasping the fundamentals of each piece that makes up the multimedia puzzle certainly doesn't hurt. As part of a team, you want to be able to communicate with the Lingo programmer, for example, and have a deep enough understanding of Director's built-in language to know what level of performance Lingo can and can't provide out of the box. For example, realizing that a client's request can be met only by developing a custom *XObject* (an external addition to Lingo) helps you anticipate the request's impact on the project's resources, budget, and estimated completion date.

It certainly doesn't hurt to be familiar with graphical user interface (GUI) guidelines either, like Apple's recommendations published in a number of formats, including a CD-ROM disc. Conforming to these guidelines is one of the more important decisions to be made on start-up of a multimedia venture, in addition to nightly flossing.

Yes, you heard right. Staying with generally accepted GUI guidelines is a decision you *make*. There's no amendment to the U.S. Constitution that I know of forcing multimedia types to conform to anyone's guidelines. Kai Krause's use of unique interfaces for his products — such as his Power Tools Photoshop plug-ins (unlike any interface previously known to humanity) — serves as a dramatic example that you can depart from the golden rules and still be wildly successful, critically and in the marketplace.

Some of the Roles You Play

Multimedia is a collaborative process, the melding of any number of areas of expertise to realize a successful product. Certainly, you want the client to consider the product a success measured in his or her own sometimes skewed terms. You look for critical and personal success, too. Part of the formula for success includes making the right decision to go it alone or to put together a team to complete the project. I've listed some of the supporting cast in a typical multimedia production team. By the way, multimedia offers plenty of parts for you readers who have little or no graphics background. (Many of my students at San Francisco State express this concern.)

Creative director

The creative director provides the main vision of the project, much like the director of a motion picture or the editor of a magazine. Having a background in film, video, computers, all three, or any two areas doesn't hurt. (With three, you get egg roll.)

Above all, the creative director communicates to all parties involved what needs to be done on a moment-to-moment, real-time basis to successfully complete the assignment. So the role of creative director involves a critical managerial aspect, a leadership ability at least as important as specific skills in the areas mentioned in the preceding paragraph.

The creative director's vision holds the project together like glue. He or she maintains continuity to the work from screen to screen and contributes to the project's ultimate look and feel. The creative director maintains a broader view of the project than the other team members working in their various specialized areas.

Art director

A multimedia project may have an art director whose vision is as broad as the creative director's, but who focuses on aesthetic issues on a real-time basis. In this sense, the art director has a significant impact on the visual outcome of the project, second only to the creative director.

The art director focuses on issues such as color schemes, typefaces used throughout the project, and the look and feel of illustrations, charts, and graphs displayed on-screen. He or she also contributes managerial skills to the project, overseeing artiste types who are contracted to provide screen illustrations, animation sequences, and specialized multimedia items such as custom icons and cursors for the project. The art director also often oversees photo shoots for quality and content.

Project manager

The success of a multimedia project is often due in large measure to the expertise of its project manager, who is contracted to help establish and meet milestones and other critical deadlines. Milestones include the beginning and ending dates of the project and due dates for *alpha versions, beta versions,* and *golden masters* of the production.

- ✔ An alpha version is like an on-screen storyboard for a project with little or no functionality, but useful for walking the client through the creative team's interpretation of the client's wishes. An alpha version is also important as a check that all the important points are included in the production as planned.

- ✔ The beta version is near final quality with all essential functionality in place. Few, if any, placeholders stand in for animation sequences or screen art, though some other rough edges may show at this point.

- ✔ The final version, sometimes called the golden master, is ready for client approval and presentation.

The project manager manipulates the resources of the project through events that inevitably occur, such as technical stumbling blocks, loss of staff from illness, and shortage of supplies from vendors. He may use software tools like Claris MacProject Pro for the Mac, Symantec's Time Line for the PC, or Microsoft Project (which is cross-platform) to help reallocate resources and reset noncritical deadlines so that the team stays on track and meets milestone commitments.

GUI designer

A graphical user interface (GUI) designer is often hired to provide the interface for the project. An extremely critical aspect of a project, the interface can make or break a multimedia production. In general, the GUI designer is responsible for adhering to generally accepted graphical user interface guidelines. Otherwise, he or she is responsible for creating an interface that's consistent with the mission of the project.

Lingo programmer

In many, if not most, Director multimedia teams, you can find at least one key Lingo programmer who has been contracted to implement scripting for a Director project. His or her background usually includes heavy experience in traditional programming languages such as C, Pascal, or Fortran. This kind of background ensures that the programmer can develop scripts optimized for

TIP

GUI GUIdelines

The heart of graphical user interface guidelines includes several generally accepted principles that you might consider:

- ✓ **Real world metaphors:** For example, using controls such as buttons, sliders, and dials as part of the interface.

- ✓ **Direct manipulation:** Giving the user control over the screen environment.

- ✓ **See-and-point:** Designing the interface to exploit visual cues rather than asking the user to remember commands.

- ✓ **Consistency:** Building on the user's expectations about how a program is going to behave from previous experience with other programs.

- ✓ **WYSIWYG:** *What You See Is What You Get*, giving the user an on-screen experience as close as possible to reality or to an experience in another medium; for example, a printout of the screen compared to the screen itself.

- ✓ **User control:** Developing an interface that places the user in control of actions.

- ✓ **Feedback and dialogue:** Maintaining communication with the user so that the computer recognizes and responds to user actions; for example, a button that highlights when the user presses it.

- ✓ **Forgiveness:** Including "outs" for the user to change his mind *without penalty* and warning the user when an action is irreversible.

- ✓ **Perceived stability:** Providing a comfort zone of predictability in the interface so that critical elements don't arbitrarily disappear or change location; for example, menu items graying out instead of vanishing when disabled.

- ✓ **Aesthetic integrity:** Basically, using the whole arsenal of available design tools and techniques to ensure user-friendliness.

---

speed and performance, which is not to say that someone without a similar background is incapable of writing excellent scripts. The key word is *ensure*. The probability of such a team member being stumped by a scripting challenge is greatly diminished, and the programmer can achieve the level of scripting required as quickly as possible.

In addition, a programmer with experience in other computer languages may be able to develop external commands, which Director calls XObjects, or new Xtras plug-ins if needed to supplement Director's built-in capabilities.

Instructional designer

Multimedia as an educational product — a self-running tutorial, for example — often means adding the services of an instructional designer to the project. The instructional designer has a background in applied learning theory and experience in developing interfaces that maximize the educational experience of a *CAI* (computer-aided instruction) or *CBT* (computer-based training) product. The instructional designer works in unison with the GUI designer, the art director, and the creative director.

Program tester

Testing is an extremely critical area for multimedia development. More often than not, a team member specializing in software testing is brought in to ensure that the product runs on all intended platforms within the given minimum specifications established at the beginning of the project. Most recently, Disney's *Lion King* CD-ROM underscored the importance of solid testing of multimedia products so that embarrassing and unnecessary software failures don't occur. Buyers reportedly discovered problems simply installing *The Lion King* and then found a number of incompatibilities with common computer configurations, reflecting the lack of rigorous testing.

Software is never perfect, but testing under different conditions helps alleviate most problems. Because users are very creative, the program tester tries to anticipate all the untraditional scenarios a user might act out while running the program and then builds in safeguards to protect the integrity of the software.

Ever Notice All Those Credits at the End of a Movie?

Was it beginning with *2001: A Space Odyssey* or earlier that the credits seemed to go on forever at the end of the movie? I don't really remember when I first realized that credits were getting longer than the movie itself, but one thing's for sure: These days, you expect credits to go by interminably. Directed by . . . Second Assistant Directed by . . . Best Boy . . . Best Boy's Third Cousin on His Mother's Side, Twice Removed . . . and on and on. At least they don't list Shoes by . . . anymore, like they used to in those old Italian movies about gladiators and the benefits of rubbing olive oil all over your pecs.

What I'm trying to say is this: Going it alone is pretty rough. I hope this chapter has given you an idea of how complex even a relatively small multimedia project can be, not to discourage you but to show you that recognizing the need for support is more typical than unusual in the wacky world of multimedia.

It's fun to fantasize about doing it all yourself, wearing all those hats and reaping all the credits. But when was the last time you saw only one name in the credits for a movie? Except for *Citizen Kane,* of course.

Part V
The Part of Tens

"NOT ONLY DID WE GET YOU AN APPLE WITH A MOUSE, LIKE YOU ASKED, WE ALSO GOT YOU A BANANA WITH A LIZARD."

In this part . . .

1f you know anything about the . . .*For Dummies* tradition, you know that these books like to leave you with a partful of chapters to peruse in sets of tens — really ten glorified bullet points. If these points were written on stone tablets, Charlton Heston would feel right at home.

Anyway, relax and enjoy my collection of Director tips and tricks. Hey, it's Miller time.

Chapter 23

Ten Common Director Questions and Answers

● ●

In This Chapter

▶ How can I cut down the size of my movie?

▶ What can I do to make my movies play faster?

▶ What's the best way to speed up digital video in Director?

▶ Why do I keep losing part of my screen when I tape my movies?

▶ How can I tape Director movies to my VCR?

▶ Why am I getting weird colors when I tape my Director movies?

▶ How can I improve the color of my movies on tape?

▶ Can I set up my movie to play at the right speed on any computer?

▶ I've never done any programming before. How do I know my Lingo scripts are okay?

▶ Can I play my Director movies on a Mac and a PC?

● ●

*P*erfect strangers come out of nowhere pleading with me to answer questions about Macromedia Director. The following are the ten most common questions they ask and my answers for your "edutainment" and "amusecation."

How Can I Cut Down the Size of My Movie?

You can use a couple of techniques to cut down the size of a Director movie, which is never a bad idea, by the way. Movies that have been cut down run faster on slower hard drives, older computers, the Web, and CD-ROM drives, should they be destined to star on a CD-ROM disc.

Rather than choosing File⇨Save, choose File⇨Save and Compact, especially after you complete a large Director movie. The Save and Compact command offers special features, including the following:

✔ **Trashing unneeded info from the Director movie:** As you develop a movie, Director tends to hang on to outdated info that it has recorded along the way, causing bloated files. Running Save and Compact makes Director dump this digital flotsam and jetsam, effectively compacting the file.

✔ **Internally rearranging Cast Members:** Choosing File⇨Save and Compact helps to further optimize the Director movie for playback. You won't necessarily see a change in the Cast window, but whatever Director does contributes to building the smallest and fastest-running Director file possible.

Another way of trimming the fat from a Director movie is to move the Score to a new movie. Here's the scoop, step by step:

1. **Choose Window⇨Score.**

2. **Choose Edit⇨Select All.**

   Selecting frames in the original Score by choosing Select All is very important. If you try selecting frames by dragging the mouse or Shift-clicking a range of frames, markers set in the Score won't be included in the selection and won't transfer to a new file with the Paste Cells command. You'll need to reestablish the markers, a chore worse than laundering underwear.

3. **Choose Edit⇨Copy Cells.**

4. **Choose File⇨New⇨Movie.**

   A new movie appears with the Score window open and active.

5. **Choose Edit⇨Paste Cells.**

6. **Choose File⇨Save As.**

7. **Type a unique name and click OK.**

   If you want to replace the original movie, enter the original movie name in the Save As dialog box, click OK, and then click OK again when your computer asks whether you really want to replace the file.

This second method actually has an advantage or two over the Save and Compact command. Copying selected cells from the Score of one movie and pasting the selection into the Score window of a new Director file fills the new Cast window only with Cast Members that appear in the Score window. Just be sure that you don't mind losing all those deadbeat Cast Members too lazy to make an appearance. Deleting unused Cast Members in this way makes an even smaller file than using the Save and Compact command. In addition, Director eliminates any empty pockets of cells that may have been present in the original movie's Cast window, because it fills consecutive cells of the new Cast window with Cast Members for the new movie.

If you're tight on memory, you can achieve the same benefits of the second method I just described without leaving the original movie by choosing Edit⇨Find⇨Cast Member and clicking the Usage radio/option button in the Find Cast Member dialog box. Director highlights all the unused Cast Members. Delete them by choosing Edit⇨Clear Cast Members. Then choose File⇨Save and Compact for a Director pick-me-up.

What Can I Do to Make Movies Play Faster?

Use a bouquet of strategies to make your movies play faster:

✔ Compact your movie with one of the methods discussed earlier.

✔ Change single-color Cast Members to 1-bit Cast Members using Director's Transform Bitmap command under the Cast menu. Then apply a color to the bitmap selected on the Stage with the Foreground Color selector in the Tools palette.

✔ Change 16-bit and 24-bit Cast Members to dithered 8-bit Cast Members using Director's Transform Bitmap command under the Cast menu. A 16-bit Cast Member asks your Mac to process roughly 32,000 colors at one time. A 24-bit Cast Member tasks your processor even further, with over 16 million colors. Dithering to 8-bit cuts down the number of colors to a mere 256, along with a special trick reminiscent of what the Impressionists accomplished with dabs of oil paint. Up close, all you see in their paintings is flecks of color, but from a normal viewing distance, the spots of color blend into new color combinations. That's the idea behind dithering, creating the illusion of seeing more than 256 colors by placing the right colored pixels, or *pels,* next to each other in an unobtrusive pattern.

✔ Take advantage of Director's memory management features. If you have tons of RAM, select all Cast Members from the Cast window and choose Purge Priority 0 from the Cast Member Properties dialog box so that they all stay in memory. Anything in memory is about 1,000 times faster to access than having Director find a Cast Member on disk and load the object into RAM. In limited RAM situations, choose Purge Priority 3 for your most important Cast Members and Purge Priority 2 for secondary Cast Members whenever possible so that Cast Members not used frequently are quickly trashed from memory. Cast members with Purge Priority 2 are released from memory before Cast Members assigned Purge Priority 3. See Chapter 4 for more on prioritizing your cast.

✔ Apply the Copy ink effect to all sprites whenever possible. With a white background, assign White Background ink to nonrectangular sprites that must pass in front of other sprites on the Stage; otherwise, choose Matte ink for these sprites. Choose Mask ink if you must have a doughnut hole effect, but *avoid* all other ink effects unless absolutely vital to your production.

What's the Best Way to Speed Up Digital Video in Director?

To speed up digital video in Director, use Director's Direct To Stage feature, which optimizes playback of digital video in a movie. Just follow these steps:

1. **Choose Window⇨Cast.**

2. **Select the desired Digital Video Cast Member in the Cast window.**

3. **Click the Cast Member Properties button at the top of the Cast window, as shown in Figure 23-1.**

   The Digital Video Cast Member Properties dialog box appears.

Figure 23-1: The Cast Member Properties button.

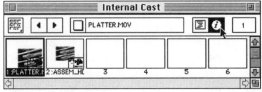

4. **Check the Direct To Stage check box, as shown in Figure 23-2.**

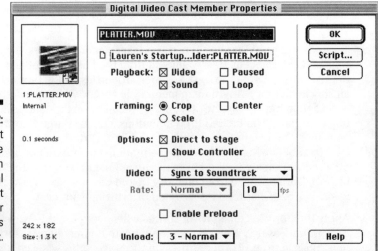

Figure 23-2: The Direct to Stage check box in the Digital Video Cast Member Properties dialog box.

When you apply Direct To Stage to a digital video, you must conform to *The Rules.* The Rules state: No other object may be placed in a higher channel than the digital video; no other object may animate across the digital video; and no special inks may be applied to the digital video. For more information about the Direct To Stage option, peruse Chapter 11.

Why Do I Keep Losing Part of My Screen When I Tape My Movies?

The differing makeup between computer video and NTSC TV reveals itself again when you tape a Director movie or print-to-video. You find that the beautiful image you carefully composed on your computer monitor partially disappears. Some of the title may be missing, resting in nether regions beyond the border of the TV screen, along with other lost details you worked so hard to perfect.

NTSC TV is designed to create an image larger than the picture area of the TV so that it fills the screen, bordered only by the physical, plastic frame of the Ray-O-Vision TV set itself. This phenomenon is called *overscan* by broadcasting types. The same thing happens to your Director movie when its video signals are converted to NTSC-compatible signals as you print to video. The image is blown up, and you lose a good inch or more of picture all the way around.

The solution is to anticipate overscan when you're planning a Director project for taping and to designate a safe title area 512 x 384 pixels or pels and centered in the Stage. Don't let titles, other copy, or important objects touch or extend beyond this area. Keep borders well within an inch of this safe area. If you set up a multiple monitor configuration as described in the section "A better way to be NTSC safe," you can visually adjust areas on the RGB display so that they don't get cut off on the TV screen.

How Can I Tape Director Movies to My VCR?

Unless you own an AV Mac or install a video edit board in your computer, there's really no effective way to put your Director movies on videotape. If you insist on trying, the simplest technique involves your computer's monitor and a camcorder.

Simple, cheap, but not terribly impressive

The simplest, most inexpensive but least effective way of videotaping a Director movie is to tape the Mac's monitor itself with your camcorder. You lose a lot of definition, color, and quality along the way. You may also get weird, shimmering patterns and vertically rolling bars in the image because of the difference in synchronization signals between the video camera and the computer monitor.

But you can minimize many of these pitfalls with a few tricks:

- If your camcorder features a variable shutter, visually adjust the shutter until the vertical roll disappears from the image on the monitor or is minimized. Many high-end consumer camcorders, especially Hi-8 and Super-VHS models, feature a variable shutter these days. Check your manual.

- To reduce distortion, shoot from a distance using the longest telephoto setting your camcorder has to offer.

- Soften the screen's pixels by shooting slightly out of focus. Better yet, shoot through a Hasselblad diffusion filter to minimize screen pixels on tape. Nikon diffusion filters are the next best choice.

- Adjust your monitor's settings to reduce contrast, and shoot in a darkened room to avoid glare.

- If at all possible, use a color laptop computer that features an active matrix LCD (Liquid Crystal Display) screen. How do you know whether your laptop has an active matrix screen? Break down and read the manual. Because LCD screens work differently than conventional computer monitors, they don't display rolling bars or annoying distortions when videotaped. LCD panels are flat, too, which helps minimize distortion.

AV Macs

If you're the proud owner of an AV-type Centris, Quadra, or Power Mac, you're all set to copy your Director movies to videotape. For highest quality, use the S-Video Video Out port from your AV Mac to the S-Video Video In port available on Hi-8 or Super-VHS camcorder and VCR models. Otherwise, use premium quality, shielded RCA-type video cables for the connection.

For first-generation AV Power Macs, you need to purchase an adapter at your friendly electronics shop to convert the stereo miniplug Audio Out port to left and right audio cables, most likely RCA-type cables. Either way, use the best-shielded cables you can afford.

Video tape is no place to skimp on cash, either. Buy the highest quality brand-name video tape you can find. And break down and buy a brand-name head-cleaning kit to clean the recording heads of your VCR before taping.

If you record in real time, the way your movie plays back on your monitor, be sure to take precautions before taping. Choose Window⇨Inspectors⇨Memory and click Purge. And remember to follow my suggestions for optimizing playback speed in "What Can I Do to Make Movies Play Faster?" earlier in this chapter.

Video boards

Without an AV Mac, you need to install a video board in your Macintosh or PC, such as Radius's VideoSpigot for the Mac's NuBus slot or one of Miro's selection of video boards for Macs and PCs. These boards do the job of converting computer video into real TV signals compatible with your camcorder or VCR. A more expensive but elegant solution for the Mac is to purchase Radius' VideoVision Studio or Telecast board, with the added benefit of creating full-screen digital video at 30 *fps* (frames per second) from incoming video.

Why Am I Getting Weird Colors When I Tape My Director Movies?

One of the biggest differences between real TV, the stuff we watch at home with our shoes off, and so-called computer video is the *gamut,* or range, of colors available on each system. (By the way, it is technically possible to watch TV with your shoes on.) If you're fortunate enough to be working with 24-bit color, you're playing with 16 million-plus colors on your monitor. With the monitor properly adjusted, any one of these colors displays relatively purely on-screen, although your monitor does have limitations of its own that I won't get into (to thunderous applause).

In comparison, Real TV color is atrocious, It's atrocious compared to just about anything, but especially compared to the beautiful images beaming off your pristine, perfectly adjusted computer monitor. Real TV's gamut of colors is extremely limited; only a small portion of the spectrum of colors displays at all. And of these colors, only a percentage display acceptably for viewing purposes. These are the so-called NTSC, or "legal," colors. "Illegal" colors that display beautifully on your computer monitor may *bloom* on TV, meaning that the colors spill over the borders of their object and in motion, smear across the rest of the television image. The colors may look DayGlo-ish and psychedelic, the way colors look on your TV when you crank up the color control. Generally, these are colors above 70 percent of their saturation (the intensity of a hue, how blue a blue sky is, for example) point.

So the answer to the question is, you're getting weird colors because so few of the colors that look fine and dandy on your computer monitor translate into NTSC colors on your Ray-O-Vision TV set at home. If you're interested in how to overcome this seemingly impossible technological hurdle, read on.

How Can I Improve the Color of My Movies on Tape?

Okay, you just installed your high-definition, surround-sound, wide-screen, 80-foot, monster Ray-O-Vision television set and antiaircraft radar detector, settled back to enjoy watching your Director *pièce de résistance* you transferred to tape, and . . . bad color! All that work for bad color. What's a videophile to do?

NTSC palette

The easiest, least technologically challenging, and least costly method to improve colors when you print to video, as multimedia types say, is to use Director's NTSC palette, one of the special collections of colors included with Director out of the box. No extra charge.

To set an entire Director movie to NTSC-legal colors, do the following:

1. **Choose Window⇨Cast from the menu bar.**

   Now you need to change the color depth of all Cast Members to 8-bit color.

2. **Choose Edit⇨Select All.**

3. **Choose Modify⇨Transform Bitmap to display the Transform Bitmap dialog box.**

4. **Choose 8 Bits from the Color Depth pop-up menu and click Transform.**

   An alert appears, telling you the transformation cannot be undone and giving you a chance to change your mind.

5. **Click OK.**

   Now you need to make certain that the display is set to 8-bit color, too.

6. **Choose File⇨Preferences⇨General.**

7. **Check the Reset Monitor to Movie's Color Depth check box and click OK.**

8. **Choose Window⇨Score from the menu bar.**

9. **In frame 1, double-click the cell in the Palette channel, as shown in Figure 23-3.**

   Director displays the Palette dialog box.

10. **Choose NTSC from the Palette pop-up menu, as shown in Figure 23-4.**

11. **Be sure that the Palette Transition radio/option button is on.**

12. **Click OK.**

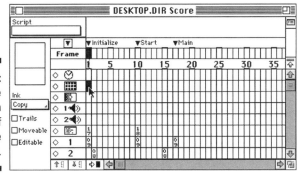

Figure 23-3:
The Palette
channel in
frame 1 of
the Score
window.

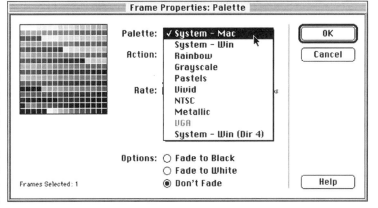

Figure 23-4:
NTSC is one
option in the
Palette pop-
up menu in
the Palette
dialog box.

Until you change palettes again, all screen images are built on the NTSC collection of "legal" colors.

The best strategy is to anticipate printing to video at the beginning of a project and to use an NTSC palette at all times. You find NTSC colors as an option in programs like Photoshop, too, where you have the opportunity to create bitmaps exclusively with "legal" colors *before* importing them into Director, which is the preferred method.

When you import a bitmap created with the default System palette, be sure to choose Remap Colors and Dither from the dialog box that appears after you click the Import button. The basic scenario plays something like the following:

1. **Choose File⇨Import.**

   The Import Files dialog box appears.

2. **Locate and select the bitmap to import in the directory, and then click Import.**

   The Image Options dialog box appears, as shown in Figure 23-5.

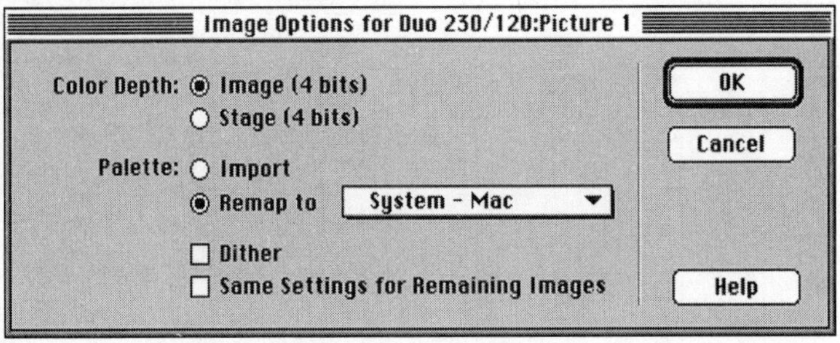

Figure 23-5:
Director lets
you remap
a bitmap's
colors
before
importing it
into the Cast
window.

> Image Options for Duo 230/120:Picture 1
>
> Color Depth: ⦿ Image (4 bits)
> ○ Stage (4 bits)
>
> Palette: ○ Import
> ⦿ Remap to   System - Mac ▾
>
> ☐ Dither
> ☐ Same Settings for Remaining Images
>
> [OK]
> [Cancel]
> [Help]

3. Choose the Remap To and Dither options.

4. Click OK.

With a Bitmap cast member built on the System palette already in the Cast, try
the following to remap the cast member to the NTSC palette:

**1. Highlight the Cast Member in the Cast window and choose
Modify⇨Transform Bitmap.**

The Transform Bitmap dialog box appears, as shown in Figure 23-6.

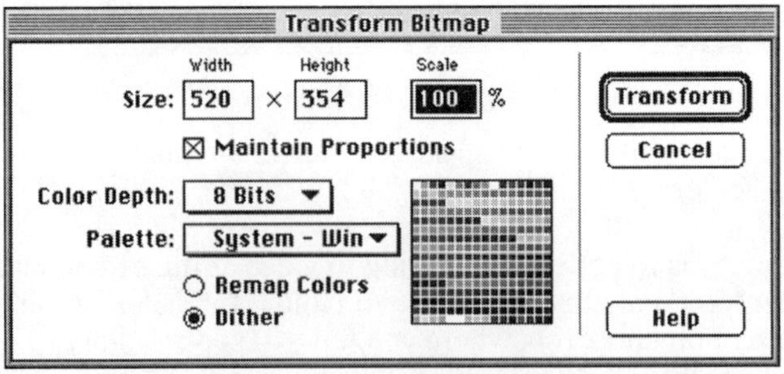

Figure 23-6:
The
Transform
Bitmap
dialog box,
where you
can remap a
Bitmap Cast
Member's
palette.

> Transform Bitmap
>
>   Width   Height   Scale
> Size: [520] × [354]   [100] %
>
>   ☒ Maintain Proportions
>
> Color Depth: [8 Bits ▾]
>   Palette: [System - Win ▾]
>
>   ○ Remap Colors
>   ⦿ Dither
>
> [Transform]
> [Cancel]
> [Help]

2. Choose NTSC from the Palette pop-up menu.

3. Click the Remap Colors radio/option button; then click Transform.

A better way to be NTSC safe

Working with an NTSC monitor is the best way to prepare a Director movie for
printing to video. If you have a 660AV Mac, 840AV Mac, or first-generation AV

Power Mac, you can switch to your TV with the Monitors control panel. (You PC-ites can purchase a video board with an extra video port for NTSC TV. Break down and read its manual.)

1. **Choose ⌘⇨Control Panels⇨Monitors.**

2. **Click the Options button in the Monitors control panel.**

    The Monitors dialog box appears. In addition to setting your monitor to different color depths (256, Thousands, Millions), you can control video output from here.

3. **Click the Display Video on Television radio button.**

    If your monitor is set to 256 colors or less, your Mac allows you the option of checking the Use flicker-free format check box so that all images are free of annoying flicker. With your monitor set to thousands or millions of colors, the check box is automatically checked and disabled.

4. **Click OK.**

    An alert appears asking whether you really want to switch monitors.

5. **Click Switch in the alert box.**

Your monitor goes black as your Mac begins sending an NTSC signal to your real TV set. When you want to return to your RGB monitor, select the Display Video on RGB Monitor radio/option button from the Options window of the Monitors control panel.

Now you can work using your TV as your computer monitor. You have instant feedback to colors in use and can instantly note the effect on your NTSC "monitor." The only problem with this setup is that the resolution is so poor on a real TV compared to the crisp pixels of a good RGB monitor that you may begin suffering eye strain and headaches in a very short time.

With the second-generation Power Mac 8500, you'll find the Monitors and Sound control panel of System 7.5.3 — as shown in Figure 23-7 — in place of the dusty old Monitors control panel. Several other windows are associated with the new control panel. Here's how you use them:

1. **Set your TV to Channel 3 (the Channel you watch videos on; in some areas, it's Channel 4).**

    Be sure to run video and audio cables from Video Out and Audio Out ports on your Mac to Video In and Audio In to your VCR or TV monitor.

2. **Choose ⌘⇨Control Panels⇨Monitors and Sound.**

    In addition to choosing the color depth for your monitor from this set of control panels, you can set up different options for running two displays at one time.

3. **Choose Window⇨Arrange Displays.**

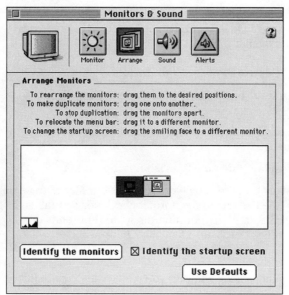

Figure 23-7:
The
Monitors
and Sound
control
panel for
second-
generation
Power
Macs,
where you
can switch
output from
your monitor
to a TV
screen.

4. In the Arrange Displays window, drag the title bar of the computer monitor thumbnail over the TV thumbnail.

Your Mac instantly moves the display on your computer monitor to your TV while keeping your computer monitor active. To your Mac, your TV and computer monitor have merged into one "virtual screen." Read the other display options available from the Arrange Displays window. For example, you may decide to "mirror" the setup so that your TV and monitor show the same display.

You PC types may access similar video drivers by following these steps:

1. Double-click Windows Setup in the Main program group.

2. In the Windows Setup dialog box, choose Options⇨Change System Settings to display the Change System Settings dialog box.

3. Click the top line in the Display list to reveal the Display options, as in Figure 23-8.

4. Click the desired video setting.

5. Click OK.

The best of all worlds is running both an NTSC TV and a computer monitor at the same time, using the NTSC screen to check regularly on the progress of your work, especially for colors and patterns. For PCs, some high-end video edit boards support running your computer monitor and an NTSC TV concurrently.

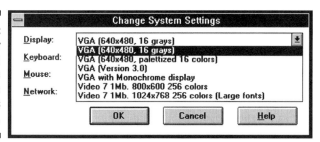

Figure 23-8:
Display
options in
the Change
System
Settings
dialog box.

Take a look at Fast Electronic's Fast video edit board featuring video input and output for VHS, S-Video, and Hi-8 tape formats. Fast Electronic U.S. Inc. claims the board performs at 30 frames/60 fields/second at 640 x 480 resolution playing AVI digital video files. Its price is around $550.

Miro Computer offers several video boards, including the miroVIDEO DC20 bundle. Miro claims performance of full-screen video (640 x 480) at 30 frames/60 fields/second with Motion-JPEG compression up to 5:1. The card outputs to VHS, S-VHS, Video8, or Hi8 with a choice of NTSC or PAL video formats. The price is just under $1,000.

The upscale candidate for video edit boards is Truevision's Targa 2000 PCI featuring built-in hardware acceleration for Adobe Premiere, 16MB of on-board memory, 30 frames/60 fields/second NTSC video capture and 24 frames/50 fields/second video capture for PAL (a European video standard). The Targa 2000 board provides a port for previewing NTSC video on a separate monitor. The price tops the $3,000 mark.

Using a setup like the preceding examples along with Director's NTSC palette is the ultimate print-to-video configuration. If you feel adventurous, you can always create a custom color within the NTSC palette and save the new palette as a custom palette. Just be sure to avoid raising the saturation level of any new color above 70 to 75 percent and you'll probably be okay.

Can I Set Up My Movie to Play Right on Any Computer?

The trick to producing your Director movie so that it plays at the right speed on any computer is twofold. First, you need to decide on the minimally acceptable configuration for playing back your movie and then reproduce the configuration in your studio. If you decide you want anyone with a Mac SE, 4MB of RAM, and a stick of bubble gum to run your movie off a high-density floppy, you must design the movie on that platform. For the sake of speed, you work in other programs and do some of the tinkering in Director on a high-powered Mac, but do the serious tempo settings and playback on the dusty, old SE when you start timing and syncing stuff for the final production. The same strategy applies to working on the PC platform.

When you've got everything timed down to the nanosecond on the sluggish SE or PC, the second ploy comes into play: locking the tempo. To prepare for locking the tempo, do the following steps with Director running on the target platform (in this example, the SE):

1. **Choose Control⇨Disable Scripts.**

2. **Choose Control⇨Loop Playback.**

3. **Press ⌘/Ctrl+Option/Alt+R to rewind the movie.**

4. **Press ⌘/Ctrl+Option/Alt+P to play back the movie once on the target computer.**

Now you're ready to lock your movie's tempo. Choose Modify⇨Movie⇨ Properties and check the Lock Frame Durations check box in the Movie Properties dialog box, as shown in Figure 23-9.

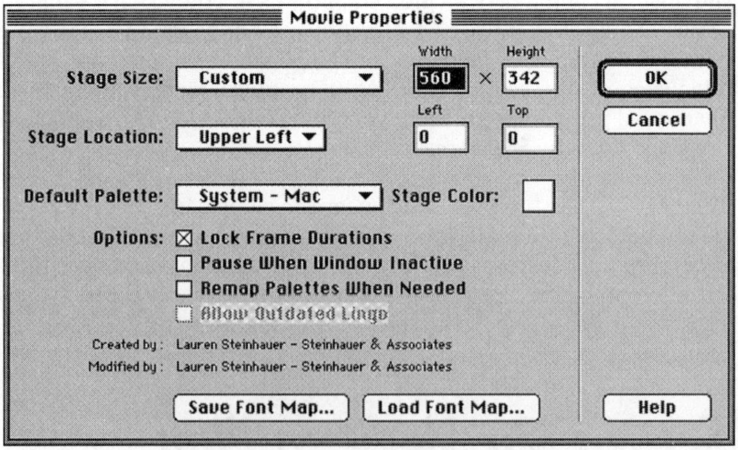

Figure 23-9:
Checking the Lock Frame Durations check box in the Movie Properties dialog box.

Remember, this technique doesn't ensure *optimal* playback. Locking the movie's tempo ensures *consistent* playback from computer to computer by designing for the lowest common denominator in mind. Sigh — this is the stuff that makes multimedia great.

I've Never Done Programming Before. How Do I Know My Lingo Scripts Are Okay?

First, go slowly with scripting; it's like learning a foreign language. Then, the best way to check your first Lingo scripts is to test them line by line in the Message window as you include them in your Director movie. For each line of Lingo you want to test, enter it in the Message window and then press Return. You don't want to wait until you amass hundreds of lines of scripts and then discover errors you need to trace back to who knows where. As you add scripts to your movie, include plenty of comments in the scripts, explaining why the line of Lingo is needed and what it's intended to do. Contrary to stories you may have heard, comments don't slow down scripts. Director simply ignores them. Remember, choose Text⇨Comment or use the keyboard shortcut, ⌘/Ctrl+>, for each line in a script you want to mark as a comment.

When you think you're finished with your movie, choose Window⇨Message or press ⌘/Ctrl+M to display the Message window, check the Trace button, and play back your movie. Don't be surprised if Director stops your movie and slaps a script error on-screen. Go to the script and look for the problem in the line with the blinking insertion point. Remember, odds are that the problem's either a simple typo or a syntax problem. Sometimes a script doesn't work because of a memory problem; check that you're allocating the best Purge Priorities to your Cast Members. Review the Lingo material in this book again (see Chapters 12, 17, and 25), and don't forget Director's wonderful online help.

Can I Play My Director Movies on a Macintosh and a PC?

One of Director's strengths is its cross-platform compatibility. You can create a projector using the Windows version of Director 5, that is virtually identical to the Mac version. In other words, you need both the Mac and Windows versions. Say you're going from the Mac to the PC. After developing your presentation on the Mac, it's a simple matter of opening Director for Windows, choosing the Create Projector command from the File menu, and selecting the Mac movies to be incorporated into the Windows projector.

The real trick is prepping Mac movies intended for playback in a Windows projector on a PC monitor (VGA or Super VGA) and vice-versa. Take the following precautions to avoid nasty surprises:

✔ **Use Windows' strictest file-naming rules:** Begin the name with a capital letter; up to eight capital letters long, not including the period and extension that Windows needs to see at the end of a filename; and no spaces or punctuation characters, including the period which is reserved to precede the file name's extension.

✔ **Use the Windows – System palette included with Director:** Jump back to the "How Can I Improve the Color of My Movies on Tape?" section in this chapter to review how to set up a custom palette for your movie.

✔ **Prepare for font wars:** PC fonts are dramatically different from Mac fonts. The easiest way to avoid problems is to turn text into bitmaps while in Director. If you must use editable text, meaning word-processing like text in a text box, stick with boring, old Helvetica and Times.

✔ **Prep your digital videos:** QuickTime mooVs may be included in a Director file destined for a Windows projector, but each mooV must be prepped in a utility program such as MoviePlayer 2.0. Open each QuickTime mooV in MoviePlayer 2.0 and then choose File⇨Save As. Click the Make movie self-contained radio/option button and check the Playable on non-Apple computers check box, as shown in Figure 23-10, and then click Save. Repeat with each QuickTime mooV featured in your Director movie. This is called *flattening* a mooV.

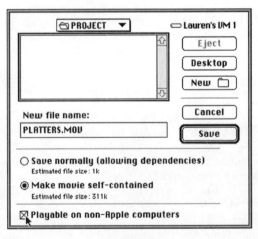

Figure 23-10:
The Save As dialog box in the QuickTime utility and player, MoviePlayer 2.0.

Chapter 24

Ten Ways to Add Animation to Your Movies

. . . .

In This Chapter

▶ Use Animation Wizard's built-in special effects

▶ Remember In-Between commands

▶ Try color cycling

▶ Buy good clip animation

▶ Turn Cast Members into moveable sprites

▶ Import digital videos

▶ Import PICS files from non-QuickTime applications

▶ Record real-time animations

▶ Use film loops

▶ Switch color palettes

. . . .

Director offers a number of techniques for adding animation to your movies, some with near push-button ease, many others only slightly more complex. Use the following list o' techniques as a useful reference for yourself. When you're stumped, just say, "Self, take a look at that useful list Lauren put together just for me."

Use Animation Wizard's Built-In Special Effects

Consider using Director's Animation Wizard Xtra, especially helpful for creating presentations on a super-tight deadline. The material in Chapter 16 can help you create impressive animation sequences with little more than a couple clicks of the mouse and a few keystrokes to enter a title and a little bit of copy.

If you missed Chapter 16 altogether, the following is a summary of Animation Wizard's features for your perusal:

- ✔ **Banners:** Text scrolls across the screen horizontally, bringing to mind Times Square and crackly old MovieTone newsreels of winning World War II and the like.
- ✔ **Bullets:** An animated bullet chart with flying type and bullets.
- ✔ **Credits:** Classic Hollywood-style film credits scrolling vertically on-screen.
- ✔ **Zooms:** Choose one of three options for creating the effect of a zoom lens, placing you closer and closer to the subject with Zoom in, Zoom out, or Zoom in then out effects.

Remember the In-Between Commands

In Chapter 5, I discuss the dark art of *tweening,* not for the faint of heart. In prehistoric days, human beans were actually hired by people with funny names like Walt Disney to tween twixt sunup and sundown. And what is tweening, you may well ask? It's the art of breaking up an animation sequence into key frames and then developing intermediate frames from key frame to key frame. In other words, tweening develops all the in-be*tween* frames, which is where the term *tweening* comes from.

Using In-Between

For example, say you want to start your movie with a car driving across the Stage from left to right in half a second. I'll describe the steps in very general terms, and you can apply the formula to whatever you like.

1. **Create a bitmap in the Paint window.**

   In this example, say you whip up a bitmap of a car in Director's Paint window with your eyes closed, automatically adding the Bitmap Cast Member to the Cast window. Actually, this happens even with your eyes open.

2. **Select the bitmap in the Paint window by double-clicking the Selection tool, and drag the bitmap onto the Stage.**

   Director automatically adds the bitmap to the first available frame in the Score. It's usually frame 1, unless you couldn't resist and clicked some other frame in the Score window before attending to step 2.

3. **Move the bitmap to some beginning location on the Stage.**

   In this example, drag the car on the Stage to the far left of the screen so that half the car is actually hidden.

4. **Select the bitmap in the Score window and choose Edit⇨Copy Cells.**

5. **In the Score window and in the same channel as the original bitmap, click on a frame representing the last frame of your animation.**

6. **Choose Edit⇨Paste Cells.**

   In this case, you paste a copy of the bitmap in frame 15 of the Score, and the car appears on the Stage in exactly the same location as the bitmap in frame 1. When you copy a bitmap, its current location, applied ink effects, and other characteristics are included in the information.

6. **While at the last frame of your epic, drag the bitmap to some other location on the Stage.**

   Shift-drag the car to the far right of the screen. You held down the Shift key to constrain the car's movement horizontally.

7. **Back at the Score window, click the bitmap in the first frame, and then Shift-click the bitmap in the last frame to create a range of selected frames.**

   In this demo, click frame 1 and then Shift-click frame 15 to create a selection ranging from frames 1 to 15.

8. **Choose Modify⇨In-Between.**

Director *tweens* the bitmaps between frame 1 and frame 15 of your movie. When you rewind the movie and play it back, the bitmap appears to move across the Stage. In this example, the toy car scoots across the screen. Its speed is determined by how many frames you chose to tween, the current tempo settings, and whether you filled up with high-octane gas.

Using In-Between Special

The In-Between Special command adds additional animation opportunities by working with a *curved* path that a bitmap follows after tweening is completed. To create a curved path, follow these steps:

1. **Follow steps 1 to 6 in the preceding section, "Using In-Between."**

   At this point, you have a bitmap in frame 1 of the Score and on the Stage its positioned at the far left side of the screen. You also have a bitmap in frame 15, which you positioned to the far right of the screen. Remember, the Clipboard still contains a copy of the bitmap.

2. **In the Score, within the same channel, click on a frame between the first and last frames of the sequence.**

In this case, click frame 8, for example.

3. **Choose Edit⇨Paste Cells.**

The bitmap appears in the selected frame and on the Stage in the original location.

4. **On the Stage, drag the bitmap to a new location different from the first or last locations.**

Drag the bitmap on the Stage to a point near the top center of the screen.

5. **Back at the Score window, click the bitmap in the first frame, and then Shift-click the bitmap in the last frame to create a range of selected frames.**

6. **Choose Modify⇨In-Between Special.**

The In-Between Special dialog box appears, as in Figure 24-1.

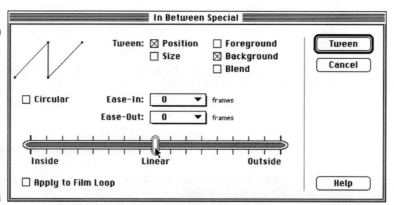

Figure 24-1:
The In-Between Special dialog box, where you can set up a curved path for a bitmap to follow.

7. **Click one or more Tween options at the top of the dialog box.**

In this case, check the Position and Background check boxes in the Tween options area. Drag the Inside/Outside sliding control to the left toward the Inside label. And from the Ease-In, Ease-Out pop-up menus, choose 4.

8. **Click Tween.**

In this example, Director incorporates the upper movement of the sprite in frame 8 with the In-Between Special command. When you play back the movie, the little car appears to drive in a curved path, up to the top of the screen by frame 8, and back down as it completes its trip across the Stage. Try experimenting with other Ease-In/Ease-Out options in the In-Between Special dialog box, too.

Try Color Cycling

Ever notice the animation happening behind your favorite weather reporter's back? You know, the little icon-like animations indicating snowfall over a particular region of the country, rain pouring here, or the sun beaming down there, with radiant energy streaming from its little happy face?

All these animations were probably created with the same kind of color cycling you can use in Director to add animation to your movie. Color cycling is especially well suited to repetitive movement, like the weather map examples above, and is very efficient because you set the whole sequence up in one custom palette placed in the Color Palettes channel of the Score.

Say you want to create an animation that features repetitive action, such as a fire crackling and popping in a beautiful brick fireplace. First, you must set your display to 256 colors. Color cycling only works with 8-bit color, so check your Monitors control panel or Monitors and Sound control panel for Macs and your System Setup in the Windows Setup control panel for PCs. See "A better way to be NTSC safe" in Chapter 23 for making these settings.

Next, create a custom palette and then import or paint your special Bitmap Cast Members.

Creating a custom palette

1. **Choose Window⇨Color Palettes.**

   For this example, check that System - Mac is the current palette for the Mac or System - Win for the PC.

2. **Choose Edit⇨Duplicate.**

3. **Enter a meaningful name for the new palette and click OK.**

   Say you name the new palette something devilishly clever like "Color Cycling Palette." Your new palette becomes the current palette in the Color Palettes window. Now you create a special blend of colors for the fire.

4. **If you want to create a special blend, click the color chip that starts the color blend or *gradient*.**

   In this case, you might choose a lemony yellow from the palette.

5. **Shift-click the ending color for your custom gradient.**

   Make sure that the second color is at least 10 to 12 chips away from the first color. The more colors between the first and last selected color chips, the smoother the gradient. For this demo, a bright red is in order to make the fiery gradient.

6. Click the In-Between icon in the Color Palettes window.

Using the first and last colors in the selected range of color chips, Director creates a smooth color gradient for the custom palette.

Painting color-cycling artwork

While the color chips making up the gradient are still selected in the Color Palettes window, you can invert the selection and reserve colors not included in the gradient. The only available colors in the Paint window are the color-cycling blend in your custom palette.

1. With colors selected in the Color Palettes window, click the Invert Selection icon to select the colors not included in the original selection.

2. Click the Reserve Selected Colors icon.

3. In the Reserved Colors dialog box that appears, click the Selected Colors radio/option button, as shown in Figure 24-2, and then click Reserve.

Figure 24-2:
With the
Reserved
Colors
dialog box,
you can
disable
selected
colors in the
Color
Palettes
window.

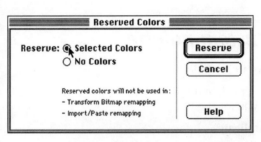

The colors you used to create a special gradient are now the only colors available for painting in the Paint window. Until you turn off Reserve Selected Colors, all imported bitmaps are remapped without including the reserved colors.

Now that the only colors available in the current palette belong to the custom blend, paint the bitmap(s) for color cycling. For example, if you're creating a fireplace scene and intend to apply color cycling to tongues of fire in a fireplace, now is the time to to paint the tongues of fire in the Paint window.

For the lowdown on importing graphics, check out the "Calling All Cast Members" section in Chapter 4. And Chapter 6 gives you the scoop on using Director's Paint tools to whip up glorious digital graphics for the amusement of family and friends.

Painting support graphics

When you complete all artwork that features color cycling, you can now alter your custom palette for painting support graphics.

1. **Choose Window⇨Color Palettes.**

2. **Click the Select Reserved Colors icon.**

3. **Click the Invert Selection icon.**

   The Invert Selection icon selects the unreserved blend colors.

4. **Click the Reserve Selected Colors icon.**
5. **Click the Selected Colors radio/option button in the Reserved Colors dialog box and click Reserve.**

   The color cycling blend in your custom palette is now reserved or disabled.
6. **Choose Window⇨Paint and create the non-color-cycling artwork to complete your scene.**
7. **Choose Window⇨Color Palettes.**
8. **Select the custom color-cycling palette from the pop-up menu.**
9. **Click the Reserve Selected Colors icon.**
10. **Click the No Colors radio/option button and click Reserve.**

Beware the following caveats. After you create a palette with reserved colors, you can import a bitmap and remap its palette to the limited custom palette currently in use. For non-people pictures, the result are probably acceptable. If people appear in your imported graphic, you may need to do some serious retouching in the Paint window to make skin tones look hunky-dory. No, I have no idea where that expression came from.

If you decide to create a bitmap from scratch for a color-cycling sequence, remember to add your custom palette to the Palette channel in the Score window.

You'll be working with a limited palette, depending on how many colors you chose to include in the color-cycling effect. This limitation may strain your creativity to the max, leading to surprise migraines and unexpected urges to impersonate Lola Montez. (Who's that? Look it up, Jack.)

Setting up for color cycling

To set up your custom palette for color cycling, follow these steps:

1. **Choose Window⇨Score and double-click the Palette channel in the frame where you want color cycling to begin.**

   The Palette dialog box appears, as shown in Figure 24-3.

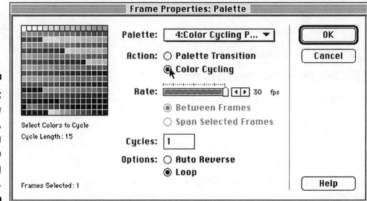

Figure 24-3: The Palette dialog box, where you can set up color-cycling animation.

2. **From the Palette pop-up menu, choose the custom palette you created for color cycling.**

3. **Drag the Rate slider control to set the frame speed.**

   Try 15 fps for starters.

4. **Click the Color Cycling radio/option button.**

5. **Drag-select the blend of colors in the palette of the Palette dialog box and click OK.**

   Clicking the Color Cycling radio/option button and the OK button in the Palette dialog box tells Director to cycle through the selected colors. The color-cycling effect continues until you change the palette in the Palette channel of the Score or turn off color cycling manually or with advanced Lingo scripting.

For color cycling to work: The monitor must be set to 256 (8-bit) colors; the color-cycling palette must be the current palette in the Palette channel of the Score; and color-cycling colors must appear in one or more bitmaps on the Stage.

6. **Drag support bitmaps from the Cast window to the Stage and position them as needed.**

7. **Drag color-cycling bitmaps from the Cast window to the Stage and position them correctly.**

8. **⌘/Ctrl-press each color-cycling sprite on the Stage to display the hidden Ink pop-up menu and choose Bkgnd Transparent.**

   Any white background surrounding the color-cycling sprite becomes transparent with Bkgnd Transparent ink.

Adding a line of Lingo

Back in the Score, add a line of Lingo to pause the playback head where your color-cycling sequence begins.

1. **Double-click the Script channel in the same frame to which you added the color-cycling Palette.**

2. **In the Script window, type the following:**

   ```
   go to the frame
   ```

3. **Click the Close box of the Script window.**

4. **Test your movie by pressing ⌘/Ctrl+1 to hide all windows and ⌘/Ctrl+Option/Alt+P to play back your movie.**

As you admire your color-cycling animation, you may find that you need to speed up or slow down the frame rate from the Control Panel for optimal effect, or return to the Palette dialog box and try a different value in the Cycles entry field or the Rate control.

Buy Good Clip Animation

Using good clip animation is not cheating. The operative word is *good.* Many packages are now available on floppies and CDs and can save a lot of development time or help you complete a project with an extremely tight deadline that you otherwise couldn't meet.

The rule of reading all the fine print applies to using clip art to ensure that you're using royalty-free material or, if not, that you understand the conditions you agreed to upon opening the package. Even if you modify the artwork substantially, you may be violating the agreement with the use of clip animation that's not completely royalty-free or in the public domain.

Turn Cast Members into Moveable Sprites

You can easily add real-time animation to your Director movie by turning Cast Members into *moveable* sprites, meaning sprites that are given the moveable property so that the person viewing the movie can drag the sprite to different locations on the Stage while the movie is playing. For example, in some of my courses, I demonstrate what I call *simulations,* real-time animations that illustrate how to disassemble various computer models. During playback, I interact with the movie, moving various components of the computer aside as if I were actually disassembling the machine before my students' eyes.

This bit of digital wizardry is accomplished by making each component a separate Bitmap Cast Member and then "assembling" the computer component by component from back to front in a frame's channels. The final step is to select all the sprites in the frame and check the Moveable check box in the lower-left corner of the Score window. By the way, to keep the playback head in the same frame, double-click the Script channel for the frame and type **go to the frame**, a variation of the go command that basically means "Stay in this frame." Don't ask me why there isn't a Stay in this frame command, please.

Import Digital Videos

In Chapter 11, I discuss what QuickTime is and how you can add QuickTime files, so-called mooVs, as Digital Video Cast Members to your Director movies. If you've played with QuickTime in Premiere or a similar application, you may be able to salvage some of your work as self-made clip art.

As I suggested in an earlier part of this chapter, tons of commercial clip art, including QuickTime mooVs, exist in the marketplace, as well as on commercial online services, private bulletin boards and numerous Internet sites. As long as you thoroughly understand your rights for using the material, you should be able to find a QuickTime mooV to satisfy any basic need of yours.

Director automatically imports a QuickTime mooV as a *linked* file, meaning that the mooV is not incorporated directly into the Director file; only a *reference* to the QuickTime mooV is established, linking the external mooV to the Director file, thus the term *link.* The QuickTime mooV remains an independent, external file that needs to be present in the same folder as the Director file referring to the mooV.

Import Bitmaps or PICS Files

Some animation programs don't offer a digital video file format when saving the document. This may be the case if you have an older version of a program and haven't upgraded. If you're working exclusively in the Mac platform and digital video is not a save option, save your work as a PICS file. PICS is a special Macintosh format that contains a series of PICTs glued together into one file; Director for Macintosh understands the PICS file format and can successfully import such an graphic, creating one Cast Member for each PICT wihin the PICS file. The new Cast Members are automatically *cast to time* in the Score window, too. Cast to time places Cast Members in the Cast window into separate frames of the Score starting with the first free frame in the Score that Director can find.

In the Import Files dialog box, be sure to choose PICS or All Files from the Show pop-up menu; otherwise PICS files won't appear in the directory.

After highlighting a PICS file in the directory, click Options to bring up the Import Options dialog box, shown in Figure 24-4. Check the Contract White Space box if you want Director to crop each PICT in the PICS file down to its smallest *bounding box.* An image's bounding box is the rectangular frame enclosing the graphic, defined by the image's maximum width and height. Contract White Space results in a smaller Director file that runs faster than a file containing PICTs with large borders of white space surrounding them.

Figure 24-4:
The Import
Options
dialog box,
where you
can direct
Director to
crop each
PICT in the
highlighted
PICS file.

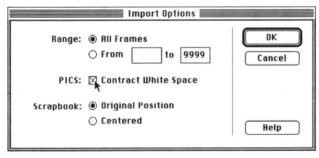

On the downside, because the PICTs are now probably different sizes, they're no longer aligned as an animation sequence and tend to jump around on playback. The best solution is to anticipate the problem and to settle on a minimal file height and width in the original application that creates the PICS file without cutting off any of the images. Barring this, in Director's Paint window, locate the first PICT in the PICS sequence, choose the Registration tool (to the left of the Eraser tool), press anywhere in the easel, and drag the Registration Point to the extreme upper-left corner of the easel. Repeat with each remaining PICT to realign the sequence.

As for the Range radio/options buttons in the Import Options dialog box, after highlighting a PICS file in the directory, you can click From and enter a set of range values. For example, entering **5** to **9** directs Director to import only PICTs 5 through 9 in the PICS file. Of course, you need to know in advance that these particular images are of interest to you.

When importing a PICS file, Director places the row of PICTs in the Score, beginning with the current channel of the current frame, eliminating any unsuspecting sprites in its path. For example, say you have channel 3 of frame 5 selected with sprites in frames 11 to 15 when you import a PICS file containing ten images. Director places the first image of the PICS file in channel 3 of frame 5, happily deleting the sprites in frames 11 to 15 as it adds the rest of the ten images from the PICS file. If you don't want this sad melodrama to happen to you, listen up. *Before* importing a PICS file, check that the currently selected channel in the Score allows enough free cells to hold each image within the imported PICS file.

Both the Mac OS and Windows can work with PICTs, an odd file format that's like a container. A PICT can hold just about any other kind of graphic document including bitmaps, drawings, and a low-resolution preview for display during production.

PCs don't take kindly to PICS, so if you're working cross-platform, follow these steps:

1. **Make a new folder/directory.**

   I usually save the folder to the Desktop so that I can find it easily.

2. **Save the animation file as a set of bitmaps or PICTs into your shiny new folder/directory.**

3. **In Director's Import Files dialog box, double-click the folderful of graphics and click Add All.**

   The graphics files fill the list at the bottom of the dialog box, ready to be imported.

4. **Click Import.**

Record Real-Time Animations

One of the most enjoyable things you can do without taking off your clothes is to record real-time animations in Director. With a Bitmap Cast Member in the Cast window, follow these directions to make those long winter nights just melt away:

1. **Choose Control⇨Loop Playback.**

2. **Choose Window⇨Cast and move the Cast window to the upper-left corner of the screen to gain a clear view of the Stage.**

3. **Choose Window⇨Score and move the Score window to the lower-right corner of the screen to gain a clear view of the Stage.**

4. **Drag a Cast Member from the Cast window to its beginning location on the Stage.**

   Notice that Director adds the Cast Member's bitmap to the Score in the selected cell. Now for the special keyboard command . . .

5. **Press Ctrl and then the spacebar.**

   Notice in the Score that Director places a special bull's-eye icon to the right of a channel number, designating real-time recording is in progress.

6. **With the Ctrl key and spacebar *still* held down, press the bitmap on the Stage and begin dragging the bitmap around.**

   Director records your movements in the Score window as successive frames until you release the mouse button.

7. **After you're finished mousing around, release the mouse button.**

   If your movie is set to loop (as in step 1), Director automatically replays all the movements of the sprite. Instant déja-vu!

Use Film Loops

Making film loops is the second-most enjoyable thing you can do with your clothes on. Actually, it's a toss-up between real-time recording, making film loops, and drinking a steaming mug of Ovaltine. For sequences of repetitive movement, film loops are invaluable and very economical because you can extend an animation sequence simply by running the film loop longer.

A classic example of applying a film loop to animation is The Flying Dove. Imagine you're videotaping a dove in flight, following its movement in the sky. If you follow it perfectly, the dove's body doesn't seem to move at all; the only movement you see and record is its wings flapping up and down. This kind of movement is perfect for making a film loop. Another classic example of repetitive movement is The Walking Man. After you have the stride captured in several frames, you're ready to make your film loop.

Say you've drawn or scanned in ten frames of the dove, ranging from its wings positioned above to below its body, and the frames are represented as Cast Members 1 to 10. To make your film loop, with or without doves, follow these steps:

1. **Press Shift and select Cast Members in the Cast window belonging to the animation sequence.**

   If the Cast Members aren't contiguous, ⌘/Ctrl-select them instead. In my example, you'd select Cast Members 1 to 10.

2. **Choose Modify⇨Cast to Time.**

   Director places the Cast Members as bitmaps in frames 1 to 10 of the Score window.

   In my example, if you played your movie you would see the dove flapping its wings from above to below its body. You want to complete the cycle of movement by adding the frames that make the dove move its wings from below to above its body, which is simply a copy of the ten frames in reverse sequence. You need to complete the cycle.

   If you don't need to create the other half of the cycle, jump to step 8.

3. **If you need to complete a cyclical sequence, Shift-select the new bitmaps in the Score window.**

4. **Option/Alt-drag the selection to the right, making a copy of the frames, and place the first frame of the copies frames just to the right of the bitmaps already in the Score.**

   In my example, you'd drop the copies on frame 11 of the Score.

5. **Choose Modify⇨Reverse Sequence.**

   Notice the 20 frames you now have in the Score. You have a couple of extra frames to delete. Currently frames 10 and 11 and frames 1 and 20 are identical and unnecessary twin frames.

6. **Click on one of the twin sprites in the center of the set of bitmaps and choose Insert⇨Remove Frame.**

   Following along, you'd select frame 10 or 11 and choose the Remove Frame command.

7. **Click on the last bitmap in the sequence and choose Insert⇨Remove Frame.**

   Now you have a complete sequence of the dove flapping its wings up and down recorded in frames 1 to 18 of the Score. You're all set to create the film loop.

8. **Press Shift and select the full set of bitmaps in the Score.**

9. **Drag the selection to an empty cell in the Cast window.**

   Director displays the Create Film Loop dialog box, shown in Figure 24-5.

10. **Enter a name for the film loop and click OK.**

11. **Delete the bitmaps in the Score and drag the film loop on the Stage.**

12. **Press ⌘/Ctrl+Option/Alt+P to play back your film loop.**

A really great thing to do with your film loop is to combine it with real-time recording. For example, using the flying dove you can make it sail across the Stage, flapping its wings along the way by placing the film loop on the Stage, pressing Ctrl+spacebar, and dragging the film loop across the Stage.

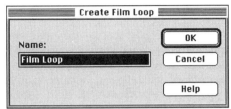

Figure 24-5:
After you
choose Film
Loop from
the Insert
menu, you
can name
your new
Cast
Member.

Switch Color Palettes

In the "Try Color Cycling" section earlier in this chapter, I walk you through setting up a custom palette in the Palette dialog box to cycle through a selected range of colors for relatively easy animation effects. Another option in the Palette dialog box allows you to create a different kind of animation by setting up a *palette transition*. This kind of animation is especially effective for situations where color changes globally on the Stage. The classic example crying out for a palette transition is The Sunset.

Say you have a beautiful desert day scene as a Bitmap Cast Member, featuring the ever-popular System palette. The image presents you with the bleached, white sand of the desert, bright green cacti hither and yon, a brilliant azure sky specked with creamy fluffs of cloud. But you want this gorgeous image to change to a cool nighttime scene filled with blues and grays *using the same bitmap.* Here's how to accomplish this miracle, beginning with creating a custom palette:

1. **Choose Window⇨Color Palettes and choose Edit⇨Duplicate.**

2. **In the Create Palette dialog box that appears, name the palette something meaningful, such as** Sunset Palette, **and click OK.**

3. **Back in the Color Palettes window, click the Zoom box in the upper-right corner so that the window zooms to full-screen size, making the color chips easier to work with.**

4. **Double-click the second color chip from the upper-left corner of the palette to display the Apple color wheel or the Windows Custom Color Selector.**

5. **Click an interesting contrasting color and alter its brightness, if you like, by dragging the scroll bar elevator; then click OK in the Apple color wheel or click Add Color to the Windows Custom Color Selector; and then click Close.**

In my example, you'd select a deep blue and deepen the color more by dragging the scroll bar's elevator down toward the bottom.

6. Repeat step 5 to alter other colors at your discretion.

In the Apple color wheel, notice the gray scale — from light gray to black — at the bottom-right corner of the System palette. Double-click the deep color just to the left of the light gray chip. In the Apple color wheel, slide the scroll bar elevator about halfway to the top. Following along, click a medium blue chip in the color wheel and click OK. In the Windows Custom Color Selector, select a medium blue color and deepen its value by sliding the scroll bar elevator toward the bottom. Click Close to return to the Color Palettes window.

Now you can make a custom blend in the Color Palettes window:

1. Shift-select two colors of differing value and/or color in the Color Palettes window.

In my example, you'd select the medium blue chip, press Shift, and click the deep blue chip that you created.

 2. Click the In-Between icon to create a custom blend.

In my example, you'd create a blend from deep blue to medium blue in your custom palette.

3. Click the Zoom box to reduce the Color Palettes window's size.

Now set up the Score for the palette transition:

1. Choose Window➪Cast.

2. Choose Window➪Score.

3. Drag the Bitmap Cast Member for the palette transition from the Cast window to a frame in the Score.

In my example, after you drag the desert scene to frame 1 in the Score, it appears centered on the Stage.

4. In the Score, Option/Alt-drag the bitmap to the right, duplicating the bitmap and placing the duplicate just right of the original.

You now have a duplicate bitmap in frame 2.

5. Double-click the Palette channel in the frame where the duplicate bitmap rests to display the Palette dialog box.

In my example, you'd double-click the Palette channel in frame 2.

6. Choose your custom palette from the Palette pop-up menu.

7. **Select (fill in) the Palette Transition radio/option button in the Action area of the Palette dialog box.**

8. **Set a frame rate with the Rate sliding control and click OK.**

   Try 6 fps to begin with.

9. **Choose Control⇨Loop Playback so that the command is *unchecked*.**

   Generally, you don't want this kind of effect to loop, so make sure that Loop Playback is turned off.

10. **Press ⌘/Ctrl+1 to hide all open windows.**

All that's left to do is to rewind the movie and play back your Director animation to thunderous applause.

Chapter 25

The Ten Most Important Lingo Words

In This Chapter

▶ Go command

▶ Play command

▶ Pause command

▶ Continue command

▶ Set command

▶ UpdateStage command

▶ DirectToStage property

▶ & and && concatenation operators

▶ Repeat while and repeat with control structures

▶ If-then control structures

*A*ttempting to sum up Lingo with just ten of its most important words may strike some in the know as quixotic at best, foolhardy at worst. On the other hand, I believe that the ten terms I've chosen to review in this chapter form a foundation that new scripters can reference to write most of their scripts and to build upon as they find the need for the more esoteric of Lingo's commands. May this be the beginning of a grand adventure for you.

Go Command

Probably the most frequently used Lingo command, the go command allows you to skip from one frame to another, as well as to go to another Director movie.

To skip to another frame, double-click the Script channel in the frame from which you want to leave and type **go to frame** followed by a space and the number of the frame; for example, `go to frame 10`.

To go to another movie, double-click the Script channel in the frame from which you want to leave and type **go to movie** followed by a space, a plain quote character ("), the name of the movie to go to, and another plain quote character: for example, `go to movie "What We Can Do for You"`.

To keep the playback head in the same frame without actually stopping playback of the movie, double-click the Script channel in the frame where you want to stay and type **go to the frame**.

Play Command

The play command is likely the second most frequently used command in Lingo. Use the play command to go to another movie and play the movie.

To go to another movie and play that movie beginning at frame 1, double-click the Script channel in the frame from which you want to leave and type **play movie** followed by a space, a quote character, the name of the movie to go to, and another quote character; for example, `play movie "Offer.dir"`.

To go to another movie and have it start somewhere other than frame 1, double-click the Script channel in the frame from which you want to leave and type **play frame** followed by a space, the number of the frame from which you want to start playing the movie, and a space. Then add **of movie** followed by a space, a quote character, the name of the movie to go to, and another quote character; for example, `play frame 10 of movie "Offer.dir"`.

To return to the original movie after playing the second movie, double-click the Script channel in the last frame of the *second* movie and type **play done**.

Pause Command

Pause is another common command, used when you want to freeze the movie's playback, allowing the user to decide when to continue the movie. As you may have guessed, the pause command is typically used in league with the command that follows: continue.

To pause a movie at a particular frame, double-click the Script channel in the frame where you want the pause to occur and type **pause** between the lines `on enterFrame` and `end`.

Continue Command

The continue command allows a movie that has been suspended with the pause command to play back again. Continue is typically placed in a button object created with the Button tool from the Tool palette. The user may click the button at will to continue playback.

For example, say your movie was suspended at frame 10. While the playback head is still at frame 10, follow these steps:

1. **Choose Window➪Tool palette or press ⌘/Ctrl+7 to display the Tool palette.**

2. **Select the Button tool from the Tool palette and drag out a button on the Stage.**

3. **Choose Window➪Score or press ⌘/Ctrl+4 to display the Score window.**

4. **Double-click the Button Cast Member in the Score to display the Button dialog box.**

5. **Click the Cast Member Script icon to display the Cast Member's Script window.**

6. **Between the lines** on mouseUp **and** end**, type** continue.

   Then close the Script dialog box.

On playback, the movie stops at frame 10, where the button becomes visible. Clicking the button initiates the continue command, and the movie plays back again.

Set Command

Set is an extremely useful, multipurpose command that you'll use often in Director. In the example script for the UpdateStage command later in this chapter, the set command is used to change the color of Cast Member 13, referring to the Cast Member residing in cell 13 of the Cast window.

Set is also used to place text in a text sprite on the Stage created with the Text tool from the Tool palette. To put the text "All the world's a Stage . . ." in a Text Cast Member named "Today's Quote," enter the following in a button:

```
on mouseUp
set the text of cast "Today's Quote" = "All the world's a
             Stage..."
end
```

During playback, pressing the button causes the text to appear instantly in the text sprite.

UpdateStage Command

Normally, Director refreshes the screen automatically as a movie plays back from frame to frame. Occasionally, you need to give Director a little nudge with the updateStage command, especially after you alter conditions on the Stage with various Lingo commands, such as changing a sprite's color. After the line of Lingo that performs the change, simply add updateStage as the next line. An example:

```
on changeMyColor
set the foreColor of cast 13 = 200
updateStage
end
```

Colors in Director are referred to by number from the set of 256 colors in the current palette. The first color in a palette is color 0, not 1, and always white, color 255 is always black, and the numbers in between refer to specific colors, depending on the current palette and their positions.

DirectToStage Property

In strictest terms, directToStage isn't a command but a property; that is, a contributing description of a QuickTime file in Director. A QuickTime mooV, as multimedia types are wont to call a QuickTime file, has the directToStage property either enabled or disabled. Turning on the directToStage property of a QuickTime mooV allows it to play at its fastest speed on the Stage, which is why the directToStage property is so important to us multimedia types.

Set a QuickTime's directToStage property in one of two ways:

✔ Highlight the Digital Video Cast Member in the Cast window, click the "i" button at the top of the window, and check the Direct To Stage check box in the Digital Video Cast Member Properties dialog box.

✔ Using Lingo, type **set the directToStage of cast 1 = true** in the Script channel of the frame where the QuickTime mooV makes its appearance in the Score. This line assumes that the QuickTime mooV is in cell 1 of the Cast window. Substitute the number 1 after "cast" with the number identifying the position of your QuickTime mooV in the Cast window.

& and && Concatenation Operators

Remember the first item under the Lingo pop-up menu, those operators such as +, −, *, and /, many of which are arithmetic operators? A few of the operators are special, such as & and &&, so-called concatenation operators that you find only in programming languages. When you use concatenation operators, you're basically doing addition with words, gluing words and phrases together.

Here's how concatenation works. Say you have three Text Cast Members on the Stage. And say, for some reason, who knows why, you simply can't have the entire phrase "All the world's a Stage" in the third Text Cast Member at the beginning of the movie. You must piece together, or concatenate, the phrase from the first two Text Cast Members when your movie begins to play back. Again, who knows why. The first Text Cast Member contains half the phrase, "All the world's"; the second Text Cast Member contains the other half, "a Stage." To glue a phrase together as in this example, you need to use the concatenation operators, along with the set command discussed earlier in this chapter. In the Script channel of frame 1, you'd enter the following:

```
set the text of cast 3 = the text of cast 1 && the text of
        cast 2
```

Now I'll go through step by step why this line makes Director do what you want it to do:

- ✔ With `set the text of cast 3 =`, you're telling Director to make the contents of Text Cast Member 3 equal to the rest of the line coming up.

- ✔ The next part of the script, `the text of cast 1`, refers to the contents of Text Cast Member 1 in the Cast window, which, in this example, contains the first half of the phrase, "All the world's."

- ✔ The last part of the script, `&& the text of cast 2`, tells Director to glue the first part of the phrase from Text Cast Member 1 together with the contents of Text Cast Member 2, which, in this example, contains the second part of the phrase: "a Stage." The script also says to add a space character between the two parts of the phrase. && stands for adding a space between two phrases. & stands for gluing parts of a phrase together without a space character in between.

Concatenation is that simple. Don't let the multisyllabic nature of the term put you off. You're just gluing bits and pieces of information together to form a whole.

Repeat While and Repeat With Control Structures

Sometimes you want Director to repeat a command as long as a certain condition is true. Other times you want Director to repeat a set of commands a certain number of times. That's when a repeat control structure comes in handy.

Say you want to hear when the user presses the mouse on a button in your Director movie. The condition you want to test for is pressing the mouse. You decide on the System beep as the sound or cue that lets you know when mouse pressing occurs. You decide to use the *repeat while* control structure in the script of the button, which winds up looking like this:

```
on mouseDown
repeat while the mouseDown
beep
end repeat
end
```

I'll go over this handler line by line.

- ✔ on mouseDown tells Director to carry out the commands that follow when the mouse button is pressed; that is, when the mouse button is down.

- ✔ repeat while the mouseDown tells Director that you want it to carry out the line that follows as long as the mouse button remains down.

- ✔ beep is the command you want Director to carry out as long as the mouse button is pressed.

- ✔ end repeat is simply a convention for how to end a repeat statement such as this one. Director must see this line after each repeat statement or it slaps an error message on-screen.

- ✔ end is another convention that you must follow when using Lingo. All so-called handlers like this one must end with the line end.

Another form of the repeat control structure, *repeat with,* is useful for repeating a command or set of commands a certain number of times. Say you want the color of a button to change from white to a rainbow of colors when a user presses it. (Remember that Director calls colors by number.) Using the repeat with control structure allows you to change a number over time, which can stand for the color of a button. The lines of Lingo in the button for this example would look something like the following:

```
on mouseDown
  repeat with n = 1 to 150
    set the backColor of cast 2 to n
    delay 100
  end repeat
end
on mouseUp
  set the backColor of cast 2 to 0
end
```

Again, I'll go over the lines step by step.

- ✔ on mouseDown tells Director that you want something to happen when the mouse button is pressed. What you want to have happen comes in the next lines of Lingo.

- ✔ repeat with n = 1 to 150 tells Director that, as long as the mouse button remains pressed down, you want Director to substitute the generic value, *n*, for numbers from 1 to 150. The next line tells Director what to do with each number. Remember, the number 150 means that the commands within the repeat statement are to be repeated 150 times.

- ✔ set the backColor of cast 2 tells Director to change the button color, called the *backcolor* in Director, of Button Cast Member 2 of the Cast window. You tell Director which color to use in the rest of this line.

- ✔ to n tells Director to set the button to the current value of *n*. set the backColor of cast 2 to n is going to be repeated 150 times. The first time Director substitutes 1 for the generic value *n* so that the real meaning of the line becomes set the backColor of cast 2 to 1, telling Director to set the color to color chip 1 in the current palette. The repeat statement makes Director repeat the set line again. The next time around, Director substitutes 2 for the generic value *n* so that the real meaning of the line becomes set the backColor of cast 2 to 2, in other words, to color 2 of the palette. As long as the user presses down the mouse button, this process repeats itself until the last repetition, the 150th repetition in this case.

- ✔ delay 100 is simply a way to slow down the process by using the delay command; Director executes the commands so quickly on a fast computer that you can't detect the color changes without slowing everything down. The number 100 in the line stands for 100 *ticks*. Director measures time in ticks; one tick equals $1/60$ of a second.

- ✔ The last two lines, end repeat and end, are Lingo conventions that you must follow when using a repeat statement and a mouseDown handler, as discussed earlier in this section.

The second handler, the mouseUp handler, simply sets the color of the button to 0 (DirectorSpeak for white) when the user releases the mouse button.

If-Then Control Structures

One of the most powerful ways to add real interactivity to your Director movies is by using if-then control structures. Basically, you're building alternate scenarios into your movie that depend on choices made by the user, or perhaps made arbitrarily by Director itself.

Earlier in this chapter, I showed how you can use Director to piece together a phrase so that when your movie begins, the phrase is placed in a third text box. What if the third text box sometimes contains text when the movie begins and is empty at other times? And what if you want Director to piece the phrase together and place it in Text Cast Member 3 only if the third text box is empty? Somehow you need to have Director check whether the text box is empty. That's when an if-then structure comes in handy. The script in the movie would look something like the following:

```
on startMovie
if the text of cast 3 = empty then
set the text of cast 3 = the text of cast 1 && the text of
          cast 2
else beep
end
```

Basically, you give Director a choice. If Text Cast Member 3 is empty, you tell Director to piece together the two halves of the phrase in Text Cast Members 1 and 2 and enter it in Text Cast Member 3. If Director finds some text in Text Cast Member 3, you don't want to lose the text by replacing it with the phrase divided up between Text Cast Members 1 and 2. Instead, you simply instruct Director to beep harmlessly. Again, I'll go over those lines one by one.

- ✔ `on startMovie` means that this kind of handler is a movie script that executes the moment your Director file begins to play back.

- ✔ `if the text of cast 3 = empty then` instructs Director to check whether anything is in Text Cast Member 3 and, if empty, to execute the next line.

- ✔ `set the text of cast 3 = the text of cast 1 && the text of cast 2` is explained earlier in this chapter in the concatenation section. Basically, you're giving Director the go-ahead to glue the phrase together and place it whole in the third text box.

- ✔ `else beep` gives Director the alternate scenario to execute should it find that some text does exist in Text Cast Member 3. In fact, you don't let Director glue the phrase together at all, as this script is written.

In more complicated if-then statements, you include an `end if` line for each if-then statement. But that's basically all you need to know — not exactly rocket science, eh?

Appendix A

I'm Ready for My Close-up, Mr. DeMille: Director 5's System Requirements

• •

*1*f Director 5 is your first copy of the program, the whole process of using it may seem overwhelming. Let me assure you, it is. Remember those wisdom tooth extractions? Well . . .

Just kidding. Running Director is no different from running any other program. But the program does ask for some mimimum configurations to run properly. In this appendix, I also give you my own set of system requirements that's a notch or two above basic.

You need the following minimum configuration to get Director 5 up and running:

- ✔ For the Macintosh, any 68030 CPU (central processing unit) Mac, including first-generation PowerBooks (other than the PowerBook 100 with a 68000 CPU), Duos, and Performas; for the PC, an IBM-compatible 386 computer

- ✔ 8MB of RAM (random access memory)

- ✔ Hard drive storage device, internal or external, with 32.4 MB of free space for a complete install

- ✔ 13-inch computer monitor

- ✔ For the Macintosh, System 7 or that copy of Copland you sneaked (just kidding, Apple); for the PC, Microsoft Windows 3.1, Windows NT, or Windows 95

Now here is my real-world minimum recommended configuration:

- ✔ For the Macintosh, a 68040 Quadra, Performa, PowerBook, or Duo — better yet, a Power Mac; for the PC, an IBM-compatible 486 machine — better yet, a Pentium computer

- ✔ 16MB or more of RAM

- 120MB hard drive storage device or better with 32.4MB of free space for a complete install

- 17-inch computer monitor or larger

- For the Macintosh, System 7.5.3 (with System 7.5 Update 2.0, the latest update as this book is being written); for the PC, Microsoft Windows 3.1 or better

Appendix B
The Mother of All Resource Lists

Books

Bove, Tony and Cheryl Rhodes, *Official Macromedia Director Studio,* Random House/New Media Series, 1994.

Burger, Jeff, *The Desktop Multimedia Bible,* Addison-Wesley Publishing Company, 1993.

Clark, Cathy and Lee Swearingen, *Macromedia Director Design Guide,* Hayden Books, 1994.

Harvey, Greg, *Shockwave For Director For Dummies,* IDG Books Worldwide, Inc., 1996.

Hoffman, Paul E., *Netscape and the World Wide Web For Dummies,* IDG Books Worldwide, Inc., 1995.

Holsinger, Erik, *MacWEEK Guide to Desktop Video,* Ziff-Davis Press, 1993.

Laurel, Brenda, *The Art of Human-Computer Interface Design,* Addison-Wesley Publishing Company, 1990.

Thomas, Frank and Ollie Johnston, *Disney Animation: The Illusion of Life,* Abbeville Press, 1981.

Vaughan, Tay, *Multimedia: Making It Work,* Osborne McGraw-Hill, 1994.

Training

American Film Institute
Advanced Technology Programs
2021 North Western Avenue
Los Angeles, CA 90027
213-856-7600

Nothing But Lingo training videos
2-Lane Media
1575 Westwood Boulevard
Suite 301
Los Angeles, CA 90024
301-473-3706

San Francisco State University
Multimedia Studies Program
The New Downtown Center
425 Market Street
San Francisco, CA 94105
415-904-7700

Vendors

Adobe Systems, Incorporated
Adobe Photoshop,
   Adobe Premiere
1585 Charleston Road
Mountain View, CA 94039
415-961-4400
http://www.adobe.com

America Online
8619 Westwood Center Drive
Vienna, VA 22182
Customer Service
800-827-6364
http://www.aol.com

Apple Computer
1 Infinite Loop
Cupertino, CA 95014
408-974-4897
http://www.info.apple.com

Apple Customer Assistance
   Center
800-776-2333
800-786-7777 for System 7
   customers
Monday through Friday,
6 a.m. – 5 p.m. PST
http://www.info.apple.com

Apple Direct
(Apple mail order purchases)
800-795-1000
http://www.info.apple.com

BMUG
Berkeley Macintosh Users Group
1442A Walnut Street #62
Berkeley, CA 94709
510-849-BMUG

BPCUG
Berkeley PC Users Group
Winner's Circle Systems
2618 Telegraph Avenue
Berkeley, CA 94709

CompuServe Information
   Services
5000 Arlington Centre Boulevard
P.O. Box 20212
Columbus, OH 43220
800-848-8199

Creative Labs, Incorporated
Sound Blaster
1909 McCarthy Boulevard
Milpitas, CA 95035
408-428-6600

Diamond Multimedia Systems
Stealth 64-bit Graphics
Accelerator
2880 Junction Avenue
San Jose, CA 95134
408-325-7000

DriveSavers, Incorporated
Data Recovery Services
400 Bel Marin Keys Boulevard
Novato, CA 94949
800-440-1904

Equilibrium
DeBabelizer
475 Gate Five Road
Suite 225
Sausalito, CA 94965
415-332-4343

GEnie Online Services
P. O. Box 6403
Rockville, MD 20849-6403
800-638-9636

Intel Corporation
Literature Sales
P. O. Box 7641
Mt. Prospect, IL 60056-7641
800-538-3373

Macromedia, Incorporated
MacRecorder sound digitizer,
    Macromedia Director 5
    animation program,
    SoundEdit 16 sound editing
    program, Extreme Three-D 3-D
    program, Swivel Art 3-D
    clip art
600 Townsend Street
San Francisco, CA 94103
415-442-0200
http://www.macromedia.com

Micropolis Corporation
Manufacturer of AV disk drives
21211 Nordhoff Street
Chatsworth, CA 91311
818-718-5308

Microsoft Corporation
One Microsoft Way
Redmond, WA 98052
206-882-8080
http://www.microsoft.com

miro Computer Products,
    Incorporated
miroVIDEO DC20 video edit
    board for the PC,
    miroMOTION DC20 video
    edit board for the PCI Power
    Macintosh
955 Commercial Street
Palo Alto, CA 94304
800-249-MIRO

Orange Micro
OrangePC Model 290 PC
    emulation board for the
    Macintosh
1400 North Lakeview Avenue
Anaheim, CA 92807
714-779-2772

Prodigy Services
445 Hamilton Avenue
White Plains, NY 10601
800-776-3449

Radius, Incorporated
Video Spigot AV video digitizer
    board, VideoVision Studio
    video digitizer board,
    VideoVision TeleCast video
    digitizer board
215 Moffet Park Drive
Sunnyvale, CA 94089
408-541-6100

Ray Dream, Incorporated
Ray Dream Designer 3-D program
1804 North Shoreline Boulevard
Mountain View, CA 94043
415-960-0768
support@raydream.com

San Francisco PC Users Group
3333 California Street
San Francisco, CA 94105
415-751-5219

Sony Corporation
One Sony Drive
Park Ridge, NJ 07656-8003
800-282-2848

Specular International
Infini-D 3.0 3-D program
479 West Street
Amherst, MA 01002
800-433-7732

Strata, Incorporated
StrataVision Pro 3-D program
2 West St. George Boulevard
Saint George, UT 84770
801-628-5218

User Group Locator
(finds local user groups)
800-538-9696

Visual Magic
Animation clip art
620 C. Street #201
San Diego, CA 92101
800-367-6240

Index

• *Symbols* •

& concatenation operator, 339
&& concatenation operator, 339
1-bit graphics, 108
8-bit color, 125
  cross-platform capabilities, 279
8-bit graphics, 108, 165
  artifacts, 176
24-bit color, 125
  modifying images, in high-level paint program, 126
24-bit graphics, 165
  color, 93

• *A* •

About This Macintosh dialog box, 28
actions, undoing, 35
activateWindow event, 245
active window, 40, 45
adaptive palette, 126–127, 165
additive and subtractive primary colors, 84, 168
Adobe Photoshop, 58
Adobe Premiere, 280
Adobe Type Manager, 104
AfterBurner, 283, 286–287
  compressing movies, 287–291
  testing files, 290–291
AIF file extension, 278
AIFC (Compressed Audio Interchange File Format) files, 79
AIFF (Audio Interchange File Format) files, 79
Air Brush Settings dialog box, 105
Air Brush tool, 104–105
Align floating palette, 36
an instance, 123
analog video, 191
animation, 12, 13, 233
  Animation Wizard Xtra special effects, 317–318
  bitmap registration point, 98–99
  building sequence, 121–122
  channels, 77
  color cycling, 321–325
  curved path for bitmap, 319–320
  file sizes, 26
  film loops, 329–330
  high-speed Web, 287
  importing bitmaps or PICS files, 327–328
  importing digital video, 326
  previewing sequence, 114–118
  purchasing clip animation, 325
  push-button sequences, 235
  recording real-time, 328–329
  setting background image, 117
  switching color palettes, 331–333
  turning Cast Members into moveable sprites, 326
  tweening, 318–320
  zoom effect, 34
Animation Wizard Xtra, 123, 191, 233–238
  built-in special effects, 317–318
  Bullets, 237
  check boxes, 238
  Credits, 237
  entry fields, 238
  fonts, 234–235
  previewing effects, 236
  radio/option buttons, 238
  setting up for, 234–235
  Style options, 237
  text options, 237
  Zooms effect, 237–238
anti-aliased text, 104
append Lingo command, 281
Apple Color Picker, 167–170
Apple HD SC Setup, 262
Apple Lisa, 19
Apple⌘About This Macintosh command, 28
Apple⌘Control Panels command, 21
application partition, 26
  changing, 28–30
applications, 11
Arc tool, 106
arithmetic operators, 241
Arrow tool, 161
art director, 295
artifacts, 176
assembly language, 239
ATM (Adobe Type Manager), 234
Audiomedia sound card, 269
Auto Distort dialog box, 121–122
Auto Filter dialog box, 120–121
AV Macintosh, 259–260
  NTSC monitors, 310–312
  sampling rates, 269
  sampling sounds, 267–269
  taping movies to VCR, 306–307
AVI (Audio Video Interleaved) file, 15
  automatically linking, 63
AVI file extension, 278

• *B* •

background color, 86, 110
baseline, 103
beep Lingo command, 212–213, 255
Berners-Lee, Tim, 284
binary system, 93
bitmap Cast Member, 91–92
Bitmap Cast Member Properties dialog box, 68–70
bitmap sprite, 92
bitmapped text, 102–104, 131–132, 140, 279

bitmaps, 58–59
  adaptive palette, 126–127
  applying effects, 94–95
  background color, 107
color depth, 108
  copying and resizing, 97
  curved segments, 106
  distorting, 121–122
  editing, 64–65
  enlarging on-screen, 101
  erasing pixels broadly, 99–100
  filled shapes, 106
  foreground color, 101, 107
  free-form painting, 104
  importing, 59, 327–328
  importing with custom palette, 158–159
  large, 113
  line width, 107
  Macintosh, 56
  moving on-screen, 149
  painting, 105–106
  pattern, 107
  pixel-by-pixel erasing, 99–100
  recentering registration point, 99
  registration point, 98–99
  resizing, 148
  sampling pixel color, 101
  scaling, 98
  scrolling large, 100
  shapes, 107
  shapes of color and splatter effects, 104–105
  straight lines, 106
  text as, 102–104
blank files, 26
bloom, 307
BMP file extension, 278
BMP files, 59
BMUG (Berkeley Macintosh User Group), 204
body text, 134
bookmarks in Help system, 34
Bookmarks⇨Edit Bookmarks QuickHelp
    command, 34
Bookmarks⇨Set Bookmark QuickHelp command, 34
bottlenecks, 172
bounding box, 83
  background transparent, 84
  color, 83
  masks, 84
  transparent, 83
breakpoints, 199, 219
brightness, 168
broadcast quality video, 258
Brush Settings dialog box, 105–106
brush shapes, 108
Brush Shapes dialog box, 108
built-in palettes, 156–157
bulletin boards and scripts, 204
button beeps when pressed script, 253
Button Cast Members Properties dialog box, 151
Button Properties (⌘/Ctrl+I) keyboard
    shortcut, 189
Button tool, 189

• C •

Cantor, Marc, 204
Cartesian plane, 222
Cartesius, Renatus, 223
Cast Member Properties dialog box, 94
  purging memory, 303
Cast Member Properties window, 68–70
  ⌘/Ctrl+I keyboard shortcut, 68
Cast Member Script button, 41
Cast Member Script dialog box, 40–41, 93
Cast Member scripts, 255
Cast Members, 83
  adding, 58–60, 80–82
  applying Xtras filters, 119–120
  bitmaps, 64–65
  Button, 151
  changing color, 337
  changing external editor, 66
  color changes, 69
  defining, 55–57
  editing in Macromedia Director, 64–65
  exchanging for sprite, 36
  linked, 62
  modifying, 68–70
  modifying properties, 94
  modifying shape, 145–146
  moving around, 63–64
  name, 93, 136
  new, 93
  organizing in meaningful way, 60
  other program editing, 65–66
  priorities, 70
  searching for, 36
  selecting multiple, 72
  selecting Text or Field on Stage, 138
  thumbnail icons, 70–72
  turning into moveable sprites, 326
Cast window, 55–57, 99, 211
  ⌘/Ctrl+3 keyboard shortcut, 36, 55, 63, 81, 120
  actual graphics and text, 26
  adding Cast Members, 58–60
  applying Xtras filters, 119–120
  Cast Member Properties button, 68–70
  Cast Members, 83
  cells, 70
  contiguous cell selection, 72
  custom features, 66–67
  defining Cast Members, 55–57
  digital video Cast Member, 184
  displaying, 36
  exchanging Cast Member for sprite in Score
      window, 36
  exploring, 66–72
  external, 60–61
  internal, 60
  linking imported files, 61–63
  listing, 94
  location of Cast Member, 94
  miniature images, 26
  moving Cast Members around, 63–64

new, 35
noncontiguous cell selection, 72
Script button, 255
selecting Cast Member, 255
selecting multiple cells, 72
thumbs, 26
Cast window (⌘/Ctrl+) keyboard shortcut, 40
Cast⇨Align Bitmaps command, 99
Cast⇨Transform Bitmap command, 303
Casts, linked and unlinked, 61
CD-ROM projects, 258–259
cells, 74
channels, 77
  hidden, 78–80
  showing/hiding, 77
  transitions, 79–80
Check box button tool, 150–151
Circle tool, 150
circles, 150
ClarisDraw, 58, 143
CLI (command line interface), 20
Clipboard, copying selection to and from, 36
Close Window (⌘/Ctrl+W) keyboard shortcut,
        227, 251
closeWindow event, 245
CLUT (color lookup table), 124, 161
color
  8-bit, 125
  24-bit graphics, 93, 125
  additive and subtractive primary colors, 84, 168
  background, 110, 153
  brightness, 168
  complementary, 170
  dithering, 126–127
  foreground, 109–110, 153
  gradients, 101, 110
  hue, 168
  index number, 161
  Macintosh, 124–127
  mixing, 84
  on-screen, 84
  PC, 124–127
  process, 168
  sampling, 161
  saturation, 168
  Stage window, 48
color cycling, 159–160, 166
  custom palettes, 321–322
  Lingo, 325
  painting artwork, 322
  painting support graphics, 323
  setting up for, 324–325
color depth, 108
color models, 167–170
color palettes, switching, 331–333
Color Palettes dialog box, 107, 124
Color Palettes window, 155–156, 322, 332
  Arrow tool, 161
  color numbers, 161–162
  Color Picker, 161
  custom palettes, 162–164
  Cycle tool, 160

Eyedropper tool, 161
H-S-B (Hue, Saturation, Brightness) controls, 161
Hand tool, 161
In-Between tool, 160
Index Color number, 161
index numbers, 161–162
Invert Selection tool, 160
NTSC palette, 263
Palette pop-up menu, 156–159
Reverse Selected Colors tool, 159–160
Reverse Sequence tool, 160
Select Reserved Colors tool, 160
Select Used Colors tool, 160
Sort tool, 160
tools, 159–161
Color Picker, 161
color still images, 176
color wheel, 161
combining movies, 205–209
commands
  Apple⇨About This Macintosh, 28
  Apple⇨Control Panels, 21
  Cast⇨Align Bitmaps, 99
  Cast⇨Transform Bitmap, 303
  Control⇨Disable Scripts, 180, 314
  Control⇨Loop Playback, 314, 328, 333
  Control⇨Play, 190
  disabled, 42
  Edit⇨Clear Cast Members, 303
  Edit⇨Copy Cells, 189, 272, 302, 319
  Edit⇨Copy Video, 188, 195
  Edit⇨Cut, 35
  Edit⇨Duplicate, 130, 321, 331
  Edit⇨Find⇨Cast Member, 303
  Edit⇨Find⇨Text, 138
  Edit⇨Launch External Editor, 62, 65–66
  Edit⇨Paste Cells, 189, 302, 319–320
  Edit⇨Paste Special, 98
  Edit⇨Paste Video, 188, 195
  Edit⇨Select All, 302, 308
  Edit⇨Undo Bitmap, 100
  enabled, 42
  File⇨Close, 38
  File⇨Create Directory, 205
  File⇨Create Projector, 38, 264, 282
  File⇨Export, 38, 173, 181
  File⇨Export⇨Flattened Movie, 280
  File⇨Get Info, 28
  File⇨Import, 38–39, 58, 61, 158, 193, 309
  File⇨New, 192
  File⇨New Folder, 205
  File⇨New⇨Cast, 38
  File⇨New⇨Movie, 282, 302
  File⇨Open, 24, 38, 193, 210
  File⇨Page Setup, 38
  File⇨Preferences⇨Cast, 39
  File⇨Preferences⇨General, 38, 135, 167, 308
  File⇨Preferences⇨Paint, 107, 111
  File⇨Preferences⇨Score, 38, 76
  File⇨Print, 227
  File⇨Quit, 27, 39

commands *(continued)*
 File⇨Revert, 38
 File⇨Save, 38, 209, 303
 File⇨Save All, 38
 File⇨Save and Compact, 38, 289, 301–302
 File⇨Save As, 38, 280, 282, 302
 format of, 4
 Insert⇨Media Element⇨Field, 133
 Insert⇨Remove Frame, 330
 Modify⇨Cast Member⇨Properties, 68
 Modify⇨Cast to Time, 330
 Modify⇨Convert to Bitmap, 279
 Modify⇨Font, 103
 Modify⇨In-Between, 189, 272–273, 319
 Modify⇨In-Between Linear, 89
 Modify⇨In-Between Special, 273, 320
 Modify⇨Movie⇨Casts, 61
 Modify⇨Movie⇨Properties, 46, 48, 83, 314
 Modify⇨Paragraph, 103
 Modify⇨Reverse Sequence, 330
 Modify⇨Space to Time, 88
 Modify⇨Sprite⇨Properties, 98, 186
 Modify⇨Sprite⇨Script, 253
 Modify⇨Transform, 98, 130
 Modify⇨Transform Bitmap, 308
 Modify⇨Tweak, 222
 New⇨Movie, 38
 repeating, 340-341
 Score⇨Space to Time, 88
 Score⇨Switch Cast Members, 189
 Text⇨Comment, 315
 toggle, 44
 View⇨Grid, 114
 View⇨Grid⇨Settings, 114
 View⇨Grid⇨Show, 114
 View⇨Grid⇨Snap To, 114
 View⇨Onion Skin, 114–115, 117
 View⇨Panel, 113
 View⇨Ruler, 114, 135
 View⇨Zoom, 101
 Window⇨Cast, 36, 40, 55, 63, 81, 99, 120, 188, 255,
   304, 308, 328, 332
 Window⇨Color Palettes, 124, 155, 162, 321,
   323, 331
 Window⇨Control Panel, 46
 Window⇨Debugger, 217
 Window⇨Field, 139
 Window⇨Inspectors⇨Memory, 25, 27, 307
 Window⇨Markers, 226
 Window⇨Message, 37, 212, 246
 Window⇨New Window, 228–229
 Window⇨Paint, 91, 102, 117, 121, 323
 Window⇨Score, 36, 74, 207, 236, 238, 253, 255, 282,
   302, 308, 324, 329, 332
 Window⇨Script, 37, 198, 251, 254, 282
 Window⇨Stage, 44, 80
 Window⇨Text, 36, 133
 Window⇨Toolbar, 31, 35
 Window⇨Tools, 189
 Window⇨Video, 181
 Xtras⇨Animation Wizard, 233, 235–236
 Xtras⇨Auto Distort, 118
 Xtras⇨Auto Filter, 120
 Xtras⇨FileFlex, 122
 Xtras⇨Filter Bitmap, 119–120
 Xtras⇨Palettes.cst, 123
 Xtras⇨PrintOMatic Lite, 122. *See also* Lingo
   commands
comparison operators, 241
complementary colors, 170
component video, 176
composite video, 176
computers, 3
 beeping, 213
 CLI (command line interface), 20
 dumb things to do with, 3
 GUI (graphical user interface), 19–20
 moving while running, 3
 plugging/unplugging cables while it is on, 3
 power for multimedia, 15–16
 starting, 20–21
context-sensitive help, 31–33, 37
continue Lingo command, 337
Control menu, 48–51
Control Panel, 40, 48–51
 ⌘/Ctrl+2 keyboard shortcut, 46
 buttons, 49–51
 icons, 49–51
Control⇨Disable Scripts command, 180, 314
Control⇨Loop Playback command, 314, 328, 333
Control⇨Play command, 190
Copy ink effect, 303
CorelDRAW!, 58, 143
CorelPHOTO-PAINT, 64
counter, 129
CPU (central processing unit), 121
Create Film Loop dialog box, 330
Create Palette dialog box, 160–161, 164, 331
Create Projector dialog box, 264
creative director, 295
cross-platform capabilities, 275
 8-bit color, 279
 digital videos, 280
 file management, 281–282
 fonts, 279
 ISO-9660 naming conventions, 277–278
 Macromedia Director cross-platform pack, 276
 platform-independent movies, 276
 playing movies, 315–316
 preparing movies for, 276–280
 project folder, 281
 stub projector, 281–282
 System - Win palette, 278–279
Custom Color Selector, 167–170
custom palettes, 156–159, 162–164, 321–322
 adaptive palettes, 165
 color cycling, 166
 flashing, 164–166
 switching palettes, 165
custom patterns, 108
custom tiles, 108
Cycle tool, 160

● D ●

data, definition of, 13
data forks, 58
data rate, 175
database program, 122
DCR file extension, 289
deactivateWindow event, 245
DeBabelizer, 56, 126–167
Debugger window, 211, 217–219
debugging, 215–219
Descartes, René, 223
decompressing movies, 286
Desktop, 20
desktop video, 172
DIB file extension, 278
digital camcorders, 258
digital paint, 144
digital video, 171–180
    Animation Wizard, 191
    Cast Member in Cast window, 184
    Cast Member sprite on Stage, 184
    controller, 186
    copying poster, 188
    cross-platform capabilities, 280
    customizing, 182
    desired color depth, 178–179
    displaying Cast Member Video windows, 194
    editing, 192–195
    editing together digital video Cast Members, 195
    exporting QuickTime options, 177–178
    floppy disks and CD-ROMs, 192
    freeware, 192
    gluing together, 181–182
    help for controller, 183–184
    importing, 193–194, 326
    linking, 195
    MOV file extension, 206
    naming, 188
    new Video window, 195
    online services, 192
    playback options, 185
    playing on multiple platforms, 178
    prebuilt, 191–192
    preloading, 187
    problems, 172
    purging memory, 187
    Real Time playback, 180–181
    scaling QuickTime movies, 179
    setting up, 184–187
    shareware, 192
    sound track, 185
    speed rate, 187
    speeding up, 304–305
    sprite bounding box, 186
    starting from scratch, 190–191
    stopping, 185
    user-created, 191

Digital Video Cast Member Properties dialog box, 184–186
    controller, 186
    Direct to Stage option, 304
    framing options, 186
    playback options, 185
    playing sprite at highest level, 186
    preloading digital video, 187
    purging memory, 187
    sound track, 185
    speed rate, 187
Digital Video Cast Member window, 188
digital video editor, 190–195
Digital Video Lite
    Lingo, 189–190
    preparing score, 188–189
    setting up window, 188
    testing video, 190
Digital Video Properties dialog box, 183–184
DIR file extension, 206, 277
Director 5.0 Get Info dialog box, 28–30
Director Help Contents window, 32
Directory dialog box, 158
DirectToStage property, 338
disabled commands, 42
Disc-To-Disk, 270
distorting bitmaps, 121–122
dithering, 126–127, 167
dithering routine, 159
DOS (Disk Operating System), 20
double-clicking, 21
drawing, 58, 144–145
DRYSTONE FOR WINDOWS, 261
DXR file extension, 277

● E ●

Edit Bookmarks dialog box, 34
Edit⇨Clear Cast Members command, 303
Edit⇨Copy Cells command, 189, 272, 302, 319
Edit⇨Copy Topic as a Picture QuickHelp command, 34
Edit⇨Copy Topic Text QuickHelp command, 34
Edit⇨Copy Video command, 188, 195
Edit⇨Cut command, 35
Edit⇨Delete Note QuickHelp command, 34
Edit⇨Duplicate command, 130, 321, 331
Edit⇨Find⇨Cast Member command, 303
Edit⇨Find⇨Text command, 138
Edit⇨Launch External Editor command, 62, 65–66
Edit⇨Paste Cells command, 189, 302, 319–320
Edit⇨Paste Special command, 98
Edit⇨Paste Video command, 188, 195
Edit⇨Select All command, 302, 308
Edit⇨Undo Bitmap command, 100
Edit⇨Undo Delete Note QuickHelp command, 34
editable text, 139
elevator, 112
Ellipse tool, 107
enabled commands, 42

Englebart, Doug, 21
enterFrame event, 245
EPS file extension, 278
Eraser tool, 99–100
essential Director topic categories, 33
Ettore, Riccardo, 271
events, 214, 245–246
Exit Movie (⌘/Ctrl+.(period)) keyboard
   shortcut, 265
exitFrame event, 245
exitframe handler, 244
Export dialog box, 173–174, 181
expressions, 199–200
Extended Display Information, 87–88
extensions, 15
external Case windows, 60–61
External Editor (⌘/Ctrl+comma (,) keyboard
   shortcut, 65
external palettes, 123
Eyedropper tool, 101, 161

• *F* •

FAQs (frequently asked questions), 33
field sprites, 76
Field tool, 139, 151
Field window, 139
File menu, 37–39
File⇨Close command, 38
File⇨Create Directory command, 205
File⇨Create Projector command, 38, 264, 282
File⇨Export command, 38, 173, 181
File⇨Export⇨Flattened Movie command, 280
File⇨Get Info command, 28
File⇨Import command, 38–39, 58, 61, 158, 193, 309
File⇨New command, 192
File⇨New Folder command, 205
File⇨New⇨Cast command, 38
File⇨New⇨Movie command, 38, 282, 302
File⇨Open command, 24, 38, 193, 210
File⇨Page Setup command, 38
File⇨Preferences⇨Cast command, 39
File⇨Preferences⇨General command, 38, 135,
   167, 308
File⇨Preferences⇨Paint command, 107, 111
File⇨Preferences⇨Score command, 38, 76
File⇨Print All Topics QuickHelp command, 34
File⇨Print command, 227
File⇨Quit command, 27, 39
File⇨Revert command, 38
File⇨Save All command, 38
File⇨Save and Compact command, 38, 289, 301–302
File⇨Save As command, 38, 280, 282, 302
File⇨Save command, 38, 209, 303
files
   blank, 26
   importing, 35, 58–59
   ISO-9660 naming conventions, 277–278
   linking imported, 61–63
   managing for cross-platforms, 281–282
   opening, 35

Filled Ellipse tool, 106
Filled Polygon tool, 106
Filled Rectangle tool, 106
film loops, 329–330
Filter Bitmap dialog box, 119–120
Find Cast Member dialog box, 36, 303
Find/Change dialog box, 139
Find⇨Global Find Again QuickHelp command, 34
Find⇨Global Find QuickHelp command, 34
Finder, 28
FireWire, 258
flattened file, 182
FlattenMooV, 281
FLC file extension, 277
FLI file extension, 277
floating palettes, 40, 46
Font dialog box, 103
FONTMAP.TXT file, 279
fonts, 234–235
   cross-platform capabilities, 279
   number installed, 234
   PostScript, 234
   previews, 234
   TrueType, 235
foreground color, 86, 109–110
Fractal Painter, 58
frame scripts, 255
frames, 76
   skipping to, 335–336
free-form painting, 104
freeware
   digital video, 192
   sound, 270
functions, 243–244
FusionRecorder, 268
FWB Hard Disk Toolkit, 262

• *G* •

gamut, 307
General Preferences dialog box, 152
getARandomNumber handler, 249
GIF file extension, 278
GIF (Graphics Interchange Format) files, 286
global variables, 248
go Lingo command, 203–204, 227, 243, 335–336
go to the frame Lingo command, 254
gradient, 101
Gradient Settings dialog box, 101–102, 106, 126
gradients
   beginning and ending colors, 107
   color, 110
   custom, 126
graphics
   1-bit, 108
   8-bit, 108, 165, 176
   24-bit, 165
   bitmapped, 58
   color still images, 176
   ink type, 26
   scaling, 98
   scrolling, 111–112

Grayscale palette, 128, 157
Grid, 114
  customizing, 114
  showing/hiding, 114
GUI (graphical user interface), 19–20
  designer, 296
  familiarity with, 20
  guidelines, 297
  mouse, 21–23
  reserving palette colors, 279
  starting your computer, 20–21

H-S-B (Hue, Saturation, Brightness) color model, 161
  additive and subtractive primary colors, 168
  Apple Color Picker, 167
  brightness, 168
  complementary colors, 170
  Custom Color Selector, 167
  hue, 168
  process colors, 168
  saturation, 168
Hand tool, 100, 112, 161
handlers, 198, 214, 244–245
  executing consecutively, 219
  executing current line, 218–219
  executing line by line, 219
  going directly to, 198
  nested, 218
  problems with, 218
  Script window, 219
  variables and properties related, 218
handles, 145
Help (⌘/Ctrl+?) keyboard shortcut, 240
Help Index window, 32
Help Pointer, 31, 37
  ⌘/Ctrl+? keyboard shortcut, 31–32
  ⌘/Ctrl+Shift+? keyboard shortcut, 32
Help system, 30–34
Help window, 31–33
hidden channels, 78–80
hidden context-sensitive menus, 67
high-level computer language, 239, 287
HiJaak, 167
hiring script programmer, 204
History palette, 32
hue, 168
hypertext, 16–17

idle event, 245
if-then control structures, 342
Image Options dialog box, 59, 127, 158–159, 165, 309
images, 14
Import dialog box, 39, 65
Import File (⌘/Ctrl+R) keyboard shortcut, 58

Import Files dialog box, 35, 58–59, 61–62, 98, 165,
    193–194, 327–328
  adaptive palette, 127
  Cast Members, 56–57
  importing sound, 270–271
Import Options dialog box, 327–328
importing
  digital video, 193–194
  files, 35, 58–59
  mooV files, 194
  sound files, 270–271
improving movie color on tape
  NTSC monitors, 310–312
  NTSC palette, 308–310
  video boards, 313
In-Between Special dialog box, 89, 320
In-Between tool, 160
inactive windows, 45
incorporated sounds, 270–271
Index Color number, 161
ink effects, 76, 83–86
  background color, 86
  background transparent in bounding box, 84
  black and white screens, 85
  color bounding box, 83
  foreground color, 86
  masks, 84, 129–130
  Paint window, 108
  pattern, 86
  selectively coloring sprite pixels, 85–86
  transparent bounding box, 83
Ink pop-up menu, 83–86
ink type, 26
Insert⇨Media Element⇨Field command, 133
Insert⇨Remove Frame command, 330
installing
  Shockwave, 286
  Xtras filters, 118
instructional designer, 297–298
interactive features, 12–13
interactive multimedia, 16–17
  scripts, 202–205
intermediate frames, 36
internal Cast windows, 60
Internet
  scripts, 204
  vs. World Wide Web, 284
Internet Explorer, 283–286
INTRO.MOV digital video, 205
Invert Selection tool, 160
ISO-9660 naming conventions, 277–278
ISP (Internet Service Provider), 285

jaggies, 148, 234
Java, 287
JavaScript, 287
Jobs, Steve, 19
JPEG (Joint Photographic Expert Group) files, 286
JPG file extension, 278

• K •

K (kilobytes), 28
kerning, 134–135
key frames, 122
keyboard shortcuts
 ⌘/Ctrl+. (period) (Exit Movie), 265
 ⌘/Ctrl+0 (Script window), 37, 198, 207, 282
 ⌘/Ctrl+1 (Show/Hide), 44–46, 325, 333
 ⌘/Ctrl+1 (View Animation), 236
 ⌘/Ctrl+2 (Control Panel), 46
 ⌘/Ctrl+3 (Cast window), 36, 40, 55, 63, 81, 120
 ⌘/Ctrl+4 (Score window), 36, 80, 236, 282
 ⌘/Ctrl+5 (Paint window), 36, 92, 117, 121
 ⌘/Ctrl+6 (Text window), 36
 ⌘/Ctrl+> (Text Comment), 315
 ⌘/Ctrl+? (Help), 31–32, 240
 ⌘/Ctrl+A (Select All), 290
 ⌘/Ctrl+comma (,) (External Editor), 65
 ⌘/Ctrl+I (Button Properties), 189
 ⌘/Ctrl+I (Cast Member Properties window), 68
 ⌘/Ctrl+M (Markers), 226
 ⌘/Ctrl+M (Message window), 37, 212
 ⌘/Ctrl+Option/Alt+← (Move Frame Right), 74
 ⌘/Ctrl+Option/Alt+→ (Move Frame Right), 74
 ⌘/Ctrl+Option/Alt+P (Play Movie), 181, 190, 210,
   236, 251, 254–256, 314, 325, 330
 ⌘/Ctrl+Option/Alt+R (Rewind Movie), 181, 314
 ⌘/Ctrl+Q (Quit), 265
 ⌘/Ctrl+R (Import File), 58
 ⌘/Ctrl+Shift (Zoom Bitmap), 101
 ⌘/Ctrl+Shift+? (Help), 32
 ⌘/Ctrl+W (Close), 227, 251
 ⌘/Ctrl+Z (Undo), 100
 listing, 33
 Macintosh and PC, 5
keyDown event, 245, 252
keyDownScript, 252
keyUp event, 245
keyword, 31–32
kiosks, 258

• L •

Lasso tool, 96
leading, 134
Line tool, 106, 110–111, 149
lines
 drawing, 149
 width, 107, 110–111, 153
Lingo, 5, 37, 189–190, 239–240, 335–342
 & and && concatenation operators, 339
 arithmetic operators, 241
 basics, 240–244
 breakpoints, 199
 color cycling, 325
 comments, 199
 comparison operators, 241
 debugging, 215
 DirectToStage property, 338

events, 214, 245–246
 functions, 243–244
 handlers, 198, 244–245
 if-then control structures, 342
 information about, 33
 instance, 123
 knowing when scripts are okay, 315
 listing operators and commands, 199
 menu, 40
 Message window, 212–214
 messages, 246–247
 online help, 240
 operators, 241–242
 properties and commands, 40–41
 repeat while and repeat with control structures,
   340–341
 script error alerts, 213–214
 Script error: Property not found message, 216
 scripting, 122–123, 152
 scripts, 93, 198–210, 249–256
 startup handler, 215
 syntax, 213–214, 240
 the date function, 243
 the time function, 243
 tracking expressions and variables, 199–200
 variables, 247–248
 vs. English, 203
Lingo commands, 242–243
 append, 281
 beep, 212–213, 255
 continue, 337
 go, 203–204, 227, 243, 335–336
 go to the frame, 254
 parameters, 213
 pause, 336
 play, 336
 play movie, 208–209
 preLoadCast, 187, 251
 put, 243
 set, 251, 337–338
 set foreColor of cast, 255
 updateStage, 338
Lingo programmer, 296–297
linked cast, 61
linked sound file, 270–271
linking imported files, 61–63
links, transparent, 16
local variables, 248
low-level computer languages, 287

• M •

MacBench 3.0, 261
machine language, 239
Macintosh
 🍎⇨Control Panels⇨Monitors and Sound
   command, 311
 🍎⇨Control Panels⇨Monitors command, 311
 ⌘+Shift+3 (Screen Shot) keyboard shortcut, 92
 About This Macintosh dialog box, 26
 active window, 40

Apple Color Picker, 162
application partition, 26
Applications folder, 23
bitmap files, 56
Cast Members, 56
changing application partition, 28–30
check boxes, 152
color, 124–127
data forks and resource forks, 58
default palette, 157
Desktop, 20–21
Director icon, 24
extensions, 15
external sound sampling, 269
File⇨Make Alias command, 63
Finder, 28
fonts, 235
friendliness of user interface, 20
Get Info dialog box, 25
GUI (graphical user interface), 19–20
hidden context-sensitive menus, 67
incorporated sound file, 271
keyboard shortcuts, 5
Macromedia folder, 118
modifier keys, 4
Mouse control panel, 21–22
PICS files, 58
PICT files, 58–59, 66
Power key, 20–21
round or square selection buttons, 152
sampling sound, 269
snd resource type, 271
sound cards, 268
sound connections, 268
sound files, 79
starting computer, 20–21
success of, 19
System 7, 2
system requirements, 343–344
trash can, 21
turning off System extensions, 261
Window⇨Arrange Displays command, 311
windows, 20
MacOpener, 276
MacRecorder, 269
Macromedia Director 5 for Macintosh, 12
Macromedia Director 5 for Windows, 12
markers, 225–227
⌘/Ctrl+M keyboard shortcut, 226
Markers window, 225–227
Mask ink effect, 303
masks, 84, 129–130
Matte ink effect, 303
mattes, 26
memory
    freeing up, 27–28
    heavy demands on, 39
    K (kilobytes), 28
    management, 70
    Macromedia Director's usage of, 25–26

physical, 25
purging Macromedia Director, 27–28
reserved for Macromedia Director, 25–26
reserved to display graphics on Stage window, 26
reserved used, 26
total in computer, 25
total used by current movie, 26
unused, 26
used by system and other applications, 26
virtual, 25
Memory Inspector palette, 25–28, 40
menu bar, 44–45
Message window, 211–216, 246, 315
    ⌘/Ctrl+M keyboard shortcut, 37, 212
    displaying, 37
    icons, 214
    Lingo commands, 212–214
    logging movie messages and scripts, 214–216
    tracing action, 214–216
    trying out Lingo functions, 243
messages, 214, 246–247
Metallic palette, 128, 157
miroMOTION video board, 260
miroVIDEO DC20 video board, 313
Macromedia Director
    launching, 19–20
    memory usage, 25–26
    online Help system, 30–33
    opening, 23–24
    Paint window, 64
    purging memory, 27–28
    reserved memory used, 26
    splash screen, 24
    system requirements, 343–344
modems, 285
modifier keys for PC and Macintosh, 4
Modify⇨Cast Member⇨Properties command, 68
Modify⇨Cast to Time command, 330
Modify⇨Convert to Bitmap command, 279
Modify⇨Font command, 103
Modify⇨In-Between command, 189, 272–273, 319
Modify⇨In-Between Linear command, 89
Modify⇨In-Between Special command, 273, 320
Modify⇨Movie⇨Casts command, 61
Modify⇨Movie⇨Properties command, 46, 48, 83, 314
Modify⇨Paragraph command, 103
Modify⇨Reverse Sequence command, 330
Modify⇨Space to Time command, 88
Modify⇨Sprite⇨Properties command, 98, 186
Modify⇨Sprite⇨Script command, 253
Modify⇨Transform Bitmap command, 308
Modify⇨Transform command, 98, 130
Modify⇨Tweak command, 222
modifying
    Cast Members, 68–70
    Stage window, 46, 48
monitors
    larger, 113
    multiple, 113

monitors *(continued)*
    NTSC, 129
    resolution, 48
    RGB color scheme, 259
    standards, 48
    VRAM (video RAM), 113
mooV files, 15
    adding, 192
    automatically linking, 63
    importing, 194
    self-contained, 280
mosaic art, 95
mouse, 21–23
mouseDown event, 245, 252
mouseDownScript, 252, 254
mouseUp event, 245, 252
mouseUp handler, 249
mouseUpScript, 252
MOV file extension, 15, 206, 278
Move Frame Left (⌘/Ctrl+Option/Alt+←) keyboard
    shortcut, 74
Move Frame Right (⌘/Ctrl+Option/Alt+→) keyboard
    shortcut, 74
movement, 15
Movie Casts dialog box, 61
Movie Properties dialog box, 46–48, 314
MovieCleaner, 175
MoviePlayer 2.1, 280
movies
    adding script, 207–209
    alternate scenarios for user, 342
    animation, 317–333
    automatically refreshing screen, 338
    casts automatically opening with, 61
    combining, 205–209
    compressing, 289–291
    current frame, 76
    cutting down size, 301–303
    decompressing, 286
    decreasing size of, 288
    DIR file extension, 206
    editing, 228
    freezing playback, 336
    halting playback, 36
    improving color on tape, 308–313
    interactive, 13
    labeling frames, 76
    losing part of screen when taping, 305
    marking important frames, 226
    moving parts to another window, 228
    moving Score to new movie, 302
    new, 35
    only one open at a time, 39
    platform independent, 276
    playback, 36
    playing, 336
    playing cross-platform, 315
    playing faster, 303
    playing right cross-platform, 313–314
    playing suspended, 337
    preparing for cross-platforms, 276–280
    printing features, 122–123

project folder, 63
removing selection to Clipboard, 35
scripts, 75
setting up for playback, 250–251
switching palettes, 164–167
synchronizing sound, 271–273
taping, 263
taping to VCR, 305–307
unable to close Stage window, 39
updating, 209
updating to disk, 35
weird colors when taping, 307
MovieShop, 175
multimedia, 13, 14
    alpha versions, 293, 296
    art director, 295
    beta versions, 296
    computer power, 15–16
    creative director, 295
    golden master version, 296
    GUI (graphical user interface) designer, 296
    hypertext, 16–17
    images, 14
    instructional designer, 297–298
    interactivity, 16–17
    Lingo programmer, 296–297
    movement, 15
    nonlinear information, 16
    program tester, 298
    project manager, 296
    real life, 293–294
    roles, 295–298
    sound, 14
    video, 258–259
multiple monitors, 48, 113
music, 14

naming
    Cast Members, 136
    digital video, 188
    markers, 226–227
narration, 14
nested handlers, 218
Netscape, 283, 285–286
New button, 33
new Cast window, 35
new features in Director 5.0, 33
new movies, 35
newbie, 285
nonlinear information, 16
Norton Utilities Speed Disk, 262
notes, 31–32, 34
NTSC monitors, 129
    AV Macintosh, 310–312
    PCs, 312
NTSC palette, 128, 157, 263
    improving movie color on tape, 308–310
NTSC standards, 158
NTSC TV, 259, 305

• 0 •

objects, 144
offset, 47
online Help system, 30
    accessing from dialog boxes, 39
    contents window, 33
    context-sensitive help, 31–33
    exiting, 34
    Help Pointer, 31
    Lingo, 240
    main menu, 30
    QuickHelp program, 33–34
onexitFrame handler, 207–208
onion skin, 98
Onion Skin floating palette, 114–118
online services and scripts, 204
Open dialog box, 65–66
Open File dialog box, 35
opening
    files, 35
    Macromedia Director, 23–24
operators, 241–242
Operators submenu, 241–242
origin, 47
overscan, 305

• *P* •

Paint Bucket tool, 101
Paint tool palette, 96–97
Paint toolbar, 94–95
paint tools
    Air Brush tool, 104–105
    Arc tool, 106
    cloning selections, 96
    Ellipse tool, 107
    Eraser tool, 99–100
    Eyedropper tool, 101
    Filled Ellipse tool, 106
    Filled Polygon tool, 106
    Filled Rectangle tool, 106
    Hand tool, 100
    hot spot, 95
    Lasso tool, 96
    Line tool, 106
    Paint Bucket tool, 101
    Paintbrush tool, 105–106
    Pencil tool, 104
    Polygon tool, 107
    Rectangle tool, 107
    Registration tool, 98–99
    Selection Rectangle tool, 96–97
    showing/hiding, 113
    Text tool, 102
    Zoom tool, 101
Paint window, 64, 86, 91–93
    ⌘/Ctrl+5 keyboard shortcut, 36, 92, 117, 121
    applying Xtras filters, 119–120
    Background color chip, 107, 110

Cast Member icons, 93–94
changing colors, 109–110
Color Depth indicator, 108
custom gradients, 126
displaying, 36, 91–93
dragging contents to Stage or Score window, 93
Foreground color chip, 107, 109–110
Gradient color chip, 110
Gradient Destination color chip, 107
Grid, 114
icons, 93
ink effect, 108
irregular selections, 96
Line Width Indicator, 107, 110–111
Next Cast Member button, 98–99
Onion Skin floating palette, 114–118
Paint toolbar, 94–95
paint tools, 95–107
Pattern chip, 107
rectangular selections, 96–97
rulers, 115
scroll bars, 112
scrolling graphics, 111–112
showing/hiding paint tools, 113
showing/hiding rulers, 114
Text tool, 132
Tool palette, 144
View menu special commands, 112–118
Xtras menu special commands, 118–123
Paint Window Preferences dialog box, 107, 111
Paintbrush tool, 105–106
Painter, 126
painting, 58, 144
Palette dialog box, 324
palettes, 109, 115, 123–129
    adaptive, 126–127, 165
    built-in, 156–157
    color numbers, 161–162
    current, 156
    custom, 156, 158–159, 162–164
    external, 123
    Grayscale, 128, 157
    index numbers, 161–162
    Metallic, 128, 157
    NTSC, 128, 157
    Pastels, 128, 157
    posterization, 165
    Rainbow, 128, 157
    switching, 164–167
    System, 124–126
    System - Mac, 157
    System - Win, 128, 157
    System - Win (Dir 4), 129, 157
    VGA, 129, 157
    Vivid, 128, 157
Paragraph dialog box, 103
parent scripts, 202
Pastels palette, 128, 157
Pattern dialog box, 107–108
patterns, 86, 153
    sampling, 108

pause Lingo command, 336
PC
  Applications program group, 23
  BMP files, 59
  Change System Settings dialog box, 312
  color, 124–127
  extended memory, 26
  external sound sampling, 269
  Fonts Control Panel, 235
  GUI (graphical user interface) with Windows, 19–20
  hidden context-sensitive menus, 67
  keyboard shortcuts, 5
  Macromedia subdirectory, 118
  modifier keys, 4
  NTSC monitors, 312
  Options⇨Change System Settings command, 312
  Print Screen key, 92
  removing TSR (Terminate and Stay Resident) programs, 261
  sampling sound, 269
  sound cards, 267–268
  sound drivers, 79
  sound files, 79
  system requirements, 343–344
  TSR (Terminate and Stay Resident) program, 15
  video boards, 259–260
  virtual memory, 25
  Windows 3.1, 2
  Windows 95, 2
  Windows NT, 2
  Windows Setup dialog box, 312
PCD file extension, 278
PCT file extension, 278
PCX file extension, 278
pels (picture elements), 48, 58
Pencil tool, 99–100, 104
Photoshop, 64, 98, 105, 126, 165, 167
PIC file extension, 278
PICS files, 58, 327–328
PICT files, 58–59, 65–66, 177
pixels (picture elements), 48, 58
  sampling color, 101
play Lingo command, 336
Play Movie (⌘/Ctrl+Option/Alt+P) keyboard shortcut, 181, 190, 210, 236, 251, 254–255, 256, 314, 325, 330
play movie Lingo command, 208–209
PNT file extension, 278
Pointer tool, 149
Polygon tool, 107
poster, 188
posterization, 165
PostScript fonts, 234
Power key, 20–21
Power Macintosh, 48, 113
prebuilt digital video, 191–192
preLoadCast Lingo command, 187, 251
presentations, 258
primary event handlers, 252–254
Print dialog box, 35, 227

printing, 35
  contents of Markers window, 227
  copy of Help system material, 34
Pro AudioSpectrum sound card, 267
process colors, 168
program tester, 298
programming, 202–203
programs, 11
project folder, 281
project manager, 296
Projector Options dialog box, 264–266
projectors, 264–266
  platform dependent files, 276
purging, 69–70
put Lingo command, 243

• Q •

QuickHelp, 33–34
QuickTime, 15, 64
  Animation codec, 175
  built-in compression schemes, 173–177
  Cinepak codec, 175
  codecs, 173–177
  Component Video codec, 176
  data rate, 175
  exporting, 177–180
  Graphics codec, 176
  mooV files, 192
  no codec, 176
  organizing PICT files, 177
  Photo - JPEG codec, 176
  scaling movies, 179
  sound, 180
  Video codec, 176
QuickTime Export Options dialog box, 177–181
QuickTime for Windows, 15, 176, 280
QuickTime Options dialog box, 174–175
Quit (⌘/Ctrl+Q) keyboard shortcut, 265

• R •

Radio/Option button tool, 151
ragged text, 134
Rainbow palette, 128, 157
Rainbow Windows palette, 123
ready-made scripts, 203
RealAudio, 287
recording real-time animation, 328–329
rectangles, 150
Rectangle tool, 107, 150
Registration tool, 98–99
repeat while control structure, 340–341
repeat with control structure, 340–341
Reserve Colors dialog box, 160, 322
Reserve Selected Colors tool, 159–160
resource forks, 58
resources
  books, 345
  training, 345–346
  vendors, 346–348

Reverse Sequence tool, 160
Rewind Movie (⌘/Ctrl+Option/Alt+R) keyboard
    shortcut, 181, 314
rich text, 132, 140, 149
Round button tool, 151
round or square selection buttons, 152
Rounded Rectangle tool, 150
RTF (Rich Text Format), 132
rulers, 114–115
    Text, 135

• *S* •

sampling, 267
saturation, 168
saturation levels, 128
Save As dialog box, 188, 195, 280, 302
Save Projector as dialog box, 266
Scale dialog box, 179
scaling graphics, 98
Score Preferences dialog box, 86–88
Score Script window, 207
    end, 208
    onexitFrame handler, 207–208
    play movie command, 208–209
Score scripts, 202
Score window, 12, 73–74, 188–189, 211, 236
    ⌘/Ctrl+0 keyboard shortcut, 207, 282
    ⌘/Ctrl+4 keyboard shortcut, 36, 236
    adding Cast Members, 80–82
    adding script to remain in frame, 253–254
    cells, 74
    customizing view, 76–77
    displaying, 36
    exchanging sprite for Cast Member in Cast
        window, 36
    frame numbers, 76
    getting Cast Member from Cast window, 88
    hidden channels, 78–80
    icons, 74–77
    ink effects, 76
    intermediate frames, 36
    Markers button, 226
    Mask Ink effect, 129–130
    moving sprites, 77
    Score Preferences dialog box, 86–88
    selecting sprite, 255
    sprites, 76, 83
    toggling with Markers window, 227
Score⇨Space to Time command, 88
Score⇨Switch Cast Members command, 189
scratch bar, 76
screen
    automatically refreshing, 338
    black and white ink effects, 85
    color, 84
    losing part when taping, 305
    multiple with Macromedia Director, 48
    offset, 47
    origin, 47
    used in this book, 8

screen buffer, 26
Script Cast Member Properties dialog box,
    200–202, 251
Script error: Comma expected message, 213
Script error: Property not found message, 216
Script toolbar, 198–200
Script window, 197–202
    ⌘/Ctrl+0 keyboard shortcut, 37, 198, 282
    breakpoints, 217
    Cast Member Properties button, 200
    displaying, 37
    handlers, 219, 249
    New Script button, 251
    Script toolbar, 198–200
    Text Cast Member, 138
scripts, 75, 198–210, 249–256
    adding to movies, 207–209
    adding to remain in Score frame, 253–254
    bulletin boards, 204
    button beeps when pressed, 253
    Cast Member, 255
    combining movies, 205–209
    debugging, 209, 217–219
    error alerts, 213–214
    frame, 255
    handlers, 214
    hiring programmer, 204
    interactive multimedia, 202–205
    Internet, 204
    knowing when they are okay, 315
    logging, 214
    movie, 202, 250–251
    moving to markers by name, 227
    naming projects, 206
    online services, 204
    operand, 209
    parent, 202
    previewing, 75
    primary event handlers, 252–254
    properties, 200–201
    ready-made, 203
    recompiling, 200
    Score, 202
    simple, 203–204
    sprite, 255–256
    testing, 210
    types, 201–202
    user-group help, 204
scroll bars, 112
scrolling graphics, 111–112
scrolling lists, 59
search string, 139
searching for
    Cast Member, 36
    text, 138–139
Select All (⌘/Ctrl+A) keyboard shortcut, 290
Select Reserved Colors tool, 160
Select Used Colors tool, 160
selection marquee, 96
Selection Rectangle tool, 96–97
set foreColor of cast Lingo command, 255

set Lingo command, 251, 337–338
Set Tempo dialog box, 273
Set Transition dialog box, 181
Shape Cast Member Properties dialog box, 145–146
shapes, 144
  editing, 146
  handles, 145
  jaggies, 148
  modifying, 145, 146
  moving on-screen, 149
  options, 146–147
  resizing, 147–148
SHARED.DIR file, 60
shareware
  digital video, 192
  sound, 270
Shockwave, 13, 182, 283, 286–287
  installing, 286
  preparing movies, 287–291
  small movies, 288
  unrecognized Macromedia Director features,
    288–289
Show/Hide (⌘/Ctrl+1) keyboard shortcut, 44–46,
  325, 333
Silverlining, 262
simple scripts, 203–204
SND files, 79
software, 11
SoftWindows, 276
Sort Colors dialog box, 160
Sort tool, 160
sound, 14, 180
  AV Macintosh, 268–269
  connections, 268
  downloading, 270
  floppy disk and CD-ROM collections, 270
  freeware, 270
  importing files, 270–271
  incorporated, 270–271
  linked file, 270–271
  music, 14
  narration, 14
  playing, 272
  sampling your own, 267–270
  shareware, 270
  sound effects, 14
  synchronizing to movie, 271–273
Sound Blaster for Windows sound card, 269
Sound Blaster Pro sound card, 267
sound effects, 14
Sound Manager 3.0, 79
Sound Mover, 271
SoundEdit 16, 79, 269
Space to Time dialog box, 88
splash screen, 24
sprite scripts, 255–256
sprites, 76, 83, 255
  aligning, 36, 114
  applying Mask Ink effect, 130
  bounding box, 83
  Copy ink effect, 303

default ink, 83
double-clicking, 92
exchanging for Cast Member, 36
masking, 130
moveable, 76, 326
moving, 77
moving in small steps, 221–223
nonlinear movements for tweened, 89
number of frames separating, 88
selectively coloring pixels, 85–86
speeding up in in-between frames, 88–89
trails, 76, 78
visually checking relationship with other
  sprites, 88
Stage
  background color, 83
  bitmaps, 148
  color sampling, 161
  digital video Cast Member sprite, 184
  displaying text, 136–137
  drawing, 144–145
  movies playing at fastest speed, 338
  selecting Text or Field Cast Members, 138
  shapes, 148
  sprite in bounding box, 83
Stage window, 24, 27, 43–46, 80, 211
  ⌘/Ctrl+4 keyboard shortcut, 80
  color, 48
  enlarging size, 26
  location on-screen, 47
  menu bar, 44–45
  modifying, 46, 48
  reserved memory to display graphics, 26
  resizing, 46–47
starting Macromedia Director, 19–20
startMovie event, 245
startMovie handler, 250
startup handler, 215
Sterne, Laurence, 17
stopMovie event, 245
stub projector, 281–282
Sutherland, Ivan, 21
switching palettes, 164–167
syntax, 240
System - Mac palette, 157, 165
System - Win (Dir 4) palette, 129, 157, 278
System - Win palette, 128, 157, 165, 278–279
System 7, 2
system board, 3
System palette, 124–127
system requirements, 343–344

• *T* •

tabs, 135
taping movies, 263
taping movies to VCR, 305
  AV Macintosh, 306–307
  taping Macintosh monitor itself, 306
  video boards, 307

Targa 2000 PCI video board, 313
ten common questions and answers, 301–316
ten most important Lingo words, 335–342
ten ways to add animation to movies, 317–333
text
  advantages and disadvantages, 140
  alignment, 134
  anti-aliased, 104, 137
  baseline, 103
  bitmapped, 102–104, 131–132, 140, 279
  Cast Member size, 137
  display-size, 134
  displaying on Stage, 136–137
  editable, 139
  field, 133, 140
  formatting, 134
  gluing words and phrases together, 339
  leading, 134
  linking, 16
  modifying, 103
  previewing, 137
  purging Cast Members from memory, 137
  ragged, 134
  rich, 132, 140, 149
  searching for, 138–139
  sizes, 134
  tracking and kerning, 134–135
  TrueType fonts, 104
  zooming, 236–238
Text Cast Member Properties dialog box, 136–138
Text Comment (⌘/Ctrl+>) keyboard shortcut, 315
Text Find dialog box, 138–139
Text ruler, 135
text sprite, 337–338
Text tool, 102, 131–132, 149
Text window, 133
  ⌘/Ctrl+6 keyboard shortcut, 36
  icons, 134–135
  rich text, 132
  Text Cast Member Properties icon, 136
Text⇨Comment command, 315
the date function, 243
the time function, 243
thumbs, 26
TIF file extension, 278
timeOut event, 246, 252
timeOutScript, 252
toggle command, 44
Tool palette, 143–148
  Background color selector, 153
  button-making tools, 150–151
  Check box button tool, 150–151
  Circle tool, 150
  Field tool, 133, 139, 151
  Foreground color selector, 153
  Line tool, 149
  Line Width indicator, 153
  Pattern pop–up menu, 153
  Pointer tool, 149
  Radio/Option button tool, 151
  Rectangle tool, 150

Round button tool, 151
Rounded Rectangle tool, 150
Shape pop-up menu, 146–147
shape tools, 150
Text tool, 132, 149
tools, 143, 149–151
toolbar, 35–37
Tools window, 86
tracking, 134–135
trails, 78
Transform Bitmap dialog box, 103, 108, 130, 310
transitions, 79–80
Tristram Shandy, 17
TrueType fonts, 104, 235
TSR (Terminate and Stay Resident) program, 15
Tweak palette, 221–224
tweening, 318–320

• U •

Undo (⌘/Ctrl+Z) keyboard shortcut, 100
undoing actions, 35
unlinked casts, 61
updateStage Lingo command, 338
updating movies to disk, 35
User Group Locator, 204
user-created digital video, 191
user-group script help, 204
US_INC.MOV digital video, 205

• V •

variables, 199–200, 247–248
VCR-like controls, 48–51
VGA palette, 129, 157
video, 257
  AV Macintosh, 259–260
  before digitizing, 261–262
  broadcast quality, 258
  CD-ROM projects, 258–259
  digital camcorders, 258
  digitizing, 262
  kiosks, 258
  moving objects hard to see, 259
  multimedia, 258–259
  on the Web, 259
  post production, 262
  presentations, 258
  production, 260–262
  projectors, 264–266
  renting equipment, 258
  taping movies, 263
  video boards, 259–260
  videotaping masters, 260–261
video boards, 259–260, 262
  improving movie color on tape, 313
  taping movies to VCR, 307
Video for Windows, 171–173, 177
Video window, 182–184
  new, 195
  smaller, 262

videotaping masters, 260–261
VideoWorks, 11, 12
View Animation (⌘/Ctrl+1) keyboard shortcut, 236
View menu special commands for Paint window, 112–118
View⊃Animation Effects QuickHelp command, 34
View⊃Director Help QuickHelp command, 34
View⊃Grid command, 114
View⊃Grid⊃Settings command, 114
View⊃Grid⊃Show command, 114
View⊃Grid⊃Snap To command, 114
View⊃Onion Skin command, 114–115, 117
View⊃Panel command, 113
View⊃Ruler command, 114, 135
View⊃Show Notes QuickHelp command, 34
View⊃Zoom command, 101
virtual memory, 25
Vivid palette, 128, 157
VRAM (video RAM), 113
VRML (Virtual Reality Markup Language), 287

• W •

wallpaper, 34
Watcher window, 219
WAV file extension, 278
WAV files, 79
Web browsers, 283, 285–286
Welcome to Director message, 212
Window menu, 48
Window⊃Cast command, 36, 40, 55, 63, 81, 99, 120, 188, 255, 304, 308, 328, 332
Window⊃Color Palettes command, 124, 155, 162, 321, 323, 331
Window⊃Control Panel command, 46
Window⊃Debugger command, 217
Window⊃Field command, 139
Window⊃Inspectors⊃Memory command, 25, 27, 307
Window⊃Markers command, 226
Window⊃Message command, 37, 212, 246
Window⊃New Window command, 228–229
Window⊃Paint command, 91, 102, 117, 121, 323
Window⊃Score command, 36, 74, 207, 236, 238, 253, 255, 282, 302, 308, 324, 329, 332
Window⊃Script command, 37, 198, 251, 254, 282
Window⊃Stage command, 44, 80
Window⊃Text command, 36, 133
Window⊃Toolbar command, 31, 35
Window⊃Tools command, 189
Window⊃Video command, 181
windows, 20
    active, 40, 45
    another representing Cast Member, 228
    inactive, 45
Windows
    active window, 40
    Cast Members, 56–57
    check boxes, 152

Custom Color Selector, 162
Desktop, 20–21
Director icon, 24
friendliness of user interface, 20
GUI (graphical user interface), 19–20
Mouse control panel, 22
round or square selection buttons, 152
starting computer, 21
windows, 20
Windows 3.1, 2
Windows 95, 2
Windows NT, 2
WMF file extension, 278
word processing. *See* rich text
World Wide Web, 283–284
    compression, 286
    hardware and software requirements, 285
    high-speed animation, 287
    speed, 284–285
    vs. Internet, 284
    video, 259
Wozniak, Steve, 19

• X •

XObjects, 263
Xtras filters
    adding palettes, 123
    Animation Wizard, 233–238
    applying to Cast Member or selection, 119–120
    automating effects incrementally, 120
    building animation sequence, 121–122
    database program, 122
    installing, 118
    number of frames building incrementally, 120–121
    printing features for movies, 122–123
    time to complete, 121
Xtras menu special commands for Paint window, 118–123
Xtras⊃Animation Wizard command, 233, 235–236
Xtras⊃Auto Distort command, 118
Xtras⊃Auto Filter command, 120
Xtras⊃FileFlex command, 122
Xtras⊃Filter Bitmap command, 119-120
Xtras⊃Palettes.cst command, 123
Xtras⊃PrintOMatic Lite command, 122

• Z •

Zoom Bitmap (⌘/Ctrl+Shift) keyboard shortcut, 101
Zoom tool, 101
zooming text, 236–238
zoomWindow event, 246